Russian
Civil Society

Russian Civil Society

A Critical Assessment

EDITORS
Alfred B. Evans, Jr., Laura A. Henry,
and Lisa McIntosh Sundstrom

M.E.Sharpe
Armonk, New York
London, England

Library of Congress Cataloging-in-Publication Data

Russian civil society : a critical assessment / edited by Alfred B. Evans, Jr., Laura A. Henry,
Lisa McIntosh Sundstrom.
   p. cm.
  Includes bibliographical references and index.
  ISBN 0-7656-1521-5 (cloth : alk. paper) — ISBN 0-7656-1522-3 (pbk. : alk. paper)
  1. Civil society—Russia (Federation) 2 Russia (Federation)—Social conditions—1991–
I. Evans, Alfred B. II. Henry, Laura A., 1971– III. Sundstrom, Lisa McIntosh, 1971–

JN6699.A15R873 2005
947.086—dc22   2005007918

Printed in the United States of America

The paper used in this publication meets the minimum requirements of
American National Standard for Information Sciences
Permanence of Paper for Printed Library Materials,
ANSI Z 39.48-1984.

BM (c)   10   9   8   7   6   5   4   3   2   1
BM (p)   10   9   8   7   6   5   4   3   2   1

Table of Contents

Part III. Civil Society in Contemporary Russia: Case Studies

Part IV. Concluding Thoughts

List of Tables and Figure

Tables

Figure

Russian
Civil Society

Introduction

Laura A. Henry and Lisa McIntosh Sundstrom

In the shabby room of an abandoned kindergarten in the town of Novozybkov, near the Russian border with Belarus, a group of twelve schoolchildren gather for the weekly meeting of their Ecology Club. The children squirm and laugh as do children everywhere, but one aspect of their lives differs from their peers elsewhere—they live within Russia's Chernobyl zone of radioactive contamination. Their club of nature lovers is led by Ksenia Klimova, a young teacher and librarian. By teaching the children an appreciation of the natural environment and basic scientific knowledge, Klimova hopes to raise environmental awareness and prevent future disasters and to give the next generation a sense of optimism about the future in a town that has had both its public health and community spirit badly damaged by the 1986 nuclear accident. She represents one of thousands of Russians who are engaged in voluntary community activities to improve the well-being of their fellow citizens or to take advantage of new formally democratic rules and institutions to persuade the government to change its policies.

The dramatic collapse of the Soviet regime in 1991 symbolized not only the transformation of Russia's political and economic institutions but also the transformation of Russian citizens' day-to-day reality. Along with new freedoms of speech and association came new challenges, including the erosion of the state welfare system that encompassed free or inexpensive education, medical care, housing, and pensions. Russian citizens have responded to these changes over the past fifteen years with a range of behaviors from apathy to activism.

This volume is dedicated to exploring those responses and the emergence of civil society in postcommunist Russia. It is particularly apropos to consider how Russian citizens are engaging in voluntary activism at the present moment. The benign neglect of civil society during the Yeltsin years has given way to a more vigorous policy of the Putin administration to engage actors in civil society in a directed way. How does the Russian state facilitate civil society development and how does it discourage citizen activism? What role is played by international actors? And what of the Soviet legacy? How does it impinge on citizens' activities in the public sphere more than a decade after the end of the Communist regime? The contributors to this volume address these questions in relation to a broad range of issue areas.

Our Approach to Civil Society

Russian civil society encompasses elements of both change and continuity, of Soviet-era practices and institutions that persist into and shape the postcommunist period, and of innovative types of societal cooperation that have arisen to address contemporary problems. Tensions within civil society include civil society actors' search for a stable resource base, efforts to mobilize public support, attempts to gain influence over state policies, and the need to reconcile the continuation of the politics of personalism with new formally democratic laws and institutions. Efforts to resolve these tensions offer a likely locus for future political and social change in Russia.

What draws scholars' attention to civil society, however, frequently is not a neutral or objective interest in political change. Our motivation is most often found in predictions of civil society's positive influence on democracy and democratization. Normative concerns for democratic politics color the study of civil society. For example, in his investigation of Italian politics, Robert Putnam demonstrates how norms of reciprocity and social trust enable social organizing and are themselves increased by active cooperation among citizens, resulting in a virtuous circle of civic engagement (Putnam 1993). Larry Diamond, looking at recent political transitions, argues that civil society plays a profound role in consolidating new democratic regimes by persistently demanding adherence to formal democratic rules and organizing petitions for continued political reform. Thus civil society enhances "the accountability, responsiveness, inclusiveness, effectiveness, and hence legitimacy of the political system" (Diamond 1999, 249). In the case of Russia and other postcommunist states, scholars seized upon the reemergence of civil society not only as a means of explaining the suddenness and peaceful nature of regime transition but also as a path to the possible consolidation of new democratic regimes.

The intention of this volume is not to assume or to argue that civil society is inherently democratic, however, but to look at the variety of ways in which citizens cooperate in the public sphere and address the state. Moreover, our authors move beyond basic assessments of *whether* civil society as it is currently developing is fostering democratic norms and behavior in order to ask *why* civil society does or does not play this role. We wish to assess the extent to which actors in civil society are strong enough to achieve their goals and to identify the constraints that limit their ability to do so. The past fifteen years have shown that extreme assumptions—optimistic and pessimistic—about the fate of Russia's civil society need to be supplanted by a more complex understanding of the patterns of interaction within civil society, of the conditions that facilitate it and constrain it, and the various ways Russians are collectively coping with the challenges of postcommunism. Considering the factors behind the development and effectiveness of civil society improves our ability both to predict and to explain political and social change and moves beyond the relatively extreme depictions of civil society in much of the scholarly literature and sloganeering use of civil society in the realm of practical politics.

As a result, this volume offers a parsimonious definition of civil society intended to capture a variety of different types of interaction, concluding that it is best to avoid an outcome-based definition of civil society (i.e., are instances of societal cooperation democracy-supporting or not?) and instead offer a relational definition in which we envision civil society as an intermediary between the public and private spheres.[1] We contend that civil society is a space of citizen-directed collective action, located between the family and the state, and not directed solely toward private profit. As a consequence, we exclude from our definition political parties (which aim to capture seats of government), business firms and organized crime groups (which are profit-oriented), groups employing violence to achieve their goals, and individual activities that are not publicly oriented. Nonetheless, we argue that it is essential to consider the role played by business elites, organized crime networks, and for-profit and state-owned media outlets in the development of Russian civil society due to their influence on governance and the broader environment in which civil society operates in postcommunist Russia, as well as outstanding debates over whether they indeed do belong within the definition of civil society.

Russian Civil Society: A Broad View

The contributions to this volume range across time, geography, and issue areas in an effort both to capture the enduring features of Russian civil society and to recognize innovative types of social cooperation. The chapters look back to pre-Soviet and Soviet history at patterns of state–society interaction. The authors also travel beyond Moscow to investigate the state of civil society in regional capitals, small towns, and rural areas. Rather than focus only on relatively well-known environmental, women's rights, and human rights organizations, these contributions also consider neglected areas of study such as disability rights, migrant resettlement, and the adaptation of Soviet-era organizations. Finally, while most scholarly attention to Russian civil society development has been directed at formal nongovernmental organizations (NGOs), many of which receive some form of foreign assistance, contributors to this volume also consider previously overlooked instances of societal cooperation through informal social networks. What follows is a brief summary of the chapters.

The first section of the volume considers the history of civil society in Russia. Mary Schaeffer Conroy's chapter on civil society in late Imperial Russia begins our exploration. Drawing on new evidence from the archives, Conroy demonstrates that, contrary to depictions of Imperial Russian society as inactive and fragmented, Russian citizens had begun to organize independent charities and hobby organizations, assert their legal rights, and participate in local representative and law-enforcement structures. Conroy points to a combination of state policies and citizen initiative to account for the rise of social cooperation in the late tsarist period.

Turning to the Soviet period, Alfred Evans questions whether civil society existed in the Soviet Union. Evans concludes that it did not; however, he reminds us that while social organizations were largely under state control during the Soviet era, many of them still provided valuable services to the general public. Evans also identifies a wide variety of efforts to influence state policy and strategies of interest representation that persist to the present day, including the use of one's official position and contacts with key individuals as a means of affecting state behavior.

The next six chapters address the contextual factors shaping civil society development. Sarah Oates chronicles the continued politicization of the media in Russia after a brief period of pluralism in the early 1990s, pointing out that the Russian state has little tolerance for media criticism. Oates argues that, due to the efforts of state and economic actors and public tolerance for a restricted media environment, the Russian media is becoming less diverse and less free, limiting its ability to play a role in civil society development.

In her chapter on organized criminal networks, Louise Shelley describes the close relations between criminal groups and state officials, arguing that this interaction leads to a new form of authoritarianism in Russia. Shelley points out several ways in which organized criminal groups undermine and usurp civil society organizations, by virtually replacing the state in some sectors and by threatening independent actors who speak out on criminal activities.

Peter Rutland's investigation of relations between civil society and private business—in particular, the economic elite—chronicles the rise of oligarchic capitalism in Russia. Rutland's analysis offers several insights into civil society development, including the continued dominance of a narrow elite uninterested in engaging other social groups yet still vulnerable to the state's intolerance of political opposition. Rutland considers the Putin administration's recent efforts to prevent opposition from oligarchs, most prominently symbolized by the legal case against Mikhail Khodorkovsky, and sees them as reflecting more general patterns of repression of civil society.

In his chapter on the Russian Orthodox Church, Edwin Bacon offers a mixed assessment of the role of Russia's dominant religion in civil society development. Bacon cites the public's trust in the Orthodox Church, the communal aspects of religious faith, and the pluralism of the Church at the local level as factors that could serve as a basis for the development of a vibrant associational life. Yet he also notes that the Orthodox Church has aligned itself closely with the state and attempted to constrain the freedom of other religious groups in Russia. Laws promulgated to reinforce the leading role of the Orthodox Church, however, occasionally have been used by other religious organizations to defend themselves against attempts to limit pluralism in the religious sphere.

Stephen Wegren considers the potential for civil society development in rural areas of Russia by looking at three spheres of rural life: attitudes, organizations, and behavior. Using survey and interview data, Wegren assesses Russian rural residents' trust in their political institutions, the number and scale of NGOs serving the rural population, and rural citizens' participation in family and public events. While he offers a guardedly optimistic prognosis, Wegren convincingly points to the significance of civil society development in understudied rural areas—which contain almost 30 percent of the country's population—for Russia's political future.

Concluding the section on contextual factors, Alfred Evans examines Vladimir Putin's policies toward civil society. Evans describes the Putin administration's incremental and often indirect use of state resources to reward loyal social organizations and to punish critical groups, in spite of Putin's rhetorical commitment to the rule of law and the development of a vigorous civil society in Russia. Evans convincingly argues that these policies illustrate Putin's vision of a civil society that is subordinate to and managed by the state, and that this model of state–society interaction—by stifling free public debate—may jeopardize the long-term stability of the regime.

The next section of the volume presents case studies of civil society organizing around various issue areas. While chronicling the proliferation of women's organizations in recent years, Valerie Sperling questions how effective these groups are at representing women's interests to the state and changing public consciousness. She points out that organizations' reliance on foreign assistance has facilitated the institutionalization of the women's movement but has also raised questions about whether the issues addressed by these groups serve to mobilize Russian women.

Lisa McIntosh Sundstrom compares Russian soldiers' rights organizations and finds that those led by soldiers' mothers are more effective—in terms of policy change and public support—than other groups critical of military policies. Sundstrom attributes this relative success of the soldiers' mothers' organizations to several factors, including the role of motherhood in Russian culture, widespread public disapproval for physical harm to new recruits, and the mothers' willingness to work cooperatively with state officials. Sundstrom contrasts these methods with more legalistic approaches to rights-based demands commonly found in the West.

In her chapter on labor organizations in Russia, Sue Davis contrasts the continued dominance of Soviet-era trade unions under the umbrella organization Federation of Independent Trade Unions of Russia (FNPR) with the new, independent trade unions that originated in the late Soviet period. While trade unions remain the largest membership organizations in Russia, they do a generally poor job of representing their members. Davis demonstrates that unions persisting from the Soviet era are more intent on defending their inherited commercial interests, while new unions struggle to counter the entrenched influence of the FNPR.

Laura Henry evaluates the ability of Russia's environmental organizations to play an intermediary role between the state and society and finds these groups to be weak on a number of measures. She argues, however, that this image of overall weakness conceals growing diversity among the types of organizations and activities that populate the green movement. Henry argues that the leaders of NGOs advocate models of state–society interaction that vary according to their different professional backgrounds and orientations toward the Soviet past.

Kate Thomson's chapter comparing organizations working on issues of disabled children highlights the role of the state in facilitating groups within civil society. Thomson's analysis shows that state agencies and officials, particularly at the local level, were instrumental in both the origination and effectiveness of disability organizations and locates this type of relationship within an interdependence model of state–society relations. Thomson speculates, however, that the closeness between organizations within civil society and the state ultimately may limit disability organizations' ability to advocate for the rights of the disabled beyond basic service provision.

In her contribution, Moya Flynn examines the situation of Russian migrants returning to Russia from the former Soviet republics. Flynn demonstrates how NGOs working on migrant issues are subject to the vagaries of shifting federal and regional policies toward migrants and therefore struggle to influence policy. Given the lack of state services, Flynn argues that many migrants make the rational decision to rely on personal networks, which then may provide migrants with a path toward integration into civic life by resolving basic barriers to civic inclusion, such as questions of housing and employment.

Janet Johnson examines the multiple roles of women's crisis centers in Russia, including their efforts to provide services, change policies, and raise public awareness. Her research reveals a complicated array of public–private cooperation on the issue of domestic violence, with organizations dealing with the issue ranging from Western-style advocacy organizations to state-affiliated semi-NGOs. Johnson suggests that a working group in the city of Barnaul, which links NGOs with responsible state agencies, offers a model for a potential "third way" between liberal and statist conceptions of civil society that promotes communication and builds new channels of interest representation.

Anne White advocates adopting a broad conception of civil society in order to examine an understudied aspect of contemporary Russian life: social cooperation in small towns. By surveying an array of topics—from NGOs to participation in town events—she finds sources of optimism in factors such as the high level of social trust in small towns. Counter to some arguments about the nature of the Soviet legacy, White also argues that in Russian small towns civic culture has "strong Soviet roots, and it could in some respects be quite promising for democratization" (Chapter 17).

Taken together, these chapters move beyond a simplistic characterization of Russian civil society as strong or weak, instead providing the reader with a more complex understanding of the varieties of civic activism that are occurring in Russia today. By analyzing these activities and organizations and the contextual factors that shape their development, we will be able to fruitfully compare contemporary Russian civil society with other regions around the world and to develop an understanding of how civil society emerges and when citizen activism is more or less likely to be effective at generating political and social change.

Note

1. For a more complete discussion of debates related to defining civil society, see Appendix.

References

Diamond, Larry. 1999. *Developing Democracy: Toward Consolidation.* Baltimore, MD: Johns Hopkins University Press.
Putnam, Robert D. 1993. *Making Democracy Work.* Princeton, NJ: Princeton University Press.

Part I

The History of Civil Society in Russia

2

Civil Society in Late Imperial Russia

Mary Schaeffer Conroy

In the popular mind, the government of Imperial Russia oppressed the citizenry, and the majority of citizens were illiterate and poverty-stricken, with no chance of bettering their lot.[1] As the Soviet Union disintegrated in the 1990s, some claimed that Russians had never known democracy, implying that they never would. Some historians, meanwhile, insisted that society in late Imperial Russia had been so fragmented as to render it inert. Others contended that society in the late imperial period was hopelessly polarized, thus precipitating revolutions in 1905 and 1917.

New evidence from the archives has allowed us to build a mosaic which reveals (Whittaker 1984, 118–19, 140–88; Lincoln 1990; Conroy 1976, 43–90) that in fact, a combination of government policies and private initiatives increased education, created a lively cultural milieu, expanded public participation in policy making, and generated a fairly robust economy that provided increased social mobility and rising living standards (Gregory 1994, 14–84), improved public health, and provided safety nets for the indigent and helpless. This chapter concentrates on the role of citizens in these endeavors, that is, on the creation of civil society. Civil society is taken here to refer to organizations and networks of cooperation that are created primarily by the initiative of citizens and draw at least in part on resources that are not granted by the state. A tentative civil society was visible in imperial Russia at least from the late eighteenth century, but civil society really burgeoned in the second half of the nineteenth and early twentieth centuries. This chapter presents evidence of a wide range of activities by Russian citizens that contributed to the expansion of cooperative endeavors in the social space between families and the state in the last decades of the imperial regime (Kassow, West, and Clowes 1991, 6). We will see that people of humble backgrounds as well as the wealthy and those of high rank, women as well as men, were engaged in a variety of pursuits that forged civil society.

It must be noted that research on civil society in Imperial Russia is not complete and historians differ in their interpretation of many facts. Disparities and vested-interest entities existed in late Imperial Russia, the more so since it was not a country but an empire comprising variegated ethnic, linguistic, and religious groups. The place of revolutionaries in civil society presents a particular conundrum, since three revolutions shook the empire in the first two decades of the twentieth century. Civil society is a "big tent," and individuals and groups of widely varying political persuasions can be a part of it. In this chapter, however, it is assumed that civil society in late tsarist Russia was composed of individuals who worked within the existing political and economic system to modify it rather than seeking to topple it by violent means. According to this rubric, we will see that on their own initiative, many individuals and groups cooperated with one another to improve the lives of their fellow citizens, eschewing the overthrow of existing political and economic institutions. Available evidence and analyses by a growing number of scholars suggest that a small but lively civil society existed in Imperial Russia before 1917.

It is true that civil society in Imperial Russia had more obstacles to overcome than civil society in contemporary America. The Imperial Russian government was domineering and intrusive and sometimes moved at a glacial pace. Records, laws, and regulations abounded throughout the imperial period. Until 1762, nobles were required to perform lengthy military and civil service, thus limiting the time they could spend on their own or societal pursuits. Before 1861, serfs, who constituted half the peasantry (peasants made up about 84 percent of the empire's population), were not judicial persons and even after emancipation in 1861 suffered from some disabilities and restrictions on their physical mobility. Jews, who constituted only about 6 percent of the population but were densely concentrated in the western borderlands, also experienced restrictions on their physical mobility and job options after 1881. In the first half of the nineteenth century, central officials curtailed businesses to some extent by making it difficult to form corporations, reportedly because of a fear of abuses in the selling of stock (Owen 1991a, 25–26); and in the second half of the nineteenth and the early twentieth centuries, the government often hampered business growth through onerous rules and tariffs. Throughout the imperial period, associations of all kinds were required to register with the government; regulations were particularly strict before 1905. Although censorship rules eased in 1905, until the end of the empire government officials supervised publications and closed down those that they deemed pernicious.

Yet, notwithstanding the visible hand of the government, the inhabitants of the Russian Empire enjoyed a surprising amount of political, cultural, and economic autonomy. It has been noted that the central Russian government, though fairly efficient and larger than the American government of that time, did not possess enough officials to govern a vast empire or adequately care for a heterogeneous populace, with transport limited by climate, and communications by the technology of the time. These factors, plus the need to share administrative and welfare costs, induced the government not only to allow but to foster local self-government of various types and to permit publicly funded schools and philanthropic and cultural organizations. The economy underwent a growth spurt in the 1890s and again from about 1908, providing wherewithal for social and cultural projects and disposable income for a broader swath of the population to participate in these projects (Gregory 1994, 27, 34, 48– 49). For example, the modest cost of the bicycle "for the middle classes, including skilled and clerical workers" in the 1880s and 1890s led to the formation of bicycle clubs in the major cities of the empire (McReynolds 2003, 96–101).

Local self-government in the towns and on the county and provincial levels also was a bridge to civil society, for local elected bodies furthered popular education and furnished examples of heterogeneous economic and social groups working in concert for common goals. The nobility's self-government was restricted in the sense that it included only nobles, and nobles with a certain income at that. Nevertheless, the nobles' assemblies did have an impact on the rest of the population, even though nobles constituted only about 1.5 percent of the whole. About half the nobles were not wealthy, did not own land, and had to work for a living (Blum 1961). Catherine the Great instituted self-government by the nobility in 1785. The nobles' assemblies were to care for indigent, orphaned, and helpless nobles. Marshals of the nobility, elected by the assemblies, were to represent nobles' concerns to the crown (de Madariaga 1990, 121–23). In the second half of the nineteenth century, marshals of the nobility convened *zemstvo* assemblies after those all-estate institutions were established in 1864 (Wallace 1961, 29–30; Conroy 1976, 4–7) and dealt with a wide variety of peasant problems. Nobles also founded and supported charities and schools, as noted below.

Townspeople, who made up about 13 percent of the population in the nineteenth and early twentieth centuries, also were given self-government by Catherine the Great in 1785. At first, all registered citizens, including small traders as well as wealthy merchants, were allowed to participate in city assemblies, although only those who had property that returned fifty rubles a year could be elected to the assembly steering committee, the city duma (de Madariaga 1990, 124–27). Following field research by "enlightened bureaucrats," the municipal government of St. Petersburg enlarged its electorate in the 1840s. Moscow did so in the 1860s; and by the 1870s, in some four hundred cities and towns, all who paid a small city tax were able to participate in city government. Representation was not equal, however. Three voting curiae gave preponderant representation to the richest and middle categories of urban dwellers. However, lesser citizens could participate and some people of modest backgrounds were elected as mayors. In the 1890s, in around seven hundred cities, the curiae were eliminated and the size of the assembly was made commensurate with the urban population. Simultaneously, suffrage requirements were raised and Jews were barred from participating in elections (Lincoln 1982, 109–16; Lincoln 1990, 134–43; Nardova 1984; Hanchett 1976, 97–114). Despite such restrictions, Daniel Brower emphasizes that civil society was visible in the towns. He documents the ways that municipal government blended classes and improved the environment for all urbanites (Brower 1990, 104–39).

Even while serfdom existed, peasants also had grassroots government, although politicking often divided the community, and officials elected from the nobility (*zemskie ispravniki*) had some police powers over peasants and nomads. Male heads of households in each peasant commune (*obshchina, mir*) elected an elder (*starosta*) (Matsuzato 2002, 27, 119). The communal assembly—or powerful groups within it—distributed strips of land to constituent families, collected poll taxes (in effect from 1724 to 1885), and chose recruits for the military (before service was made more equitable in 1874). After the serfs were emancipated, communes collected land payments to reimburse the state treasury, which had compensated nobles for the land and labor they lost. Throughout the imperial period, communes settled small-scale crimes and disruptions of public peace (Wirtschafter 1997, 104–5). That system obtained among state peasants in Siberia, Cossacks, Finnish and Turkic nomads, and foreign colonists.

Law courts, although separate for each free *soslovie* (estate, pl. *sosloviia*) and technically closed to serfs before the mid-1860s, nevertheless helped foster civil society by making citizens aware of their separateness from the state and giving them a tool to protect private and public space. Serfs were not legal persons before 1861, but they circumvented that restriction and, utilizing a law that allowed serfs possessed by non-nobles to sue for freedom, generated over thirty-five thousand lawsuits in provincial courts and the Senate (supreme appellate court) between 1835 and 1858 (Wirtschafter 1997, 120–23). The judicial reforms of 1864 increased recognition of citizens' rights by establishing regular courts open to all classes on the county and provincial levels, with the possibility of jury trials for nonpolitical cases, and justice of the peace courts at the township level in thirty-four provinces. The judges in the latter courts were not trained, so justice was sometimes rough and ready, but the courts were more accessible. Juries, used in civil and nonpolitical criminal cases in thirty-four out of fifty regular courts after 1864, stimulated the growth of civil society by forging cooperation (albeit temporary) on common problems among disparate social and economic groups (Kucherov 1953, 72–73, 80–86).

Zemstvos or local councils, established in thirty-four out of fifty provinces and their counties in 1864, greatly strengthened civil society. They supplanted the Boards of Welfare, where from the time of Catherine the Great, representatives from the nobility, townspeople, and free peasants had assisted governors in caring for the indigent and helpless. The new local governing bodies did not employ the procedure of "one man, one vote." Owners of independent property, business properties, and property in communes voted in separate curiae. Governmental authorities supervised the zemstvos. They were supposed to eschew political discussion and were prevented from combining with other zemstvos. The zemstvos were able to levy taxes, and their frequent tax hikes particularly irritated peasant constituents. Nevertheless, zemstvos welded together former serfs, nobles, free peasants, and business people (Wallace 1961, 27–48). Women property owners could vote through male relatives. Zemstvos markedly increased elementary schools and improved health care. Because they handled the same matters as local bodies in the United States, Charles Timberlake views them as authentic, participatory local governments (Timberlake 1991, 164–79; Timberlake 1998, 53–54).

The zemstvos also encouraged change on the national level. Zemstvo work honed citizens' negotiating skills in dealings with one another and with government officials. Zemstvo achievements supported demands for a national parliament. Flaunting official rules, zemstvos cooperated with each other in times of crisis, as when they assisted the central government during the Russo-Japanese War. Their record of achievements, coupled with popular upheavals and the advice of former Minister of Finance Sergei Witte, prompted Nicholas II to institute a national parliament in 1906 and permit political parties (Porter and Gleason 1998a).

Businessmen and businesswomen contributed to the development of civil society, since they operated in a space distinct from government power; personified entrepreneurship, determination, and self-confidence, traits that are requisite for civil society; and subsidized the organizations that enlightened and benefited society. The tsarist government was a driving engine of large-scale industry during the reign of Peter the Great and again in the third quarter of the nineteenth century. Not only merchants and burghers—typical bourgeoisie—but also peasants (women as well as men) and nobles manufactured and sold products of all kinds for the domestic market and for export (de Madariaga 1990, 155; Edelman 1980, 16–17; Blum 1961, 290–92, 343, 390–413; Platonov 1995; Ruckman 1984, 50–51; Glickman 1992, 54–72). Entrepreneurs evaded restrictions on corporations and raised capital by forming closed partnerships (*tovarishchestva*) or expanding small-business (*kustar'*) operations into larger ones (Owen 1991b; Conroy 1994, 137–61; Ruckman 1984, 50–62). Property and profits gave entrepreneurs autonomy. Business owners provided the bulk of funds for philanthropy, schools, and cultural projects. Employment raised living standards and increased numbers of those participating in extracurricular activities.

Associations formed by and for citizens of all types, usually initiated without stimulus from the government, were the chief component parts of the abstraction that we call "civil society." Emerging in the late eighteenth century, such associations particularly proliferated by the second half of the nineteenth century, due to the emancipation of the serfs; tolerance by the central (and sometimes local) governments; the government's need for financial and administrative assistance; increased prosperity, education, and self-awareness on the part of the populace; and more convenient transportation and communication.

A few caveats must be noted. As has been mentioned, the central government did hover over civic associations. To operate legally, they were supposed to be officially chartered. However, some societies operated for a few years before becoming registered. They were not illegal or revolutionary but simply ignored cumbersome rules. Most civic associations were not large and did not involve the majority of the populace. But they did connect different *sosloviia* or groups for the benefit of a larger good, and they proved that the inhabitants of late Imperial Russia were self-starting and capable.

Adele Lindenmeyr regards private charitable organizations, which supplemented charity doled out by the central and local governments, as seedbeds of civil society. Including both sexes from all walks of life, private charities grew remarkably in the nineteenth and early twentieth centuries. In 1803, there were 389 registered charitable institutions; by 1862, there were 768 (Lindenmeyr 1996, 233). The Orthodox Church was active in philanthropy. In 1878 there were about 11,500 parish guardianships, although Lindenmeyr asserts that they devoted 85 percent of their monies to church construction and only paltry sums to charity (ibid., 160). In general, according to Lindenmeyr, most charity offered in cities came from private sources. Wealthy merchants gave generously, particularly those in Moscow (ibid., 58, 207–8). In 1895, there also were 16,500 noble "trusteeships," with property worth 243 million rubles; Moscow nobles alone sponsored 61 institutions. Twenty-eight independent societies that still existed in 1901 had been founded in the first quarter of the nineteenth century. By 1855, these had nearly doubled to 40 private charity organizations funding 73 institutions. By 1880, private charity organizations had increased nearly eightfold, to 348, and supported 225 institutions. By the beginning of the twentieth century private philanthropic organizations doubled again to 750, sponsoring some 3,224 charitable institutions, more than half those in the empire (ibid., 122). In 1900, Moscow spent more per capita on charity than Paris, Berlin, or Vienna (Ruckman 1984, 88).

An educated populace is the foundation of civil society. The enormous percentage of peasants in the empire meant that, in the aggregate, their education programs pushed civil society forward. Ben Eklof considers peasants "the driving force behind the progress in literacy registered in official statistics" between 1864 and 1890 (1986, 84), for peasants supplemented state, local, and Orthodox church schools by learning on their own, or on their own initiative inviting teachers to their villages. Peasant village communes paid for schools, voluntarily or involuntarily, in fact supporting many schools attributed to the zemstvos (Eklof 1986, 83–87; Seregny 1996, 172), The most dramatic example of an individual peasant's contribution to national education in the eighteenth century was Mikhail Lomonosov. In the nineteenth century, that honor belonged to Ivan Sytin, whose rise from illiterate state peasant to millionaire publisher is recounted compellingly by Charles Ruud (1990). Merchants, above all, subsidized schools. Isabel de Madariaga enthuses that "some merchants had already made substantial gifts for the setting up of schools" even before the Statute on National Schools appeared in 1786. Following the statute, "more voluntary gifts to the schools were made by merchants and townspeople than any other social group; eminent citizens of Moscow . . . each gave five hundred rubles." At the end of the eighteenth century, the majority of pupils in six central provinces "where support for the schools was particularly noticeable were children of merchants or townspeople" (de Madiaraga 1990, 158).

Nobles complemented merchants in advancing education for society at large. In the early nineteenth century, merchants and nobles on their own initiative founded primary parish schools and secondary country schools and, as significantly, pledged to fund them over the long term (Walker 1984). In the reign of Nicholas I, according to Cynthia Whittaker, "the financial contributions of landowning nobility were largely responsible for doubling the number of parish schools . . . and for supporting forty-seven *pansions* and six noble institutes. At the same time," she continues, "non-nobles . . . contributed to the gymnasia and, along with various strata of the 'obligated' [poll-tax-paying] middle classes, supported private institutions which came to represent 27 percent of all the schools under the educational ministry." Indeed, in the middle of the nineteenth century, private lower and middle schools were more numerous than state-supported schools and the over one thousand parish schools were entirely privately funded (Whittaker 1984, 151). Various voluntary societies founded schools and fostered literacy in other ways in the nineteenth century (Brower 1990, 165–87). At the end of the empire, business people were active in supporting trade schools, teacher training schools, and schools and hospitals for peasants (Ruckman 1984, 94, 98). Most girls' schools were privately financed, often by businessmen, so that by the early twentieth century, according to Patrick Alston, one out of three girls attended secondary school versus one out of four boys (the latter, of course, often left school for work) (Alston 1969, 202–4). Cooperation between central and local governments, the State Duma, the Orthodox Church, and the private sector resulted in the near doubling of teacher-training and elementary schools between 1908 and 1914, although Russia still needed twice as many lower schools again to achieve universal primary education (Seton-Watson 1967, 639). All eight dental schools in the empire were privately established and supported by tuition, women forming a sizable proportion of the student body, although the Ministry of Internal Affairs regulated the schools, and students completing the courses were required to take state qualifying examinations. ((*Zubovrachenyi vestnik* 1885, 1891, 1892, 1897).

Fewer handicapped children—blind, deaf, and retarded—were in special schools in Imperial Russia than in West European countries in the nineteenth and early twentieth centuries, but a number of Russian schools were established and supported privately, supplementing those sponsored by the Empress Marie Trusteeship, the imperial family, Boards of Welfare, and subsequently zemstvos (Conroy 1985; McCagg 1989, 40, 48–49; Ruckman 1984, 94).

Russians' efforts to promote education among indigenous peoples of the empire represented a facet of civil society, for that process linked the dominant ethnic group with minorities and enabled the latter to become more vocal and take more control over their own lives. Educator N. I. Il′minskii and the Brotherhood of St. Gurii pioneered private bilingual schools for Finns and Turkic-Tatar Muslims in the Volga region in the mid-nineteenth century. By 1870, there were 43; by the early twentieth century there were some 120 schools with an enrollment of over 4,000 (Dowler 2001, 33–45, 54–61, 90–97). Orthodox clergy furthered literacy among national minorities of the Ural-Volga region, particularly the Mordvin, Cheremi, and Mari peoples, for example, by writing and publishing a Mordvinian–Russian dictionary (Matsuzato 2002, 38–39).

National minorities were not passive recipients of Russian culture. Some Polish, Estonian, and Jewish societies were revolutionary. Nationalist organizations that were not overtly revolutionary, though, ought to be considered under the rubric of civil society, for they represented popular as opposed to official initiatives. Sizable numbers of Poles lived outside Russian Poland; there were about seventy thousand in St. Petersburg in the early twentieth century. They established a Catholic school next to St. Catherine's Church on Nevskii Prospect. The Polish Benevolent Society, established in 1884, conducted fund raisers and social activities and published a newspaper

(Conroy 1994, 114–15). In the second half of the nineteenth century, Estonians formed agricultural societies and clubs for "the advancement of music, theater, adult education, and temperance," although Estonian song festivals, some of which included thousands of participants, were more ambiguous politically (Raun 1987, 70, 76). The Finnish peoples in Kazan, Viatka, and Kostroma provinces maintained a strong sense of their identity. Their prayer services, sometimes attended by four to five thousand people, at which they sacrificed horses and sheep and venerated a sacred stone, caused conflict with tsarist officials (Matsuzato 2002, 67–73, 84–95, 117–21). Although this would seem to confirm the arguments of historians who charge that divisions tore Imperial Russia apart, it also must be acknowledged that Russian outreach programs enlarged the world of the indigenous peoples and improved their ability to articulate their needs and rights. The Finnish animists, for example, insisted that "[t]he tsar himself could not change their beliefs" (ibid.).

Mutual aid societies for clerks, printers, and members of other occupations, which existed since the first half of the nineteenth century, showed working people taking charge of their own fate, an important ingredient of civil society (McKean 1990, 163–68; Ramer 1996, 120; Seregny 1996, 178). Professional societies of engineers, feldshers, teachers, and physicians testified to the growth of civil society in the second half of the nineteenth century (Balzer 1996a; Ramer 1996; Seregny 1996). The first society of pharmacists had opened even earlier, in 1818. By 1913, there were some 10,000 pharmacists (out of a total population of some 144 million), and pharmacy societies functioned in eighteen cities of the empire, disseminating information on developments in the field through meetings and journals (Conroy 1994, 219–28). The Pharmacists' Pension Fund amassed 0.5 million rubles from staff pharmacists and pharmacy owners and was quite effective in succoring members during the first decade of its existence, before revolutionary pharmacists took over its assets (Conroy 1994, 229–53). Dentists organized their first professional society in January 1885. In the 1890s, they appealed to the Governing Senate to prevent unqualified persons from assuming the title *zubnoi vrach* (dental doctor) (*Zubovrachebnyi vestnik* 1885, 1897).

Some historians imply that associations of business owners like the Association of Southern Coal and Steel Producers, the Russian Industrial Society, and the Baku Petroleum Association were too exclusive and even xenophobic to qualify as components of civil society (Friedgut 1994, 25–40; Owen 1991a, 75–89). Yet, indisputably, they do belong under that rubric, for they reflected the cohesion of individuals, albeit with a specific agenda, acting independently from the government—the definition of civil society.

A number of societies contributed to the protection and promotion of public health. Pharmacy societies cooperated with cities in promoting clean water and unadulterated foodstuffs (Conroy 1994, 193). The Society for the Preservation of Public Health was small, with only three hundred members and a treasury of about 1,900 rubles in 1880. The society had been formed in St. Petersburg, but branches, duly approved by the government, gradually fanned out across the empire—to Odessa, Kazan, and

Theodosia on the Black Sea. The society sponsored research and was engaged in raising public awareness of health and hygiene (ibid., 196). The Free Economic Society was a particularly lively example of an emerging civil society. Founded in the eighteenth century, the society cooperated with Orthodox parishes, zemstvos, feldsher schools, and other institutions to promote smallpox vaccination until it closed in 1906. It was largely self-funded (Pratt 2002, 566, 568, 573, 575).

Religious groups were somewhat exclusive, yet they promoted civil society through their social and educational activities. The Orthodox Church, the favored religion, was connected to the government, since a board (the Holy Synod) headed by a government-appointed layman, managed the Church and fulfilled government mandates, such as establishing elementary schools. Nevertheless, the Orthodox Church was not an extension of the government. In implementing social programs, Orthodox parishes operated fairly autonomously, especially as they were privately funded. In addition to educational activities, some clerics were involved in working for social justice, although they sometimes blurred the line between constructive and revolutionary activity, the best-known exponent of this ambiguity being Father Gapon (Sablinsky 1976).

Brenda Meehan's sensitive study of five Orthodox nuns notes that the women's "monastic communities" that "spread throughout rural Russia in the second half of the nineteenth century . . . were self supporting, primarily through the communal labor of the sisters." These communities "offered" poor as well as prosperous "women an opportunity to develop their leadership abilities and to exercise considerable responsibility." Women's religious communities "managed and worked large agricultural properties." They also "ran schools, almshouses, and orphanages, and supervised the feeding, housing and religious life of the community." Religious communities increased members' literacy and gave them some business training, such as making and selling icons, handicrafts, and decorating churches (Meehan 1992, 13–14).

Despite the preeminence of Orthodoxy, other religions operated in Russia and engaged in secular activities. Those of Catholic Poles have been noted. Baron Gintsburg's Society for the Spread of Enlightenment among the Jews of Russia (the OPE) could be classified as a civic organization, one of whose purposes was to bring Christians and Jews closer (Klier 1995, 245–62). Pavel Riabushinskii likewise tried to mainstream the "Old Belief" (West 1991, 41–56).

Masonic societies, which emerged in the eighteenth century, were only quasi-religious. Nevertheless, those societies, as well as the philosophical circles of the 1830s and 1840s (such as the Slavophiles and Westerners) and occult groups that appeared especially in the late nineteenth and early twentieth centuries, were elements of civil society. Some philosophical groups, like the Durov circle to which Fedor Dostoevsky belonged, had revolutionary proclivities but others focused on the gradual betterment of society within the prevailing system. Slavophiles like Aleksei Khomiakov tried to work out the finances of emancipating the serfs in the first half of the nineteenth century (Christoff 1961, 240–42). W. Bruce Lincoln details how informal groups emerging from salons and circles of the 1830s and 1840s produced the "enlightened bureaucrats" who orchestrated the Great Reforms of the 1860s and 1870s (Lincoln 1982, esp. 139–67).

Spiritualists and Theosophists, though considered aberrant by the Orthodox Church and the tsarist government, nevertheless pushed civil society forward. According to Maria Carlson, "hundreds of occult societies and circles, registered and unregistered, were formed in every major city and in the provinces" in the last decades of the nineteenth century and the first decades of the twentieth. The societies provided private space for members' activities such as seances but also galvanized the public through lectures, the publication of "more than eight hundred occult titles" between 1881 and 1918, and other activities. They introduced Russians to Buddhism and Hinduism, if in garbled form. Following the October Manifesto's proclamation of greater civil liberties in 1905, the Moscow Spiritualist Society, which had operated openly since 1897, applied for official registration, was duly chartered in 1906, and held a congress that attracted about seven hundred people later that year. The Theosophical Society gave public lectures, had its own academy, restaurants, and a dacha near St. Petersburg, and engaged in many philanthropic projects. Members established a dormitory for working women in St. Petersburg; managed vegetarian cafeterias and food kitchens for the poor; organized kindergartens and day care centers; assisted in hospitals; helped the elderly; distributed food, books, and toys to children; implemented Maria Montessori's educational methods; and promoted peasant handicrafts. During World War I, the society assisted soldiers and their families, often in conjunction with other relief organizations, such as the International Red Cross (Carlson 1993, 22, 24, 26, 28, 66–69, 76, 78–80).

Groups focusing on art, theater, and music proliferated in the late nineteenth and early twentieth centuries. They furthered civil society because they originated and operated independently from the government and, in some cases, educated the public and provided jobs. Through traveling exhibits of paintings that focused on Russian history, nature, and sometimes the plight of the poor and political dissidents, the Wanderers (*Peredvizhniki*) sought to raise the social awareness as well as the artistic sensibilities of provincial dwellers (Valkener 1977). The Artistic Circle, founded in 1867 by Aleksandr Nikolaevich Ostrovskii, and the Moscow Association of Russian Playwrights, organized in 1870 and chartered by the Senate in 1874, helped protect the material interests of playwrights and translators and encouraged aspiring writers. By 1876, the Moscow society had some seventy members and contracts with seventy-two theaters. By 1884, the society had 330 members and working capital of 67,000 rubles (McReynolds 2003, 39–42). The less commercial World of Art movement advanced civil society by blending together businessmen and -women, male and female painters, theater actors, opera and ballet artists, and impresarios. The nucleus of the group, which was fascinated with eighteenth-century subjects and the clarity of realistic as well as the curvilinear Art Nouveau style, began holding meetings in the 1880s. In the 1890s and the early twentieth century, they established a journal, held art exhibitions, and sponsored musical performances. The World of Art group did not register with the authorities, and some members propounded radical political as well as cultural ideas (Kamensky 1991, esp. 18–19).

A number of Moscow businessmen consciously combined cultural patronage and social responsibility. Savva Mamontov, Petr Ivanovich Shchukin, Stepan Riabushinskii, and Pavel Tret'iakov amassed impressive collections of art and in Shchukin's case, historical artifacts. Mamontov and his wife also supported music and Vladimir Nemirovich-Danchenko's Moscow Art Theater. Extending personal enjoyment of their acquisitions, Shchukin donated his collection of manuscripts and books to the Historical Museum; and Tret'iakov built an art museum to display his icons and paintings. Savva Mamontov not only gathered painters at his estate of Abramtsevo near Moscow and fired ceramics himself but also established workshops to promote peasant handicrafts, both to preserve Russian heritage and increase peasant income (Bradley 1991, 137–41; Norman 1991, 93–107; Ruckman 1984, 84, 89, 97–98, 103, 105, 155–58).

Leisure pursuits helped construct civil society, in Joseph Bradley's opinion. Whereas in the early nineteenth century, aside from charitable organizations, Moscow had only a handful of clubs for the elite, by 1912 there were "more than six hundred societies, organizations, clubs, and associations," including vocational, technical, and medical societies; automobile, aviation, and other hobby clubs; Chautauqua-like self-improvement clubs; and voluntary societies such as those devoted to science or to founding museums, which bound together the middle and lower classes (Bradley 1991, 135–48). Self-improvement and recreational clubs sprouted in other cities as well (Hamm 1993, 164–72). Louise McReynold's delightful *Russia at Play* details the burgeoning of societies devoted to leisure and reminds us that while recreational societies might be considered frivolous, they reflected the growing self-confidence of the middle classes, increased living standards, and popular initiative and independence.

Equestrian-related activities had a long history. As early as 1739, there were 10 private stud farms; by 1814, there were 1,339. The Moscow Hunting Society was established in 1834. Horse races were held in the Moscow Hippodrome in the 1830s; in 1880, races took place in twenty-four cities; and by 1905, there were races in fifty-nine cities, with prizes amounting to 2.75 million rubles (www.horse.spb.su/history). "Between 1854 and 1907," McReynolds adds, "the number of registered [horse]-breeding societies jumped from 96 to 3,700; the number of race horses" increased from 260 to 3,000; and "the number of hippodromes nearly tripled, from 20 to 54" (McReynolds 2003, 81). In contrast to elitist British hunting societies, Russian hunting societies were egalitarian, including peasants among their members. The Moscow Hunting Society received a charter in 1862. "The charter underscored civic concerns" related to gaming laws, protection of the environment, and "the breeding of hounds"(ibid., 83). There were over thirty hunting societies in the early twentieth century (ibid., 83–87). Physical culture and wrestling gained popularity in the late nineteenth century, fueling the establishment of amateur athletic societies. These strengthened civil society as well as the physiques of their members because "they offered opportunities for participation across a broad social spectrum," "pulled thousands of Russians into the public sphere," and at least psychologically, helped knit together disparate socioeconomic groups, since "virtually all club charters declared themselves open to membership of all social estates" (ibid., 92–93, 88, 90, 94–95).

Soccer clubs were first organized in 1879 by British managers at Russian factories. By 1911, there were thirteen clubs in Moscow. These "football" clubs had a leveling effect because they were associated with factories and neighborhoods and included workers as well as engineers and junior management (ibid., 102–5). Bicycle clubs also included members of different social classes. The first was established in Moscow by 1888; there were nineteen clubs by 1892. By 1897, the St. Petersburg club had five hundred members (ibid., 96).

McReynolds points out that women pursued sport (ibid., 107–8). It should be noted that women also promoted education, health care, and culture, increasing the viability of civil society in the bargain. Women established schools for girls in the early nineteenth century. In the second half of that century, women lobbied for admission to institutions of higher education (Johansen 1987, 29, 35–40, 60). Over two thousand women were certified as medical practitioners from the 1870s on. About seven hundred finished medical courses and became certified midwives. Over sixteen hundred women were enrolled in medical schools in the early twentieth century. Women were heavily involved in the new field of school hygiene, and they established medical clinics and schools for peasants. In the late nineteenth and early twentieth centuries, women received permission from the tsarist government to publish journals and establish societies, the foci of which included self-improvement, facilities for training destitute women and prostitutes, and the general betterment of society (Clyman and Vowles 1996; Ruane 1994, 93–113; Figner 1991, 54–56; Conroy 1981; Noonan and Nechemias 2001, 3–123).

Some individuals stand out among female social activists. Antonina Lesnevskaia, one of the first women pharmacists, founded a pharmacy entirely staffed by women in 1901 and in 1903 started a women's pharmacy school that graduated around two hundred pharmacists by the time of World War I. The school helped professionalize pharmacy, and some graduates contributed to medical research (Conroy 1994, 109–36, 396, 410).

Wendy Salmond depicts the prominent role that women played in preserving traditional wood carving, lace making, embroidery skills, and patterns, while buoying up peasant women financially by establishing *kustar'* industries, retail shops selling crafts, and international exhibitions publicizing them. Although there were some fissures, in addition to furthering culture, those activities strengthened civil society, for they created links among women from various socioeconomic groups, and with male patrons and ultimately the government. Wealthy nobles and merchant wives like Princess Maria Tenisheva, Elizaveta Mamontova, and Mariia Iakunchikova, whose workshops were founded during the famine of 1891–92, relied on the artistic talents of Elena Polenova, the product of an upper-middle-class family of artists and intellectuals, and on Sofiia Davydova and Natalia Shabel'skaia and her daughters, historians and promoters of Russian arts and crafts from humbler backgrounds. These famed women inspired Ekaterina Chokolova, a railroad engineer's wife, to promote traditional art. All the patronesses depended on nameless peasant women in Tver, Vitebsk, and other Russian and Ukrainian provinces to execute their designs and produce wares.

The women's arts and crafts movement stimulated the Moscow zemstvo to open a *kustar'* museum in 1885, which sold peasant handicrafts, and on the eve of World War I prompted the central government to establish official agencies to promote peasant handicrafts, bureaucratizing the movement but giving it wider scope (Salmond 1996, esp. 15–45, 65–66, 82–83, 115–45, 164).

Women's civic activities propelled them into the political arena. The Russian Women's Mutual-Philanthropic Society counted sixteen hundred members at its high point in 1899. Some women joined subversive groups. Over two thousand became Social Democrats before 1905, railed against the Russo-Japanese War, and orchestrated strikes in 1905, May Day parades in 1914, and strikes during World War I. The women's suffrage movement was more mainstream, although it included Social Democrat Alexandra Kollontai, supporters of the Socialist Revolutionaries, and supporters of the Constitutional Democrats (Kadets, then fairly radical) like Anna Miliukova and Ekaterina Shchepkina. Only one woman spoke for female suffrage at the banquets that radical liberals organized in the fall of 1904 to demand a parliament and expanded civil rights. In January 1905, however, some 150 women signed a petition for women's suffrage, and in the spring of that year the Union of Equal Rights for Women began to push for women's civil and political rights (Edmondson 1992, 79–80, 81, 85–87; Conroy 1994, 125–26, 129). Only in Finland, however, were women permitted to participate in elections for the unicameral regional parliament, the Sejm, that was established in 1906.

Civil society did not wither during World War I despite some shortages and problems. Peasants did not seize estate land, probably because they already owned 80 percent of the arable land, and an estimated 20 percent of the peasants were prosperous (Matsuzato 1998; Gatrell 1994, 226–28; Wheatcroft and Davies 1994, 62). Large-scale industry increased productivity and output (Davies 1994, 135; Conroy 1994, 320–48). A flourishing film industry, theater, and the arts (Tsivian et al. 1989; Jahn 1995; McReynolds 2003, 1–3) document that many citizens lived a fairly normal life during the war. About 1,000 to 1,600 strikes erupted in 1915 and 1916, but organizers labored to call them and many workers were cool to revolutionary blandishments (Friedgut 1994, 221, 224, 228; McKean 1990, 369–94; Conroy 1994, 350–63). Refugees strained the infrastructure in some cities, but civic as well as governmental organizations assisted them (Gatrell 1999). Unfortunately, civil society began to weaken in 1917, partly due to demagogues who stressed inequality between socioeconomic strata rather than the possibility for social and economic advancement. The fate of civil society in Russia after the Bolshevik Revolution in October 1917 is the subject of the next chapter.

Conclusion

The examples above do not exhaust the potentially relevant evidence. They do not purport to prove that all was harmonious in late Imperial Russia or that civil society was stronger than the government. However, they indicate that many Russian citizens were self-starters and joined in cooperative activities to bring about educational, social, and cultural improvements. In broad terms, this analyis implies that Russian society was symbiotic and synergistic as well as adversarial. There were those who worked to destroy the existing political and social order but also various socioeconomic groups that worked in concert for larger goals within the system. The embryonic civil society was buttressed by the ownership of private property; a growing economy (Gregory 1994, 14–84; West and Petrov 1998; Crisp 1976; Davies 1994, 32–135); a government that, although authoritarian, abided by a codified system of rules; and a fairly responsive and honest judicial system. Though the tsarist state was far from democratic, it allowed space for many independent initiatives by citizens, and in many cases even encouraged nonstate organizations as a means of gaining assistance in serving national interests. It is the consensus of a large number of scholars that during the last decades of tsarist Russia, the efforts of a wide variety of people had generated the vibrant associational activity that indicated the emergence of a nascent civil society.

Note

1. This generalization is based on the author's conversations with students and citizens during thirty years of teaching Russian history.

References

Alston, Patrick. 1969. *Education and the State in Tsarist Russia.* Stanford, CA: Stanford University Press.
Balzer, Harley D. 1996a. "The Engineering Profession in Tsarist Russia." In Balzer 1996b, 55–88.
Balzer, Harley D., ed. 1996b. *Russia's Missing Middle Class: The Professions in Russian History.* Armonk, NY: M. E. Sharpe.
Blum, Jerome. 1961. *Lord and Peasant in Russia from the Ninth to the Nineteenth Century.* Princeton, NJ: Princeton University Press.
Bradley, Joseph. 1991. "Voluntary Associations, Civic Culture, and *Obshchestvennost'* in Moscow." In Clowes, Kassow, and West 1991, 131–48.
Brower, Daniel R. 1990. *The Russian City between Tradition and Modernity, 1850–1900.* Berkeley: University of California Press.
Carlson, Maria. 1993.*"No Higher Religion Than the Truth": A History of the Theosophical Movement in Russia, 1975–1922.* Princeton, NJ: Princeton University Press.
Christoff, Peter K. 1961. *A. S. Khomjakov: An Introduction to Nineteenth-Century Russian Slavophilism.* S-gravenhage, UK: Mouton and Co.
Clowes, Edith W., Samuel D. Kassow, and James L. West, eds. 1991. *Between Tsar and People: Educated Society and the Quest for Public Identity in Late Imperial Russia.* Princeton, NJ: Princeton University Press.
Clyman, Toby W., and Judith Vowles, eds. 1996. *Russia through Women's Eyes: Autobiographies from Tsarsist Russia.* New Haven, CT: Yale University Press.
Conroy, Mary Schaeffer. 1976. *Peter Arkad'evich Stolypin: Practical Politics in Late Tsarist Russia.* Boulder, CO: Westview Press.
———. 1981. "School Hygiene in Late Tsarist Russia." *Slavic and European Education Review* vol. 5, no. 2: 17–26.

————. 1985. "Education of the Blind, Deaf, and Mentally Retarded in Late Tsarist Russia." *Slavic and European Education Review* vol. 9, nos. 1–2: 29–49.

————. 1994. *In Health and In Sickness: Pharmacy, Pharmacists, and the Pharmaceutical Industry in Late Imperial, Early Soviet Russia.* Boulder, CO: East European Monographs (distributed by Columbia University Press).

Conroy, Mary Schaeffer, ed. 1998. *Emerging Democracy in Late Imperial Russia.* Niwot: University Press of Colorado.

Crisp, Olga. 1976. *Studies in the Russian Economy before 1914.* London: Macmillan.

Davies, R. W. 1994. "Industry." In Davies, Harrison, and Wheatcroft 1994, 131–57.

Davies, R. W., Mark Harrison, and S. G. Wheatcroft, eds. 1994. *The Economic Transformation of the Soviet Union, 1913–1945.* Cambridge, UK: Cambridge University Press.

De Madariaga, Isabel. 1990. *Catherine the Great: A Short History.* New Haven, CT: Yale University Press.

Dowler, Wayne. 2001. *Classroom and Empire: The Politics of Schooling Russia's Eastern Nationalities, 1860–1917.* Montreal: McGill-Queen's University Press.

Edelman, Robert. 1980. *Gentry Politics on the Eve of the Russian Revolution.* Brunswick, NJ: Rutgers University Press.

Edmondson, Linda. 1992. "Women's Rights, Civil Rights, and the Debate over Citizenship in the 1905 Revolution." In *Women and Society in Russia and the Soviet Union,* ed. Linda Edmondson, 77–110. Cambridge: Cambridge University Press.

Eklof, Ben. 1986. *Russian Peasant Schools: Officialdom, Village Culture, and Popular Pedagogy, 1861–1914.* Berkeley: University of California Press.

Eklof, Ben, and Lynne Viola, eds. 1992. *Russian Peasant Women.* New York: Oxford University Press.

Figner, Vera. 1991. *Memoirs of a Revolutionist.* DeKalb: Northern Illinois University Press.

Friedgut, Theodore H. 1994. *Iuzovka and Revolution,* vol. 2. Princeton, NJ: Princeton University Press.

Gatrell, Peter. 1994. "The First World War and War Communism, 1914–1920." In Davies, Harrison, and Wheatcroft 1994, 216–37.

————. 1999. *A Whole Empire Walking: Refugees in Russia during World War I.* Bloomington: Indiana University Press.

Glickman, Rose L. 1992. "Peasant Women and Their Work." In *Russian Peasant Women,* ed. Beatrice Farnsworth and Lynne Viola 1992, 54–72. New York: Oxford University Press.

Gregory, Paul R. 1994. *Before Command: An Economic History of Russia from Emancipation to the First Five-Year Plan.* Princeton, NJ: Princeton University Press.

Hamm, Michael F. 1993. *Kiev: A Portrait, 1800–1917.* Princeton, NJ: Princeton University Press.

Hamm, Michael F., ed. 1976. *The City in Russian History.* Lexington: University Press of Kentucky.

Hanchett, Walter. 1976. "Tsarist Statutory Regulation of Municipal Government in the Nineteenth Century." In Hamm 1976, 91–114.

Jahn, Hubertus. 1995. *Patriotic Culture in Russia during World War I.* Ithaca, NY: Cornell University Press.

Johansen, Christine. 1987. *Women's Struggles for Higher Education in Russia, 1855–1900.* Montreal: McGill-Queen's University Press.

Kamensky, Alexander. 1991. *The World of Art Movement.* Leningrad: Aurora.

Kassow, Samuel D., James L. West, and Edith W. Clowes. 1991. "Introduction: The Problem of the Middle in Late Imperial Russian Society." In Clowes, Kassow, and West 1991, 3–14.

Klier, John Doyle. 1995. *Imperial Russia's Jewish Question.* Cambridge: Cambridge University Press.

Koniushennyi prikaz, gosudarstvennoe konnozavodstvo i pervye ippodromy. 2003. www.Horse.spb.su/history, pp. 1–2; *Gosudarstvennoe konnozavodstvo v XIX veke,* ibid., p. 1.

Kucherov, Samuel. 1953. *Courts, Lawyers, and Trials under the Last Three Tsars.* New York: Praeger.

Lincoln, W. Bruce. 1982. *In the Vanguard of Reform: Russia's Enlightened Bureaucrats, 1825–1861.* DeKalb: Northern Illinois University Press.

Lincoln, W. Bruce, ed. 1990. *The Great Reforms: Autocracy, Bureaucracy, and the Politics of Change in Imperial Russia.* De Kalb: Northern Illinois University Press.

Lindenmeyr, Adele. 1996. *Poverty Is Not a Vice: Charity, Society, and the State in Imperial Russia.* Princeton, NJ: Princeton University Press.

Matsuzato, Kimitaka. 1998. "Interregional Conflicts and the Collapse of Tsarism: The Real Reason for the Food Crisis in Russia after the Autumn of 1916." In Conroy 1998, 243–300.

Matsuzato, Kimitaka, ed. 2002. *Vesna narodov: Etnologicheskaia istoriia Volgo-Ural'skogo regiona. Sbornik dokumentov.* Sapporo: Hokkaido University Press.

McCagg, William O. 1989. "The Origins of Defectology." In *The Disabled in the Soviet Union: Past and Present, Theory and Practice,* ed. William O. McCagg and Lewis Siegelbaum, 39–61. Pittsburgh, PA: University of Pittsburgh Press.

McKean, Robert B. 1990. *St. Petersburg between the Revolutions.* New Haven, CT: Yale University Press.

McReynolds, Louise. 2003. *Russia at Play: Leisure Activities at the End of the Tsarist Era.* Ithaca, NY: Cornell University Press.

Meehan, Brenda. 1993. *Holy Women of Russia: The Lives of Five Orthodox Women Offer Spiritual Guidance for Today.* San Francisco: Harper.

Melancon, Michael. 1990. *The Socialist Revolutionaries and the Anti-War Movement, 1914–1917.* Columbus: Ohio State University Press.

Nardova, V. A. 1984. *Gorodskoe samoupravlenie v Rossii v 60–kh–nachale 90–kh godov XIX v.* Leningrad: Nauka.

Noonan, Norma Corigliano, and Carol R. Nechemias, eds. 2001. *Encyclopedia of Russian Women's Movements.* Westport, CT: Greenwood Press.

Norman, John O. 1991. "Pavel Tret'iakov and Merchant Art Patronage, 1850–1900." In Clowes, Kassow, and West 1991, 93–107.

Owen, Thomas C. 1991a. *The Corporation under Russian Law, 1800–1917.* Cambridge: Cambridge University Press.

———. 1991b. "Impediments to a Bourgeois Consciousness in Russia, 1880–1905: The Estate Structure, Ethnic Diversity, and Economic Regionalism." In Clowes, Kassow, and West 1991, 75–89.

Platonov, O. 1995. *1,000 let russkogo predprinimatel'stvo.* Moscow: Sovremennik.

Porter, Thomas, and William Gleason. 1998a. "The Zemstvo and the Transformation of Russian Society." In Conroy 1998, 60–87.

———. 1998b. "The Democratization of the Zemstvo during the First World War." In Conroy 1998, 228–42.

Pratt, Joan Klobe. 2002. "The Free Economic Society and the Battle against Smallpox: A 'Public Sphere' in Action." *Russian Review* vol. 61, no. 4 (October): 560–78.

Ramer, Samuel C. 1996. "Professionalism and Politics: The Russian Feldsher Movement, 1891–1918." In Balzer 1996b, 117–42.

Raun, Toivo U. 1987. *Estonia and the Estonians.* Stanford, CA: Hoover Institution Press.

Ruane, Christine. 1994. *Gender, Class, and the Professionalization of Russian Teachers, 1860–1914.* Pittsburgh, PA: University of Pittsburgh Press.

Ruckman, Jo Ann. 1984. *The Moscow Business Elite: A Social and Cultural Portrait of Two Generations, 1840–1905.* DeKalb: Northern Illinois University Press.

Ruud, Charles A. 1990. *Russian Entrepreneur: Publisher Ivan Sytin of Moscow, 1851–1934.* Montreal: McGill-Queen's University Press.

Sablinsky, Walter. 1976. *The Road to Bloody Sunday.* Princeton, NJ: Princeton University Press.

Salmond, Wendy. 1996. *Arts and Crafts in Imperial Russia*. New York: Cambridge University Press.
Seregny, Scott J. 1996. "Professional Activism and Association among Russian Teachers, 1864–1905." In Balzer, 1996, 169–95.
Seton-Watson, Hugh. 1967. *The Russian Empire, 1801–1917*. Oxford: Clarendon Press.
Timberlake, Charles E. 1991. "The Zemstvo and the Development of a Russian Middle Class." In Clowes, Kassow, and West 1991, 164–79.
———. 1998. "The Tsarist Government's Preoccupation with the 'Liberal Party" in Tver' Province in 1890–1905." In Conroy 1998, 30–59.
Tsivian, Yuri, Paolo Cherchi Usai, Lorenzo Codelli, Carlo Montanaro, and David Robinson, eds. 1989. *Silent Witness: Russian Films, 1908–1919*. London: British Film Institute.
Valkener, Elizabeth. 1977. *Russian Realist Art: The State and Society. The Peredvizhniki and Their Tradition*. Ann Arbor, MI: Ardis.
Walker, Franklin A. 1984. "Popular Response to Public Education in the Reign of Tsar Alexander I (1801–1825)." *History of Education Quarterly* vol. 24, no. 4: 527–43.
Wallace, Sir Donald Mackenzie. 1961. *Russia on the Eve of War and Revolution*. First published 1877. New York: Vintage Press.
West, James L. 1991. "The Riabushinsky Circle: *Burzhiaziia* and *Obshchestvennost'* in Late Imperial Russia." In Clowes, Kassow, and West 1991, 41–56.
West, James L., and Iurii A. Petrov, eds. 1998. *Merchant Moscow: Images of Russia's Vanished Bourgeoisie*. Princeton, NJ: Princeton University Press
Wheatcroft, S. G., and R. W. Davies. 1994. "Population." In Davies, Harrison, and Wheatcroft 1994, 57–80.
Whittaker, Cynthia H. 1984. *The Origins of Modern Russian Education: An Intellectual Biography of Count Sergei Uvarov, 1786–1855*. DeKalb: Northern Illinois University Press.
Wirtschafter, Elise Kimmerling. 1997. *Social Identity in Imperial Russia*. DeKalb: Northern Illinois University Press.
Zubovrachebnyi vestnik, vol. 1, no. 1 (1885), p, 45; no. 5, 142; no. 10, 153; no. 231; vol. 13, no. 10 (1891), 24; no. 11, 429; vol. 14, no. 1 (1892), 41; no. 6, 241; no. 8, 331, 332; no. 9, 373; no. 10, 419; vol. 19, no. 4 (1897), 206; and no. 7, 367.

3

Civil Society in the Soviet Union?

Alfred B. Evans, Jr.

In recent years there has been a great deal of discussion of the condition of civil society in postcommunist Russia (Evans 2002).[1] It must be noted, however, that there are some large gaps in our understanding of the historical background of civil society in contemporary Russia. There has been a boom in scholarly works describing the gradual development of civil society in late tsarist Russia (Clowes, Kassow, and West 1991; Conroy 1998), but there has been no corresponding expansion of studies by Western scholars dealing with the possible precursors of civil society under the Soviet regime. The reasons for the neglect of that subject may be related to the two contending views of the character of social organizations in the Soviet system that are commonly found in the scholarly literature. The first view is that the Soviet state's mechanisms of control were pervasive, so that there were no independent social organizations (Biddulph 1975, 102; Pavlova 1998, 114), which for some implied that Soviet citizens were completely subjected to direction by the political regime. The second view is that by the late 1980s, an embryonic civil society had taken shape in the Soviet Union (White 1999, 41),[2] which for some observers of that period raised the hope that a full-fledged civil society would soon become dominant over the Soviet state (Starr 1988, 35; Lewin 1991, 80, 157). The analysis offered in this chapter takes issue with both these conclusions, or at least with the more simplistic versions of each one.

Most scholars have agreed that civil society, as usually defined by Western theoretical approaches, did not exist in the Soviet Union, because no sphere of formal organization in society was sufficiently independent of control by the party-state regime to be considered fundamentally self-governing. Nevertheless, there were three distinct arguments in favor of expecting the future emergence and flourishing of civil society in Russia. First, for a long time some scholars had asserted that the main historical accomplishment, and indeed the principal historical function, of the Soviet regime was that of directing the social and economic modernization of the USSR (Von Laue 1964). The awareness that the Soviet Union had become an industrialized society raised the hope that an urbanized society with an educated population and a complex social structure would be the basis for the gradual transition to a more pluralistic political system that would accept diversity in society as a natural consequence of modernization (Hough 1977, 22–24).[3] Second, in consistency with that argument, by the 1970s some scholars contended that "proto-interest groups" presented their demands within the limited but expanding pluralism of the Soviet political system (Ploss 1968; Skilling and Griffiths 1971). Those scholars assumed that if there were a breakthrough of rapid liberalization in that system, the networks of interest articulation that had developed cautiously under Communist rule would assume a form similar to that of interest groups in pluralist democracies. A third argument came from those who focused on trends among the creative and scientific intelligentsia in the post-Stalin years and hoped that the currents of dissatisfaction and dissidence that began to widen in the 1960s foreshadowed the beginnings of civil society. Those analysts thought that they saw the confirmation of their optimistic expectations in the rapid proliferation of independent organizations or "informal groups" during the period of perestroika in the late 1980s under Gorbachev (Starr 1988; Lewin 1991). With the wisdom of hindsight gained from the observation of trends in Russia since the end of Communist rule, it now seems clear that by the end of the 1990s, all three of those avenues of exploration had led to the disappointment of the most optimistic hopes.

After more than a decade of change in postcommunist Russia, it is apparent that the expectations for the imminent triumph of civil society in that country were exceedingly optimistic. Social and economic modernization were not sufficient to create the attitudes and behavior that are essential for the operation of secondary associations that is expected in a civil society. The proto-interest groups that exerted the greatest influence on policy makers in the USSR operated primarily within the state, and while such institutional interest groups have adapted to the changes in the postcommunist Russian political system with varying degrees of success, their existence did not guarantee the birth of organizations formed by the initiative of citizens and drawing on society's independent resources. The dissident movement and most of the informal groups proved to have shallow roots in Russian society, and the boom of activity that the unofficial groups enjoyed during the late 1980s was followed by a slump in their energy and effectiveness during the 1990s. In a preliminary assessment, it may be said that in Russia in the period since the breakup of the USSR and the collapse of the Communist Party's monopoly of control, the hopes that were based on those arguments for the emergence of Western-style pluralism have not been fulfilled. That realization suggests the need for a careful reexamination of the experience of social organizations in the USSR.

This chapter will direct most of its attention to the subject of social organizations (*obshchestvennye organizatsii*) in the Soviet Union.[4] During the last decades of the Soviet regime, those who looked for the beginnings of civil society in the USSR paid far less attention to those organizations, since it was widely assumed that such structures were only the "transmission belts" of the Communist Party's will, and therefore that the organizations lacked any autonomous life. Fortunately, since the beginning of the 1990s, some Russian historians have produced scholarly writings of high quality dealing with social organizations of various sorts in the Soviet Union; and this chapter draws on their findings, as well as on the writings of a number of Western scholars who have written about trade unions, women's groups, religious organizations, scientific societies, and other types of organizations that in theory were distinct from the state in the USSR. Among Russian historians, Irina Il'ina in particular stands out for her pathbreaking research on Soviet social organizations, and this chapter is greatly indebted to her major book (2000) on that subject. Also, a substantial number of studies of social organizations and networks in the Soviet Union have been conducted by Western scholars, though admittedly there are still numerous gaps in the historical coverage of such organizations, and little effort has been made to provide a general assessment of the organizations' experience (Bradley 1994, 34). In this chapter, the survey of the history of social organizations in the USSR emphasizes that during the earliest years of the Soviet system the Communist Party began its efforts to suppress independent social groups and confirms that the party's control of social organizations intensified from the early 1920s through the 1930s. The dream of the Bolsheviks was a society permeated with groups created from above. Even so, the social organizations that were designed to implement decisions that had been made at the highest level did perform functions that were useful for their members, and such organizations also took on the function of representing the interests of their members, if only in a limited fashion and within narrow boundaries. Most of those organizations have survived into the postcommunist period, usually with sharply reduced resources, but in any case bearing the marks of the dualistic legacy of both subordination to the state and service for their members that they inherited from the Soviet system.

Periods in Soviet History

The First Years of the Soviet Regime

In some ways it might seem that the early years after the October 1917 Revolution in Russia were not unfavorable for independent social organizations, since many prerevolutionary associations continued to operate, and some new, independent organizations were founded between 1917 and 1921 (Il'ina 2000, 59–60). Lynn Mally has said that in the initial period after the October Revolution, there was "an explosion in the number of new cultural groups and organizations," as "independent clubs and societies spr[a]ng up" (1990, 33). The burst of independent social activity reflected the liberation of energy among citizens of many ranks in society, however, rather than the intentions of the Bolshevik leadership. As Irina Il'ina has emphasized, the new government almost immediately began to introduce restrictions on social activity, closing many preexisting social organizations during 1918–19 (2000, 31). E. G. Gimpel'son, another contemporary Russian historian, reports that as early as 1918 the leadership of the Communist Party intended to subordinate not only state structures but also social organizations to the party (1995, 139). Geoffrey Hosking (1993, 88) points out that the rules of the Communist Party that were adopted in December 1919 stipulated that when there were three or more party members in any organization, they were required to form a party cell as a means of ensuring effective party supervision of the organization. E. A. Sikorskii (1999, 78) sees Lenin as having been the principal architect of the ideal of thorough domination of society by the Communist Party. In practice at the local level, however, it appears that the relationships between the soviets' executive committees (*ispolkomy*) and local social organizations varied substantially from one region to another (Sobolev 1985, 61). The direction in which the national political leadership wished to move was indicated in May 1918 when a decree of the All-Russian Central Executive Committee set up a new government agency, the Central Board of Universal Military Training (Vsevobuch), which was to control all sports clubs and societies and disbanded clubs that resisted its direction (Riordan 1977, 69–71). In the spring of 1919, the All-Russian Professional Union of Workers of the Arts (Vserabis) was formed, with the intention of ensuring Communist Party coordination of culture (Borisova 1993, 97), though it was to take a long time to achieve that goal. As A. I. Shchiglik unabashedly wrote during a time when Soviet historians had to follow the party line, after October 1917, prerevolutionary organizations would be allowed to exist, but only if they were subjected to thorough restructuring (*perestroika*), as "the dictatorship of the proletariat in our country 'digested' (*perevarila*) various old organizational forms and subordinated their work to the construction of socialism" (1977, 107).

Perhaps the most important social organizations inherited from prerevolutionary Russia were religious organizations, and the largest and most influential of those was the Russian Orthodox Church. In the first years after the October Revolution, that denomination was the particular target of the hostility of the Bolshevik regime (Walters 1988, 69). During the Russian Civil War, the state confiscated much church property, prohibited the levying of dues for church members, converted many churches to other uses, and prohibited religious instruction of children, while large numbers of priests were subjected to violent attacks (Pipes 1993, 339; Service 1998, 94). The nationalization of church property in 1918 severely restricted the potential for further charitable activity by religious organizations, though charitable work by religious associations was not officially banned until 1929 (Oliver 1992, 96). After 1918, all religious instruction of children outside the family was forbidden, and all religious publications were outlawed (Hosking 1993, 228). Providing a broader perspective, Iu. V. Aksiutin and his colleagues argue that after coming to power, the Bolsheviks not only liquidated the institutions of civil society but also largely destroyed the social strata that supported those institutions (1996, 113).

The 1920s

Despite the intentions of the consensus of the Bolshevik leadership, which from the outset foresaw the coordination of the whole range of social organizations, the 1920s are often remembered as the "golden age" of voluntary associations in the Soviet Union because thousands of varied associations arose and persisted during that decade (Il'ina 2000, 4). Not only did many prerevolutionary organizations continue to operate, but also a number of completely new ones came into existence. The number of social organizations in the USSR actually increased during the 1920s (ibid., 122).[5] Joseph Bradley points out that, though "many prerevolutionary associations disappeared" during the first few years under the Communist government, many other organizations that had been founded before 1917 continued to function in accordance with their prerevolutionary charters until 1929 (1994, 35–36). From 1918 until the late 1920s, not only the Communist Party but also factory committees, trade unions, and the movement for proletarian culture founded workers' clubs (Siegelbaum 1999, 79). The high degree of freedom among writers in the early 1920s opened the opportunity for the creation of a number of writers' organizations, each with its own artistic values and ideological outlook (Simmons 1961, 469).

On the other hand, the Communist state's response to the evidence of widespread activism in independent associations was to move toward a greater degree of "direct administrative interference in the process of creation of social organizations," as Il'ina says (2000, 110). She adds that the party leadership formulated the conception of a "new public" (*novaia obshchestvennost'*), in which social organizations were to be founded by the initiative of the political regime (ibid., 111). Il'ina documents the ways in which the Communist Party's guidance of social organizations was deliberately intensified during the 1920s, with insistence that party members form the core in each association and that the party organizations engage in detailed regulation of the activities of associations, including the convening and agendas of their congresses (ibid., 66, 68). Clearly the means of control that were to be well recognized in the mature Soviet system of later decades, in which the primary party organization in each social association coordinated the efforts of that association and reported to the higher party officials (Hill and Frank 1986, 131), reflected the design that the party leadership had adopted by the early 1920s. Lynn Mally points out that the Communist Party leadership, and Lenin foremost among that leadership, "distrusted any institution that demanded independence" (1990, 227). We must agree with Il'ina's thesis that, though a variety of social organizations continued to flourish for a few more years, the "basic vector" and predominant tendency of the 1920s in the Soviet Union was toward suppressing spontaneous social initiatives and directing all organizations to the achievement of the goals of the state (2000, 133).

As a concrete result of the political leadership's striving to suppress independent civic activism, steps were taken to decrease the number of active organizations during the 1920s, as reflected in legislation that was adopted during 1925, 1926, and 1928 (ibid., 82–83). To attempt to guarantee party control of those organizations that survived, the *nomenklatura* system began to develop after 1920, so that the top officials in all social associations (and indeed in all institutions in society) would be chosen or approved by the party Secretariat (Hosking 1993, 89). The inevitable result of that system would be that the officers of an organization like the Communist Youth League (*Komsomol*) would be appointed from above, and would owe their primary allegiance to their superiors in that organization and the party apparatus, rather than to the rank and file of the Komsomol (Kassof 1965, 125). Another sign of the tendency toward the tightening of control over social associations was the requirement of June 1922 that all societies and unions register with the People's Commissariat of Internal Affairs, or NKVD (Il'ina 2000, 61). From that time on, the NKVD, which controlled the police throughout the country, would have to grant associations permission to hold their congresses and national meetings and had the right to approve the charter of each organization and supervise its activity (Bradley 1994, 37). The drive to eliminate independent associations and replace them with organizations controlled by the Communist Party required the liquidation of all non-Communist organizations for children and youth, which entailed the suppression of the Boy Scouts and the consolidation of a monopoly by the Komsomol and its affiliated organizations (Krainov 1993, 207–8, 211).

Toward the middle of the 1920s, in Joseph Bradley's words, a "new network of organizations" began to arise, consisting of new mass membership organizations that were founded and structured by the Communist Party (1994, 37). Already in 1919, the party leadership had approved the establishment of the Women's Department (*Zhenotdel*) of the Central Committee Secretariat, which was subordinated to the party committees at the corresponding levels and was intended to carry out work among women as determined primarily by the goals of the political regime (Buckley 1989, 65, 70). Gail Lapidus specifies that the Zhenotdel was intended to remove obstacles to the political mobilization of women, and to function as a "female auxiliary of the party" (1978, 64, 66). However, the Zhenotdel was constantly hampered by interference from party and state officials who feared that the organization would serve as a channel for bourgeois feminism, and that arm of the party was finally abolished in 1929 (Jancar 1978, 59, 106). Though the Communist regime's general aims for social organizations were clear and the main mechanisms of control had already been created, the party was still learning by trial and error what organizations would be worth maintaining and what tasks each could accomplish.

The Bolshevik regime's fundamental attitude toward religious institutions had already been apparent from an early point, as we have seen, but the precise means of carrying out the struggle against organized religion had not yet been discovered by the end of the Russian Civil War. Until the end of the 1920s, the Russian Orthodox Church was the main target of persecution, while other religions faced varying degrees of restriction (Jancar 1975, 193). Yet even the attacks on the Orthodox Church were subjected to greater restraint by the middle of the 1920s, as emphasis shifted to indirect methods of splitting and demoralizing the Orthodox believers (Service 1998, 135). During the 1920s, the laws of the Soviet state specified that the only remaining activity that was permitted for churches and other religious organizations consisted of holding worship services and performing sacraments (Ellis 1986, 43).

Issues concerning the role of trade unions were the source of heated controversy among the party leadership, as noted in the chapter in this volume by Sue Davis. E. G. Gimpel'son has emphasized that even during the first years after the October Revolution there was a strong tendency toward integrating the unions with state structures and assigning them state functions, such as setting labor norms and wage rates and striving to fulfill productive tasks (1992, 48; 1995, 138). The debate about the unions reached its peak at the Tenth Congress of the Communist Party in March 1921, at which three contending proposals were presented and the one favored by Lenin was adopted (Ruble 1981, 10–11). In *Pravda* in 1921, Lenin delivered the famous dictum that the unions must serve as "the transmission belt from the Communist Party to the masses" (Ruble 1981, 12). Nevertheless, Lenin was the main source of the thinking that assigned dual roles to the unions, since they were supposed to implement the party's goals while also serving the workers' interests and protecting their rights (McAuley 1969, 10; Pravda and Ruble 1986a, 1–2; Ruble 1986, 24). The dualistic legacy of the unions proved to be long-lasting. Donald Filtzer points out that in the post–World War II years, "unions played a bifurcated role," since they supported management in seeking fulfillment of the plan, while "they would often defend individual workers if the latter pursued grievances" against management, though they refrained from advocating the interests of workers collectively in opposition to factory directors (2002, 202). As Blair Ruble described the situation, "a factory union leader in the Soviet Union must both mobilize workers behind production goals and defend those same workers against unscrupulous administrators" (1981, 9). The interpretation that was accepted by most Western scholars for several decades, and is now supported by the consensus of contemporary Russian historians, is that the control function of the unions was always primary, though the balance between the two functions varied over time. Under the New Economic Policy (NEP) until 1929, Soviet trade unions enjoyed a greater degree of independence than they had during the Civil War, so that workers could now call strikes in their enterprises, and many unions engaged in collective bargaining with management (Ruble 1981, 12). The dualistic orientation of the unions was paralleled in other social organizations in the Soviet Union, with somewhat different styles of operation in different organizations.

The party leadership also faced questions concerning the degree of independence of cultural institutions and organizations. The founders of *Proletkul't* (Proletarian Cultural-Educational Institutions) had intended that their organization would be completely independent from the Communist Party and state and would provide opportunities for the expression of the autonomous, creative force of the working class (Mally 1990, 36–38; Hosking 1993, 180). Richard Pipes contends that Proletkul't enjoyed greater autonomy from the Communist Party than any other group and that its leaders openly regarded themselves as subject only to their own supervision (1993, 291). Its leaders still expected that Proletkul't would receive extensive financial support from the state, however (Husband 1997, 288). As Daniel Orlovsky says, Proletkul't "was culture 'from below,' inevitably representing an alternative to party dogma and inviting different readings of Marxism itself" (1997, 261). Lynn Mally finds that Proletkul't allowed a remarkable degree of eclecticism in cultural innovation and lacked any unified aesthetic direction, in large part because participants in the movement were unable to agree on the precise purpose of their organization (1990, 152). The central core of the organization had little authority over its local affiliates and was not even very competent in collecting information about its growing network of groups, so that the grass roots influenced the national leadership much more than that leadership influenced the local branches (ibid., 67–68). Such autonomy, decentralization, and eclecticism were unacceptable to those at the highest level in the Communist Party, and Lenin took the lead in obtaining a decree from the Central Committee in October 1920, ordering that Proletkul't be integrated into the state's Commissariat of Enlightenment (Siegelbaum 1992, 56; Pipes 1993, 291). During the next two years, the central and regional offices of Proletkul't were closed and most of its activities were curtailed. Though the organization was not formally abolished until 1932, after late 1920 its activities were severely diminished (Read 1990, 145). In 1928, the party presided over the founding of the Russian Association of Proletarian Writers, or RAPP, an organization that was intended to impart a direction to literature that would be in accordance with the party's wishes (Simmons 1961, 470; Hosking 1993, 181).

The Academy of Sciences of the USSR was perhaps unique in that it was the only prerevolutionary institution that retained almost complete independence until the late 1920s. For several years after 1917, the Communist leaders had no clear conception of what they wanted to do with the Academy of Sciences, and did not try to subordinate it to party control, though they did seek to undermine its dominance in the direction of science in the Soviet Union (Vucinich 1984, 93–94, 101). Even in 1927, not a single academician was a Communist Party member, there was not a single party cell in the Academy, and its press was uncensored, even with respect to works in the social sciences. Loren Graham has said aptly that at that time, the Academy of Sciences "was an anomaly in Soviet society" (1967b, 30). That anomaly and other deviations from the pattern prescribed by the political regime would be eliminated during the next few years as Stalin's transformation of Soviet society unfolded.

The 1930s

The relative freedom of operation that many social associations enjoyed throughout most of the 1920s and the variety in the goals of such organizations came to an end during the First Five-Year Plan period, as the party and state tightened control of society to an extreme degree. A 1928 law on nonprofit organizations and groups provided the legal basis for contracting the range of social organizations (Il'ina 2000, 56, 83, 90). Il'ina points out that "of the enormous quantity of social organizations of the 1920s, the overwhelming majority were liquidated by 1932" (ibid., 95). Under legislation passed in 1930, there was a trend of merging and consolidation of societies, supposedly to avoid duplication (Bradley 1994, 40). The requirement that all existing voluntary associations register anew with the state helped to ensure that the number of such organizations would decrease (Il'ina 2000, 56). Such changes were in accordance with the central political authorities' explicit goal of restructuring the work of social organizations in order to attract voluntary associations to "active participation in socialist construction," naturally implying strict political supervision of such organizations (ibid., 57).[6] By 1932, official policy decreed that where there were multiple societies of writers, artists, composers, or film makers, the existing societies should be disbanded and replaced in each area of cultural activity by one united (*edinyi*) creative union (Korzhikhina 1981, 115). Of course, that policy also brought a sharp reduction in the number of voluntary associations. During the First Five-Year Plan period and the accompanying "Cultural Revolution," voluntary associations were replaced by mass organizations created by the Communist Party (Bradley 1994, 42) of the sort for which models had been created in the 1920s but not yet widely imposed. Even the majority of mass organizations that had arisen during the 1920s were abolished during the early 1930s, however (ibid., 43). After 1934, almost all remaining social organizations that had been in existence before 1929 were closed, and it became virtually impossible to found new organizations unless the initiative came from the Communist political leadership (Il'ina 2000, 95).

On the basis of research by contemporary Russian historians, it seems clear that a crucial test case for the change in policy during the period of the institutionalization of full Stalinism was that which sealed the fate of the *kraevedy*. The kraevedy were the devotees of local lore and history in a wide variety of districts of Russia, and their society was one of the largest voluntary associations in the Soviet Union. The suppression of the society of the kraevedy began in Voronezh in later 1930, when the State Political Directorate, or OGPU, began arresting its members in that region on false charges, and by 1937 the government of the USSR officially eliminated all organizations that were dedicated to the study of local lore (Akinyshin 1992, 174–77; Il'ina 2000, 92). Political control over culture also was tightened in the early 1930s, as RAPP, which earlier had supplanted Proletkul't, was formally abolished in 1932 so that it could be replaced by the Union of Soviet Writers, which was expected to be amenable to direction by the Communist faction within its ranks (Simmons 1961, 471; Siegelbaum 1997, 305).[7] Geoffrey Hosking characterizes that organization as typical of the "monolithic professional unions set up by the state and run by a mixture of 'Old' and 'Red' specialists under strict party guidance" (1993, 225). Similarly, after April 1930, a new All-Union Physical Culture Council attached to the government's Central Executive Committee was charged with the task of controlling all sports councils and clubs, so that supervision of sports was not entrusted to nongovernmental organizations after that point but was directly carried out by agencies of the state (Riordan 1977, 122–23).

The late 1920s were a turning point for trade unions in the USSR (Ruble 1981, 13). During 1928 and 1929, under orders from the party leadership, union leaders who had pushed for relative independence and had emphasized the defense of workers' rights were removed from their offices (Brown 1966, 52). Merle Fainsod's investigation of the documents in the Smolensk archive also marks 1929 as the turning point in the history of Soviet labor, because of "a marked tightening of labor discipline, a strengthening of managerial prerogatives, [and] an atrophy in the powers of the trade unions" that took place at that time (1963, 309). As Blair Ruble summarizes the situation, by the end of the 1930s "the unions served as agents of state and party control over the Soviet population" (1981, 20). Emily Clark Brown, who, in general, offers an exceptionally favorable depiction of Soviet trade unions, concludes that by the late 1930s "there was widespread feeling among workers that the unions were chiefly agencies of management and the party, not able or willing to do much for their members" (1966, 56–57).

The political regime also sought to structure an officially supervised institutional framework for leisure activities by creating workers' clubs and palaces of culture (Siegelbaum 1999, 89). Lewis Siegelbaum has astutely observed that the more enterprising participants in the workers' clubs managed to appropriate those state-sponsored institutions for their own purposes (1999, 79), but it is important to realize that such capable citizens were able to achieve their objectives by working within the channels provided by the regime rather than attempting to found independent organizations, which would have been suppressed by the state. Indeed, the citizens who led the workers' clubs were able to take advantage of the material resources and legitimacy granted by the state to facilitate the pursuit of their goals. Another sign of the tightening of control over social organizations in the late 1920s and early 1930s was the dramatic decline of the independence of scientific societies during those years. The Academy of Sciences and other scientific societies were subordinated to control by the Communist Party after 1928 (Brooks 1997, 363; Graham 1967a, 89–90; Vucinich 1984, 129). The party abolished the Zhenotdel in 1930, ending the nation's only organization for women, ostensibly because women had already been liberated (Lapidus 1978, 71; Buckley 1989, 103).

The campaign against religious organizations was intensified sharply, starting in 1928, with all religious denominations now targeted for suppression (Walters 1988, 74). The relative moderation of official policy during several previous years, when it was hoped that education, propaganda, and discrimination would guarantee that religion would gradually fade, gave way to "a frontal assault" that was intended "to diminish the power and influence of all forms of religious organization" (Fainsod 1963, 434). Legislation that was adopted in 1929 increased the Soviet state's direct control over religious organizations and explicitly prohibited charitable work by such organizations (Jancar 1975, 194; Oliver 1992, 96; Il'ina 2000, 51). By 1929, it became evident that the League of the Godless, one of the state-sponsored mass organizations that had been created in the 1920s, would be a direct extension of the authority of the Communist Party in the struggle for total victory over religion (Peris 1991, 723). Robert Service reports that the number of clergy who were killed during the First Five-Year Plan even exceeded the total of those who had been murdered during the Civil War (1998, 203). A second wave of arrests of clergy and closing of churches followed during the great purges of 1936–39 (Hosking 1993, 235). As a result of repeated campaigns of persecution, the Russian Orthodox Church had been reduced to a shadow of its former existence by the end of the 1930s. Service estimates that by that time, only one in forty churches continued to function, while no new churches were being built in the new cities and towns that were growing rapidly across the country (1998, 204). Philip Walters considers it likely that in the territory under Soviet control before September 1939, only one hundred to two hundred Orthodox churches were still open, compared with about forty-six thousand such churches before the October Revolution, while Nathaniel Davis estimates that by 1939, from two hundred to three hundred churches remained open in the Soviet Union (Walters 1988, 75; Davis 1995, 13).Though Islam in the USSR had a relatively docile leadership and was better able to survive through informal and underground activities (Bourdeaux 1975, 171), all religious organizations found their opportunities for operating openly to have been severely curtailed by the institutionalization of Stalinism.

By the end of the 1930s, the Soviet regime had destroyed almost all independent organizations that had furnished mediating linkages between citizens and the state and had channeled all organized, overt public activism into structures that were controlled by the party-state regime (Bonnell 1990, 66). A contemporary Russian historian who has examined the records in the Smolensk archive concludes that "control by the party and state organs of state security over conduct, word, and thought was ubiquitous" (Koshkin 1999, 293). I. V. Pavlova says that it is impossible to discern elements of civil society in the Stalinist order, since the social organizations of the 1930s were not acting independently of state power but transmitted the directives of political authority (2001, 50). It seems clear that the organizations that had constituted a nascent civil society in late tsarist Russia and had fought to continue their existence in the first years after the Communist takeover of power had been effectively eradicated and replaced by a system of public organizations permeated by party and state control by the late 1930s.

The Wartime Period

The most significant shift in the relationship between the state and social organizations during World War II (the Great Patriotic War) was in the area of the regime's treatment of organized religion, especially the Russian Orthodox Church. In September 1943, Metropolitan Sergei was summoned to the Kremlin to meet Stalin, the Church was allowed to reestablish the patriarchate, and the government set up a Council for the Affairs of the Russian Orthodox Church, which would deal directly with the church hierarchy, giving de facto recognition to the Church as an institution (Walters 1988, 77; Service 1998, 282). The administration of that denomination was revived, and a large number of churches that had been closed in earlier years were allowed to reopen for services (Hosking 1993, 237). However, the Church was still subordinated to the state, and indeed the regime's control of all religious organizations was strengthened (Jancar 1975, 194; Oliver 1992, 97). To a greater extent than ever before, the hierarchy of the Orthodox Church was assimilated to the *nomenklatura* system of appointments (Hosking 1993, 237), and that church became an instrument for gaining greater popular acceptance of Stalin's rule (Service 1998, 282). Thus relatively more favorable conditions for the operation of the Orthodox Church and some other religious bodies did not signify a retreat from the state's penetration of social organizations.

The Post-Stalin Period

In the decades after Stalin's death in 1953, most of the state-sponsored social organizations continued their operations, and the Communist Party generally succeeded in maintaining close control over such associations (Hill and Frank 1986, 131–32). It must be recognized, however, that there was some change in social organizations in the post-Stalin period, though different organizations changed to different degrees (Kassof 1965, 176). Allen Kassof presents the Komsomol (Communist Youth League) as an example of an association that did not change much, and his interpretation seems quite plausible on the basis of other analyses and evidence. The Komsomol remained thoroughly subordinate to the Communist Party (Gimpel'son 1995, 3); and its main tasks of political control, indoctrination, and organization of physical culture were determined by the party leadership (Fainsod 1956, 240; Kassof 1965, 5).

To facilitate the party's supervision of the Komsomol, the hierarchical structuring of the youth league exactly mirrored that of the Communist Party (Fainsod 1956, 251), and elections of Komsomol officials at all levels were carefully arranged in advance by higher-level functionaries in the Komsomol or party leaders, or both (Fainsod 1961, 157). Jerry Hough, however, has argued that the Komsomol did provide its youthful members some opportunities to try to affect the conditions in which they studied, worked, and lived (Hough and Fainsod 1979, 300).In comparison with some other public organizations, however, the Komsomol probably had less independence and was less important in satisfying group demands. Kassof reported that many young people resented being compelled to enroll in the organization in order to enter higher educational institutions or advance their careers and that, as a result, widespread apathy among its members was a serious problem for the league (1965, 121–22). His conclusions are consistent with the later reality of the rapid disappearance of the Komsomol toward the end of Communist Party rule, when it became apparent that membership in the organization was no longer necessary for educational admissions or professional employment.[8]

Labor unions experienced more significant change in the post-Stalin period. Though the unions had been effectively subordinated to the Communist Party during the 1930s, Donald Filtzer cites instances of unions' asserting demands on behalf of workers even before the end of Stalin's life, in reaction to inadequate wages and food shortages after World War II (Filtzer 2002, 81, 86). Already by the time of the Tenth Congress of the All-Union Central Council of Trade Unions in 1949, speeches at the congress and articles in union publications demanded that the unions become more responsive to their members' expressed needs (Ruble 1981, 24). Under Khrushchev after 1957, there was greater official emphasis on the unions' tasks connected with improving conditions for workers and safeguarding their rights (Brown 1966, 61; McAuley 1969, 66). Walter Connor confirms that the scope of union activity and the resources at the disposal of the unions increased after 1957 (1991, 209). The unions continued to be under the control of the Communist Party, however; and the principal objectives of the unions' work still reflected the initiative of the party (Brown 1966, 63; Hill and Frank 1986, 130). Within a factory, union officials usually worked in close cooperation with management; and when the workers' rights came into conflict with the imperative of plan fulfillment, the union leaders tended to give top priority to production goals (Ruble 1979, 79). Trade union offices were included in the nomenklatura system, so that Communist Party leaders effectively determined the outcome of the elections to fill such positions (Ruble 1979, 72), creating a substantial gap between union officials and the rank-and-file members of the unions. According to Robert Conquest (1967, 151), the position of the unions as "transmission belts" of the party's directives was not fundamentally altered in the post-Stalin period; and contemporary Russian historians such as Iu. V. Aksiutin and his colleagues (1996, 594) suggest that Conquest's conclusion was correct.

Despite that argument, scholars who specialized in studying Soviet trade unions found that factory union committees often did make efforts on a case-by-case basis to protect individual workers from "specific abuses by individual managers" (Ruble 1986, 27; Connor 1991, 209). The unions' capacity for the defense of workers as a group was much more limited, since the major potential issues between management and labor in any factory or any industry were not subject to dispute, due to the limits imposed by Soviet legislation and the centralized control of economic enterprises (McAuley 1969, 249). From the viewpoint of the individual worker on the shop floor, it probably remained true, as it had been in the Stalin years, that the most attractive options for workers persistently dissatisfied with some conditions were individual responses, primarily in the form of absenteeism, insubordination, or job changing (Filtzer 1986, 2; Filtzer 2002, 9, 202, 243); or an appeal to the union committee to defend against an illegal infraction by management; or attempts to take advantage of informal personal connections (Ruble 1986, 31). Most Soviet workers probably did not perceive the unions as having a powerful effect on conditions in the workplace, but some probably saw the unions as having some beneficial effect. In the sample of émigrés interviewed in the Soviet Interview Project in the 1980s, of those who answered a question about the effects of trade unions on workers' welfare, 37.3 percent said that unions made things better, 0.9 percent answered that unions made things worse, and 61.7 percent said that unions had no effect (Gregory 1987, 250).

Under Khrushchev the Communist Party introduced women's councils, or *zhensovety*, to address issues of specific concern to women (Browning 1987, 52–53), as part of a "differentiated approach" to meeting the needs of various groups in society (Buckley 1989, 144, 147). The party had taken the initiative in founding the zhensovety, and it attempted to ensure that they worked within the framework of its policies (Browning 1987, 73, 74). According to Mary Buckley, the zhensovety "followed directions specified by the party," and the activities of their sections "reflected official party priorities for work among women" (1989, 149–50). In the conception of the leaders who authorized the creation of the zhensovety, one of the most important functions of those councils was to mobilize women in their workplaces in order to increase the quantity and improve the quality of production (Browning 1987, 83–85).

Even so, the zhensovety studied by Mary Buckley showed every evidence of striving to address the needs of women workers, based on the expression of those needs by the women themselves (1989, 211–15). Genia Browning found that zhensovety frequently attempted to enhance working conditions for women and placed considerable emphasis on improving child care, medical care, and cafeterias at places of work, even though such efforts sometimes brought zhensovety activists into conflict with management (1987, 113–15). The programs of the zhensovety often included classes on knitting, sewing, cooking, and other aspects of homemaking, obviously in accordance with conventional stereotypes of a gender-based division of labor but evidently also in consistency with the wishes of many women (Browning 1987, 97). Thus the zhensovety could be credited with some genuine accomplishments on behalf of women on a modest scale, by helping somewhat to ease the notorious double burden on Soviet women as workers on the one hand, and mothers and homemakers on the other, and by obtaining some benefits for individual women and small groups of women (Browning 1992, 102). They were not able to confront the political leadership at the national level or to challenge official policies on the basis of competing conceptions of the interests of women as a whole. Thus Browning argues that the role of the zhensovety as a pressure group was very limited (1987, 116), but that did not prevent them from offering some useful services to women at the local level. Mary Buckley observes that the members of the zhensovety themselves often had "a hazy idea about what they should be doing and frequently hesitate to take the initiative without being told to do," which won them the reputation of being rather docile organizations when frank discussion of such matters was permitted in the late 1980s (1989, 215–16).

In the post-Stalin period, the Academy of Sciences of the USSR enjoyed qualitative growth in the degree of its independence from the party and state, so that control over the direction of research in most of the Academy's institutes in the natural sciences shifted from party functionaries to senior scientists (Graham 1967a, 155–57). Jerry Hough says that there were instances in which high-ranking party officials even failed to win election to membership in the Academy (Hough and Fainsod 1979, 397). The Academy of Sciences, and particularly the natural sciences, apparently won an unparalleled degree of autonomy from the detailed control of some of their professional activities, though the social science institutes were much more subject to political interference. Alexander Vucinich emphasizes that even in the post-Stalin period the Academy of Sciences of the USSR functioned both as a part of the scientific community and as "an integral part of the Soviet state" (1984, 1). Indeed, he argues that during the post-Stalin decades "the Academy became more firmly integrated into the system of Soviet government," while it "also acquired unprecedented strength in influencing the government's decisions on the development of national science policy" (ibid., 198, 308–9).[9] In fact, the scientists who had influence on public policies worked in institutions that were funded by the state, and they used their officially granted status to advantage in their lobbying efforts, because their institutional positions gave them direct access to key decision makers.

Religious organizations did not enjoy the relatively benign treatment by the state or the expansion of independence that were granted to natural science institutes. The best that the Russian Orthodox Church could hope for in exchange for its faithful support of the political regime was a modest degree of freedom in managing its internal affairs (Walters 1988, 82). In 1959, however, the Orthodox Church and other denominations sustained a traumatic shock as Khrushchev launched a major assault on religion. The persecution of religion was renewed, and churches of all Christian denominations were demolished in most regions of the USSR (Service 1998, 369). The Orthodox Church again was the main target; from 1959 to 1964, two-thirds of the Orthodox churches that had been operating legally in the country were closed, and many priests and active lay persons were arrested and tried (Walters 1988, 81). After Khrushchev's fall, overt persecution of the Orthodox Church decreased; in Geoffrey Hosking's words, "the Soviet state . . . was no longer trying to destroy the church but to use it as a pliant instrument" (Hosking 1993, 440). State officials were more hostile toward some smaller religious groups such as the Baptists and Pentecostalists.

There are widespread reports that during the 1950s and 1960s, a number of informal social groups, mostly nonpolitical in orientation, began to take shape quietly without sponsorship by the Communist Party (Alekseeva and Fitzpatrick 1990, 3; Smith 1996, 69). Under Brezhnev, Soviet authorities tended to look the other way instead of actively moving to suppress most of these groups. It appears likely that many of the new groups that were not sponsored by the political regime were founded by young people (Bonnell 1990, 64; Hosking 1990, 64), most often to give an outlet to their desire for new forms of leisure activities. Unofficial associations included clubs of sports fans, rock music enthusiasts, poets, amateur actors, and aficionados of basketball, yoga, and break dancing. Some other unofficial organizations of citizens attempted to satisfy unfulfilled social needs, including those of people with various sorts of disabilities (White 1993, 790; White 1999, 17, 54–64). It is said that the number of independent associations increased in the 1970s and early 1980s (Alekseeva and Fitzpatrick 1990, 4), though it is impossible to give a precise estimate of the number of such groups. Some ideologically unorthodox groups such as the nationalistic and racist group, Pamiat', were on the borderline of being defined as dissidents and risking suppression by the authorities (Petro 1991, 119), but they were quietly tolerated by the state, perhaps because of protection from some patrons in the Communist leadership. In the 1970s, demands by many citizens that the state improve its efforts toward the protection or restoration of buildings of historical significance led to the founding of the All-Union Society for the Preservation of Historical and Cultural Monuments, which acquired a huge number of members within a short time (Petro 1991, 107). That society seemed to reflect genuine grassroots initiative, though it was not entirely free of party control, and its very existence seemed to be due to sympathy from some factions in the political leadership.

In the early 1960s, the warnings voiced by writers and scientists about such problems as pollution in Lake Baikal brought attention to the beginnings of an environmental movement in the Soviet Union (Ziegler 1987, 53; Hosking 1990, 51–52; Peterson 1993, 208–9). For many years (until the Gorbachev period), most of those who were able to raise issues concerning the environment occupied positions in research institutes, institutions of higher education, or government bureaus; in other words, the articulation of interests in that area of policy came from within the state or organizations closely integrated with the state (Ziegler 1987, 62–63). When scientists sought to influence environmental policy by making written statements, they published their findings in books, journals, magazines, and newspapers that were approved by the state or in internal documents directed to officials in the government. Environmentalists did not attempt to create separate, much less independent, groups. They were able to gain some access to decision makers in part because of divisions within the political leadership that left those on each side seeking justification for their stance (Hosking 1990, 53).

After Stalin's death and even more after Khrushchev's "secret speech" denouncing Stalin at the Twentieth Congress of the Communist Party of the Soviet Union in 1956, the range of permitted subjects for creative literature expanded, and some writers sought to test the limits further (Hosking 1993, 409–10). By the early 1960s *samizdat* (self-published) writings began to appear, initially consisting of poetry but subsequently including other types of material. After the trial and sentencing of Andrei Siniavskii and Iulii Daniel in 1965 for the offense of publishing fiction abroad, an organized dissident movement emerged, as intellectuals, mainly writers and scientists, protested against that punishment and asserted the right of freedom of expression (Hosking 1993, 413–14). Further arrests stimulated further protests, in the form of letters, petitions, and occasional public demonstrations. In 1965–67, an organized movement of dissenters took shape, insistently raising issues of human rights and acting independently of the state by gathering signatures on petitions and disseminating multiple copies of samizdat writings (Reddaway 1975, 125–26, 147). By 1968, various samizdat writings were regularly collected and published in the main journal of the dissident movement, *Chronicle of Current Events* (Hosking 1993, 418).

In response to the state's efforts to repress dissent, after 1968 the movement's demands became directly political, it attracted wider circles of active supporters, and it became better organized (Aksiutin 1996, 593; Freeze 1997a, 379). Soviet dissidents also learned how to use means of communication to take their case to the world outside the borders of the USSR (Tökes 1975a, 24). After the invasion of Czechoslovakia in 1968, the KGB cast aside its former caution and moved to arrest as many dissidents as possible (Reddaway 1975, 147–48). By 1971, the KGB attempted to suppress all samizdat publications; and by 1974, many of the first generation of dissenters had been imprisoned or driven into emigration. Most scholars agree that by the middle of the 1970s, repression had taken a serious toll on the dissident movement (Tökes 1975a, 12). The ranks of the movement were fragmenting, and its remaining participants engaged in intermittent and uncoordinated actions (Tökes 1974, 28). Evidently the Communist leadership was determined to eliminate organized dissent altogether.

Though the dissident movement had grown during the late 1960s, Theodore Friedgut argues that the "active democrats" were "at best a tiny percentage of the intelligentsia" (1975, 123). The dissident movement remained isolated from the majority of Soviet citizens, as most people saw the vocal dissenters as reckless, and feared being associated with them (ibid., 129; Lane 1985, 271). Walter Connor asserts that most of the population of the Soviet Union had little knowledge of the dissidents who received a great deal of publicity in the West, and that most of those who had heard of the dissenters reacted "with hostility or incomprehension" toward them, so that dissidents failed "to strike a responsive chord among the masses" (Connor 1975, 155). The dissident movement did survive in the early 1980s (Alekseeva and Fitzpatrick 1990, 4), but with fewer participants and with sharply decreased capacity to express its demands openly (Hosking 1993, 425).

Dissenting elements also appeared within Soviet trade unions and the Russian Orthodox Church, both of which had become pillars of support for the political regime and had been fairly quiescent for a few decades. During the late 1970s, there were three different attempts to found independent trade unions (Connor 1991, 225). Those efforts were the product of small, isolated groups that were quickly suppressed by the authorities. The leaders of the official unions cooperated in blocking the formation of an independent labor movement, since the outlook of those leaders was, as Connor maintains, "antithetical to the development" of opposition to the political regime (ibid., 246). Vocal dissatisfaction with the Orthodox Church's docility was more widespread than open discontent within the unions, though evidently it was shared by only a minority of priests and laity. In 1976, some dissident Orthodox priests and lay persons created a Christian Committee for the Defense of Believers' Rights, which used samizdat and Western publications to publicize violations of the rights of religious believers (Hosking 1993, 441). Most of the leaders of that group were arrested and sentenced to prison or labor camps. During the 1970s and 1980s, a reportedly growing number of the Orthodox faithful demanded that the state's control of their denomination be eased (Bourdeaux 1975, 164–66; Walters 1988, 83). More vigorous and persistent discontent was articulated by a group of Baptists who became known informally as the *Initsiativniki*; these dissidents even founded unregistered churches and operated underground printing presses (Hosking 1993, 441). Before Gorbachev came to power, the Russian Orthodox Church was unique in Soviet society as an organization whose hierarchy accepted the compromise that gave the Church a very limited degree of freedom to perform functions of little practical concern to the state, in exchange for the Church's loyal support for the political regime (Walters 1988, 88, 90).

Gorbachev: Perestroika and the Rise of Independent Organizations

Mikhail Gorbachev took power as head of the Communist Party of the Soviet Union in the spring of 1985, and by the summer of 1986 he called for the radical restructuring (*perestroika*) of all the institutions in the Soviet system. His program for the limited democratization of that system allowed the founding of "informal" groups (*neformalye*), which were created by the initiative of citizens rather than the dictates of the party apparatus, and which Gorbachev expected to furnish public support for his reforms (Brovkin 1990; Hosking 1993, 466). Within a short time the number of such groups had grown with startling rapidity (Bonnell 1990, 64), and the range of their interests was quite broad, including everything from stamp collecting to heavy-metal rock music (Petro 1991, 102). In 1988 the Communist Party newspaper *Pravda* estimated that there were about thirty thousand informal groups in the USSR, and in 1989 *Pravda* reported that there were around sixty thousand of those groups in the country (Butterfield and Sedaitis 1991, 1; White 1995, 1354). Anne White points out, however, that since the creation of voluntary associations was favored by official policy at that time, those numbers were probably exaggerated (ibid.; White 1999, 12). She notes that in 1990 the *Moscow News* suggested that there were from two thousand to three thousand "informals" in the USSR, and she adds that the number of such organizations in existence at that time cannot be determined precisely, but a realistic estimate would be on the order of thousands rather than tens of thousands.

There is general agreement on the crucial point that, whether they were oriented toward political objectives or absorbed in leisure activities, the informal groups were a new phenomenon in the Soviet Union, since they were social organizations that were not directed by the Communist Party but pursued activities chosen by their members (Alekseeva and Fitzpatrick 1990, 1). Also, a substantial number of those groups (if only a minority of them) were increasingly politicized, as they openly pressed demands for actions by the state, and in some cases called for radical changes in policy. For example, the *Pamiatnik* society was founded in 1987 (Adler 1993, 51; Smith 1996, 84) to advocate the construction of a monument to the victims of Stalin's terror, and it soon expanded its goals to seek broad acknowledgment of the human costs of the terror (White 1995, 1344). Movements opposing the construction and operation of nuclear power plants gathered strength rapidly in Russia and three other republics of the USSR from 1987 to 1991 and achieved some distinct successes in influencing decision making (Dawson 1996, 3). Some of the already existing women's councils found that they had the freedom to pursue more independent initiatives (Browning 1992, 103), while a large number of new women's groups attempted to raise women's consciousness and address immediate problems, though those groups did not achieve a great deal of impact on policies (Noonan 1996, 84). Workers began to use strikes as a means of pressing their demands, and strikes became more frequent over time during the late 1980s (Connor 1991, 240). By the beginning of the 1990s, some scholars contended that the relationship between state and society had shifted critically (Butterfield and Weigle 1991, 190–91) and that elements of a civil society had begun to emerge in the Soviet Union (Hosking 1990, 75, 126; Peterson 1993, 193). Some suggested that the retreat of the "totalitarian" state in the face of pressure from voluntary associations had gone beyond the point of no return, so it was highly likely that the triumph of civil society would come in the near future.

In 1988, Gorbachev began a sharp change in relations between church and state in the USSR (Davis 1995, 64–67), in accordance with his positive evaluation of pluralism in Soviet society. By the summer of 1990, thousands of churches had reopened and others had been established for the first time, increasing the number of functioning churches in the Soviet Union by almost 50 percent (Powell 1991, 328). New legislation of September 1990 attempted to guarantee freedom of conscience and worship, and removed most restrictions on religious activities (Hosking 1993, 461).

Religious organizations were also allowed to engage in charitable work for the first time since the 1920s (Oliver 1992, 102–6). Independent charitable organizations had begun to appear as early as 1987, and the *Miloserdie* movement soon became "a nationwide phenomenon," with groups forming in many cities in the USSR even in the absence of any central organization (White 1993, 292). However, as Steven Fish has pointed out, most of the organizations created by citizens had "hyperdemocratic" internal structures that lacked clear lines of authority and responsibility, and such groups generally had little capacity to establish relationships with state organs in a manner that would enable them to articulate group interests on a regular basis (1995, 56–57). For such organizations, success in influencing public policy still depended heavily on winning the favor of individuals in powerful positions within the state; according to Anne White, reliance on personal contacts compromised the independence of social groups, and "perpetuated the arbitrariness and dependence on figures of authority which marked the Soviet period" (1999, 168).

Conclusion

The historical evidence that has been examined in this chapter supports the conclusion that civil society was almost completely eradicated in the Soviet Union with the consolidation of mature Stalinism during the 1930s. In fact, recent studies by Irina Il'ina and other historians have demonstrated that from the period of the founding of the Communist regime, the dominant elements in the Bolshevik leadership embraced the conception of a comprehensive network of mass organizations dedicated to the service of the goals of the party and state, and they almost immediately began to lay the cornerstones for a system of party control of such organizations throughout the whole society. During the 1920s, which are remembered as a period of relative freedom when a variety of social groups continued to operate, the political regime moved to prepare for the elimination of prerevolutionary voluntary associations and their replacement by mass organizations controlled by the party apparatus. The breakthrough toward the realization of the goal of comprehensive subordination of social organizations to the state came during the First Five-Year Plan of the late 1920s and early 1930s. By the late 1930s, the elimination of independent, organized social activity was almost complete, and civil society was hardly even a memory in Soviet society.

Despite the notions fostered by some earlier theories, Soviet society was not entirely passive in reaction to initiatives by the political regime, even after the full consolidation of Stalinism. People in the USSR were not automatons who obediently followed all directives from the state and internalized all the party's values and goals as their own. The members of Soviet society proved inventive and often energetic in finding ways to achieve objectives that were of importance to them personally or to their families. There is an empirical basis for concluding that the informal connections and tradeoffs that were used by Soviet citizens to make the system work for them became more important from one generation to another in the post-Stalin period (Millar 1987a, 28; Zimmerman 1987, 349–50). Soviet citizens became highly accomplished in evading authority and subverting the rules of the system, which reinforced the perception of a wide gap between public norms and practical necessity, fostering an underground popular culture pervaded with cynicism concerning the validity of ethical guidelines for behavior outside the circles of intimacy and trust among family members and close friends (Shtromas 1984; Jowitt 1992). When social organizations like the trade unions or the women's councils of the post-Stalin (and pre-Gorbachev) years did genuinely attempt to represent the interests of their members, they usually defended the rights of individuals on a case-by-case basis, rather than challenging the policies that were adverse to their constituents as groups of people. In the post-Stalin period, when small clusters of citizens in key positions sought to influence policies on such issues as environmental protection or nuclear weapons development, they did not try to found independent organizations but instead took advantage of their positions in organizations that were sponsored by the state, and indeed used the resources and connections attached to those divisions of the official network of control. Also, any instances of success in such attempts to influence decision making—and there were some successes, as documented by Charles E. Ziegler (1987), Matthew Evangelista (1999), Douglas R. Weiner (1999), and others— reinforced the lesson that ties with individuals in key posts of authority were crucial assets for those seeking to make an impact on public policies.

As we have seen, the dualistic functioning of social organizations in the Soviet Union meant that each organization worked toward achieving the goals set by the Communist Party and also devoted some attention to serving the interests of its members (Hill and Frank 1986, 133–34). (In an analogous fashion, the organs of local government in the USSR had the primary function of achieving the objectives that were chosen by the Communist Party and the secondary function of providing channels for representing citizens' interests [Hahn 1988, 169, 260–61].) The degree of commitment to fulfilling the needs of members varied from one organization to another. There is general agreement among contemporary scholars that the function of implementing the directives of the party usually was of primary importance. For that reason and because there were more than adequate mechanisms of control of social organizations, it is understandable that as those organizations operated within the Soviet system, Western observers could not regard them as harbingers of pluralist democracy or components of an emerging civil society. The limitations on the way that such organizations could articulate the interests of their constituencies were crucially important from the point of view of democratic theory. In the perspective of the people who belonged to such organizations, however, those organizations might have been seen as providing some services that were useful in their daily lives, though those citizens may have been perfectly aware of the limits on the independence of such structures and the pressures on their leaders to be subservient to the party apparatus. It is likely that for millions of Soviet citizens, a factory union, a women's council, or their chapter of the organization of deaf people had a more apparent impact on their well-being than a brave group of dissidents who struggled against the state's restrictions on freedom.

The character of the formerly party-controlled and state-subsidized organizations, such as organizations of the disabled and youth, that have persisted in postcommunist Russia is a subject that has been largely neglected by scholars, but the analysis in this chapter suggests that it deserves to be the focus of investigation. It is possible that in the absence of Communist Party control after 1991, with drastically reduced financial support from the state, organizations that are holdovers from the Soviet system might adopt a more independent stance in representing their members' interests, and might be of continued or even heightened importance in serving the members' everyday needs. The degree of such adaptation and of viability in changed circumstances may vary substantially from one organization to another and could be influenced by such factors as the resources at the disposal of the organization, the strategy adopted by its leaders, and above all else the practical importance of its services for its members. Those organizations that are seen by their members as delivering valuable benefits may survive with a base of support and incentives for cooperation that could allow them to play a significant role in society and become participants in more genuine social pluralism. It is possible, however, that such organizations of a previously quasi-governmental nature may still be so dependent on some level of government for financial assistance that they feel limited in their freedom to voice the demands of their members, if that means criticizing those who provide support for them. It is also possible that if the state's funding for those organizations decreases markedly, the organizations will find it difficult to sustain an adequate level of services for their members.

Was there a civil society in the Soviet Union? The information that has been presented in this chapter impels a negative answer to that question. The concept of civil society that has been elaborated in the West assumes a sharp distinction between the state and society. Indeed, the scholarly literature on civil society implies that there is not only some separation between state and society but also some degree of opposition between the two. The amount of separation between state and social organizations that is taken for granted in the West, and had begun to grow in Russia during the late tsarist period, disappeared in the Soviet Union by the end of the 1930s because of the extensive penetration of social organizations by the party-state regime. By that time, all social organizations in the USSR had either been created by the Communist Party or had been brought under the domination of the party.[10] By the time of the consolidation of Stalinism, all social organizations in the Soviet Union were either part of the state or were closely integrated with it. A social organization such as a trade union, the Komsomol, or an institute of the Academy of Sciences, received resources and gained the potential for influencing decision making in the same way as a government ministry. In each case, resources came from the state and the potential for influence depended on access to leaders within the state. According to Douglas Weiner, "it can be argued" that the scientists who operated as nature protection activists, and who were exceptionally successful in realizing their objectives even under Stalin, "had an investment in the perpetuation of an authoritarian, centralized state regime," and that because of "their wish to participate in, and not destroy, the

Leviathan-state, the scientists of the nature protection movement could only hope to persuade and enlighten these bureaucrats to invite them into the circles of power" (1999, 10).Weiner adds that the elitist character of the nature protection movement with its insider connections even led those scientists to fear the prospect of a mass base of support for their cause (ibid., 10).

Some of the most optimistic assessments during the last years of the Soviet regime (Starr 1988; Lewin 1991) implicitly assumed that the only possible outcomes of the changes and conflicts precipitated by perestroika were the triumph of the state (if it returned to the imposition of authoritarian control) or the victory of civil society (which would bring a liberal democratic political regime). Now we know that there was a third possibility. As Aleksander Smolar perceptively observed on the basis of the experience of Eastern Europe several years after the demise of that region's Communist regimes, elements of the old system found a refuge in society, the area that had been the source of opposition to the authoritarian state (1996, 36). The third possibility, rather than the decisive victory of civil society or the restoration of Brezhnevian authoritarianism, was that many members of the elite would survive and thrive, and some key institutions would manage to retain authority, by adapting to changing circumstances. It is well established that members of the political elite and economic administration were able to manipulate economic transformation in Russia in the 1990s to their advantage, for instance by gaining control of enterprises that were subjected to privatization (Rutland 2001, 4–9), so we should ask whether elements in the elite have been able to influence changes in social organizations in a manner designed to protect their interests. In any case, the degree of reliance on personal ties with authority figures in a system of patron–client relations that was fostered by the Soviet system has not enhanced the potential for the success of independent social organizations in the postcommunist period but, on the contrary, has detracted from the development of the networks of trust and cooperation that would be essential for the growth of a vigorous civil society.

Notes

The author would like to thank Aryeh Unger, Mary Conroy, and Blair Ruble for their perceptive comments and suggestions.

1. In this chapter, civil society is defined as the sphere of self-activating, self-governing social organizations that are largely independent of the state.

2. Actually, White has been much more cautious than some other authors in her assessment of the growth of civil society in the Soviet Union under Gorbachev. Her point of view is close to that of the equally sophisticated analysis that had been offered by Lapidus (1989).

3. Moshe Lewin's writings also articulated a point of view consistent with that argument. This chapter puts his analysis in another category, which is described below, but his works could be included in support of both the first and third arguments that are delineated here.

4. This chapter usually refers to such organizations as "social organizations." The corresponding term in Russian, *obshchestvennye organizatsii*, can also be translated as "public organizations." Though that term was suitable for usage by Soviet Communist theoreticians (as we will see, however, it had somewhat deceptive implications), it seems also to fit well in a new

context in which the concept of civil society is explored, although the term takes on some different connotations in that context. For variety in wording, this chapter will use the term "voluntary associations" as virtually interchangeable with "social organizations." The term "nongovernmental organizations" may also have a similar meaning. Each of those terms comes from a different disciplinary background, but each describes essentially the same kind of entity.

5. Maksimenko notes that the number of voluntary associations in Petrograd/Leningrad increased between 1920 and 1925 (1999, 27).

6. Recent revisionist historical research may be justified in asserting that in some cases the tightening of political control over social organizations in the Soviet Union in the late 1920s and the 1930s was supported enthusiastically by some citizens at the lowest level, and by a number of activists at intermediate levels (Peris 1991, 725). That thesis is not highly relevant to the arguments in this chapter, however, since the salient conclusion for our purposes pertains to the result that state control was intensified and the independence of almost all social organizations was sharply decreased, leaving a legacy of pervasive, authoritarian control of such organizations. This chapter does not attempt an exploration of the interaction of forces at various levels that sought such tightening of control. It should be noted that most contemporary Russian historians are not very sympathetic to Western revisionist scholars' attempts at what is perceived as the softening of the characterization of the Stalinist system as having imposed radical, traumatic changes from the top down (Pavlova 1998, 110). Nevertheless, this author sees a great deal of merit in the argument that the Stalinist transformation was a revolution from below as well as a revolution from above (Fitzpatrick 2000, 6–7), though he would add that the pressures from above were dominant at every critical juncture.

7. The Union of Soviet Writers was not actually organized until 1934.

8. In Russia, the Komsomol has been succeeded by the Russian Union of Youth (RSM), which has inherited many of the officers and facilities of the Komsomol. However, the RSM has only a fraction of the membership of the Komsomol.

9. Vucinich (1984, 361) asserts that even in the post-Stalin period in the Soviet Union, "the idea of autonomous scientific associations defending the professional interests of scientists and voicing the views of the scientific community on public policies continued to be a far cry from the stark reality of academic existence."

10. To be more precise about one exception, the transformation of the Russian Orthodox Church into an organization supporting the Soviet state, controlled by the state, and allowed to carry out narrowly limited functions was not completed until a little later, during World War II.

References

Adler, Nanci. 1993. *Victims of Soviet Terror: The Story of the Memorial Movement*. Westport, CT: Praeger.

Akinyshin, A. N. 1992. "Sud'ba kraevedov (konets 20–kh—nachalo 30–kh godov)." *Voprosy istorii*, nos. 6–7: 173–78.

Aksiutin, Iu. V., et al. 1996. *Politicheskaia istoriia: Rossiia—SSSR—Rossiiskaia Federatsiia*, Vol. 2. Moscow: Terra.

Alekseeva, Liudmila, and Catherine A. Fitzpatrick. 1990. *Neformaly: Civil Society in the USSR*. New York: Human Rights Watch.

Biddulph, Howard L. 1975. "Protest Strategies of the Soviet Intellectual Opposition. In Rudolf Tökes 1975, 96–115.

Bonnell, Victoria A.1990. "Voluntary Associations in Gorbachev's Reform Program." In *Can Gorbachev's Reforms Succeed?* ed. George Breslauer, 63–76. Berkeley: University of California Press.

Borisova, L. V. 1993. "Teatral'naia intelligentsiia i sovetskoe gosudarstvo v 20–e gody." *Otechestvennaia istoriia*, no. 2: 94–106.

Bourdeaux, Michael. 1975. "Religion." In Brown and Kaser 1975, 152–80. London: Macmillan.

Bradley, Joseph. 1994. "Dobrovol'nye obshchestva v Sovetskoi Rossii, 1917–1932 gg." *Vestnik Moskovskogo Universiteta, Seriia 8, Istoriia*, no. 4, 34–44.

Brooks, Nathan M. 1997. "Chemistry in War, Revolution, and Upheaval: Russia and the Soviet Union, 1900–1929." *Centaurus* 39, no. 4 (November): 349–67.

Brovkin, Vladimir. 1990. "Revolution from Below: Informal Political Associations in Russia 1988–1989." *Soviet Studies* 42, no. 2 (April): 233–57.

Brown, Archie, and Michael Kaser. 1975. *The Soviet Union Since the Fall of Khruschev*. London: Macmillan.

Brown, Emily Clark. 1966. *Soviet Trade Unions and Labor Relations*. Cambridge, MA: Harvard University Press.

Browning, Genia. 1987. *Women and Politics in the USSR: Consciousness Raising and Soviet Women's Groups*. New York: St. Martin's Press.

———. 1992. "The Zhensovety Revisited." In *Perestroika and Soviet Women*, ed. Mary Buckley, 97–117. Cambridge: Cambridge University Press.

Buckley, Mary. 1989. *Women and Ideology in the Soviet Union*. Ann Arbor: University of Michigan Press.

Butterfield, Jim, and Judith B. Sedaitis. 1991. "The Emergence of Social Movements in the Soviet Union." In Sedaitis and Butterfield 1991, 1–12.

Butterfield, Jim, and Marcia Weigle. 1991. "Unofficial Social Groups and Regime Response in the Soviet Union." In Sedaitis and Butterfield 1991, 175–95.

Clowes, Edith W., Samuel D. Kassow, and James L. West, eds. 1991. *Between Tsar and People: Educated Society and the Quest for Public Identity in Late Imperial Russia*. Princeton, NJ: Princeton University Press, 1991.

Connor, Walter D. 1991. *The Accidental Proletariat: Workers, Politics, and Crisis in Gorbachev's Russia*. Princeton, NJ: Princeton University Press.

———. 1975 in Tökes, Rudolf, L. 1975, p. 155.

Conquest, Robert. 1967. *Industrial Workers in the U.S.S.R.* New York: Praeger.

Conroy, Mary Schaeffer, ed. 1998. *Emerging Democracy in Late Imperial Russia: Case Studies on Local Self-Government (the Zemstvos), State Duma Elections, the Tsarist Government, and the State Council before and during World War I*. Niwot: University Press of Colorado.

Davis, Nathaniel. 1995. *A Long Walk to Church: A Contemporary History of Russian Orthodoxy*. Boulder, CO: Westview Press.

Dawson, Jane I. 1996. *Eco-Nationalism: Anti-Nuclear Activism and National Identity in Russia, Lithuania, and Ukraine*. Durham, NC: Duke University Press.

Ellis, Jane. 1986. *The Russian Orthodox Church: A Contemporary History*. Bloomington: Indiana University Press.

Evangelista, Matthew. 1999. *Unarmed Forces: The Transnational Movement to End the Cold War*. Ithaca, NY: Cornell University Press.

Evans, Alfred B., Jr. 2002. "Recent Assessments of Social Organizations in Russia." *Demokratizatsiya* 10, no. 3 (Summer): 322–42.

Fainsod, Merle. 1956. *How Russia Is Ruled*. Cambridge, MA: Harvard University Press.

———. 1961. "The Komsomol: Youth under Dictatorship." In Inkeles and Geiger 1961, 147–64. First published in *American Political Science Review* 45, no. 1 (March 1951): 18–40.

———. 1963. *Smolensk under Soviet Rule*. New York: Vintage Books.

Fish, M. Steven. 1995. *Democracy from Scratch: Opposition and Regime in the New Russian Revolution*. Princeton, NJ: Princeton University Press.

Filtzer, Donald. 1986. *Soviet Workers and Stalinist Industrialization: The Formation of Modern Soviet Productive Relations, 1928–1941*. London: Pluto Press.

———. 2002. *Soviet Workers and Late Stalinism: Labour and the Restoration of the Stalinist System after World War II*. Cambridge: Cambridge University Press.

Fitzpatrick, Sheila. 2000. "Introduction." In *Stalinism: New Directions*, ed. Sheila Fitzpatrick, 1–14. London: Routledge.

Freeze, Gregory L. 1997a. "From Stalinism to Stagnation, 1953–1985." In Freeze 1997b, 347–82.

———. 1997b. *Russia: A History*. Oxford: Oxford University Press.

Friedgut, Theodore. 1975. "The Democratic Movement: Dimensions and Perspectives." In Tökes 1975b, 116–36.

Gimpel'son, E. G. 1992. "Nachal'nyi etap skladyvaniia administrativno-komandnoi politicheskoi sistemy (1918–1920)." In *Formirovanie administrativno-komandnoi sistemy*, ed. V. P. Dmitrenko, 34–55. Moscow: Nauka.

———. 1995. *Formirovanie sovetskoi politicheskoi sistemy, 1917–1923* gg. Moscow: Nauka.

Graham, Loren R. 1967a. "Reorganization of the U.S.S.R. Academy of Sciences." In *Soviet Policy-Making: Studies of Communism in Transition*, ed. Peter H. Juviler and Henry W. Morton, 133–61. New York: Praeger.

———. 1967b. *The Soviet Academy of Sciences and the Communist Party, 1927–1932*. Princeton, NJ: Princeton University Press.

Gregory, Paul R. 1987. "Productivity, Slack, and Time Theft in the Soviet Economy." In Millar 1987, 241–75.

Hahn, Jeffrey W. 1988. *Soviet Grassroots: Citizen Participation in Local Soviet Government*. Princeton, NJ: Princeton University Press.

Hill, Ronald J., and Peter Frank. 1986. *The Soviet Communist Party*, 3rd ed. Boston: Allen and Unwin.

Hosking, Geoffrey. 1990. *The Awakening of the Soviet Union*. Cambridge, MA: Harvard University Press.

———. 1993. *The First Socialist Society: A History of the Soviet Union from Within*, 2nd ed. Cambridge, MA: Harvard University Press.

Hough, Jerry. 1977. *The Soviet Union and Social Science Theory*. Cambridge, MA: Harvard University Press.

Hough, Jerry, and Merle Fainsod. 1979. *How the Soviet Union Is Governed*. Cambridge, MA: Harvard University Press.

Husband, William B. 1997. "The New Economic Policy (NEP) and the Revolutionary Experiment, 1921–1929." In Freeze 1997b, 263–90.

Il'ina, I. N. 2000. *Obshchestvennye organizatsii Rossii v 1920-e gody*. Moscow: RAN, Institut rossiiskoi istorii (Institute of Russian History, Russian Academy of Sciences).

Inkeles, Alex, and Kent Geiger, eds. 1961. *Soviet Society: A Book of Readings*. Boston: Houghton Mifflin.

Jancar, Barbara Wolfe. 1975. "Religious Dissent in the Soviet Union." In Tökes 1975, 191–230.

———. 1978. *Women Under Communism*. Baltimore, MD: Johns Hopkins University Press.

Jowitt, Ken. 1992. *New World Disorder: The Leninist Extinction*. Berkeley: University of California Press.

Kassof, Allen. 1965. *The Soviet Youth Program: Regimentation and Rebellion*. Cambridge, MA: Harvard University Press.

Kodin, E. V., ed. 1999. *Stalinizm v rossiiskoi provintsii*. Smolensk: Smolenskii gosudarstvennyi pedagogicheskii universitet (Smolensk Educational Institute).

Korzhikhina, T. P. 1981. "Istoriia dobrovol'nykh obshchestv i soiuzov SSSR v sovetskoi istoriografii." *Voprosy istorii*, no. 3: 114–23.

Koshkin, A. P. 1999. "Stalinotsentriia v gosudarstvennom regulirovanii rossiiskogo obshchestva." In Kodin 1999, 291–98.

Krainov, G. 1993. "Skauty v Rossii." *Otechestvennaia istoriia*, no. 5: 207–12.

Lane, David. 1985. *State and Politics in the USSR*. New York: New York University Press.

Lapidus, Gail Warshofsky. 1978. *Women in Soviet Society: Equality, Development, and Social Change*. Berkeley: University of California Press.

———. 1989. "State and Society: Toward the Emergence of Civil Society in the Soviet Union." In

Politics, Society, and Nationality inside Gorbachev's Russia, ed. Seweryn Bialer, 121–47. Boulder, CO: Westview Press.

Lewin, Moshe. 1991. *The Gorbachev Phenomenon: A Historical Interpretation*, exp. ed. Berkeley: University of California Press.

Maksimenko, L. V. 1999. "Obshchestvennye organizatsii Petrograda 20–kh godov." In *Obshchestvo i vlast' v istorii Rossii: Sbornik nauchnykh trudov*, ed. I. I. Rogozin et al., 27–29. St. Petersburg: Nestor.

Mally, Lynn. 1990. *Culture of the Future: The Proletkult Movement in Revolutionary Russia*. Berkeley: University of California Press.

McAuley, Mary. 1969. Labour Disputes in Soviet Russia, 1957–1965. Oxford: Clarendon Press.

Millar, James R. 1987a. "History, Method, and the Problem of Bias." In Millar 1987b, 3–30.

Millar, James R., ed. 1987b. *Politics, Work, and Daily Life in the USSR: A Survey of Former Soviet Citizens*. Cambridge: Cambridge University Press.

Noonan, Norma C. 1996. "The Bolshevik Legacy and Russian Women's Movements." In *Russian Women in Politics and Society*, ed. Wilma Rule and Norma C. Noonan, 77–93. Westport, CT: Greenwood Press.

Oliver, Suzanne. 1992. "Charity and the Churches." In *Soviet Social Reality in the Mirror of Glasnost*, ed. Jim Riordan, 95–111. New York: St. Martin's Press.

Orlovsky, Daniel. 1997. "Russia in War and Revolution, 1914–1921." In Gregory Freeze 1997b, 231–62.

Pavlova, I. P. 2001. "Vlasti i obshchestvo v SSSR v 1930–e gody." *Voprosy istorii*, no. 10: 46–56. Translated in *Russian Studies in History*, Fall 2001

Pavlova, I. V. 1998. "Sovremennye zapadnye istoriki o stalinskoi Rossii 30–kh godov: kritika revizionistskogo podkhoda." *Otechestvennaia istoriia*, no. 5: 107–21.

Peris, Daniel. 1991. "The 1929 Congress of the Godless." *Soviet Studies* 3, no. 4 (October): 711–32.

Peterson, D. J. 1993. *Troubled Lands: The Legacy of Soviet Environmental Destruction*. Boulder, CO: Westview Press.

Petro, Nicolai. 1991. "Perestroika from Below: Voluntary Sociopolitical Associations in the RSFSR." In *Perestroika at the Crossroads*, ed. Alfred J. Rieber and Alvin Z. Rubinstein, 102–35. Armonk, NY: M. E. Sharpe.

Pipes, Richard. 1993. *Russia under the Bolshevik Regime*. New York: Knopf.

Ploss, Sidney I. 1968. "Interest Groups." In *Prospects for Soviet Society*, ed. Allen Kassof, 76–103. New York: Praeger.

Powell, David. 1991. "The Revival of Religion." *Current History* 90, no. 558 (October): 328–32.

Pravda, Alex, and Blair A. Ruble. 1986. "Communist Trade Unions: Varieties of Dualism." In Pravda and Ruble 1986b, 1–21.

Pravda Alex, and Blair A. Ruble, eds. 1986b. *Trade Unions in Communist States*. Boston: Allen and Unwin.

Read, Christopher. 1990. *Culture and Power in Revolutionary Russia: The Intelligentsia and the Transition from Tsarism to Communism*. New York: St. Martin's Press.

Reddaway, Peter. 1975. "The Development of Dissent and Opposition." In Brown and Kaser 1975, 121–55.

Riordan, Jim. 1977. *Sport in Soviet Society: Development of Sport and Physical Education in Russia and the USSR*. Cambridge: Cambridge University Press.

Ruble, Blair A. 1979. "Factory Unions and Workers' Rights." In *Industrial Labor in the U.S.S.R.*, ed. Arcadius Kahan and Blair A. Ruble, 59–84. New York: Pergamon Press.

———. 1981. *Soviet Trade Unions: Their Development in the 1970s*. Cambridge: Cambridge University Press.

———. 1986. "Industrial Trade Unions in the USSR." In Pravda and Ruble 1986b, 23–52.

Rutland, Peter. 2001. "Introduction: Business and the State in Russia." In *Business and the State in Contemporary Russia*, ed. Peter Rutland, 1–32. Boulder, CO: Westview Press.

Sedaitis, Judith B., and Jim Butterfield, eds. 1991. *Perestroika from Below: Social Movements in the Soviet Union*. Boulder, CO: Westview Press.

Service, Robert. 1998. *A History of Twentieth-Century Russia*. Cambridge, MA: Harvard University Press.

Shchiglik, A. I. 1977. *Zakonomernosti stanovleniia i razvitiia obshchestvennykh organizatsii v SSSR*. Moscow: Nauka.

Shtromas, Alexander. 1984. "Dissent and Political Change in the Soviet Union." In *The Soviet Polity in the Modern Era*, ed. Erik P. Hoffmann and Robbin F. Laird, 717–45. New York: Aldine Publishing.

Siegelbaum, Lewis H. 1992. *Soviet State and Society between Revolutions, 1918–1929*. Cambridge: Cambridge University Press.

———. 1997. "Building Stalinism, 1929–1941." In Freeze 1997b, 291–318.

———. 1999. "The Shaping of Soviet Workers' Leisure: Workers' Clubs and Palaces of Culture in the 1930s." *International Labor and Working Class History* 56 (October): 8–92.

Sikorskii, E. A. 1999. "Iz istorii stanovleniia v Smolenskom krae totalitarnogo rezhima v gody grazhdanskoi voiny (Noiabr' 1917 g.–1920 g.)." In Kodin 1999, 67–78.

Simmons, Ernest J. 1961. "Political Controls and Soviet Literature." In Inkeles and Geiger 1961, 469–78. First published in *Political Quarterly* 23, no. 1 (January–March 1959): 15–31.

Skilling, H. Gordon, and Franklyn Griffiths, eds. 1971. *Interest Groups in Soviet Politics*. Princeton, NJ: Princeton University Press.

Smith, Kathleen. 1996. *Remembering Stalin's Victims: Popular Memory and the End of the USSR*. Ithaca, NY: Cornell University Press.

Smolar, Aleksander. 1996. "From Opposition to Atomization." *Journal of Democracy* 7, no. 1 (January): 24–38.

Sobolev, V. S. 1985. "Sovety i obshchestvennye organizatsii v usloviiakh diktatury proletariata (po materialam Verkhnogo povolzh'ia pervykh let sovetskoi vlasti)." In *Gosudarstvennye uchrezhdeniia i obshchestvennye organizatsii SSSR: Istoriia i sovremennost'*, ed. N. P. Eroshkin et al., 61–67. Moscow: MGIAI.

Starr, S. Frederick. 1988. "Soviet Union: A Civil Society." *Foreign Policy*, no. 70 (Spring): 26–41.

Tökes, Rudolf L. 1974. "Dissent: The Politics for Change in the USSR." In *Soviet Politics and Society in the 1970s*, ed. Henry W. Morton and Rudolf L. Tökes, 3–59. New York: The Free Press.

———. 1975a. "Introduction: Varieties of Soviet Dissent: An Overview." In Tökes 1975b, 1–31.

Tökes, Rudolf L., ed. 1975b. *Dissent in the USSR*. Baltimore, MD: Johns Hopkins University Press.

Von Laue, Theodore H. 1964. *Why Lenin? Why Stalin?* Philadelphia: Lippincott.

Vucinich, Alexander. 1984. *Empire of Knowledge: The Academy of Sciences of the USSR (1917–1970)*. Berkeley: University of California Press.

Walters, Philip. 1988. "The Russian Orthodox Church." In *Eastern Christianity and Politics in the Twentieth Century*, ed. Pedro Ramet, 61–91. Durham, NC: Duke University Press.

Weiner, Douglas R. 1999. *A Little Corner of Freedom: Russian Nature Protection from Stalin to Gorbachev*. Berkeley: University of California Press.

White, Anne. 1993. "Charity, Self-Help, and Politics in Russia, 1985–91," *Europe–Asia Studies* 45, no. 5 (September): 787–810.

———. 1995. "The Memorial Society in the Russian Provinces." *Europe–Asia Studies* 47, no. 8 (December): 1343–66.

———. 1999. *Democratization in Russia under Gorbachev, 1985–91: The Birth of a Voluntary Sector*. New York: St. Martin's Press.

Ziegler, Charles E. 1987. *Environmental Policy in the USSR*. Amherst: University of Massachusetts Press.

Zimmerman, William. 1987. "Mobilized Participation and the Nature of the Soviet Dictatorship." In Millar 1987b, 332–53.

Part II

The Context of Civil Society Development

4

Media, Civil Society, and the Failure of the Fourth Estate in Russia

Sarah Oates

Debates rage around the world about the value of the media as a pillar of civil society. There is widespread concern that the trend toward "infotainment" and "dumbing down" of the news leads to a lack of a real civic engagement or knowledge of politics. In addition, there is concern that commercial and media interests are too often intertwined, depriving viewers, readers, and listeners of the level of professional, disinterested information that they need to be informed citizens. This debate about the role of the media, however, does not fit well into the ongoing concerns about the media in Russia. Despite a brief period of plurality at the end of the Soviet regime, the Russian media remain polarized between various political views rather than becoming an arena for free expression and discussion. As the presidential administration and the business elite continue to consolidate their power, the media have become less varied, less open, and much less free. Particularly on state-run television, the most popular medium in the country, there is little unbiased or disinterested political information for viewers.

How did the media fail to contribute to civil society in Russia? At first glance, it would appear that Russia has a rich and varied media environment. There are prominent, state-run media, including the flagship Russian Public Television (Obshchestvennoe rossiiskoe televidenie or ORT) on Channel 1. There is a wide range of state-run and commercial television stations across the vast country. There are several major newspapers and a wealth of specialty publications. There are both state and commercial radio stations. The Internet, albeit currently with low usage, is growing rapidly and features many news, politics, and entertainment sites.

What this plethora of media outlets masks is a lack of commitment to journalism as either a contender or watchdog in the political arena. Any broadcaster or publisher that has consistently challenged the monopoly of power in a narrow band of elites is attacked by the state through questionable legal maneuvers, by smear campaigns, or even with violence. After shareholders friendly to the Kremlin seized control of the commercial television channel NTV in 2001 over the issue of unpaid loans, the channel ceased its sharp criticism of the Putin administration and the war in Chechnya. It would appear that at every level of the media environment—from government offi-cials to journalists to the audience themselves—there is a lack of support for and understanding of a free and fair media. As a result, with every passing month, Russian citizens are less informed about critical issues such as elections, the economy, and their own civil war. Currently, the media environment in Russia is coming to resemble the Soviet style of ideological bias more than any Western model of interaction be-tween media and audience.

Fitting Russia into the Debate about Media and Civil Society

W. Lance Bennett has developed a particularly useful way of conceptualizing the media's relationship to political power when assessing the impact of media on civil society (2000, 204). Bennett derives three aspects of perceptions of political power from Lukes's (1974) typology of power in society: people either accept political ac-tions that affect them as legitimate, they resist them, or they resign themselves to being powerless about these actions. The media can feed into these conceptions in three ways. First, the media can frame coercive power within societies in ways that can "encourage, discourage, hide, or expose" this power (205). In addition, the media can be selective in presenting political news, covering some politicians and their ac-tivities and ignoring others. Finally, the media are important for "transmitting values, problem definitions, and images of people in society that provide resources for people in thinking about their lives and their relations to government, politics, and society" (205). This final definition is particularly important in a transitional society. Yet it is also dangerous, in the sense that an emphasis on values that divide the population or fail to foster civil society—such as a focus on nationalism of the dominant group or strong leadership over mass preference—can have a detrimental effect on the devel-opment of civil society.

However, if the mass media choose to "lead" their audience by attempting to challenge majority beliefs too strongly, they run the risk of losing both the audience's attention and its trust. This is complicated by the fact that it is often hard to gauge the opinion or mood of a media audience, particularly when journalists become somewhat isolated from average citizens. In addition, both public and commercial media outlets cannot act in isolation from the competition. Even if their state fund-ing allows them to ignore popular trends, if they lose audience share to a point at which they fail to communicate a message to a significant number of people, they have become marginalized.

There are four important issues to consider if we are to understand how the pos-sible early promise of a rich, varied media environment never came to fruition in Russia. First, it is important to assess the motivations for media behavior during the glasnost years from 1985–91 in the Soviet Union. While many observers and analysts interpreted this era as a flowering of media freedom, a retrospective view could see it as more of a cacophony of dissenting voices rather than an advance in the disinter-ested role of the Fourth Estate in a civil society. Second, it is critical to track just how much—or how little—the media managed to transform themselves from the authoritarian system by the time the Putin administration launched its serious offensive against media freedom. Third, it is impossible to overlook the realities of the media environment in Russia, one of the most dangerous countries on earth to work as a journalist. Fourth, how has the Russian media audience responded to these changes? Evidence suggests that Russian audience expectations from the media have more to do with societal control and nation building than with creating an informed, empowered citizenry.

Comparative Media Studies and the Russian Case

Trying to fit the media into models in comparative politics is a difficult task, even in countries that have far more stable and predictable media systems than Russia. One of the classic ways to attempt to model the mass media comes from work by Siebert, Peterson, and Schramm (1963). They divided the world's media into four normative models: authoritarian, Soviet, libertarian, and socially responsible. Although the models have been criticized as both too simplistic and an artifact of the Cold War, they do provide a useful starting point for a discussion of the Russian media. Siebert et al. argued that the Soviet press model required that the press support the Marxist-Leninist view of reality; the authoritarian model had the press in service to the state; the libertarian model supported the notion that opinions should be aired freely; and the social responsibility model held that the media should work proactively to include all segments of society in its coverage.

Yet was the "Soviet" model an accurate representation of the relationship between the mass media and the state in the USSR? In fact, the distinction that Siebert et al. made between "Soviet" and "authoritarian" was quite useful. In more specific studies of the Russian media, particularly Mickiewicz (1980, 1988), it was clear that the need to support the tenets and policies of the Communist Party was paramount in the Soviet media prior to the introduction of glasnost in 1985. While there was censorship and the threat of imprisonment for disseminating information that deviated from the party line, it was much more the deep indoctrination into the Soviet information system that made Soviet journalism docile to the party. Journalists, particularly on the main evening news broadcast such as *Vremia* (Times) on Channel 1 or on key central newspapers, were integral parts of the party apparatus. They did not need to be continually subjugated and controlled by the party, as they already were a functioning part of the party system. Although control and content varied somewhat during the Soviet regime, top Communist Party officials defined the acceptable limits. Thus the Soviet media could contribute little to civil society, as the mass media did not function outside the state. While it was possible to glean additional information or insight from some variations in the coverage among newspapers, television, and radio, it was a difficult and Aesopian task.

If the Soviet model fits the Russian media before 1985, do the other models from Siebert et al. help to inform the understanding of the system either during the glasnost era (1985–91) or after the collapse of the USSR in 1991? Here these theories are less useful. After Soviet leader Mikhail Gorbachev announced a new "transparency" or *glasnost'* for the Soviet media in 1985, news outlets began gradually to produce news more critical and open about Soviet society. The first newspaper articles were relatively tame, but the pace and the breadth of glasnost increased enormously until the media had written or aired stories on the futility of the war in Afghanistan, atrocities by Russian troops in World War II, and the misuse of psychiatric hospitals to punish dissidents. Ultimately, they questioned the entire value of Leninist philosophy. Glasnost quickly outstripped Gorbachev's perception of its role, that of a productive debate on the merits and problems of the system. Eventually, the Soviet mass media came to question the merit of the system itself.

How much, at this point in Soviet history, were the media striving to create a civil society? On many levels, the media outlets were functioning as a conduit through which citizens could express their opinions. One youth program on national television even featured a live call-in show, in which viewers discussed a wide range of societal issues.[1] Newspapers published views from citizens on a variety of subjects. But while there was an enormous amount of information and opinion offered on a broad variety of topics, there was relatively little interest aggregation. Some loose political affiliations were formed, mostly on the ideological basis of dislike of the Communist Party, but no dominant political force emerged to challenge the Communist Party. Rather, the Communist Party of the Soviet Union imploded from within, as reactionaries who wished to end Gorbachev's reforms fought with his supporters within the party elite. A closer reading of the newspaper coverage of the glasnost era shows that much of the plurality of opinion was in fact a reflection of this elite struggle for power. For example, the prominent national newspaper *Sovetskaia Rossiia* (Soviet Russia) supported the reactionary faction, while *Moskovskie novosti* (Moscow News) was behind the Gorbachev reformers for much of the glasnost era.

How did the Soviet media in its final years fit into the models suggested by Siebert et al.? In a sense, the media were libertarian, in that a wide range of views were published and broadcast during glasnost. Yet it is important to remember that notions of balance or objectivity were not central to the dissemination of information. Rather, particular media outlets—ranging from television shows to newspapers to literary magazines—chose to pursue particular political lines. Fact and opinion often were not delineated in program and text. While the media certainly broke with the authoritarian model, it could not be deemed socially responsible. While there was a great deal of political discussion, it did not seek to include all strata of society. Rather, the debate tended to center on issues that were particularly important to the urban elite. There was, for example, relatively little discussion of how the disintegration of the Soviet social system would affect rural, poorer communities or the more vulnerable members of society, such as the elderly and children.

If there has been one moment in Soviet/Russian history in which the media have acted as a direct conduit between information and the masses, it would be in August 1991. In that month, reactionary members of the Politburo staged a coup, arrested

Gorbachev, seized control of the central television stations by force, and mobilized troops into the streets. Proclaiming themselves leaders of the Soviet Union, the coup makers forced television journalists to announce an end to the experiment in openness and free-market economy. They then shut down all other television stations and broadcast an old production of the classic ballet *Swan Lake*. In numerous acts of personal bravery, journalists evaded the armed guards at the main television tower in Moscow and elsewhere to broadcast opposition to the reactionary coup. The coverage included a speech by Soviet Russian Federation President Boris Yeltsin calling for a return of Gorbachev and the rule of law; soldiers showing empty bullet clips in their guns; barricades thrown up by citizens across the main streets of Moscow; and children climbing over the tanks to make friends with the soldiers. Competing newspapers banded together to publish the latest news. At this moment in history, the media played a key role in informing the public, consolidating opinion, and defusing the coup. Tens of thousands of people were mobilized onto the city streets. Within days, the coup makers were arrested and Gorbachev was rescued from house arrest, albeit only to face the dissolution of his country a few months later.

Can the central role that the media played in the collapse of the reactionary coup in 1991 be used as proof that the media played a key role in civil society in the final years of the Soviet Union? This is a puzzling question, because arguably the Russian media have not played a major role in democratization since the new Russian state was established in December 1991. It is more logical to see the actions of the Soviet media during the coup under what Doris Graber describes as the "mirror" model of the media (2002). She perceives the media as operating under four broad models that describe their behavior: mirror, political, organizational, or professional. When the media merely reflect events, they serve as a mirror. When they choose to present events for ideological reasons, they are using a political model to lead their actions. If they choose to produce news based on prerequisites of the newsroom and the media business, this is the organizational model of the news. Finally, those who choose news based on its value and importance are following the professional model of the news.

There are times of crisis when the mirror model is inescapable, particularly when there are dramatic, unprecedented events, according to Graber. Unable to cope with both the magnitude of the event and the demand for information, news outlets tend to rush forward with information that has not been carefully checked or edited. As a result, there are often errors or misjudgments in news coverage. In addition, there is little attempt at "framing" or editing, sometimes because of time constraints and other times because there may be no news precedent, such as with the terrorist attacks in the United States on September 11, 2001. This results in a large volume of unmediated news coverage, which can be very unfamiliar—albeit liberating—to viewers used to a more professional or even a more politicized news product.

In many ways, the mirror model is particularly relevant for Russia, because the Soviet news media dealt with an increasing number of unprecedented events and journalistic challenges during glasnost. Soviet citizens enjoyed increasingly broad direct access to events, as television news featured major strikes, depressing war news from Afghanistan, and the first publicly contentious party congresses. In this sense, citizens were shown an enormous amount of information about the real machinations of the Soviet state, which certainly informed public opinion and action. But while this is all relevant to social change in the late Soviet era, the real question is whether the relationship among state, media, and audience was changed fundamentally. There is relatively little evidence of this more than a decade after the end of glasnost. Thus, while the coverage of the 1991 Soviet coup has been hailed as a triumph of free journalism, it was not a function of a permanent change in the relationship among the journalist, the state, and citizens. Rather, it was more a reflection of unusual events in the twilight of the Soviet state, coupled with a power vacuum as the Politburo was discredited. This gave media organizations the opportunity to present the story (although at considerable personal risk) and the audience an intense interest in the unfolding events. The result was a very strong bonding between the media and the citizenry for a short time period.

Russian Media: Transformation or Stagnation?

This intense and powerful force of the media to effect change—or at least to serve as its catalyst—did not endure in the young Russian state. Although there remained a wide variation of opinions within the Russian media for several years, most media outlets remained more voices for particular political or economic patrons than sources of information for building a civil society. Indeed, the particular polarization in the mass media appears to work against building a coalition of citizens and state actors interested in improving Russian society. In the Russian political tradition, there is no sense of a loyal opposition or even a Habermasian "sphere" in which discussion and debate can take place. Rather, the political style is one of winners and losers, friends and enemies. In many ways, this parallels the Soviet style of the media, which portrayed the world through its ideological lens.

While the new Russian Constitution of 1993 made important guarantees regarding freedom of information and the banning of censorship, the period from 1991 to 1993 can best be described as a time of benign neglect of the mass media. Although President Yeltsin objected to many of the reports on him in the mass media, he did not broadly impose controls or pressure the mass media with dubious legal maneuvers (aside from briefly banning the media that supported the reactionary factions). The central conflict in the young Russian state revolved around a reactionary parliament and a presidential administration determined to effect rapid economic and social change. This conflict ended in violence in late 1993, when Yeltsin illegally dissolved the parliament, shelled the rebels out of the building, and called for immediate elections of a new parliament.

The Russian parliamentary elections of 1993 are perhaps another example of unprecedented events overwhelming a media system, producing unlikely outcomes for the media audience. Russia passed a liberal campaign law, allowing parties and candidates free and equal access to state-run television and newspapers. Most of the campaigning focused on the race for the lower house of the Russian parliament, the 450-seat Duma. Half the seats were to be given to candidates elected in Russia's 225 single-member districts and the other half were to be allocated to parties gaining more than 5 percent in a national party-list contest. The campaign rules included an hour of free broadcast time for all thirteen parties in the election, as well as free space in major newspapers to campaign. In addition, parties and candidates were allowed to buy paid advertising, including on television. Technically constrained by campaign spending limits, the financial rules were largely ignored. Several parties, including the pro-government Russia's Choice and nationalist Liberal-Democrats, bought large amounts of paid advertising (European Institute for the Media 1994). Although the campaign law called for fair and equal coverage of political parties, Russia's Choice received an excessive amount of coverage on *Vremia* while the Communist Party of the Russian Federation received virtually no coverage (Helvey and Oates 1998; European Institute for the Media 1994; Oates 1998). During the 1993 campaign, journalists generally ignored the flamboyant nationalist Vladimir Zhirinovsky, who made several wild xenophobic and racist claims during his free-time speeches and paid advertising. Opinion polls showed him with little support, while Russia's Choice appeared to be doing moderately well leading up to the December elections. However, the polls turned out to be fairly inaccurate.[2] People were attracted to both the nationalist policy and rhetoric of Zhirinovsky as well as the ideals of the Communist Party. In retrospect, the news coverage was a poor reflection of the interests or needs of the voters.

If lack of knowledge could be used as excuse for skewed coverage in the 1993 Duma elections, this excuse was no longer possible for the increasingly biased and unfair coverage in subsequent Duma elections in 1995, 1999, and 2003. The news coverage continued to be unfair in three basic ways. First, pro-government parties and candidates—even those with little voter appeal—continued to receive an inordinate amount of coverage. They tended to be framed in more positive situations and able to speak in their own voices in television coverage. Second, the Communists and others seen as a challenge to the Russian government received substantially less coverage, and often it was less positive. For example, an analysis of news content on ORT and NTV in the 1999 campaign found that the Communists received just 5 percent of the election news coverage on ORT and just 3 percent of the election news coverage on NTV—despite winning the largest number of votes in the Duma party-list contest.[3] In addition, by 1999 journalists were practicing the dubious tactics of "black propaganda" and *kompromat* (a Russian abbreviation of "compromising materials"), smearing candidates with scandal-laden stories with little journalistic integrity and not allowing for a proper reply from the victims. By the 2003 campaign, the level of kompromat had decreased, but so had the level of political opposition to the Kremlin. The presidential campaigns of 1996, 2000, and 2004 featured fewer "dirty tricks," but state-run ORT used kompromat against liberal presidential contender Grigory Yavlinsky in 2000 by suggesting that his campaign was financed by the West and that he had undergone cosmetic surgery (Oates forthcoming, 2006). Many times, the failure of television, particularly ORT, to report on the basic issues or facts in the presidential campaigns is startling as well. The 1996 coverage of Yeltsin's campaign against Communist Party leader Gennady Zyuganov was particularly noteworthy for the failure of any major television station to report on Yeltsin's heart attack during the campaign (European Institute for the Media 1996a, 1996b, 2000a, 2000b; Oates 1998; Oates 2000; Oates and Roselle 2000; Mickiewicz 1999).

The Role of Commercial Media

It is important to stress that all media in Russia are not run by the state. There is a sizable commercial media industry, although the last national commercial television station that openly opposed the Putin regime was taken off the air in 2003.[4] Although commercial media have worked against a government monopoly on information, the structure of the media environment in Russia has militated against those efforts. Many who study the media believe that the commercial media are critical to maintaining a balance of information. Although commercial media can be constrained by ownership or advertising needs, a quality commercial media outlet will be concerned with objectivity and fair reporting in order to meet the needs of a demanding and discerning audience (Graber 2002). In this way, commercial media have a particular advantage over the state-run media, a critical distance and ability to criticize without the fear of retaliation from political patrons. One of the most significant problems with employing this concept in the Russian case is that there has never been a creation of a sphere separate from the government in Russia, although one commercial television station did play an important role in society for a time. NTV, a commercial network, was founded by the Media-Most banking concern in 1993. Media-Most head Vladimir Gusinsky had close ties with the Yeltsin government and was able to obtain a national frequency from the failing St. Petersburg channel for a minimal fee. Eventually, Media-Most took over the entire channel and, through agreements with regional channels across Russia, was able to broadcast to about 75 percent of the Russian population by 2001 (see Table 4.1).

Much in the way that the introduction of commercial television in Britain spurred innovation at the state-run British Broadcasting Corporation, the new Russian commercial channel quickly challenged the post-Soviet broadcast style. The new station, dubbed only with the initials NTV by its founders, adopted a faster-paced, more informal style. While *Vremia* had updated its personnel since Soviet days, it still retained a more traditional appearance. NTV news segments on its flagship *Segodnia* (Today) nightly news tended to be shorter and livelier. More important, the NTV news crews were more aggressive about covering stories that the Russian government was not keen to air. In particular, NTV made its reputation by covering the first Chechen War of 1994–96 (Mickiewicz 1999). The NTV news teams were not afraid to tackle the official Russian line on the war, which was a threadbare premise of happy Chechens being liberated from an oppressive regime by brave Russian soldiers. NTV showed the brutality of the war, the despair of the poorly trained young soldiers, and the anger

Table 4.1

National Television Channels in Russia

Channel	Name	Ownership	Daily reach* (percent)
1	Russian Public Television (ORT)	51 percent owned by the state, the rest by a mix of public and private corporations	84
2	Russian Television and Radio (RTR)	100 percent state-owned	71
3	TV-Center	Funded primarily by the city of Moscow	16
4	NTV	Commercial but now controlled by state interests	53
5	Culture	State-owned; cultural channel created by presidential decree in 1997. Only television channel not to carry paid advertising	8
6	Sports Channel TVS (formerlyTV-6)	Commercial. Formerly TVS or TV-6 commercial channel. Inherited NTV news team when NTV taken over by state interests, but was then itself closed for alleged fiscal mismanagement in 2003	N/A

*Figures on daily audience are taken from the April 2001 survey (2,000 respondents across Russia).

of the Chechens. Some NTV reports directly contradicted news aired the same evening on *Vremia* (Mickiewicz 1999; Oates 1998). Studies showed that NTV's 1995 parliamentary election coverage was more even-handed as well (European Institute for the Media 1996a, 1996b; Helvey and Oates 1997; Oates and Roselle 2000; Oates 1998).

Yet NTV showed that it was still linked to the notions of patronage and self-interest by choosing to support Yeltsin overtly in his bid for reelection in 1996. In fact, the president of NTV joined Yeltsin's campaign team (Mickiewicz 1999). The station heads explained this breach of journalistic good practice by claiming that they had to champion Yeltsin, or the Communist candidate would have won, returning media control completely back to the state. NTV returned to challenge the presidential administration after Yeltsin's reelection with criticism of his policies and those of Putin. Studies showed that NTV news in the 1999 and 2000 elections gave more coverage than state television to the government's political opponents (European Institute for the Media 2000a, 2000b; Helvey and Oates 1998; Oates 2003). In 2001, the Russian tax police raided NTV's offices and Gusinsky was arrested on charges of fraud. The ownership and editorial control of NTV were removed from the control of Media-Most and Gusinsky eventually fled the country. Although some of the NTV news team moved to a smaller commercial station, it was shut in 2003 (see Table 4.1). While commercial television had provided, for a time, a broader range of information and openness, objectivity and balance were missing over the long term. An analysis of the news coverage on ORT and NTV in the 2003 Duma elections shows that coverage still varied, but NTV's coverage had become markedly less confrontational towards the Putin regime (Oates forthcoming, 2006).

When discussing the Russian media, it is important to remember that virtually all media systems are widely criticized by political elites and citizens alike. Many concerns are linked to notions of media ownership. In Europe, where the general consensus is that state or public-funded television is critical to society, there are quite serious conflicts about the control of the broadcasts. In addition, there is widespread criticism of the U.S. media in elections, claiming that the coverage has become little more than a "horse race" with candidates gaining less and less time to speak for themselves (Patterson 1993). Arguably, the U.S. media are continuing the tradition of covering elections, yet offering less useful and unbiased information to the voters. If established democracies and media systems such as the United Kingdom and the United States face serious issues in terms of openness and control, the problems for the Russian media are even starker.

Yet there are three particularly worrying features about the sleaze, or the use of compromising materials, in the Russian mass media. First, the Russian mass media do not have a good track record for objective, fair reporting. In depressingly many of the cases of sleaze reported in democratic countries, there is usually a fairly good basis for the reports. Despite President Bill Clinton's vociferous protests to the contrary, he had in fact engaged in sexual activity with a White House intern. The incident and the president's reaction raised serious questions about credibility and presidential conduct that were far broader than some sexual indiscretion. With the Russian style of kompromat, facts are selectively reported and exaggerated, often with little evidence, to create an impression of scandal. For example, the reporting on Moscow Mayor Yuri Luzhkov's lavish country home during the 1999 Duma campaign gave the impression that Luzhkov was misappropriating funds to provide himself with a huge estate in the country. But the flashy report on the popular Sunday commentary program on Channel 1 relied on aerial shots of the complex with an ironic voice-over, but no real discussion of the financing of the estate. There was no rebuttal from Luzhkov or his associates; there was no serious discussion of the broader issues of the lavish lifestyles of many public servants.[5]

The second problem with a focus on individuals and a generally negative view of opposition leaders is that it undermines the development of political parties in Russia. If the news focuses on individual achievements or scandals, then there is little chance to air information on party policies or even ideologies. More problematic is that readers and viewers can be left with the impression that political parties are little more than vehicles for scandal, self-aggrandizement, or self-enrichment. In fact, political parties consistently receive some of the lowest ratings of trust of any institution in Russia.[6] Parties are reduced to followings around certain people, usually men who once served in government. The lack of a public debate on critical issues, notably the future of the Russian economy, retards the development of civil society.

Finally, and most worryingly, it is clear that the Russian mass media target particular individuals for negative coverage while meting out positive coverage to others. In this way, contemporary Russian television parallels Soviet television, with its firm support of Communism and denigration of capitalism. Yet who is controlling whether a particular candidate or politician gains favorable or negative coverage? At one point, different television channels in Russia picked their own candidates and politicians to champion. As channels have been forced to shift ownership or shut down altogether, it is clear that positive coverage is reserved for President Putin and his supporters and negative coverage for those who can challenge Putin. Other politicians, who are deemed too minor to challenge the president's hegemony, are either ignored or covered in a superficial manner.

Where does this pattern of coverage originate in Russia? This is a difficult area in which to conduct research. Reporters, editors, and producers are not keen to say that their editorial coverage is "directed" in a Soviet fashion. Although media analysts acknowledge bribery as widespread, it is not something that is openly discussed. In addition, it is a point of professional pride. Journalists may genuinely feel that they are reporting political news in a good fashion or at least in a way in which the audience expects it to be reported. Just because they are catering to a taste for kompromat and scandal does not mean that their reporting is necessarily flawed. Nor does this take into account the constant threat of violence and even murder, which continues to this day. Journalists are at particular risk due to a lack of rule of law and links among organized crime, big business, and the ruling elite in Russia. There have been several high-profile assassinations of top journalists and media executives, beginning with the slaying of popular television personality and Channel 1 advertising head Vlad List'ev in 1995 and the murder of Dmitrii Kholodov, who was killed in 1994 by explosives hidden in a briefcase. List'ev was presiding over a financial shake-up at state-run television, while Kholodov was investigating corruption in the military for a prominent Moscow newspaper at the time of his death. In addition, there has been a spate of media-related violence in the regions, in particular aimed against journalists who challenge the corrupt administrations of local elites.[7]

Certainly the role of the media "patron" cannot be underestimated in the Russian case. Just as different Communist Party organs were the patrons of various news outlets in Soviet times, political factions and oligarchs became patrons of news outlets in post-Soviet times. Particularly since Putin's first election in 2000, political interests have increasingly consolidated behind the president, reducing the variation of coverage in the media. As business interests are intertwined with the approval of the presidential administration, it is not surprising that commercial voices even mildly critical of the president and his policies have been silenced as well. It would appear that the editorial line is, in the first instance, dictated by the needs of the media outlet patron. Much as in Soviet times, tight control is not needed at every link in the chain of command. Rather, there is a good understanding of the "line" throughout the news organization. Journalists who choose to question this line, such as by writing a story that is not in step with the needs of the patron, will not long work for the organization. They also can be threatened by semilegal and criminal interests. As a result, it is more a system of disincentives to free, far-ranging journalism rather than censorship or direct orders that produces slanted, incomplete reports.

What does the Russian audience think of this problematic news coverage? Although several studies have pointed out that political coverage on Channel 1 is particularly biased (European Institute for the Media 1994, 1996a, 1996b, 2000a, 2000b; Oates 2003; Helvey and Oates 1998; Oates and Roselle 2000), the majority of Russians prefer this state-run channel. In fact, state television in general received the highest rating of trust (65 percent) of any institution in Russia in a 2001 survey. Meanwhile, commercial television stations (including NTV) that have often provided more professional and less biased coverage received a much lower level of trust.[8] While on the one hand puzzling, focus groups held in Russia in 2000 illuminated some reasons for this. Many of the respondents criticized the more sensational aspects of the NTV news, preferring a more calm, orderly presentation of current events in Russia. Although they were often quite shrewd about the ways in which the news was slanted or skewed, they also supported the notion of not airing political scandals in public. In addition, they were suspicious about the motivation of the owners of the commercial media. As one respondent pointed out, commercial owners were also part of the ruling elite, although it would appear their first priority was profit as opposed to the public interest. While state-run television was biased, many respondents felt that this was for the good of the country.[9]

Despite initial optimism on the part of Western and some Russian analysts, the Russian mass media have failed to develop as a tool for the masses. Rather, after a brief period of plurality, they are still firmly entrenched as a tool for the elites, as in Soviet times. The people who remain unsurprised—and surprisingly accepting—at this fate of the Russian media appear to be the Russian audience. Through focus-group discussions and survey responses, it is clear that they expect a certain collusion between the power elite and the media. Colin Sparks (2000) suggests in his work that neither state nor commercial media elites serve the interests of the public and many Russians agree with this notion. In particular, though, Russians see little to recommend the possible disinterested community service of a commercial media owner. In fact, they prefer state-run television to all other major types of media—and imbue it with greater trust. While some evidence makes it clear that they are aware of the distortion and lies in the state media, other discussion shows that they accept this as a part of the state-building exercise. Weary of the political and economic chaos of the late 1980s and the 1990s, they are ready to accept state television as a political Leviathan. Sparks recognized that his theory of both the commercial and public media working in the service of political elites fits the Russian situation particularly well, citing Russian media expert Ivan Zassoursky as identifying television as critical "political capital" (Sparks 2000, 43). In addition, "reflection . . . suggests to us that this situation of close links between political economic actors is very far from being some strange aberration unique to post-Communist societies" (Sparks 2000, 45).

All this leaves the Russian journalist in a particularly vulnerable state. On the one hand, if he or she reports on the very real conflicts of opinion within the elite and indeed the masses, he or she runs the risk of contributing to the destabilization of the nation. This is true even if the dissenting voices could be heard in the controlled media environment. On the other hand, if the mass media choose to champion a particular leader, party, policy, cause, or ideology, they run the risk of alienating a large part of their audience or simply failing in their job to inform rather than indoctrinate their audience. There is the middle ground, a system in which media outlets choose to champion a range of causes. In this way, the audience can be informed by choosing to watch, read, or listen to a range of media sources. This is essentially what has happened in Russia, although the plurality and useful range of reporting is being increasingly curtailed. What the Russian media experience suggests in theorizing about the media and civil society is that the debate about freedom is not simply a debate about ownership, "infotainment," or the "dumbing down" of the news. The focus should be on whether journalists retain the power and ability to inform the public. Russia lacks the capacity for this on a number of levels, ranging from politicians who are unwilling to accept a critical press, to journalists who lack a professional tradition, to an audience willing to accept sanitized news broadcasts. The opportunity for the Russian mass media to contribute to civil society is weak—and growing steadily weaker.

Notes

1. This show, *Twelfth Floor*, is discussed in Mickiewicz (1999, esp. 67–69). I am grateful to Professor Mickiewicz for letting me see her recorded clips of this and other Soviet-era shows.

2. For example, a survey of 1,062 people conducted between November 25, 1993, and December 7, 1993, by Russian Public Opinion and Marketing (ROMIR) found that 12.4 percent of the population planned to vote for Russia's Choice and only 6.9 percent planned to vote for the Liberal Democrats. On election day on December 12, 1993, however, Russia's Choice received 15.5 percent of the vote and the Liberal Democrats an astonishing 23 percent. The survey also underestimated the support for the Communists, showing just 4.8 percent support in the survey, while they won 12.4 percent in the election. The sample for the survey was Russia-wide, and this gap between prediction and results held across several surveys by respected public opinion research groups. Analysts believe that Russians in 1993 still were reluctant to express real voting preferences, particularly for groups seen as out of favor with the state (i.e., nationalists and Communists).

3. Author's research. For details on this analysis, see Oates and Roselle 2000.

4. The Russian Press Ministry cited the channel's long-term financial and management problems as the reason for its closure on June 23, 2003. However, the station was shut down without due process or a court order. The TVS broadcasts had virtually stopped in mid-June after Moscow authorities took it off the air, claiming it was $8 million in debt, according to Internews. For more detail on the closure, see a report by Internews (a nongovernmental organization in Russia supporting media freedom) at www.internews.ru/en/rumedia/2003/tvs4.html.

5. *The Sergei Dorenko Program*, Channel 1, Moscow, December 1999.

6. In a survey of 2,000 Russians conducted in March–April 2001, respondents reported the following levels of "full" and "considerable" trust in state television (57 percent), radio (53 percent), the army (50 percent), the Church (48 percent), the print media (47 percent), commercial television (38 percent), the government (30 percent), the parliament (16 percent), political parties (11 percent), and the Internet (7 percent). The survey was funded by the Economic and Social Research Council of the United Kingdom and conducted by Russian Research Ltd. under the direction of the author and professor Stephen White at the University of Glasgow. The nationwide sample was representative.

7. This violence has been highlighted by groups such as the European Institute for the Media, the Committee to Protect Journalists, and the Center for Journalists in Extreme Situations in Moscow. The international Committee to Protect Journalists reported that three journalists were murdered for their work during 2002 and documented fourteen other cases of journalists who were killed for reasons "unrelated to their reporting." The committee called this a "reflection of the rampant crime and violence that prevails in Russian society." For more details, see the committee's annual report on Russia, at www.cpj.org/attacks02/europe02/russia.html.

8. In the survey of 2,000 Russians cited above, respondents were asked to rank their feelings of trust for television channels. ORT and NTV were the most trusted, with 31 percent choosing ORT and 24 percent choosing NTV. State-owned RTR (Rossiiskoe televidenie i radio) on Channel 2 was a distant third, with 12 percent choosing it as the most trustworthy television station. A similar survey conducted in December 2003 through January 2004 suggested that trust in NTV had slipped, but the questions were not quite the same.

9. These focus groups were conducted in the spring of 2000 in Moscow, in a rural hamlet near Voronezh on the Volga River, and in Ul'ianovsk (about 600 miles east of Moscow). Half the focus groups took place just before the 2000 presidential elections and the other half immediately after the contest. The questions for the focus groups were designed to target themes that

had become apparent during fieldwork, particularly during media monitoring for the 1999 Russian parliamentary elections conducted by the European Institute for the Media. The fieldwork was carried out by Russian Research Ltd. (Moscow and London). The author gratefully acknowledges funding for this work from the U.K. Economic and Social Research Council (Grant R000223133, Building a New Democracy? Television, Citizens and Voting in Russia, 2000–2001, University of Glasgow).

References

Bennett, W. Lance. 2000. "Media Power in the United States." In Curran and Park 2000, 202–20.

Curran, James, and Myung-Jin Park, eds. 2000. *De-Westernizing Media Systems*. New York: Routledge.

European Institute for the Media. 1994. *The Russian Parliamentary Elections: Monitoring of the Election Coverage of the Russian Mass Media*. Düsseldorf: European Institute for the Media.

———. 1996a. *Monitoring the Media Coverage of the 1995 Russian Parliamentary Elections*. Düsseldorf: European Institute for the Media.

———. 1996b. *Monitoring the Media Coverage of the 1996 Russian Presidential Elections*. Düsseldorf: European Institute for the Media.

———. 2000a. *Monitoring the Media Coverage of the December 1999 Parliamentary Elections in Russia. Final Report*. Düsseldorf: European Institute for the Media.

European Institute for the Media. 2000b. *Monitoring the Media Coverage of the March 2000 Presidential Elections in Russia. Final Report*. Düsseldorf: European Institute for the Media.

Graber, Doris A. 2002. *Mass Media and American Politics*. 6th ed. Washington, DC: CQ Press.

Helvey, Laura Roselle, and Sarah Oates. 1998. "What's the Story? A Comparison of Campaign News on State-Owned and Independent Television Networks in Russia." Paper presented at the American Political Science Association Annual Meeting, Boston, MA, September.

Lukes, Steven. 1974. *Power: A Radical View*. London: MacMillan.

Mickiewicz, Ellen Propper. 1980. *Media and the Russian Public*. New York: Praeger.

———. 1988. *Split Signals: Television and Politics in the Soviet Union*. Oxford: Oxford University Press.

———. 1999. *Changing Channels: Television and the Struggle for Power in Russia*. 2d ed. Durham, NC: Duke University Press.

Oates, Sarah. 1998. "Voting Behavior and Party Development in New Democracies: The Russian Duma Elections of 1993 and 1995." Ph.D. dissertation, Emory University, Atlanta, Georgia.

———. 2000. "Russia's Parliamentary Elections: The Dirty Road to the Duma." *Problems of Post-Communism* 47, no. 3 (May–June): 3–14.

———. 2003. "Television, Voters and the Development of the 'Broadcast Party.'" In *The 1999–2000 Elections in Russia: Their Impact and Legacy*, ed. Vicki Hesli and Bill Reisinger, 29–50. New York: Cambridge University Press.

———. Forthcoming 2006. *Television and Elections in Russia*. London: RoutledgeCurzon.

Oates, Sarah, and Laura Roselle Helvey. 1997. "Russian Television's Mixed Messages: Parties, Candidates and Control on *Vremya*, 1995–1996." Paper presented at the American Political Science Association Annual Meeting, Washington, DC, August.

Oates, Sarah, and Laura Roselle. 2000. "Russian Elections and TV News: Comparison of Campaign News on State-Controlled and Commercial Television Channels." *Harvard International Journal of Press/Politics* 5, no. 2 (Spring): 30–51.

Patterson, Thomas E. 1993. *Out of Order*. New York: Knopf.

Sparks, Colin. 2000. "Media Theory after the Fall of European Communism: Why the Old Models from East and West Won't Do Anymore." In Curran and Park 2000, 35–49.

Siebert, Frederick S., Theodore Peterson, and Wilbur Schramm. 1963. *Four Theories of the Press.* Urbana: University of Illinois Press.

Zassoursky, Igor. n.d. "From Public Sphere Utopia to Public Scene Reality: The First Seven Years of the New Russian Press." Unpublished paper. Quoted in Sparks 2000, 43–45.

———. "Media and Politics in Russia in the Nineties." Unpublished paper available at www.polito.ubbcluj.ro/EAST/East6/zassoursky.htm.

5

Business and Civil Society in Russia

Peter Rutland

Private business is a vital element in any civil society. Business has the resources and expertise to defend and advance its interests in the face of pressure from the state. In most countries there is concern that business interests may be too strong and successful as players in civil society. Business groups may be able to overpower labor unions, exploit and cheat unorganized consumers, and even "capture" state institutions and political parties, thereby turning the state into an instrument for the advancement of its corporate interests rather than the common good.

In the Soviet Union, legally independent business corporations did not exist. All industrial institutions were owned and controlled by the state and tried to advance their interests through a dense network of bureaucratic bargaining. In the fifteen years since the collapse of the Soviet Union, the institutional structure of the Russian economy has been dramatically transformed. Large private business corporations dominate the economic scene and are active players in political life.

However, since Vladimir Putin's accession to the presidency at the end of 1999, the Russian state has been reasserting its power, forcing Russian business to retreat. It is still unclear how far Putin will go in his campaign to bring Russian business back under state control. Certainly, Putin has demonstrated that he will not allow business leaders to pose a political challenge to the Kremlin, by funding opposition political parties, for example. But it does not look as if Putin has the intention or the ability to dismantle the system of oligarchic capitalism that grew up under President Boris Yeltsin and replace it with centrally controlled "state capitalism." Although many Russian politicians are calling for such a system, Putin himself seems to believe that private ownership ensures the most effective economic system and that an attempted return to central planning would be counterproductive.

Understanding Civil Society: The Anglo-Saxon Model

Civil society is a contested concept. It has a variety of meanings, and has itself become a tool of political struggle, both in the West and in Russia itself. Broadly speaking, the term refers to organized groups representing social interests that are independent of the state and may pose a check on its power.

One of the most influential versions of the concept of civil society arose in eighteenth-century Scotland in response to the spread of capitalism, which saw the growth of merchants and manufacturers independent of the state. Civil society is closely connected to the concept of the rule of law, entailing an independent judicial system that can fairly administer the law. The rule of law provides a framework for the adjudication of disputes between members of civil society. Also, in a society governed by the rule of law, even state institutions must obey the law. The capitalists of nineteenth-century Scotland wanted to protect their interests against one another and against the sovereign state.

Thus from the very beginning, the concept of civil society saw independent business interests as an essential component. Only if there is a significant part of society earning its livelihood outside the state can one hope to see a dispersal of political power. Members of this capitalist class were among the most active proponents of the virtues of civil society, which they saw as serving their own interests as well as the public good.

The Anglo-Saxon model is often invoked as the ideal type of civil society. It presupposes a broadly developed market economy with a large and diverse population of market actors: independent farmers, small businessmen, and the like. From the writings of James Madison to the pluralist school of the 1950s, the emphasis was on competition among independent economic and political actors, producing a rough equilibrium in the political marketplace. At the same time, there was a fear that business and other private interests could threaten civil society if they became too powerful and exerted disproportionate influence over the state (recall James Madison's warning of the evils of faction). These fears materialized during the era of "robber barons" in late nineteenth-century America. In response there arose the doctrine of pluralism, the belief that there should be a diversity of business interests and a variety of organizations representing them, to ensure that no one group would achieve a dominant position, at least not on a permanent basis.

Pluralist theory assumed not just a plurality of actors within the business sector but also a plurality of dimensions of interest representation. Business interests would compete along with groups representing labor, consumers, regional interests, religious confessions, and so on. It was recognized that civil society was imperfect; that some groups would be better able to advance their interests than others. But in the pluralist paradigm, the social system has self-correcting tendencies, such that no one group would be able to enforce its interests all the time.

Civil Society in Russia

How does Russia measure up against that ideal type of civil society (Khlopin 2002)? On the one hand, post-Soviet Russia does have a large number of social, economic, and political actors (companies, labor unions, social organizations, etc.) that exist outside the state apparatus—both in law and in reality. On the other hand, the rule of law is exceptionally weak, and the state is able to exert strong influence over the conduct of most social actors. There is a contradiction, then, between the rapid appearance of civil society actors and their limited power in practice.

That paradox is particularly sharp if one looks specifically at the business component of civil society. After 1991, Russia very rapidly gave birth to several dozen successful and internationally prominent business corporations. In fifteen years, Russia went from a society where entrepreneurship was a crime to one that had produced thirty-six individual billionaires, the third highest number in the world ("Rising Tide" 2004).[1] In a World Bank study of industrial concentration, the country's twenty-three largest firms were estimated to account for 30 percent of Russia's gross domestic product (GDP), and these firms were effectively controlled by a mere thirty-seven individuals (World Bank 2004).[2] By international standards, that is an astonishing concentration of wealth and industrial power in such a large country, all the more surprising since this entire economic elite did not exist fifteen years ago.

In July 2003, however, prosecutors started arresting top executives of Russia's largest oil company, Yukos, on various fraud charges. On October 25, 2003, the richest man in Russia, Yukos head Mikhail Khodorkovsky, was himself jailed on vague charges of tax evasion, and he has remained in prison ever since. At the end of May 2005 he and his colleague and codefendant, Platon Lebedev, were found guilty, and each was sentenced to nine years in prison (Belton 2005). One could not ask for a more vivid illustration of the limits of civil society in Russia.

This chapter explores the contradictory evidence for the presence or absence of civil society in Russia, as exemplified by the Khodorkovsky case. Does the arrest of Khodorkovsky prove that civil society is dead in Russia, and that all businesses are subservient to the state? Or is his case an exception that shows the limits of business power but does not reflect the real, day-to-day influence of the business community?

The Russian Transition to Capitalism

Russia's transition to democracy was accompanied by a remarkably rapid transition to capitalism. In the space of a decade, Russia went from an economy where more than 90 percent of activity was under state control to an economy where 70 percent of assets and employment were in legally private corporations. Yet Russia somehow managed to make the leap from state socialism to capitalism without developing the rule of law and civil society. One can divide the Russian economic transition into three phases: 1992–94, 1995–98, and 1999–2004.

The First Phase, 1992–1994

The first period of chaotic liberalization and voucher privatization (1992–94) saw the rapid emergence of a multitude of independent economic actors, from street traders, now allowed to buy and sell in public markets, up to factory directors, now free to "privatize" their still state-owned factory cash flows by routing sales through inter-mediary firms (Rutland 2001). That process saw a leakage of power from state to nonstate actors and from the federal center to the regions. Individual regional leaders signed bilateral "treaties"with President Boris Yeltsin on the division of reponsibilities with the federal center, beginning with Tatarstan in 1994. (By 1996, forty-six of Russia's eighty-nine regions had signed such treaties.) The period also saw the breakdown of respect for the law and a surge of crime and corruption.

These processes resulted in a weak state and the dispersal of power but did not lead to the appearance of civil society in the classic sense of the term. In the chaos of transition, power shifted from formal political institutions to informal networks of influence among individuals who had political connections or economic resources at their disposal.

The process of dismantling formal institutions was actively encouraged by the liberal leaders of the state, such as Egor Gaidar (prime minister in 1992). They saw it as a way of preventing a return to Communist power. The reformist leaders gave higher priority to avoiding a return to the past than building new institutions for the future (Gel'man 2003). Promoting respect for the law, effective regulatory institutions, or a healthy civil society was simply not on their agenda. The architects of the new decentralized political economy hoped that it would be a transitional stage, a painful but short interlude that would open the door to the eventual emergence of civil society and a stable democracy.

While market forces penetrated large sections of economic activity, the Russian economy as a whole was only partially marketized by the Yeltsin reforms. In the face of runaway inflation, a cash squeeze, and the breakdown of bank credits, a parallel economy sprang up, where factories traded goods with one another through physical barter or using pseudo-currencies such as bills of exchange or tax credits. This parallel economy accounted for perhaps half of all business-to-business transactions (Ledeneva 1998; Woodruff 1999). The interface between polity and economy was mediated by corruption and mutual favors, instead of by political orders as under the old regime. It did not involve the sort of transparent political bargaining and legal adjudication characteristic of a civil society ruled by law. Alarmingly, businesses started using criminal groups and not the courts to enforce contracts and secure their property rights (Varese 2002).

Yulia Latynina (2003) vividly explained the process:

> Back in the late 1980s, when the future oligarchs were just getting started in a frenzy of dirt and blood, each faced an impossible task: dealing with the thugs who walked into their offices, stuck guns to their heads and demanded money. They solved this problem by amassing security forces and privatizing the state along with the cops and the prosecutors. Then, instead of disarming and disbanding their privatized police forces, the oligarchs began to battle one another. They taught the prosecutors how to use criminal investigations to pry factories away from their owners. They created Frankenstein, but Frankenstein did not obey his master for long.

The existence of organized crime by itself neither proves nor disproves the existence of civil society. (Robert Putnam's book on Italy [1993], which reawakened

American interest in civil society, does not discuss whether the presence of the Mafia weakens or strengthens social capital.) But as Latynina suggests, the criminalization of Russian business was a highly volatile process that opened the door to a counter-offensive by state security organs.

The lack of a firm legal basis for their rapidly acquired wealth made the new business elite vulnerable to attack by the state, the guardian of legality (especially in the Russian historical context). The rapidity and rapaciousness of their enrichment meant that they lacked a strong social basis of support, so that when the state came knocking on their door it would be with general public approval.

The Second Phase, 1995–1998

Second, there was a phase of gradual consolidation (1995–98). More powerful competitors pushed out their weaker rivals, and a system of "oligarchic capitalism" emerged in which influence was concentrated in the hands of a small number of powerful individuals. Those figures headed business corporations but had close connections to the political leadership at the national or regional level. Russia had dismantled an autocracy, but instead of rule by the many (democracy), it had arrived at rule by the few (oligarchy).

Most of those oligarchs headed private corporations formed on the basis of former state enterprises, such as regional oil companies, banks, or metallurgical plants. They typically made their first million through commodity trading, imports of scarce goods, or financial brokering, then grew by acquiring state assets as they were privatized (Brady 1999; Freeland 2000; Klebnikov 2000; Brzezinski 2001). Alfa Group, Inkombank, Rosprom, SBS-Agro, and Rossiiskii Kredit all had their origins in enterprises formed under the auspices of the Communist Party of the Soviet Union or its youth branch, the Komsomol. Vladimir Potanin's Oneksimbank came out of the foreign trade ministry, but it grew into the most extensive and diversified of the oligarchic holdings, Interros, which owns the minerals giant Noril'sk Nickel (Lysova 1998). Among the top oligarchs only Vladimir Gusinsky's Most Group and Boris Berezovsky's Logovaz can be regarded as relatively independent start-up operations.[3] Berezovsky began with a chain of auto dealerships, then went on to acquire the international operations of Aeroflot, the ORT television station, and the Sibneft' oil company. Vladimir Gusinsky began with an information service, then moved into publishing and banking.

A pivotal event in the transition to oligarchy was the loans-for-shares auctions in 1995–96, when key firms such as Noril'sk Nickel and Sibneft' were sold off at bargain prices to politically favored businessmen. In return, these oligarchs helped Boris Yeltsin win reelection in June 1996 by putting their financial and organizational resources at the president's disposal. Above all, it was the mobilization of their press and television empires that pulled Yeltsin through to victory. Some of the businessmen were rewarded for their help by being appointed to government positions in the fall of 1996. Thus Boris Berezovsky became deputy secretary of the Security Council and Vladimir Potanin became deputy prime minister, although each lasted less than a year.

The oligarchic consolidation in 1994–96 coincided with a degree of macroeconomic stabilization. Inflation came down from 1,500 percent in 1992 to 25 percent in 1996 and 12 percent in 1997. GDP even recorded a slight growth of 0.7 percent in 1997, after seven years of decline. It was at that point that the term "oligarch" entered the Russian political lexicon.[4] In the spring of 1997 it was taken up by Boris Nemtsov, a deputy prime minister who was pushing for a new round of liberal reforms, along with fellow deputy premier Anatolii Chubais. Nemtsov and Chubais wanted to cut corruption and introduce more competition into the "crony capitalism" that had been forged between the newly emerged oligarchs and the weakened state.

Had Nemtsov and Chubais succeeded, perhaps Russia's oligarchic capitalism could have evolved into something like a civil society. The Russian state was weak, having leaked political power to the regions and economic power to the oligarchs. The 1997 reform drive failed in the face of energetic opposition from regional governors and business oligarchs, who mobilized their supporters in the State Duma. Moreover, the macroeconomic stabilization proved illusory. The government was borrowing heavily to cover its budget deficit. The Asian financial crisis in 1997 caused a slump in world oil prices that in turn eroded Russia's current account surplus. That problem, together with the ballooning budget deficit, led to a run on the ruble and the dramatic devaluation and debt default in August 1998.

We will never know for sure, but one can argue that the demise of oligarchic capitalism was due to deep contradictions in the model, and not merely to contingent factors such as Yeltsin's incompetence or the August 1998 financial crash. Two contradictions stand out. First, the oligarchs were parasitic on the Russian state. They were draining it of assets and revenues, to the point where the budgetary imbalance and profiteering from high-interest treasury bonds helped trigger the 1998 crash. Second, the oligarchs were deeply divided among themselves. They did not trust one another, fighting bitterly over the privatization of the telecommunications holding company Sviazinvest in the summer of 1997 (Fortescue 2002). By September, the feuding—in the form of personal attacks and corruption allegations in rival newspapers—was so intense that Yeltsin called the six leading bankers to a meeting and persuaded them to declare a truce (Pinsker 1997).

It seemed that crony capitalism was here to stay. The reform process was stalled in midstream (Hellman 1998). Powerful leaders had a vested interest in preserving the status quo, and there was no significant coalition of groups with a stake in further reform. The economy had been sufficiently liberalized to enable the oligarchs to enrich themselves, but not so much as to expose them to effective competition (from foreign companies, for example). Ordinary citizens were dissatisfied but felt powerless to change the status quo. They retreated into their family survival strategies and private networking—which included cheating on taxes and paying bribes, further corroding the social values necessary for civil society to flourish.

There was no question that the new business corporations were very powerful political actors, with considerable economic resources, a strong identity within each corporation, and access to the political power elite. But the headlong speed of their rise meant their legitimacy was fragile and their social base weak (Peregudov 2002, 2003). Both state and society are suspicious of business, a value orientation that has deep roots in Russian culture: pre-Soviet, Soviet, and post-Soviet. Big business is associated with injustice. According to a 2003 ROMIR poll, 45 percent consider the influence of big business on the economy to be negative and 25 percent consider it positive, and on politics 49 percent negative and 17 percent positive (Gorin et al. 2003).[5] In a Public Opinion Foundation (FOM) poll of June 2003, 71 percent agreed with the statement that you cannot earn a lot of money without breaking the law (ibid.).

In most societies, capitalists were forced to overcome their differences and act collectively to ward off a challenge from the rest of society, in the form of organized labor or socialist parties seeking power through the ballot box. In post-Soviet Russia labor was weak and demoralized, and the left wing of the political spectrum was dominated by the backward-looking Communist Party, which found it difficult to win votes beyond its hard-core supporters, who made up 25 to 30 percent of the elector-ate. The presidential election of 1996 was the only point at which Russian business faced a serious left-wing challenge that forced it to act in a cooperative fashion in defense of the Yeltsin presidency. Otherwise, the oligarchs were fiercely independent and suspicious of one another. They devoted most of their energies to competing with one another for favors from the state and rarely worked together to protect or advance their common interests, or even to discuss what those common interests might be.

The oligarchs did not have a mechanism for resolving disputes among themselves. The only "mechanism" they had was to appeal to Boris Yeltsin. Given that Yeltsin was often physically incapacitated, that meant they competed for the favor of the Kremlin courtiers (the "Family") who controlled access to the president. Yeltsin's second and final term as president was scheduled to end in March 2000, and the oligarchic sys-tem did not have any mechanism in place for picking a successor to Yeltsin.

The Third Phase, 1999–2004

The tremendous uncertainty over the Yeltsin succession triggered mounting instabil-ity. Yeltsin went through a series of prime ministers in 1998–99, searching for a reli-able successor who could maintain the political system that he had created. (Sergei Kirienko was followed by Evgenii Primakov, then Sergei Stepashin.) The State Duma elections scheduled for December 1999 were seen as a sort of presidential "primary," since it was assumed that the leader of the winning party would be well placed for a run at the presidency. The oligarchs funded rival parties in the Duma election, which was fought through a bitter and dirty media campaign.

Ousted Prime Minister Primakov joined forces with regional bosses Yuri Luzhkov (mayor of Moscow) and Mintimer Shaimiev (president of Tatarstan) to form the Fatherland–All Russia alliance. In the wake of the Chechen terrorist raid on Dagestan in August 1999, Yeltsin appointed yet another new prime minister: Vladimir Putin, the head of the Federal Security Service. After a wave of apartment house bombings, in September Putin sent federal forces back into Chechnya. The Kremlin slapped together a pro-Putin Unity party, and Berezovsky's ORT TV channel rallied to the Kremlin cause, launching blistering attacks on Luzhkov and Primakov. Meanwhile Gusinsky's NTV backed Fatherland–All Russia. Unity finished second in the Duma election with 23 percent of the vote, only just behind the Communists, pushing Fatherland–All Russia into third place with 13 percent. Yeltsin preempted the race for the presidential succession by resigning ahead of schedule on December 31, 1999, making Putin acting president. Putin proceeded to sweep the March 2000 presidential election.

At first, it looked as if Putin was going to preserve the essential features of Yeltsin's oligarchic capitalism. He said that his intention was to continue market reform and to leave the results of Yeltsin's privatization program in place. Many key figures from Yeltsin's inner circle or "Family" were kept on in the Kremlin, such as chief of staff Aleksandr Voloshin and Prime Minister Mikhail Kas'ianov. Berezovsky gave out the impression that he personally had been the architect of Putin's rise to power. However, one week before the election Putin sent a warning signal. Speaking to Radio Maiak on March 18, 2000, he attacked the oligarchs who had been "merging power with capital" and declared that "such a class of oligarchs will cease to exist."

Putin proved more independent than many observers had supposed, and he was unwilling to preserve the privileged political role that the oligarchs had carved out during the Yeltsin years. In the summer of 2000, Putin moved quickly to win control of the national television stations, driving their owners, Boris Berezovsky and Vladimir Gusinsky, into exile. He did that through a shrewd combination of threats of criminal investigation and economic pressure by loyal oligarchs (Fossato and Kachkaeva 2000). Masked tax and security police staged a dramatic raid on Gusinsky's Media-Most offices in downtown Moscow on May 11, just four days after Putin's inauguration. That was followed by the Gazprom company's calling in $400 million it had lent to Gusinsky's NTV. In July, Gusinsky made a secret deal with Press Minister Mikhail Lesin and the head of Gazprom-Media, Alfred Kokh, under which he agreed to cede control over NTV in return for the cancellation of its debts to Gazprom and the dropping of criminal charges. He then fled the country.

At the same time, Putin created a new system of federal districts headed by presidential plenipotentiaries, with the goal of forcing the regional governors to obey federal laws and directives. On May 31, 2000, Berezovsky published an open letter denouncing Putin's federal reform plans. In June, under pressure to repay a $100 million loan from state-owned Vneshekonombank, Berezovsky agreed to transfer his 49 percent stake in the ORT television company back to the state. In July, prosecutors started an investigation of Berezovsky in connection with Aeroflot's foreign currency accounts, and by November 2000, he too had gone into exile.

Although some saw Putin's summer 2000 offensive as signaling the end of the oligarchs, Putin's crackdown was limited to Gusinsky and Berezovsky, who controlled media empires that had directly challenged Putin's rule (Caryl 2001). The other oligarchs assumed that so long as they kept away from the mass media (television in particular) it would be business as usual. In 2001, Aleksandr Tsipko (2001) argued that "just as under Yeltsin, Russia is still ruled by a group of oligarchs via their proteges in the president's administration, the government and the security services."

Yeltsin's system was roughly pluralistic, with a competition for influence among several centers of power—the oligarchs, the Kremlin, regional governors, and political parties in the State Duma. At first, it looked as if Putin wanted to strengthen the power of the state but not break the pluralistic character of the system as a whole (Arkhangel'skaia 2001). But as time went on, it became increasingly clear that Putin wanted to replace pluralism with a centralized, authoritarian hierarchy, the "power vertical." The Yeltsin system could perhaps have evolved into a civil society, but the Putin project is its antithesis.

The pivotal confrontation that revealed the contours of Putin's regime was the showdown with oil oligarch Mikhail Khodorkovsky in 2003 (Bianova and Litvinov 2003). By 2004, it was clear that oligarchic capitalism had given way to a system of state capitalism.

The Limits of Oligarchic Capitalism

Why did the system of oligarchic capitalism prove unstable? Several factors were involved. First, the economic fate of the individual oligarchs was just too closely tied to the course of state policy. Who would be given the right to acquire the remaining assets of state industry as they were put up for privatization? How long would the government retain control over the "natural monopolies" such as the railways, Gazprom, Unified Energy System, the oil pipeline operator Transneft' and the telecommunications holding Rostelekom?

Second, there is the matter of pride and envy. Some of the oligarchs envied the power of the president and sought some of that glory for themselves. Berezovsky and Gusinsky controlled media empires and reveled in playing the political game until they were forced into exile. Then in the spring of 2003, Mikhail Khodorkovsky, the founder of the Yukos oil company and the richest man in Russia, started signaling his interest in a political career. In Putin's quarterly meeting with businessmen in February 2003, Khodorkovsky reportedly railed against corruption and quizzed Putin about a deal in which the state-owned Rosneft' oil company was buying the smaller Severnaia Neft' for $600 million, a price that he contended was excessive. Later that month, rumors began circulating that Khodorkovsky intended to run for the presidency in 2008, if not in 2004. Yukos was active in buying the loyalty of Duma deputies, and it did not hesitate to use its leverage to block legislation that it disliked, such as higher oil excise taxes and revisions to the law on production sharing. During the campaign leading to the December 2003 State Duma election, Khodorkovsky was pouring money into parties across the political spectrum (as was Berezovsky, from exile in London). Yukos-linked analysts were floating the idea of introducing a parliamentary system of government, in which the government would be answerable to the State Duma (presumably oligarch-controlled) rather than to the president ("Oligarkhizagov-orshchiki" 2003; Sovet po natsional'noi strategii 2003).

The oligarchs' envy of the Kremlin's political power was matched by the bureaucrats' envy of their wealth and arrogance. Many state officials, especially those in the security services, resented the erosion of their own privileges and prestige since the collapse of the Soviet Union, while the oligarchs grew fabulously rich. They felt it was time to even out the distribution of benefits from the transition to capitalism. Putin was one of them, in terms of his career and probably his mentality, and was seen as their standard-bearer.

The third reason for the oligarchs' unstable hold on power is the international dimension. The Russian political economy is not a closed system. It is very open to international influences and opportunities. Both Putin and his oligarch rivals sought international support as part of their strategy to acquire and consolidate power. This made the balance of forces between Putin and the oligarchs inherently unstable.

The oligarchs had an exit strategy: they could always cash out and live on the French Riviera. Some of them also considered an exit-and-return strategy: the West could offer both political legitimation and practical support. The latter strategy was exemplified by Berezovsky, and subsequently Khodorkovsky.

In 2002–3 Khodorkovsky tried to strengthen his position by adopting international accounting standards and adding Westerners to the Yukos board, with a view to offering a large stake in the company to a Western oil major (ExxonMobil was reportedly interested) (Romanova 2003). That maneuver would have enabled him to cash out some of his share holdings, valued at their peak at $15 billion. To increase Yukos's attractiveness he tried to develop new export possibilities outside the state-owned Transneft' pipeline system. He sought permission to build a new export pipeline to Murmansk and symbolically shipped a tanker of crude from there to Houston. He also pursued an agreement with China to finance a $3 billion pipeline project to carry oil from Angarsk in Siberia to Daqing in China. In addition, he mounted an aggressive international public relations campaign, funding international charities and getting himself appointed to worthy foundation boards, such as that of the International Crisis Group. He thought that these steps would make it too risky for Putin to take him down, but he miscalculated.

Prosecutors started arresting top Yukos executives in July 2003, presumably with Putin's approval. At first, the arrests focused on the 1994 privatization of a fertilizer company, Apatit—in which Yukos had actually reached an out-of-court settlement the previous year. Then the investigations widened, to accusations that Yukos fraudently hid its earnings through a network of offshore shell companies, enabling it to evade taxes illegally.[6] Khodorkovsky had the chance to go into exile quietly, but he refused to back down, instead launching a political offensive in defense of his arrested colleagues. Khodorkovsky himself was detained in October 2003 and went on trial in June 2004.

Why did the system of oligarchic rule collapse so quickly in the face of Putin's assault (Tret'iakov 2003; "Vlast i oligarkhiia" 2003)? First, the oligarchs failed to act collectively in their common self-defense, preferring to use their connections to try to make individual deals. "The oligarchs slept through the past four years, thinking that dealing with the Kremlin individually would cost them less than investing in civil society" (Fedorin 2003).

Second, they underestimated Putin's political acumen and his desire to break away from the political traditions established by his predecessor. In part they were lulled into a false sense of security by the fact that Putin retained the two leading officials of the Yeltsin era: Chief of Staff Aleksandr Voloshin and Prime Minister Mikhail Kas'ianov. Their presence was seen, erroneously in retrospect, as a guarantee that the Yeltsin rules of the game would be preserved. Voloshin resigned in November 2003 after Khodorkovsky's arrest, and Putin fired Kas'ianov one month before the March 2004 presidential election.

Third, the oligarchs underestimated the political resources at Putin's disposal. As chief executive, Putin had the vast resources of the Russian state at hand, a cornucopia of sticks and carrots that soon won the loyalty of virtually all the regional bosses and business leaders. Putin also enjoyed huge popular legitimacy, having been elected first in March 2000 and again in March 2004, and enjoying approval ratings above 70 percent in every intervening month. Both the oligarchs and Putin claimed to speak for the interests of Russia and the Russian people. But Putin was elected, and the oligarchs were not. Putin was popular, and the oligarchs were not.

Putin was also welcomed by international leaders and quickly became a prominent figure on the international diplomatic stage, a factor that bolstered his domestic authority and limited the effectiveness of the campaigns by Berezovsky and Khodorkovsky to discredit Putin internationally.[7] Finally, Putin was boosted by the fact that the Russian economy finally turned around in 1999, and enjoyed five years of 7 percent annual growth, in part fueled by rising world oil prices. This eased the pressure of social protest and gave the state extra resources to buy off regional leaders.

The New Rules of the Game

> I am absolutely convinced that the much talked-about equal distance between various business representatives and the authorities has been achieved in our country in the past few years. Today, those who disagree with this position, as they used to say, "are no longer with us" (Gazeta.ru 2003).
>
> —Vladimir Putin

> I keep hearing here and there that the laws were complicated and that it was impossible to observe them. Yes, the laws were complex and knotty, but it was quite possible to respect them. If five or seven people broke the laws it does not mean that everyone did (Startseva 2003).
>
> —Vladimir Putin

Back in 2000, observers imagined that the relationship of Putin to the oligarchs would be that of primus inter pares, something akin to King Arthur and the Knights of the

Round Table. However, that kind of horizontal bargaining between equals has been replaced by a vertical hierarchy of power. Aleksei Zudin (2001) argues that Putin set out from the beginning to fundamentally weaken the oligarchs and turn them into a subordinate group, an instrument of state rule.

Zudin's argument is not completely persuasive. Sergei Peregudov (2002), in contrast, sees more of a balance, an "iron triangle" of a bureaucratic elite, the presidential apparatus, and business corporations. Zudin glosses over the oligarchs' grip on the State Duma, a problem not solved until the December 2003 election. He does not cite the many cases where government policy conformed closely to oligarch interests, such as the tax loopholes or the blocking of production-sharing legislation. He cites only one example of an oligarch policy proposal being defeated—the ambitious bank reform plan prepared by a commission of the Russian Union of Industrialists and Entrepreneurs (RSPP) headed by Aleksandr Mamut in the summer of 2001.

As Roland Nash (2003), chief strategist for Renaissance Capital, succinctly explains:

> In general, successful policy was either that which was mutually beneficial to both [the Kremlin and the oligarchs] (tax reform, land reform, pension reform), or that in which the other side had little interest (reform of the Federation Council, centralizing regional influence, improving corporate governance). Anything that either side actively didn't want to see passed was mostly blocked. The Kremlin prevented the expansion of a privately funded oil pipeline network, the breakup of Gazprom, and some of the oligarchs' wilder notions for utility sector restructuring. Big business successfully lobbied against increased effective taxes on the oil sector, Gref's plans for pension reform (the final adopted legislation was a compromise version), and the original version of banking reform.

Institutional Channels

What, then, will be the role of business in the state capitalist system that Putin is fashioning? It is not only that oligarchs must now be loyal to the Kremlin and stay out of politics. They must conduct their business in a more transparent way, following Russian laws and paying Russian taxes. They are also expected to play an active role in helping the Kremlin realize its political, economic, and social agenda—at home and abroad. In the words of Economic Development and Trade Minister German Gref (the leading liberal in Putin's government), "With great wealth comes great responsibility" (Sitnina 2003). Putin told the Chamber of Commerce and Industry that "business cannot and must not avoid resolving social problems." The Chamber in turn released a statement calling on all businesses "to fully share with the government the responsibility for the social and economic situation in Russia" (Startseva 2003). Finance Minister Aleksandr Kudrin—another liberal—explained the "normal rules" for business as honest payment of taxes, charitable giving, and "support for the political forces that care about the development of the country and promote its democratic values" (Rossiia TV 2004).

This "social responsibility" ranges from contributing funds to the Kremlin's pet projects, such as paying for the renovation of St. Petersburg in preparation for its three hundredth anniversary, to investing in energy infrastructure in politically sensitive regions such as Armenia and Georgia. While companies are more than willing to boast about the former, they are understandably reticent about discussing the political context of the latter, actions that are typically portrayed as purely business decisions.

The Kremlin has tried, in a rather halfhearted way, to put the state's new relationship with the business community on a more institutionally sound footing. The first vehicle for this relationship was regular face-to-face meetings between the president and leading executives. On July 28, 2000, Putin met with twenty-one leading businessmen in the Kremlin, mostly from energy companies (Slavutinskaia 2000). In contrast to previous meetings between Yeltsin and business leaders, this time it seemed to be the president laying down terms to the oligarchs, rather than the other way around. Putin cautioned the oligarchs to stay out of politics and pledged to maintain an "equidistance" from them as president, not favoring one over the others (Vishnevskii et al. 2001).

A sense that the Kremlin was not listening to the business community led to calls from Oleg Kisilev (Impeksbank) for an "oligarch trade union" in September 2000. In response, in November 2000 Putin selected the RSPP as the designated interlocutor. He "issued a 'royal command' for all Russian business leaders to unite in the RSPP and to submit all complaints via this body, collectively, after working out a common opinion" (Bogaturov 2003; Efimov 2003).

The RSPP was "a rather staid, decade-old organization representing traditional state-owned factories and headed by a Gorbachev-era functionary, Arkady Volsky" (Germanovich 2001).[8] The RSPP had been critical of the liberal reforms and forged a strong link with the labor unions. In 1993, Gaidar created the Association of Private and Privatized Enterprises as a balance to the "red directors" who had taken refuge in the RSPP. But in 2001 the RSPP found itself taken over by the brash new oligarchs. As none of the new billionaire members could agree on one of their number to head the organization, they left Volsky in charge. Alarmed by the oligarch influx, some of the traditional RSPP members, such as the League of Defense Enterprises headed by Anatolii Dololaptev, threatened to quit the organization. The RSPP remains deeply split between neoliberals and neostatists, which inhibits their ability to give clear advice to government development plans (Peregudov 2004b).

At the same time, the Kremlin decided to spread its bets, lest the RSPP become too influential or independent-minded. The Putin leadership promoted the influence of rival groups that would provide some checks on the RSPP's role. Delovaia Rossiia was a group of business deputies that Igor Lisinenko, the head of the Maiskii Chai company, formed in the Duma that was elected in December 1999. The Kremlin persuaded Lisinenko to break his ties with the RSPP and work directly with (and for) the Kremlin. Delovaia Rossiia's founding congress came in October 2001, one month after the creation of another body, the United Entrepreneurs' Organizations of Russia (OPORA). This body was created by the Kremlin to reach out to small and medium enterprises, a group that RSPP had tended to ignore. OPORA was organized with branches in each of the new federal okrugs—without the participation of RSPP. Then in December 2001 former prime minister Yevgenii Primakov was appointed head of the Chamber of Commerce and Industry (TPP), a moribund organization with roots in the Soviet era, but one that could now be activated as a tame business lobby to do the Kremlin's bidding (*Izvestiia* 2001). The Kremlin was trying to create an institutional framework to formalize and streamline its relations with the business community, although in practice, informal connections with individual businessmen still seemed to be the preferred modus operandi of the presidential apparatus.

The possible utility of the new institutional arrangements was illustrated by the Kremlin's handling of the controversy regarding TV6, a television company with a team of journalists, led by Evgenii Kisilev, who had fled NTV, formerly owned by Gusinsky. In March 2002, Volsky's RSPP and Primakov's TPP dutifully joined a consortium to bid for the broadcasting license of TV6. The bid failed, but TV6 was shut down anyway.

The regular meetings between Putin and the businessmen continued to take place two or three times a year, but they were usually low-key affairs discussing issues like trade policy and customs reform (Kozhakhmetova 2001). Even those modest gatherings ground to a halt in the wake of the Yukos affair.

The business community was paralyzed by the Yukos affair. At first, the wave of arrests of Yukos executives triggered some mild protests from their business colleagues. But after Khodorkovsky was arrested, and Putin spoke out against "speculation and hysteria" surrounding the affair, the business community fell silent ("Stability? What Stability? 2003). At a meeting with 800 Russian business leaders on November 14, 2003, Putin said that the Yukos case was an isolated example, but at the same time, he warned that Russian businesses "must develop a system of new social guarantees for the population in line with the new demands of the time" (Interfax 2003).

Respected economist Evgenii Iasin described the state of business–state relations in the wake of the Yukos affair as "like a traffic accident, when the two drivers stand around thinking about what they need to do" (Korop 2004). United Russia organized a round table with business leaders on the theme "Repentance" in May 2004. But almost nobody showed up, except Igor Iurgens, deputy head of the RSPP, who said: "The terms will be more strict for business. I don't think another business leader will risk playing politics" (Siluianova 2004). Business leaders were fearful that Putin would give in to pressure from the nationalists in the Duma and the security bloc (*siloviki*) in his own administration and embark on wholesale renationalization of the industries privatized in the 1990s. Igor Bunin argues that this threat remains "a sword of Damocles hanging over business" (ibid.).

The assault on Yukos also had an impact on the broader realm of Russian civil society, since business groups had been an important source of funding for independent political and civic organizations (Tsygankov 2003). Khodorkovsky and Berezovsky had been funding hundreds of civic groups, and these ties would now bring these groups unwelcome attention from the authorities who sought to root out the political networks of these renegade oligarchs.

One should not exaggerate the significance of these institutional channels for the collective representation of business interests. Most business lobbying, under Putin as under Yeltsin, takes the form of direct approaches to government officials by business groups, either individually or by industrial sector. They lobby for tax breaks, for protective tariffs, and for government contracts. Their efforts ebb and flow depending on national and international trading conditions. Thus representatives of the steel industry, dominated by the Big Four companies (Novolipetsk, Severstal, Magnitka, and Evrrasholding), were lobbying for state protection in 2001, but by 2004 they were born-again free traders (Butrin 2004).

The Role of Parliament

One important vehicle for business to exert leverage over the government apparatus is (or was) the Federal Assembly.[9] While Yeltsin had tended to ignore the State Duma, relying heavily on rule by decree, Putin's agenda has included an ambitious program to overhaul Russia's legislation and introduce major structural reforms in the legal system, local government, and public administration. Hence, for Putin, establishing control over the legislature was an important goal.

In the elections of 1995 and especially 1999, many businessmen spent hefty sums to try to win a seat in the Duma. Their motives were often more individual than political. A Duma deputy is immune from prosecution unless the body votes to strip him or her of this privilege. In addition, a Duma seat brought contacts useful for spreading the scope of a business beyond its home region. It also came with certain costs, such as the risks of public scrutiny and political competition and the need to withdraw from business activities, at least formally (Zhavoronkov 2003). Business-connected deputies were so influential in the Duma, and in the Federation Council (where they held more than half the seats), that they were effectively substituting themselves for the role conventionally played by political parties.

Leading corporations like Yukos and Gazprom were also the most politically active. Yukos director Leonid Nevzlin was selected as a Federation Council member from Mordova, while Vladimir Dubov, a major Yukos shareholder, entered the Duma in 1999 on the Fatherland–All Russia ticket and became chair of its tax committee. Gazprom supported an estimated 130 candidates in the 1999 elections (Kolmakov 2003). Yukos seemed to get a good return on its political investments. For example, over Kremlin objections the Duma left in the Tax Code a profit tax exemption for investment agreements between companies and regional governments. Mordova, Chukotka, and Kalmykia signed such agreements with Yukos and other companies, saving them $1.5 billion a year (Visloguzov 2003).

In the 2003 election, roughly 20 percent of the candidates were directly linked to business corporations, even including many Communist nominees (24 percent of whose candidates were thus identified) (Mereu 2003). In August 2003, *Fortune* quoted Khodorkovsky as saying "I'm going to try to buy a democratic future for my country . . . And I have enough money and energy to do that" (Guyon 2003). The Yukos affair, closely followed by the victory of the pro-Putin United Russia in the December 2003 Duma elections, radically changed that state of affairs. When United Russia stunned observers by pulling off a sweeping victory, Putin managed to put the oligarchs in their place and drive the left and right opposition parties out of their niches in the parliament: 54 percent of the Duma incumbents who ran for reelection lost their seats (Rudakov 2003).

The failure of the two independent right-wing parties, Yabloko and the Union of Right Forces, to clear the 5 percent threshold and win seats in the party-list contest was a particularly heavy blow to oligarch interests. Between them these parties won only seven seats in the single-mandate races, down from a total of forty-nine seats in the outgoing legislature. The two parties had included the most intelligent and experienced advocates of liberal reforms and had the closest ties to business lobbies. After December 2003, Russia's businessmen suddenly found themselves shut out of both the Kremlin and the Duma, constituting what Peregudov jokingly describes as the "new *lishentsy*" (people deprived of political rights, a term from the 1930s) (Peregudov 2004a).

State Corporations

It is important to remember that not all Russian industry is owned by private businessmen. Alongside the private oligarchs there are also state oligarchs, individuals who manage state-owned companies, such as Rem Viakhirev at Gazprom. The managers of state-owned firms grew personally wealthy through various ways. They could channel sales through middleman companies controlled by their relatives. They were legally allowed to buy from 2 to 5 percent of the shares in their companies at nominal prices and could acquire even more through semilegal means. Even some of the Russians on the *Forbes* list of billionaires (Viktor Chernomyrdin, Rem Viakhirev) made that money in companies like Gazprom in which the state was still the controlling shareholder.

In 2004, the state still held a 100-percent stake in some 100 companies, including the oil company Rosneft´, the oil pipeline monopoly Transneft´, the aircraft maker Sukhoi, and the Russian Railways Corporation. It holds shares in about 4,000 other companies, including majority stakes in the savings bank Sberbank (62 percent), Aeroflot (51 percent), and the electricity giant Unified Energy Systems (51 percent) and a significant stake in the natural gas monopoly Gazprom (38 percent) (Aliakrinskaia and Dokuchev 2004). The state is not a very active stakeholder, typically leaving the top management of these companies free to run them as they see fit. Many state officials, such as government ministers and even Kremlin staffers, sit on the boards of these companies. That arrangement gives them an extra source of income and career opportunities once they leave government service.

This means that many Russian business corporations occupy a gray area—they are not fully independent of the state but not fully part of it either. Decision making is opaque and hidden from public view, brokered in face-to-face meetings between the leaders of state corporations and top government officials. The government will put its foot down over publicly visible and politically sensitive decisions, such as the annual announcement of price increases for the electricity, gas, and railway monopolies. But more detailed discussions about which trading companies to use to buy and sell company products are presumably made by the corporate executives themselves.

Putin slowly but steadily moved to ensure that the leading state corporations were headed by people loyal to him. In May 2001, he ousted the long-standing head of Gazprom, Rem Viakhirev, and replaced him with a young and trusted economist from Putin's home town of St. Petersburg, Aleksei Miller. Gazprom's $15 billion in exports make it Russia's largest cash earner. Later in 2001, Putin removed the head of Russian Railways, Nikolai Aksenov, who was dogged with accusations of corruption. He also removed Viktor Gerashchenko, head of the Central Bank, in March 2002 and replaced him with Sergei Ignat'iev, who was serving as deputy finance minister. Russia's largest company, Unified Energy System (UES), has been headed since 1998 by Anatolii Chubais, another Petersburger whom Putin apparently trusts, and who has been left in place to oversee its privatization.

Oligarchs in the Regions

Space does not permit a full discussion of the role of business groups in Russia's eighty-nine regions. Suffice it to note that the degree of economic and political pluralism varies greatly among those regions. Some regions have a concentration of political and economic power in a tight circle, while others (a minority), have a divided elite and political contestation.

In the early 1990s, the typical pattern was for local business leaders to collude with regional leaders against the Moscow center. The pattern grew more complex as the decade wore on. One saw the emergence of business groups operating across several regions, and getting actively involved in governors' elections. Increasingly, those cross-regional business groups started to serve in cooperation with Moscow, supporting state moves to spread market relations to the backward and subsidized regions—for example, when negotiating over regional energy debts with governors (Zubarevich 2002). According to one analyst, "The Moscow-based businesses, which are now taking over the major regional economic resources (and supplanting the local economic elites), are in fact assisting in the reestablishment of Kremlin control over the regions" (Yorke 2002).

In 1996, Gazprom ran candidates in ten governor's races but only won one, in Iamalo-Nenets. In some small and sparsely populated regions, individual oligarchs got themselves elected governor and effectively took over the region. The relevant examples are Roman Abramovich (Sibneft') in Chukotka, Yukos's Boris Zolotarev in Evenkiia, and Khazret Sovmen, the owner of a gold mine and president of Adygea. Aleksandr Khloponin, the former director of Noril'sk Nickel, became governor of Krasnoiarsk after the death of Aleksandr Lebed'. Nine of the current governors, or 10 percent, are former business executives. It has been more common for a corporation to become a close supporter of an incumbent, such as Lukoil backing Iurii Trutnev in Perm (in 2004 he was appointed federal minister of natural resources). Regional leaders would also appoint representatives of powerful businesses to their teams. For example, Samara Governor Konstantin Titov made a Yukos first vice president his deputy governor, while Irkutsk Governor Boris Govorin included representatives from both Russian Aluminum and Alfa Group on his staff (Tsentr politicheskikh tekhnologii 2002). Local businessmen usually established a strong foothold in regional legislatures, accounting for 60 to 70 percent of the deputies (Kryshtanovskaia 2003). But only in a few regions, such as St. Petersburg and Voronezh, do local parliaments have much power.

All the organized groups in Russian political life were to a degree energized by the additional resources generated by the post-1998 economic growth. But overall, the federal center was capturing more of the revenue stream from energy exports and growing more powerful. It is possible that as business leaders are marginalized from political power at the federal level, they may be able to consolidate their positions at the regional level (Gaman-Golutvina 2004), though the power and independence of regional leaders is decreasing under Putin.

Conclusion

Economic and political power in Putin's Russia is not distributed horizontally and constrained by the rule of law, as a civil society would require. Rather, power is structured vertically, with a chain of command leading to President Putin. The pattern of interactions between business and the state does not correspond to bargaining in a market-like environment of multiple and changing buyers and sellers. Rather, it is consistent with a patrimonial system where favors are distributed in reward for loyalty. In Putin's Russia, as Lilia Shevtsova puts it, "not only democracy but capitalism itself is managed by the Kremlin" (*Financial Times* 2003). This new hierachical model is more flexible (and more unstable) than the old Communist Party model. It is authoritarian, not totalitarian, and it is compatible with a market economy and a fairly high degree of personal freedom, though it poses limits on freedom of speech and association. But it is not clear to what extent this state-led capitalism can allow the development of a civil society in the Western sense of the term, or create the conditions for the emergence of civil society in some future crisis.

Clearly, the building of civil society in Russia cannot be isolated from the processes of globalization that preceded, accompanied, and followed the Soviet collapse. International factors both strengthened and weakened the role of business as an element in Russia's emerging civil society. The rise of the oligarchs as a class was driven by domestic developments, the opening of a vacuum of power within which entrepreneurial individuals with political connections were able to create new business empires. However, most of their wealth came from the export of Russian resources overseas—and their ability to hide their profits in offshore banks, far from the Russian tax authorities. Mikhail Khodorkovsky sought to strengthen this international dimension even further, by turning Yukos into a globally recognized (and foreign-owned) corporation. It was his Icarus-like desire that triggered the crackdown by Putin, shattering the illusions, and the realities, of oligarchic capitalism in Russia.

Russia illustrates the familiar pattern of the "resource curse" (Karl 1997). Countries that depend on the extraction of natural resources, especially oil, typically see political and economic power concentrated in the hands of a narrow elite, closely tied to the state. The elite that controls the lucrative extractive industries has huge resources at its disposal and does not feel obliged to enter into a dialogue or share power with broader social groups, whether industrial workers or small business. In the Russian case, this tendency to concentrate power in energy-rich economies comes on top of a long and deep history of state domination of society, under the tsars and the Communists.

The collapse of central planning and its replacement by a rough-and-ready form of market capitalism opened the door to the emergence of civil society in Russia. It helped create a plurality of social actors by leading to the emergence of a group of powerful business oligarchs. However, the new Russian business elite was closely tied to the state apparatus, and when Yeltsin was replaced by Putin, the new president laid down clear limits to their political independence, which restrict the capacity of business to serve as a check on state power and a force to promote the flourishing of civil society. President Putin sought to use Russia's new capitalists to serve the interests of the state and its own agenda of socioeconomic modernization. Thus a student of Russian business would be inclined to conclude that in many respects a true civil society in Russia seems no closer in 2004 than it was in 1991.

Notes

1. Some of the people on the list complained that *Forbes* exaggerated their wealth, although Boris Berezovsky said he was richer than *Forbes* reported (Osetinskaia et al. 2004). *Forbes* listed twenty-five billionaires in February, then increased the number to thirty-six in May, reflecting new estimates of their stock holdings ("Forbes" 2004). *Forbes* counted zero Russian billionaires in 2000, and seventeen in 2003.

2. See also the explanation of the report by the lead author Christof Ruehl (Federal News Service 2004). The study was conducted in 2003 and was looking at company structure as of 2001.

3. Other, less politically prominent oligarchs who were start-up billionaires include Igor Iakovlev of the Eldorado retail chain and cell phone magnates Dmitrii Zimin (VimpelCom) and Vladimir Evtushenkov (MTS).

4. The word "oligarch" was first used by Aleksandr Privalov of *Ekspert* magazine, who started a regular poll of elites, publishing rankings of those who were seen as the most influential political and business figures (Romanova 2002).

5. The only "positive" element in these polls is that respondents are just as suspicious of state officials as they are of businessmen.

6. A Paris-based former Yukos associate, Elena Collongues-Popova, started revealing details of the myriad offshore companies through which Yukos had evaded taxes (Whalen 2004).

7. Here Putin was only partly successful. For example, British courts refused Russian requests to extradite Berezovsky.

8. Leading figures in the RSPP included Kakha Benukidze, Oleg Deripaska, Aleksandr Mamut, Vladimir Potanin, Mikhail Fridman, Mikhail Khodorkovsky, and Anatoly Chubais (Germanovich 2001).
9. Many thanks to Thomas Remington for helpful advice on this section.

References

Aliakrinskaia, Natalia, and Dmitrii Dokuchev. 2004. "State = Board of Directors." *Moscow Times*, June 9.
Arkhangel'skaia, Natalia. 2001. "Estestvennyi klannovyi otbor." *Ekspert* 46 (December): 19–21.
Belton, Catherine. 2005. "Shock and then Boredom in Court." *Moscow Times*, June 1.
Bianova, Natalia, and Andrei Litvinov. 2003. " Oligarkhicheskii pogrom." *Gazeta*, December 24.
Bogaturov, Aleksei. 2003. "The Kasianov Cabinet Is Finishing Its Game." *Rodnaia gazeta*, June 27, translated in What the Papers Say, June 28, LexisNexis, web.lexis-nexis.com/cis.
Brady, Rose. 1999. *Kapitalizm: Russia's Struggle to Free Its Economy*. New Haven, CT: Yale University Press.
Brzezinski, Matthew. 2001. *Casino Moscow: A Tale of Greed and Adventure on Capitalism's Wildest Frontier*. New York: Free Press.
Butrin, Dmitrii. 2004. "Gosplan ekonomicheskogo rosta." Gazeta.ru, April 26, www.gazeta.ru.
Caryl, Christian. 2001. "Twilight of the Oligarchs." *Newsweek International*, February 5: 20–22.
Efimov, Aleksei. 2003. "Oligarkhi pripolzli na koleniakh." *Nezavisimaia gazeta*, October 23.
Federal News Service. 2004. World Bank press conference, April 7, www.fednews.ru.
Fedorin, Vladimir. 2003. "Chelovek nedeli." *Vedomosti*, December 8.
Financial Times. 2003. December 24.
"Forbes: Richest 36 Own 24% of GDP." 2004. *Moscow Times*, May 13.
Fortescue, Stephen. 2002. "Pravit li Rossiei oligarkhiia?" *Polis*, no. 5: 64–73.
Fossato, Floriana, and Anna Kachkaeva. 2000. "Russian Media Empires VI." Radio Free Europe/Radio Liberty, September, www.rferl.org/specials/russia/media6/.
Freeland, Chrystia. 2000. *Sale of the Century: Russia's Wild Ride from Communism to Capitalism*. New York: Crown Business.
Gaman-Golutvina, Oksana. 2004. "Regional'nye elity v Rossii." *Polis*, no. 2: 6–19.
Gazeta.ru. 2003. June 20, www.gazeta.ru.
Gel'man, Vladimir. 2003. "Institutsional'noe stroitel'stvo i neformal'nye instituty v sovremennoi Rossiiskoi politike." *Polis*, no. 4: 6–25.
Germanovich, Aleksei. 2001. "Oligarkhi pokaiutsia." *Vedomosti*, February 14.
Gorin, N. I., et al. 2003. "Obshchestvo, biznes, vlast'. *Obshchestvo i ekonomika*, no. 12 (December): 36–63.
Guyon, Janet. 2003. "The Game Goes On." *Fortune* 148, no. 11 (November 24), LexisNexis, web.lexis-nexis.com/cis.
Hellman, Joel. 1998. "Winners Take All: The Politics of Partial Reform in Post-Communist Transitions." *World Politics* 50, no. 2 (January): 203–34.
Interfax. 2003. November 14, www.interfax-news.com.
Izvestiia. 2001. December 11.
Karl, Terry Lynn. 1997. *The Paradox of Plenty: Oil Booms and Petrostates*. Berkeley: University of California Press.
Khlopin, Aleksandr. 2002. "Grazhdanskoe obshchestvo v Rossii." *Pro et Contra* 7, no. 1, www.carnegie.ru/en/pubs/proetcontra.
Klebnikov, Paul. 2000. *Godfather of the Kremlin: Boris Berezovsky and the Looting of Russia*. New York: Harcourt, 2000.

Kolmakov, Sergei. 2003. "The Role of Financial-Industrial Groups in Russian Political Parties." *Russia Watch*, bcsia.ksg.harvard.edu/publication.cfm, no. 9, January.
Korop, Elena. 2004. " Novoe pravitel'stvo poidet starim kursom." *Izvestiia*, May 13.
Kozhakhmetova, Al'mira. 2001. " Poslushnye oligarkhi skhodili v Kreml'." *Novye izvestiia*, June 1.
Kryshtanovskaia, Ol'ga. 2003. " Liudi Putina." *Vedomosti*, June 30.
Latynina, Yulia. 2003. "Who Is the Biggest Loser?" *Moscow Times*, October 29.
Ledeneva, Alena V. 1998. *Russia's Economy of Favours: Blat, Networking, and Informal Exchanges.* Cambridge: Cambridge University Press.
Lysova, Tat'iana. 1998. " Reforma oligarkhov." *Ekspert*, March.
Mereu, Francesca. 2003. "Business Will Have Big Voice in Duma." *Moscow Times*, November 13.
Nash, Roland. 2003. "Who Needs Politics Anyway?" *Prime TASS*, December 17.
"Oligarkhi-zagovorshchiki." 2003. *Stolichnaia vecherniaia gazeta*, May 29.
Osetinskaia, Elizaveta, et al. 2004. "Milliarderov uzhe 36." *Vedomosti*, May 13.
Peregudov, Sergei. 2002. "Korporativnyi kapital i instituty vlasti." *Polis*, no. 5: 74–84.
———. 2003. *Korporatsiia, obshchestvo, gosudarstvo*. Moscow: Nauka.
———. 2004a. "Delovaia elita kak novye lishentsy." *Nezavisimaia gazeta*, January 20.
———. 2004b. "Korporatsiia kak sotsial'nyi institut." *Nezavisimaia gazeta*, March 23.
Pinsker, Dmitrii. 1997. " Moskovskii Anti-Davos." *Itogi*, September 22.
Putnam, Robert D. 1993. *Making Democracy Work.* Princeton, NJ: Princeton University Press.
"Rising Tide." 2004. *Forbes*, May 13: 91.
Romanova, Liudmila. 2003. "O strategii Khodorkovskogo." *Mirovaia energeticheskaia politika*, May 31: 18–21.
Romanova, Ol'ga. 2002. "Novoiaz." *Vedomosti*, January 29.
Rossiia TV. 2004. April 25.
Rudakov, Vladimir. 2003. "Bez politiki—bez konkurentsii." *Profil'*, December 22: 14–17.
Rutland, Peter. 2001. "Introduction: Business and the State in Russia." In *Business and the State in Contemporary Russia*, ed. Peter Rutland, 1–32. Boulder, CO: Westview Press.
Siluianova, Polina. 2004. "Neobkhodimo peregruzit' matritsu." *Gazeta*, May 14.
Sitnina, Vera. 2003. "My—vedomstvo—razdrazhitel'." Interview with German Gref. *Vremia novostei*, December 22.
Slavutinskaia, Inessa. 2000. "Liberalissimo." *Profil'*, August 7: 14.
Sovet po natsional'noi strategii. 2003. "V Rossii gotovitsia oligarkhicheskii perevorot." www.utro.ru, May 26.
"Stability? What Stability?" 2003. *Economist.com*, October 31.
Startseva, Alla. 2003. "Putin Threatens to Revisit Sell-Offs." *Moscow Times*, December 24.
Tret'iakov, Vitalii. 2003. "Vlast': Imperativy Putinina." *Literaturnaia gazeta*, November 5.
Tsentr politicheskikh tekhnologii. 2002. *Politika v regionakh: gubernatory i gruppy vliianiia.* Moscow: www.politcom.ru.
Tsipko, Aleksandr. 2001. "The Family Takes Control of Domestic Politics." *Prism* (Jamestown Foundation) 7, no. 9 (September 30).
Tsygankov, Valerii. 2003. "Den' grazhdanskogo neposlushaniia." *Nezavisimaia gazeta*, October 28.
Varese, Federico. 2002. *The Russian Mafia.* New York: Oxford University Press.
Vishnevskii, Boris, et al. 2001. " Ravnoudalennost'v raznye storony." *Obshchaia gazeta*, June 7–13.
Visloguzov, Vadim. 2003. "Deputat barrelia." *Kommersant-Vlast'*. December 12.
"Vlast' i oligarkhiia" (extracts from Kul'tura TV discussion program). 2003. *Rossiiskaia gazeta*, November 27.
Whalen, Jeanne. 2004. "A Jilted Banker's View of Khodorkovsky's Empire." *Wall Street Journal*, January 2.

Woodruff, David. 1999. *Money Unmade: Barter and the Fate of Russian Capitalism.* Ithaca, NY: Cornell University Press.

World Bank. 2004. *From Transition to Development* (draft). April, www.worldbank.org.ru.

Yorke, Andrew. 2002. "Putin and the Oligarchs: More Cooperation than Conflict So Far." *Russian Regional Report* (EastWest Institute) 7, no. 5, February 6. www.isn.ethz.ch/researchpub.

Zhavoronkov, Pavel. 2003. "The Price of the Problem." Pravda.ru, english.pravda.ru, September 10.

Zubvarevich, Natalia. 2002. "Prishel, uvidel, pobedil? Krupnyi biznes i regional'naia vlast'. *Pro et Contra* 7, no. 1, www.carnegie.ru/en/pubs/proetcontra.

Zudin, Aleksei. 2001. "Neokorporativizm v Rossii?" *Pro et Contra* 6, no. 4, www.carnegie.ru/en/pubs/proetcontra.

6

Organized Crime Groups

"Uncivil Society"

Louise Shelley

Organized crime groups may be considered an "uncivil" part of society. Ironically, criminal organizations were the only form of organized nonstate society that existed until the late Soviet period. In the post-Soviet period, they have emerged as major financial actors. They share significant financial interests with state officials, and many state officials use criminals to provide the security for their personal financial interests. A criminal–political nexus has occurred, promoting the mutual economic and political interests of state officials and crime groups (Shelley 2003).

Post-Soviet organized crime groups represent a new form of authoritarianism, because they are able to enforce compliance and intimidate their countrymen without fearing reprisals (Shelley 1997). Unlike contemporary Russian civil society in the area of human rights, women's groups, or the environmental arena, who seek a more open and democratic society, the crime groups do not favor a more transparent and freer society (McFaul 2003). Instead, they seek an unaccountable and ineffective legal system, corruptible government officials, and lack of conflict-of-interest laws. If a more democratic society became achievable, it would deny them the economic monopolies they enjoy, limit their political influence, and reduce their possibility of intimidating fellow citizens to achieve their economic and political objectives.

Not only are organized crime groups not civil society organizations because of their close linkages to the state; organized crime groups also work actively to undermine legitimate forms of civil society in the former Soviet Union. Organized crime groups have usurped and undermined some of the functions of civil society. For example, they have exploited charities to promote their economic interests (Shelley 1994). They have provided services for their fellow citizens that the state does not provide, as have the Colombian crime groups and the *boryodukan* in Japan after the Kobe earthquake (Abadinsky 2003, 172, 209). These are not acts of kindness but acts that mimic the goals of civil society—social activism and community engagement—in an effort to blunt any citizen resistance. Crime groups are preventing the rise of civil society in many parts of Russia and undermining the rule of law through their corruption of the legal system. Citizens cannot expect protection from the state.

Recent attacks by Putin on civil society further undermine the protection of the citizenry against the authoritarianism of the state. Crime groups remain potent actors, particularly on the regional level, where they carry enormous influence with local governors and political authorities. With the attacks on nongovernmental authorities by the central state in early 2004, citizens face even fewer protections from the powerful crime groups, which have their interests rather than those of the larger society at stake.

Historical Precedents

During the long years of Stalinist rule in which millions were incarcerated, the criminal world was able to benefit in two ways. It was able to absorb some of the *besprizorniki* (homeless children) who were so numerous and to recruit from the large numbers of convicts confined in the camps. With the end of the draconian measures of the Stalinist period, the criminal underworld also was able to benefit from this "thaw" in society. These new opportunities for the criminals particularly manifested themselves in the Caucasus.

Under the Soviet system, entrepreneurship was criminalized from its outset, not only through its prohibition under the criminal law but also through its association with the professional criminal class (Shelley 1992). The links between entrepreneurship and crime groups observed first in Georgia and some of the Asian republics after the Stalinist period became a pattern observed subsequently in Russia and throughout the former USSR. Developments in Georgia provide a good picture of how Caucasian criminal groups influenced future Russian organized criminals.

In the middle of the 1970s, the underground second economy fell under the scrutiny of the Georgian criminal underworld, one of the most powerful parts of the Soviet criminal underworld. The criminals perceived the profit-making potential of exploiting these black-market entrepreneurs (Rawlinson 1997, 44). In a meeting in Kislovodsk in 1979, the criminals decided that their take of these businesses should be 10 percent of their revenues (Kostiukovskii n.d.). As a result, a new criminal structure emerged that combined the interests of the shadow economy with those of the criminal world. This merger had great significance for the development and subsequent criminalization of the Soviet and transitional economies.

The attitude toward the criminal world that developed in the 1970s is important to understanding criminal groups' role within contemporary Russian society. The youth of the 1970s, now Russia's middle-aged population, began to be attracted by the myth of the criminal world—the group of professional criminals who lived outside the regimented Soviet state. Many appreciated the traditions of the criminals—their songs and their folklore. Many law-abiding citizens also looked to this world for its utilitarian contributions—its ability to return stolen merchandise, its ability to mediate conflicts, and its role in controlling crime (MVD Georgia 1982, 4; Lebedev and Kozlov 1988, 20).[1]

A crucial transformation occurred in the criminal world in the 1980s. In 1982, at the end of the Brezhnev period, a meeting was held in Tbilisi, at which the thieves contemplated their role in a transformed society. With the imminent death of the long-term president, the criminal underworld considered greater involvement in politics and the economy. The originator of this idea was Dzaba Ioselani, a man who served decades in Soviet-era labor camps and presided over the Georgian professional criminal world (Glonti 1998, 138; Podelesskikh and Tereshonok 1994).

In the 1980s, Georgians represented approximately half of all identified thieves-in-law (*vory v zakone*)—professional criminals emerging from the Soviet gulag who worked solely within the criminal underworld and rejected the legitimate world. At the 1982 meeting, Ioselani proposed a fundamental change that would enhance the financial opportunities of the criminals in this transition (Mikheladze and Shevelev 1993). His proposal for greater collaboration with the state derived from the situation in Georgia, where criminal clans had already developed close ties with the regional government. Bribery and other forms of corruption flourished because of the structured links between the criminals and the state. Others from outside the region, where the ties were not yet so solidified, questioned this fundamental change as a threat to the criminal law and the criminal subculture. In Georgia, at least, this conflict was resolved in favor of Ioselani's proposal. After Georgian independence, he became a member of parliament from 1992 to 1995 and the right hand of President Shevardnadze. At Ioselani's death in 2003, the Georgian patriarch buried him, and leading government officials were at his funeral. Russian television described the funeral as that of a leading "thief-in-law" (Petriashvili 2003).

By the mid-1980s, the Russian criminal world was peopled not only by the ethnic groups that had figured so prominently in the criminal cultures of the labor camps. New groups emerged at this time, primarily out of the world of professional athletes, Afghan veterans, and juvenile delinquents (Volkov 2002, 11). Groups such as the Tambov mafia, originating out of the sports world of this southern Russian city, would become powerful actors in St. Petersburg (67). Juvenile groups in Kazan became active not only in their city but in many parts of Russia. The professional criminal world became more diverse and less tied to the practices and standards of conduct that had characterized the criminal underworld for decades.

With their new focus on economics and politics, the criminal underworld was well positioned for the changes that occurred in the decade preceding the collapse of the Soviet Union. They benefited from the prohibition of alcohol in 1986, which quickly professionalized the once small-scale bootlegging. With the onset of private entrepreneurship in the late 1980s through the adoption of the law on cooperatives, there was an enormous opportunity for organized crime groups to launder their dirty assets into the legitimate economy (Jones and Moskoff 1992). It is no coincidence that 60 percent of the owners of cooperatives had criminal records for a range of offenses. Their predominance in the cooperative sector denied the opportunity for other cooperatives to compete legitimately because they used violence and other techniques to remove their potential economic competitors (ibid.). Therefore, rackets and corruption became integral parts of business activity from the onset of private business in the Soviet state (Gurov 1990). Consequently, organized crime was poised to assume a predominant role in the new capitalist activity. This position has not weakened in the decade of transition.

Russian Organized Crime and the Transition

Russian organized crime groups increased in number and membership throughout the 1990s. Russian law-enforcement authorities estimated that there were 785 groups operating in 1990 and 8,000 by mid-1996. At a minimum, 120,000 people were thought to be involved in these groups, and many estimates put the figures in the millions (Dunn 1997, 63). The number of crimes attributed to members of these crime groups grew throughout the 1990s (Luneev 1997). At the present time, estimates suggest that a third of the crime groups are local in nature, slightly more are national in scope, and a smaller share operates internationally. These international groups have become powerful actors in the international crime arena. They have managed to survive because they are untouchable at home due to their high-level political protection, which prevented prosecutors from cooperating in international cases. This was evident in the Bank of New York case but in many others as well (Shelley 2002). This prevents prosecution at home and the international cooperation needed to prosecute them abroad.

Diversity of Crime Groups

There are many types of crime groups with different structures, functional areas, and capabilities. The traditional thief-in-law groups, with large numbers of members of ethnic minorities, have receded in importance as the transition has continued. Instead, major economic actors are such crime groups as the Tambov mafia in St. Petersburg, the Solntsevo group in Moscow, and the Uralmash crime group in Ekaterinburg (Volkov 2002, 108–16; Handelman 1995, 75). The membership of these groups is more Russian than the traditional elite of the criminal world, the thieves-in-law. Younger, less bound by the established rules of the criminal world, and not distinctive in physical appearance, they can more easily function within Russian society. Just as the tradition-bound Cosa Nostra has been less financially successful than the newer crime organizations out of Colombia that are not as bound by traditional hierarchy, the same has occurred in Russia, where the new, more flexible crime groups have been more successful in adapting to the opportunities of the new environment.

Ethnic Composition

Ministry of Internal Affairs sources from the beginning of the 1990s, before the collapse of the USSR, revealed that there were 716 thieves-in-law, the top of the criminal hierarchy. Of these, 339 were registered in different republics but operated on Russian territory. Russians represented 33.1 percent of known thieves, Georgians 31.6

percent, Armenians 8.2 percent, and Azerbaijanis 5.2 percent, while Uzbeks, Ukrainians, Kazakhs, Abkhaz, and others represented 21.9 percent of the total (Glonti 1998, 140; Nicaso 2001). In the USSR, non-Russian ethnic minorities were often disproportionately represented in organized crime because they had fewer opportunities for legitimate advancement.

Cooperative relationships among these ethnic groups did not preclude conflicts over monopolies and leadership. The most noted conflicts within the criminal world were between the two largest groups—the Russians and the Georgians. This rivalry for markets preceded the political conflicts between the Russian and Georgian states. In 1985, the Ministry of Internal Affairs observed the first noted criminal conflict where Russian resentment of "Caucasians" surfaced (MVD USSR 1985).

There is much cooperation between Russians and Georgians in the crime groups, and with Russian officials of Georgian origin who have assumed prominent positions in the Moscow city government and the Georgian and Russian governments. A modus vivendi now exists among Russian and Georgian crime groups in the conflict regions of North and South Ossetia and Abkhazia on the southern border of Russia. For the crime groups on each side of the border, the failure to resolve these conflicts contributes to their profits. Moreover, the profits of the crime groups may be contributing to the lack of political resolution of these regional conflicts (Kukhianidze 2003).

The predominant role of non-Slavs in the criminal world recalls the analysis of organized crime in the United States, Japan, and the Netherlands (Abadinsky et al. 1998; Kaplan and Dubro 1986). In these countries, organized crime groups arise disproportionately from minority groups. The absence of legitimate paths for economic success in these societies is seen as contributing to the rise of ethnic crime. The theory of ethnic succession has been used in the United States to explain the displacement of certain crime groups by others. This has not occurred in the former Soviet Union. The same groups have been involved in criminal activity over extended periods of time.

Structure of Different Crime Groups

The Caucasian crime groups need to be differentiated from those of other crime associations by the fact that they are based on family structure and clan, rather than the friendship relations of the Afghan veterans, sports associations, or veterans of the labor camps. These newly formed crime groups are characterized more by their ethnic diversity than their homogeneity.

The criminal world can be divided into three levels of crime groups. The lowest and most specialized level operate only locally or regionally while the others have ties across the Soviet successor states and internationally. The simplest form of these groups, called "buffer" thieves, consists of three to ten people. Each of them has his appointed role within the organization. The structure is relatively democratic, without a strict hierarchy. Their activities consist of theft, burglary, swindling, armed robbery, and racketeering. Their corrupt ties are limited and mostly with the lower levels of the law-enforcement apparatus. It is these groups that assume powerful roles in the labor camps.

The mid-level groups of thieves, known as *Chestniaki*, are much more sophisticated structures. Within their ranks they have enforcers, intelligence operatives, bodyguards, and watchmen. These organizations have more than fifty members and the capability to carry out much more complex criminal activities. For example, they can run larger-scale rackets, trade in narcotics, smuggle illegal alcohol and contraband, and run illegal credit operations in the financial sphere. These individuals have much higher-level ties with the government and acquire a protector, or *krysha*. They are not found in labor camps because they are protected by their governmental krysha and have sufficient assets to buy off members of the law-enforcement apparatus, ensuring their release after detention, their acquittal, or dismissal of their charges if a case proceeds to trial (Gvetadze interview 2003; Maisuradze interview 2003).

At the next level are the criminal organizations controlled by the so-called authorities, leading figures of the crime world. These figures control very significant criminal organizations and have large network-like structures reporting to them. They have two or three levels of hierarchy coordinating the significant networks below. These groups have large financial interests in banks, real estate, joint ventures, casinos, restaurants, and private protection services. They have established norms of conduct and penalties for breaching these norms. They have a hierarchical structure that organizes them across regions: a governing council, bodyguards, and an intelligence service, in addition to a common jargon. They have an informational network that includes a means of collecting and disseminating information, including their own television stations and newspapers. They have their own personnel in positions of authority, including the law-enforcement system and courts (Gvetadze interview 2003; Maisuradze interview 2003). As in traditional mafia structures, high-level criminal groups divide their spheres of influence among gambling, prostitution, and drugs. Furthermore, they have extensive involvement in many sectors of the legitimate economy, particularly time-sensitive businesses such as construction and transport. They seek out sectors with maximum profitability and avoid sectors with limited profits such as agriculture.

Methods of Russian Organized Crime

The Russian criminal world is particularly violent. Russian organized criminals have become important actors internationally because of their ability to deploy violence. They have done this successfully within Russia and also have been able to retaliate overseas by sending hit men to execute orders for contract killings and to threaten individuals abroad with reprisals against family members within Russia. This has been particularly true in extorting money from Russian athletes abroad and women who have been trafficked overseas.

The reason that Russian organized criminals have so successfully utilized violence is that they are not employing mere thugs, but individuals that the Soviet state trained in the application of violence. Within the ranks of Russian organized crime are many who served in the Soviet military during the Afghan war or were part of the security services in the Soviet period (Volkov 2002, 129–42).

During the early years of the transition period, the violence was less directed than it is today. Presently the killing is more targeted with few random victims. In the early to mid-1990s, there were very large numbers of contract killings. The initial high level of contract killings was a consequence of violent conflicts over the division of property, which occurred in the early years of privatization. Yet with the end of this initial division of property, the number of contract killings has not abated. Rather, contract killings and high levels of violence appear to be an enduring characteristic of Russian organized crime (Nomokonov and Shulga 1988). In fact, crime more generally in Russia has one of the highest levels of violence in the world, as its homicide rate is approximately 27 homicides per 100,000, almost three times the level in the United States (Andrienko and Shelley 2002).

High levels of both corruption and violence characterize Russia. Although organized crime internationally requires corruption to survive, in Russia the level of corruption is so significant that it is possible to speak of a political–criminal nexus in which the criminals and government have merged. Organized crime appears to be particularly linked with the high level of corruption. This has occurred through the election of criminals to local, regional, and national office; the financing of political campaigns by crime groups; and the representatives of crime groups serving in appointed positions in government. The World Bank refers to a "high level of state capture" within Russia (Hellman et al. 1999). Consulates of the United States government have turned down members of local and regional governments and members of the Duma for visas to the United States because they have determined that they are part of criminal organizations. The most noted of these is the singer Iosif Kapzon, who presently serves in the Russian Duma; he is not the only case—just the most visible.

The close connection between criminal groups and the state undermines the concept of organized crime groups representing a type of nonstate actor. The desire of the crime groups to penetrate and influence the state suggests that they no longer wish to be autonomous actors. In fact, their success is dependent on their close ties to government.

Significant Crime Groups

In the decade since the collapse of the former Soviet Union, certain crime groups have risen to commanding positions in the criminal world. These are not like the "families" of the mafia but organizations based on nonfamilial ties with more network-like structures than the strict hierarchies of organized crime. These crime groups differ by region and have been formed through control of different sectors of the economy. At the present time, they control a diverse range of industries in their home regions.

These crime groups, established within the past fifteen years, are very different from the crime groups based on thieves-in-law. They eschew their own jargon and do not sport tattoos. Their culture is not based on the labor camps of the former Soviet Union. They do everything to neutralize the impact of the justice system. Furthermore, they strive to appear as "legitimate" businessmen. But behind this veneer of legitimate business lies pervasive corruption and control of markets achieved through the deployment of violence.

Significant crime groups exist in many regions of Russia. The members of these groups have often moved from other cities in Russia to major metropolitan areas where they can exploit more affluent business communities. Examples of this would be the Tambov and Kazan groups in St. Petersburg (Volkov 2002, 111). The Tambov group has proven more successful in the long term because it exploited violence in more sophisticated ways than the Kazan group, who were youthful thugs who employed knives, metal rods, and truncheons rather than the more measured violence of the athletes of the Tambov group.

The Tambov group, by 1990, already had between three hundred and five hundred members. It was a diversified criminal group that was involved in protection in every aspect of the economy, and it ran import businesses and prostitution rings. Concerted efforts by law enforcement weakened its activities in the early 1990s, but it reemerged with renewed strength in the mid-1990s and moved into legitimate sectors of the economy such as banking, computers, the timber trade, and entertainment. Its members acquired strength by moving into positions of political power. They also established powerful private security firms that helped mediate conflicts in the energy sector and became major investors in the fuel infrastructure of St. Petersburg. Their influence on politics increased. In 1995, Mikhail Glushchenko, a founding member of the group, became a deputy of the State Duma (Volkov 2002, 108–18).

At the end of the 1990s and in 2000, associates of the Tambov group were killed in very visible ways. This violence suggested neither that the control of major business interests was solidified, nor that the city had "stabilized" in relation to organized crime. The renewed violence in the crime world was not unique to St. Petersburg at this time but was observed in several cities with important crime groups. This may suggest that the end of the Yeltsin period and the transition to the Putin administration forced realignments between crime groups and politicians.

With the three hundredth anniversary of St. Petersburg in 2003 and Putin's emphasis on investment in the city, real estate has appreciated significantly in value. Members of the Tambov crime group continue to use violence or threats of violence against those they seek to oust from desirable real estate (Dobrynn 2001). Their continued active presence in St. Petersburg, the home base of President Putin, suggests that despite presidential efforts to emphasize the rule of law in Russia, Putin has not been able to wrest political and economic power from one of the city's major crime groups. The failure to promote greater accountability by the courts and the protection of citizens' interests suggests that the crime group is undermining the daily life of citizens, who can expect no protection from the state. This group is, therefore, a major force in preventing the rise of civil society in one of Russia's major cities.

Crime groups in the Russian Far East, far from the power of the central state, have been able to wrest control over the region's economy. The long-term governor of Primorskii Krai, Evgenii Nazdratenko, was propelled to power and maintained there by crime groups. This situation is different from cities, such as Ekaterinburg and Moscow, where representatives of the crime groups merely work closely with local and regional governments or place their representatives in key positions in the government. In the Far East, particularly the key port city of Vladivostok, crime groups run the government. Far East crime groups, basing their existence on the extraction of natural resources, the sale of military technology, and transport, have achieved political and economic power that reaches far beyond their region. This is evident in Nazdratenko's political trajectory. Despite Kremlin efforts under Putin to oust Nazdratenko, he moved from the governorship to a powerful and lucrative position as head of the Ministry of Fisheries and subsequently a position on the National Security Council, from which he has only recently been ousted (Russian Regional Report 2004).

As governor, Nazdratenko displayed no concern for providing citizens with basic services such as heat and electricity in winter. Even now, nongovernmental organizations and journalists who attempt to expose the activities of the crime groups, such as human trafficking, are infiltrated or exposed to threats. In 2002, a journalist was hospitalized after being attacked for writing on trafficking rings in the region. Additionally, the director of an organized crime research center in Vladivostok has recently received intimidation from the criminal mayoral candidate (Russian Regional Report 2004).

Ekaterinburg, in contrast, represents the convergence of the interests of the major crime groups and the state. The Uralmash crime group developed in Ekaterinburg, one of Russia's largest cities, during the early 1990s. In the early years of the transition, there were four major crime groups operating in this strategic Urals city striding the border between Europe and Asia. With crime membership numbering more than twelve thousand individuals, there were visible battles for control of the economy. With the crime groups enjoying a firm grip on local politics, Ekaterinburg resembled Chicago in the depression era, when violence and corrupt ward politics characterized the city (Handelman 1995, 110–11).

Local politics in Ekaterinburg had national importance because the city furnished many of the top leaders of Russia, the most important of whom was President Yeltsin. Drawing on his circle of party cronies, he moved many of his long-term associates into key positions in national government.

The Uralmash crime group, which emerged from the massive machine-building plant in the city, provided "protection" for many firms, extorting fees of 20 to 30 percent of revenues (Volkov 2002, 116). They faced off the competition of the "central" (*tsentral'naia*) crime group, as well as others, in gun battles that eliminated many of the youthful gangsters and led to the establishment of a large gangster "sculpture" park in one of the city's leading cemeteries. With their accumulated capital and the elimination of their rivals, the Uralmash group became leading investors in heavy industry, technology, and the food and alcohol production sectors. With close ties to the city and regional government, for whom they helped deliver the vote, they were exempt from prosecution. The close ties of the Ekaterinburg elite to national politics also provided a further buffer for the criminal elite.

The vast majority of the Ekaterinburg population, according to opinion polls in the later 1990s, saw the ruling elite as a "criminal structure" (Volkov 2002, 121). The author of this chapter observed the distribution of campaign literature for a member of the crime group running for public office in Ekaterinburg in December 2000. Vote purchases were also reported.

Ekaterinburg, a center of the military-industrial complex and Communist Party power, does not have the civic traditions of St. Petersburg. The predominance of crime groups in this major city has distorted civil society in one of Russia's largest cities. Sports teams, cultural events, and other manifestations of civil society have been supported by crime groups since the middle of the 1990s.

Moscow, the financial capital of Russia, has had numerous crime groups operating within the city. Some of these groups have been ethnically based, while others have been based on military, security, and sports backgrounds. Early in the 1990s, there was a division of urban territory among the different crime groups and significant territorial battles occurred, resulting in numerous fatalities. These groups have chosen different spheres of operation. The ethnic crime groups operate in the food markets and the restaurant, hotel, and casino sectors. They are not alone in these operations but cooperate with law enforcement, city officials, and other crime groups. The most important crime groups, such as the Solntsevo, which are multi-ethnic, are truly diversified crime organizations, spanning the illegitimate economy from drugs and prostitution to the weapons trade, construction, and transport sectors. They operate closely with the city government, particularly the mayor's deputies who have control over the development of key sectors of the economy (Various interviews 2003). For example, the deputy mayor in charge of overseeing casinos interacts primarily with the ethnic crime groups that operate in this area, whereas the mayor's deputy responsible for real estate interacts with other criminal groups.

The close association between the Moscow crime groups and the mayor's office recalls the ward politics of the Chicago crime groups in the prohibition era. In Moscow, however, the criminal–political relations are not at the level of ward politics or subunits of urban government, but with the central city administration. Furthermore, important Russian crime figures in the United States, discovered through wiretaps, also had links in the mid-1990s with the Kremlin administration. Crime groups lobbied for their economic and political interests and in this way mimicked civil society, which seeks to exert influence on government.

The organized criminals are less visible than they were in the early part of the transition, when their clothes, gestures, and cars set them very much apart. Representing themselves as "businessmen" and often philanthropists in the community, some having forged close links with the oligarchs, they have legitimated themselves in the eyes of many. Russian citizens in need of financial assistance for church reconstruction, educational institutions, or social welfare programs often do not question the origin of the capital that finances their activities.

Crime Groups and Daily Life

Leaders of contemporary crime groups have lifestyles that mimic those of elite figures in the legitimate world. They purchase large and expensive apartments, buy new and costly imported cars, and appear at artistic and diplomatic events. With this lifestyle, they mimic the robber barons of the capitalist age in the United States. This is not a genuine transformation but one that allows them to operate more successfully internationally and to enroll their children in the most exclusive schools because they are seen to have abandoned their youthful life of crime.

Members of crime groups oversee charitable functions supporting sports teams, musical ensembles, or youth programs. Yet this philanthropy is not of the kind associated with the robber barons, who left a lasting legacy for society. Rather, it resembles the charitable activities of the Colombian cartels or the Japanese yakuza during the Kobe earthquake.

The Russian Orthodox Church has particularly benefited from the charitable largesse of the crime groups. After seven decades of Soviet rule, most churches and monasteries were in a state of total collapse. Many buildings returned by the Russian state to the Church had been abandoned or used as warehouses. There were no resources made available by the state for their restoration, and church assets had been confiscated by the Russian state during Communist rule. Therefore, Russian church officials had no resources on which to draw to provide usable churches to satisfy the pent-up demand for organized religion following the Soviet period, when no one who desired a party career could show any sign of religiosity. The strains of the transition also made many turn to the Church for support.

Therefore, many church officials accepted donations from questionable figures because they felt that the goal justified the means. Churches were reconstructed with money from organized crime bosses, often arranged by intermediaries so that the local church officials only knew that the money came from "believers in Moscow." In many regions, new churches were built by money provided by highly questionable figures; and in Georgia, Russia-based organized crime figures have sent home significant sums to construct new churches.

The links between the Church and organized crime recall the situation in Sicily, where for many years priests baptized the babies of crime bosses and administered last rites to those who they knew were part of organized crime. While some local members of the Church struggled against organized crime, the church hierarchy in Sicily accepted the Mafia as part of local life. The same situation may be developing in Russia if the past ten years provides any evidence (Catanzaro 1988).

Conclusion

Civil society is an important sign of democratization because it establishes powerful forces outside of state control. Furthermore, it allows citizens to express their interests in structured ways that are not subordinate to the government. Many hoped that

Russia, after abolishing the Communist system, would develop a strong civil society that would serve as a buffer against authoritarianism. Despite the involvement of millions of Russian citizens in independent associations, civil society has not developed as the buffer to state authority that was expected by political science theory. Civil society has not had this desired effect not only because of the legacy of authoritarianism, but also because powerful local and national crime groups are closely tied to all levels of government. By undermining existing civil society and co-opting its functions, crime groups have undermined the transition to democracy and contributed to nonstate-based authoritarianism (Shelley 1997).

Crime groups often substitute for the failure of the state to provide for the basic needs of the citizenry. The crime groups intervene where there is no alternative. By currying the favor of the citizenry in a time of need, they neutralize potential citizen collaboration with the state. Thereby the crime groups are not building a cultural life or educational system but merely ensuring their continued role within the state. They are neutralizing the potential impact of the state, a process that could continue even if the state under Putin continues to enhance its capacity. Yet they are not creating a space for civil society to grow in Russia, which is a keystone of democratization.

Foreign assistance providers have focused on funding a vibrant civil society but have not realized the centrality of organized crime. For development specialists, organized crime was a peripheral issue to state development rather than a central issue that would undermine their efforts at democratization. They failed to understand that organized crime groups would undermine or even attack the activities of civil society groups such as associations of independent journalists, women's organizations, and environmental activists because the activities of these associations threatened the financial interests of the crime groups. Because crime groups were buying newspapers and radio and television stations, trafficking in women, and harvesting the rich natural resources of the Russian state, it is hardly surprising that leading journalists have been killed throughout Russia, while anti-trafficking activists from Miramed and even visible organized crime specialists have been targets of organized crime.

The attacks on civil society reveal that organized crime groups perceive these citizen organizations as a threat to their interests. Citizens, by confronting the abuses of the crime groups, are no longer complicit in their exploitation as was the case in the Soviet period. Their willingness to stand up against crime groups that traffic in women or reach for political power, despite the enormous costs, shows that citizens are no longer submitting to authority, as was the case in the Soviet past.

Are the crime groups themselves an "uncivil" part of society? Their initial and continued violence continues to make them uncivil. In addition, their close involvement with the state in places like Vladivostok and their merger with or co-optation of the state in many other areas denies their role as nonstate actors. Their role is certainly more than that of lobbyists for political power. The objectives of the crime groups are personal profit and political influence rather than a wider public goal, and this distinguishes them from civil society.

Thieves-in-law swore to be autonomous from the state. By abandoning this philosophy just before the end of the Soviet period, they were major beneficiaries of one of the greatest property redistributions in history. Their pivotal role in privatization and capitalist activities, achieved and sustained through their criminal–political links, have made them powerful economic and political actors in contemporary Russia. They are not a counterbalancing force to the state, as is civil society, nor are they interested in the rise of democracy in Russia. Rather, crime groups are major obstacles to the rise of civil society, democracy, and free markets.

Note

1. Authors have pointed out the similarity between Russian organized crime of the transitional period and the Sicilian mafia, but organized crime's role in Soviet society suggests that the utilitarian functions of Russian-speaking organized crime predated the demise of the Soviet regime (Gambetta 1993; Varese 2001).

References '

Abadinsky, Howard. 2003. *Organized Crime.* 7th ed. Belmont, CA: Wadsworth.

Abadinsky, Howard, Cyrille Fijnaut, Frank Bovenkerk, and Henk van den Bunt. 1998. *Organized Crime in the Netherlands.* The Hague: Kluwer.

Andrienko, Yuri, and Louise Shelley. 2002. "Crime and Political Violence in Russia." Presentation prepared for Workshop on Case Studies of Civil War, Yale University, April 12–15.

Catanzaro, Raimondo. 1988. *Men of Respect: A Social History of the Sicilian Mafia.* New York: Free Press.

Dobrynn, Konstantin. 2001. "Moshnichestvo v sfere nedvizhimosti v Sankt-Peterburge: priamaia vzaimosviaz s organizovannoi prestupnost'iu i korruptsiei." www.jurfak.spb.ru/centers/traccc/article/mochen.htm.

Dunn, Guy. 1997. "Major Mafia Gangs in Russia." In Williams 1997, 63–87.

Gambetta, Diego. 1993. *The Sicilian Mafia: The Business of Private Protection.* Cambridge, MA: Harvard University Press.

Glonti, Georgi. 1998. *Organizovannaia prestupnost' kak odin iz osnovnykh istochnikov nasil'stvennoi prestupnosti i etnicheskikh konfliktov.* Tbilisi: Azri.

Gurov, A. I. 1990. *Professional'naia prestupnost': proshloe i sovremennost'.* Moscow: Iuridicheskaia literatura.

Handelman, Stephen. 1995. *Comrade Criminal: Russia's New Mafiya.* New Haven, CT: Yale University Press.

Hellman, Joel S., et al. 1999. "Measuring Governance, Corruption and State: Capture How Firms and Bureaucrats Shape the Business Environment in Transitional Economies." World Bank Working Paper no. 2312. www.econ.worldbank.org/docs/1066.pdf (accessed August 27, 2004).

Jones, Anthony, and William Moskoff. 1992. *Ko-ops: The Rebirth of Entrepreneurship in the Soviet Union.* Bloomington: Indiana University Press.

Kaplan, David E., and Alec Dubro. 1986. *Yakuza: The Explosive Account of Japan's Criminal Underworld.* Reading, MA: Addison-Wesley.

Kostiukovskii, Iakov. n.d. "Istoriia Rossiskoi organizovannoi prestupnosti." St. Petersburg Branch, Instititute of Sociology. Russian Academy of Sciences. www.narcom/ru/ideas/socio (accessed July 15, 2003).

Kukhianidze, Aleksandr. 2003. "Georgia: Internal Conflicts and Contraband Trade through Abkhazia and South Ossetia." Paper presented at the Third Annual Conference of the European Society of Criminology, August 27–30.

Lebedev, S. Ia., and O. E. Kozlov. 1988. "'Vor v zakone' kak traditsionnyi lider prestupnoi sredy (na materialakh Armianskoi, Gruzinskoi soiuznykh respublik)." In *Problemy professionalizma organizovannoi prestupnosti*. Omsk: NIO, RIO, Omskaia Vysshaia Shkola Militsii.

Luneev, Viktor V. 1997. *Prestupnost' XX veka*. Moscow: Norma.

McFaul, Michael. 2003. "Introduction: Russian Civil Society." *Demokratizatsiya* 10, no. 2: 109–16.

Mikheladze, Akaki, and Mikhail Shevelev. 1993. "Ia izvestnyi vor." *Moskovskie novosti*, May 30.

Ministry of Internal Affairs, Republic of Georgia, USSR (MVD Georgia). 1982. "O sostoianii bor'by OVD respubliki s litsami, priderzhivaiushchimisia vorovskikh traditsii i merakh po ee usilenii." Order No. 0152 (August 31).

Ministry of Internal Affairs, USSR (MVD USSR). 1985. "Ob osobennostiakh prestupnoi deiatel'nosti lits iz chisla 'vorov v zakone' i rekomendatsiiakh po usileniiu bor'by s etoi kategoriei ugolovnogo elementa dlia prakticheskogo ispol'zovaniia." Form No. 324, 24.4379s (October 12).

Nicaso, Antonio. 2001. "The Violent Birth of the *Vory v Zakone*: Part 12—How Petty Thieves Have Taken Control of the Russian Economy." *Tandem*, June 24. www.tandemnews.com/viewstory.php?storyid=93 (accessed August 27, 2004).

Nomokonov, V. A., and V. I. Shulga. 1988. "Murder for Hire as a Manifestation of Organized Crime." *Demokratizatsiya* 6, no. 4 (Fall): 676–80.

Petriashvili, Diana. 2003. "V Tbilisi umer Dzhaba Ioseliani." *KP-Tbilisi*, July 10.

Podeesskikh, Georgii and Andrei Tereshonok, eds. 1994. *Vory v zakone: brosok k vlasti*. Moscow: Khudozhestvennaia literatura.

Rawlinson, Patricia. 1997. "Russian Organized Crime: A Brief Story." In Williams 1997, 28–52.

Russian Regional Report. 2004. www.isn.ethz.ch/researchpub/publihouse/rrr/docs/rrr040608.pdf (June 8).

Shelley, Louise. 1992. "Entrepreneurship: Some Legal and Social Problems." In *Privatization and Entrepreneurship in Post-Socialist Countries*, ed. Bruno Dallago, Gianmaria Ajani, and Bruno Grancelli, 307–25. New York: St. Martin's Press.

———. 1994. "Post-Soviet Organized Crime," *Demokratizatsiya* 2, no. 3 (Summer): 341–58.

———. 1997. "Post-Soviet Organized Crime: A New Form of Authoritarianism." In Williams 1997, 122–38.

———. 2002. "Transnational Crime: The Case of Russian Organized Crime and the Role of International Cooperation in Law Enforcement," *Demokratizatsiya* 10, no. 1 (Winter): 49–67.

———. 2003. "Russia and Ukraine: Transition or Tragedy?" In *Menace to Society: Political-Criminal Collaboration Around the World*, ed. Roy Godson, 199–230. London: Transaction.

Varese, Frederico. 2001. *The Russian Mafia: Private Protection in a New Market Economy*. Oxford: Oxford University Press.

Volkov, Vadim. 2002. *Violent Entrepreneurs: The Use of Force in the Making of Russian Capitalism*. Ithaca, NY: Cornell University Press.

Williams, Phil. 1997. *Russian Organized Crime: The New Threat?* London: Frank Cass.

Interviews

Gvetadze, Iurii. 2003. Head of the Georgian Ministry of Internal Affairs unit charged with fighting thieves-in-law. Tbilisi, Georgia. July.

Maisuradze, Iurii. 2003. Head of the Georgian card file on thieves-in-law. Tbilisi, Georgia. July.

Various. 2003. Anonymous interviews. Tbilisi, Georgia. July 1.

7

The Church and Civil Society in Russia

Edwin Bacon

Four Paradoxes

Civil society is that realm between the state and the private sphere where social organizations operate.[1] Many definitions of civil society exclude particular realms of activity, such as the economic, the familial, or—particularly pertinent to this chapter—the religious. Religious believers, especially those in faiths not linked directly to the state, have an allegiance to a deity and/or a system of beliefs separate from the temporal authorities. Religious believers are also overwhelmingly communal; meeting together is usually essential to their identity. Religious believers normally function, too, in identifiable groups in the space between society and the state. Given all of the above, the claim could be made that religious believers constitute an archetypal element of civil society.

Such a claim can be said to be strengthened in the particular circumstances of postcommunist Russia. The Soviet state's totalitarian tendency to seek to control all of society led many to argue that there was no such thing as civil society in the Soviet Union, since "the Soviet state's most salient characteristic became the virtual destruction of the space between the individual and the state" (McFaul and Treyger 2004, 142). However, during this period many communities of faith were dissident in nature and therefore comparatively autonomous groupings that managed to continue in existence separate, for the most part, from the state. Such communities arguably served as a repository for civil society during the Communist era. The fact that then, as now, the relationship of some religious bodies with the state was closer than some definitions of civil society would allow is simply a factor of Russia's history and, as McFaul and Treyger put it in relation to studying civil society in Russia, "insisting on strict autonomy from the state would not be sensible" (ibid., 139).

Although almost any definition of civil society will locate it in the space between the private realm and the state, it is also the case that academic analysis of civil society, in Russia at least, tends to concentrate on the relationship between society and the state, rather than society and the individual. This chapter is no exception. What I am interested in here is the role that the state has played in relation to religious civil society in the period since the mid-1990s. The focus is on the Christian church, in its various forms, with a particular emphasis on the place of the Russian Orthodox Church and its relationship with the state. In particular, this chapter identifies and investigates four apparent paradoxes in conceptualizations of religion and civil society in Russia today, namely:

- Russia has a very low rate of participation in organized religion. At the same time, religion, and particularly Russian Orthodoxy, is apparently highly valued in the social and political sphere.
- The Russian Orthodox Church is a widely respected and trusted organization with the potential to benefit from a strong civil society, and yet it has arguably acted to prevent the growth of religious civil society in general.
- The Russian Orthodox Church is an independent organization that could offer a clear and authoritative voice from its place between the private and state realms, but it has increasingly drawn near to the state in recent years.
- The actions of the state have made a contribution to the weakness of religious civil society in Russia. However, it could be argued that some apparently negative moves in this regard—notably the promulgation of the 1997 law on religion—have actually provided a structure that has been used to protect elements of religious civil society.

The resolution of these paradoxes lies to some extent in an understanding of civil society that takes particular account of Russia's temporal and cultural context. It is perhaps unreasonable to expect the first dozen years or so of the postcommunist era to produce a flourishing and independent civil society. As Marc Howard (2003) details, a number of features of postcommunism hinder such an immediate outcome. With regard to religious civil society, the immediate post-Soviet prognosis was promising, with religion largely seen as a public good denied to the people by the Communists and now freely available. Interest in and contact with religion in a range of forms grew rapidly in the early 1990s, and yet specific contextual features have helped frustrate the transition from widespread interest and contact to large-scale formal engagement in religious civil society. In particular, in exploring the paradoxes outlined above, this chapter repeatedly notes two features: first, the continuing impact of "postcommunist" negativity toward belonging to formal groups; and second, the role of the state in overseeing civil society. This latter point raises the question of whether civil society in Russia can be judged in the same terms as in the West. To echo the debate surrounding democratic transition, is civil society in Russia today en route to becoming a strong independent sector of activity akin to that found in Western democracies? Or is it settling into a more Russian form, where the role of the state removes a degree of independence, but nonetheless distinct groups and movements remain, with a voice, a legal identity, and—not universal, but nonetheless real in a number of cases—political influence? For now, the second route is the one being taken by religious civil society, and an exploration of our four paradoxes serves to elucidate this view.

Paradox One

My starting point is the fact that in comparative terms Russia has a weak civil society. Measuring the strength of civil society by means of participation in nonstate organizations reveals that membership in such organizations in general is notably low in Russia in comparison with most other countries. Data from the University of Michigan's World Values Survey of sixty countries place Russia in the bottom three in terms of membership of a range of selected organizations that make up civil society (sports or recreational clubs, cultural and educational groups, political parties and pressure groups, professional associations, charities, environmental organizations). The only exception to this trend is membership in trade unions, where Russia scores highly—a fact that is largely due to the role played by trade unions during the Soviet era, when, far from being independent associations defending the rights of the employee against the state-employer, unions were state-controlled bodies through which an array of benefits and essential services were distributed (Howard 2003, 65–66).

Turning to the religious sphere, figures from the same World Values Survey place Russia at the bottom of the list of regular church attendance, that is, once a week or more (University of Michigan 1997). Clearly, if we measure the strength of civil society by organizational membership, then Russia scarcely registers on the international scale, and the church in Russia is particularly weak in terms of popular membership and involvement. However, although rates of regular church attendance are low, opinion polls consistently record high levels of self-identification with the church (specifically the Russian Orthodox Church).[2] The place of the Church in the life of the state is increasing in the ceremonial sense, and in terms of formal links between government ministries (for example, defense and education) and the Orthodox Church. The use of religious discourse in the political sphere is not uncommon (Bacon 1997; 2002). Recent poll data reveal that 66 percent of the Russian population identify themselves as believers, with 58 percent of those calling themselves Russian Orthodox (Fond obshchestvennogo mneniia 2002).

This, then, is the first paradox to note in terms of the church and civil society in today's Russian Federation—engagement with religious organizations is markedly low in international terms, and yet self-identification as a religious believer is common, and the influence of religion in the political sphere is apparently significant, with the Church interacting with the state at a number of levels (see below) and the state repeatedly offering general support for religion. For example, in August 2002, President Putin affirmed his belief in the unique role played by religion in building today's Russia. During a visit to Tatarstan he declared that he had "become increasingly convinced that now that we have no work collectives or party organizations, such as those of the Communist Party of the Soviet Union, or educators at places of work, nothing but religion can make human values known to people" (Ekho Moskvy 2002).

The key to understanding the first apparent paradox noted in our consideration of religious civil society in Russia today is to view the contemporary situation against its historical background. A number of issues within the historical context help explain how very low levels of church membership sit alongside much higher levels of religious self-identification among the Russian population and a clear role for religion in the political discourse of the state. It has become commonplace to note that one of the freedoms gained by citizens in Russia after the collapse of the Soviet Union was the right *not* to participate (White, Rose, and McAllister 1997, 131–51; Howard 2000). Within the framework of Soviet life, citizens were expected to engage with the pseudo-civil society established by a regime that discouraged individualism and encouraged community activities. Independent associations of citizens were not permitted; and, although motivations varied from person to person, participation in professional, political, or leisure groups controlled by the state was often impelled by fear of reprisals, either direct or (more commonly) indirect, such as missing a promotion or being passed over on the list for a new apartment.

When the Communist system collapsed at the beginning of the 1990s, it left in its wake a mistrust of organizations. According to Howard's research, "increasing mistrust of organizations during the communist period seems to be closely associated with decreasing levels of organizational membership today" (2003, 107). Such, then, was the general legacy of the Soviet era in relation to civil society, and the low level of committed church membership in Russia may be a further demonstration of this phenomenon.

It also seems likely that there is a link between the level of self-identification as a believer and the role of religion in the political discourse of contemporary Russia. As noted earlier, two-thirds of Russia's population identify themselves as having a religious faith, and overwhelmingly that faith is Russian Orthodoxy. Their expressed faith therefore serves as a nonpartisan point of identification for politicians. Furthermore, the lack of actual involvement with a church among the large majority of professed believers suggests that identification with Orthodoxy may not be primarily a spiritual matter. Again the context is crucial.

First of all, Russian Orthodoxy stands as a symbol for Russian nationalism. Such nationalism need not be of the extreme type, though there is a vociferously anti-Semitic nationalist wing of the Orthodox Church. Orthodoxy, in the words of the 1997 religion law, has a special role in the history of Russia, and as Presidents Yeltsin and Putin have sought to establish a distinctly Russian path in domestic and international politics, Orthodoxy has stood as a symbol of that distinctiveness. Second, throughout the post-Soviet period, an appeal to religion has been used by political leaders as an attempt to fill a spiritual and moral vacuum. As the moral codes of the Soviet era disappeared along with the Soviet state's official "religion" of Marxism-Leninism, issues such as crime, corruption, pornography, prostitution, and drugs became increasingly relevant politically. President Putin, as noted earlier, has declared that "nothing but religion can make human values known to people" (Ekho Moskvy 2002). Similarly, in January 2001, he said:

> We have stepped over the threshold of the two thousandth anniversary of the history of Christianity and are convinced that once and for all we have done away with spiritual nihilism and moral poverty and with the century of fierce struggle for the individual's right to believe. We enter the new millennium with hope, which, I am convinced, will be a time of historic and spiritual transformation of our motherland, Russia (Sluzhba kommunikatsii OVTsS MP 2001).

To accurately quantify the extent of religious belief, definitions are vital. The two main definitions used are "self-identified believers" and "regular attenders." Religion can be a matter of birth or belief, and the former definition will produce a larger number of adherents than the latter. In other words, an ethnic Russian citizen of the Russian Federation might identify herself as a Christian to indicate that she is not a Muslim or a Jew. She might further identify herself as a Russian Orthodox Christian as a statement of nationality. Despite such identifying statements, however, that citizen might never attend church nor have a grasp of, let alone belief in, the doctrines of Christianity in general or Russian Orthodoxy in particular. Indeed, an opinion poll in August 2002 established that of the 58 percent of respondents who identified themselves as Russian Orthodox, 42 percent had never even been in an Orthodox church (*RFE/RL Newsline* 2002).

Using the criterion of self-identification, opinion polls in Russia in the 1990s showed that around 50 percent of the Russian population called themselves believers. Despite the decades of state-sponsored atheism under the Soviet regime, nominal adherence to religion has far from died out. Nonetheless, taking a narrower definition of believers produces different results. The same surveys that tell us that two-thirds of Russians consider themselves religious believers also reveal that only about 3 percent of the population regularly (once a month or more) attend a place of worship. Of those, around half (1.5 percent) attend Russian Orthodox churches affiliated with the Moscow Patriarchate (Shevchenko 1998). This definition of a believer reflects active participation rather than cultural identity, and therefore is more relevant to the potential for the development of civil society.

So, excluding the obvious exceptions of Russia's five Islamic republics and one Buddhist republic, can the Russian Federation be described as a Russian Orthodox country? In terms of the broadest definition of self-identified believers, the answer is yes, with the figures cited above meaning that over eighty-four million people identify themselves as Russian Orthodox. Using the narrower definition of regular attenders, though, not only are around half of the practicing Christians in Russia today not Russian Orthodox, but the actual percentage of practicing Orthodox within the population is only around 1.5 percent. This becomes significant when considering, as we shall do later, the implementation of a law on religious associations that appears to privilege the Russian Orthodox Church.

Table 7.1

Do You Consider Yourself a Believer, and If So, to Which Confession Do You Belong? (as %)

	October 1992	August 2000	August 2002
Nonbeliever	28	31	31
Orthodox	51	56	58
Other Christian denomination	1	2	2
Muslim	1	5	5
Other religion	1	1	1
Hard to say	20	5	4

Source: Fond obshchestvennogo mneniia 2002.

Paradox Two

The second paradox with which this chapter deals concerns the role of the Russian Orthodox Church in the formation of civil society in Russia. As can be seen from the data noted above, if we take the broadest category of self-identified believer, not only does Russia seem to be a relatively religious country, but the Russian Orthodox Church also ranks far ahead of all other denominations and religions (see Table 7.1). What is more, in surveys throughout the 1990s and beyond, the Russian Orthodox Church has been the most trusted public institution in the Russian Federation (White, Rose, and McAllister 1997, 52). If, as recent research has shown, mistrust in organizations has been a key factor inhibiting the growth of civil society in the postcommunist world (Howard 2000, 33), then the relatively high levels of trust in the Orthodox Church may indicate that it starts from a privileged position in establishing itself as a key element of Russian civil society.

At the same time, though, the Russian Orthodox Church at the official level has been the prime mover behind attempts to restrict the freedoms enjoyed by other Christian churches, the most significant of such moves being the relatively restrictive 1997 Law on Freedom of Conscience and Religious Associations, which I consider in more detail later. What then is the contribution of Russian Orthodoxy to civil society? It represents a powerful voice separate from the state with a claim to speak for well over half of the population. It could be said to be one of the largest organizations making up civil society in Russia today. At the same time, however, elements within it appear to be intent on holding back the very pluralism and democratic values on which civil society thrives.

The second paradox then concerns the role of the Orthodox Church, both as one of the largest organizations making up civil society in Russia today and as an organization in some ways attempting to discourage pluralism in the sphere of religion. Can such an entity be deemed to be positive for the development of civil society? Indeed, can it be accepted as a part of civil society itself? Before answering these questions, let us consider the details and context of the charge against the Orthodox Church that it has not accepted a fundamental principle underlying civil society, namely, the right of other groups to exist.

Religious civil society differs from other manifestations of civil society in that the focus of its members is partly or wholly not of this world. Although the content of religious belief does not easily lend itself to social science analysis, it would be wrong to ignore what is, in theory at least, the central reason for religious organizations to meet together. The beliefs of almost all religions are mutually exclusive, and consequently the demand that such groups should accept the right of other groups to exist is a little more problematic in the religious sphere than in, say, the realm of sports clubs or charitable foundations. This mutual exclusivity is particularly an issue in Russia on an intra-religion, rather than inter-religion, level. The Russian Orthodox Church at the official level finds it far easier to share the souls of Russia's citizens with other "traditional" religions, such as Islam and Buddhism, which in any case have their own geographically identifiable areas within Russia, than it does to share its spiritual space with other Christian denominations. Such denominations are often identified in Orthodox literature as "sects and cults," regardless of their longevity in Russia, their history, or their global popularity. In particular, the post-Soviet period has seen a fierce debate on proselytizing, with the Orthodox Church claiming the right to lead the people of Russia to Christ and seeing other Christian groups, for the most part, as encroaching into its spiritual territory (*Emory International Law Review* 1998).

The second point to make with regard to whether a group that actively works against peaceful coexistence with other groups can be said to be a part of civil society is that the Russian Orthodox Church is not monolithic. Much that is written about Russian Orthodoxy demonstrates, in the words of Zoe Knox:

> the proclivity of Western analysts to paint the Church as a monolithic body, one that uniformly "does not support liberalism." It is true that the traditionalist current, which emphasises powerful authority and limits on pluralism, is strong, both within and outside the Church structures. The statement in an editorial in *The Times* (London), however, that "[t]he Russian Orthodox Church is in the grip of extreme nationalists and anti-Semites" is overblown and reduces the movement among reformist clergy and laity for *perestroika* in Orthodox life to inconsequence (Knox 2005, 8–9).

Reformist movements do exist. Many Orthodox parishes across Russia work happily with other Christian denominations, or at least do not seek to harass or ban them. Of course, there are also those who vehemently oppose Roman Catholics, Baptists, Pentecostals, charismatics, Seventh Day Adventists, and so on, but to tar the whole of the Russian Orthodox community with the brush of intolerance and bigotry would be grossly unfair. In particular, the distinction needs to be made between official pronouncements and the views and work of the "unofficial" Church.

In my view, the context of religious civil society and the recognition that the

Russian Church is not a monolithic body act together to strengthen the case for accepting the Orthodox Church as a key part of civil society in Russia. Of course, its official position, and in particular the actions of some of its priests in relation to other denominations, could be more liberal. It is difficult, though, either to claim that the Church as a whole is uniformly illiberal in belief and action (in the same way, for example, as an avowedly racist or supremacist group), or to deny that for many of its members it represents an independent organization, performs socially beneficial charitable work, and serves to create a local community.

It is too easy to view the Russian Orthodox Church simply through the prism of its political role and relations with the state, mediated through its hierarchy. For the old woman in the congregation or the young man in the youth group, the Church is a spiritual and social organization, rather than a political one. In early 2003, Patriarch Aleksii gave an interview in which he noted examples of the charitable work of the Church, including a boarding school run by monks for children without parental supervision, girls' orphanages established by nuns, facilities for supporting the victims of AIDS, and soup kitchens for the poor. As the patriarch concluded, "such examples could be multiplied many times" (Korobov 2003). The corruption, xenophobia, and intolerance to which the Church is also home represent only part of the picture and should not obscure the whole.

Paradox Three

The third and fourth paradoxes to note in our discussion of religion and civil society in Russia today revolve around the question of the relationship between civil society and the state. Much discussion of civil society in Russia places it in opposition to the state, with the underlying assumption being that the Russian state, particularly since the election of President Putin, is keen to suppress independent civil society (Pinsker 2001; Fein 2002; Nikitin and Buchanan 2002). Whether this is the case or not is a question for elsewhere in this volume and beyond (Bacon 2003). Nonetheless, it is important to establish here, in accordance with much literature on the topic, that the relationship between the state and civil society is not a zero-sum game (Hall 1999; Howard 2003, 16–17). A supportive state can create conditions that encourage the growth of civil society.

In the sphere of religion, the role of the state in postcommunist Russia raises the two paradoxes noted above. The first of these concerns the Russian Orthodox Church's relationship with the state. Russia is officially a secular state, but the state is for the most part happy to identify itself closely with the Moscow Patriarchate of the Russian Orthodox Church. Although this relationship is mutually beneficial, neither the church nor the state wishes to see a more formal linkage.

From its point of view, the Russian Orthodox Church defends its official separation from the state, although mutual interests, and perhaps to some extent financial benefits, mean that the church–state relationship deserves nurturing and protection. However, the means by which the authorities can "lean on" the Orthodox hierarchy in the early twenty-first century differ vastly from the brutal tactics and administrative control of previous eras. The Orthodox Church is self-governing and conscious of the advantages of this independence as well as of relations with the state, which are by and large positive. Patriarch Aleksii spelled out the position in March 1998: "I am convinced that the church must be separate from the state, but it must not be separate from society. The church must have the right to evaluate from ethical positions what is happening in the country, and sometimes this evaluation will not agree with the state's" (Pravoslavie v Rossii 1998).

Nonetheless, the closeness between the church and the state in Russia is repeatedly evident. A duality exists. On the one hand, in many areas of religious policy, particularly on a day-to-day basis, the state appears willing to allow the Russian Orthodox Church to take the lead. This is especially the case at the regional level, where most of the difficulties faced by non-Orthodox confessions have resulted from complaints against them to the local authorities by the Orthodox hierarchy. It is also the case on occasion at the national level, with the anti-Catholic stance of the Moscow Patriarchate apparently influencing national policy with regard to such matters as the state's attitude toward any official visit by the pope and to the issuing of visas for Catholic clerics. Indeed, in some areas of activity the relationship between the Moscow Patriarchate and the state at the national level is sufficiently close to apparently cause Sergei Kovalev, the former presidential human rights envoy, to approach the state procuracy on occasion, arguing that constitutional violations have taken place.[3] Church–state interaction takes such forms as the agreement between the Ministry of Education and the Russian Orthodox Church over religious education in schools, the blessing of a Ministry of Health building by the patriarch, and a formal relationship between the Church and the armed forces, which includes the training, since 2003, of regimental priests who work with troops, providing spiritual and moral support (Poroskov 2003).

In relation to civil society then, the paradoxical situation is that those associations of citizens that constitute civil society must by definition occupy the space between the state and the private spheres. How close can an organization, in this case the Russian Orthodox Church, be to the state while still being said to occupy this intervening space?

It is undeniable that there is a closeness between the state and the Russian Orthodox Church that does not sit easily with Russia's secular constitution. The constitution forbids any official state ideology (Article 13) and asserts that "the Russian Federation is a secular state. No religion may be established as the state religion" (Article 14). Despite that declaration, the patriarch has taken part in numerous state occasions at the highest level, such as the signing of the "treaty of union" between Belarus and the Russian Federation in April 1996, and the inaugurations of Presidents Yeltsin and Putin. Much has often been made of such closeness, but although it might be seen as inconsistent with the spirit of the constitution, it does not amount to the establishment of a state religion. From the point of view of the historical context and the avowed personal faith of the leaders involved and the majority of the Russian people, it is perhaps more understandable. Furthermore, it is not as if President Putin ignores all other faiths. In January 2001, Putin awarded state medals to Christian clergy in a Kremlin ceremony. Although the majority of the recipients were Orthodox, medals were also awarded to leaders of other denominations. Putin's commitment to a plurality of religions in a multiconfessional state seems clear, and was backed up by his widely reported statement in August 2002: "We must not tell religious figures what to do, who to choose, and how to form associations. We must create favorable conditions for their activities and do our best to prevent the building of barriers between them and citizens" (Ekho Moskvy 2002).

Speaking in the predominantly Muslim Republic of Tatarstan, and not singling out any particular group, Putin demonstrated his commitment to a multiconfessional state that values religion per se. In terms of the relationship between Orthodoxy and the state insofar as it impinges on the Church's claim to be a part of civil society, then, it is clear that though the Russian Orthodox Church enjoys a privileged position, the relationship is not so close as to make the Church not independent. In fact, given the Church's history of control by the state and severe persecution at the hands of the state in the twentieth century, two conclusions may be drawn. First, the Church is more independent now than it has been for centuries; and second, it has no more desire to lose that independence than the state has to adopt an official religion.

Paradox Four

The fourth and final paradox that we consider here also relates to the role of the state in relation to the church. I noted above that the state and civil society should not necessarily be viewed as in opposition to one another, and that the former can play a key role in encouraging the growth of the latter. According to Marc Howard's 2003 monograph on civil society in postcommunist Europe, "in the postcommunist context, particularly in Russia, it is clear that the state has all too frequently *not* provided the necessary resources and support for the organizations of civil society" (17). In the case of religion in Russia, this is a position supported by many, with the standard view over the past few years being that the 1997 law on religion has had a negative effect on civil society, undermining the constitutional freedoms that religious groups had up until then enjoyed.

The 1993 Russian constitution guarantees a secular state and freedom of religion. It further states that all religious associations are equal before the law. Article 28 guarantees freedom of religion, including the right to profess and disseminate any religion, and Article 13 states that there should be no national ideology in Russia. To this constitutional base a law "On Freedom of Conscience and Religious Associations" was added in September 1997. This created two different categories of religious association. Its preamble sets the tone of the law in general, in that it repeats the freedom of religion line of the constitution while placing some faiths above others. It reads:

> The Federative Assembly of the Russian Federation—affirming the right of each
> person to freedom of conscience and freedom of creed, as well as to equality before
> the law irrespective of attitudes to religion and convictions; basing itself on the fact
> that the Russian Federation is a secular state; recognizing the special role of Ortho-
> doxy in the history of Russia and in the establishment and development of its spiri-
> tuality and culture; respecting Christianity, Islam, Buddhism, Judaism, and other
> religions, constituting an integral part of the historical heritage of the peoples of
> Russia; considering it important to cooperate in the achievement of mutual under-
> standing, toleration, and respect in matters of freedom of conscience and freedom of
> religious profession—adopts the present federal law.

There are elements of the 1997 law that are exactly in line with the constitution,
and indeed the law explicitly repeats the rights guaranteed by the constitution. Other
elements of the law, however, appear to contradict both the constitution and earlier
articles of the law. The most obvious example is the contradiction of the constitutional provision in Article 14, Paragraph 2, repeated in Article 4, Paragraph 1, of the
1997 law, which states that "religious associations are separated from the state and
are equal before the law." Article 6, Paragraph 2, of the law on religious associations, however, demonstrates the somewhat Orwellian nature of such equality, as
some religious associations are more equal than others. It states that "religious associations may be formed as religious groups and religious organizations." This
apparently directly contradicts the earlier statement and constitutional provision
that religious associations are equal before the law, as the distinction between
"groups" and "organizations" is the pivot on which the 1997 law turns and the basis
for allegations that religious freedom has been seriously curtailed. The majority of
the text of the law is devoted to the differing rights granted to religious groups and
religious organizations.

The complexity of the 1997 law requires deeper analysis than the present chapter
allows (*Emory International Law Review* 1998). Nonetheless, the main features of
the law can be identified. Religious organizations are officially registered associations. They receive a number of rights along with their registration. An unregistered
religious association is termed a "religious group" and simply has the right to exist,
conduct its activities in premises provided by its members, and teach its own adherents. The benefits of registration are a whole raft of rights granted to religious organizations and not to religious groups. These include the rights to: own property; establish
and maintain buildings; employ people; conduct services in hospitals, homes for the
elderly, children's homes, and prisons, at the request of citizens in them; produce and
distribute literature; conduct charity work; establish and maintain international communication; and contact and issue invitations to foreign citizens. Unregistered religious groups do not have those rights.

A religious organization can be dissolved by a court or forbidden from practicing
for a number of reasons, including: violation of public security and public order;
incitement of social, racial, national, or religious enmity and misanthropy; compulsory dissolution of the family; infringement of the person, rights, and freedom of

citizens; infringement, as defined by the law, of the morality and health of citizens, including the religious use of drugs and psychotropic substances and hypnosis and the performance of lewd and other illegal actions; encouragement of suicide or refusal of medical care for religious motives for persons whose life or health are threatened; prevention of acquiring obligatory education; compulsion of members and adherents of a religious association and other persons to alienate property owned by them for the use of a religious association; and encouragement of citizens to refuse to fulfill civic duties required by law and to perform other illegal actions. There are then clearly listed circumstances that, according to the law, must occur before a religious organization can be shut down. Attempts to close an organization in the absence of such actions are open to legal challenge.

Bringing together the standard view of the law on religion and the finding of Marc Howard's extensive research that in terms of civil society as a whole, the Russian state has not been supportive, the situation seems clear: Russia has a weak religious civil society, and the state is partly to blame. Where then is the paradox? The paradox comes in considering what theorists think a state should do to encourage civil society. According to Howard, the formal organization of a group might well be seen as a defining characteristic of civil society. He contrasts "loose organizations" and "formal organizations," asserting that "in my view, if they are formally organized, then they belong to civil society" (Howard 2003, 40). At a stretch, this distinction might be mapped onto the law on religion's distinction between "religious groups," with no formal legal identity, and "religious organizations," which register and enjoy the rights of legal personage. Whether this correlation holds or not, it is certainly the case that when the question of what the state can do to support civil society is asked, one common answer is that it can provide a legal framework offering protection for groups against the state. Viewed from this perspective, the paradox is clearer. Could it be that the 1997 religion law, despite those features that have been widely condemned, and in opposition to the apparent intent of its supporters within the Orthodox hierarchy, actually *strengthens* religious civil society by providing a framework of legal protection and a badge of state support for those organizations that gain registration under its provisions?

The case against the Russian state is that it has offered little in the way of support but rather has sought to control and excessively oversee nascent civil society. However, as is argued below, the paradox is that the flip side of control may be protection. In the realm of religion, the specific charges explored above are that the state and the Russian Orthodox Church are too close for the Church to be seen as truly independent, and that the religion law of 1997 favors the Orthodox Church and hedges religious groups around with a complex set of over-detailed regulations and demands that enable the state to move against particular groups should it so choose. To register as a religious organization requires a detailed charter including information on members, purposes, tasks, and basic forms of activity; the procedure for creation and cessation of activity; the structure of the organization, its administrative bodies, and the procedure for their formation; sources of finance; and "other information pertaining

to the distinctive features of the activity of the given religious organization"
(*Federal'nyi zakon o svobode sovesti,* Article 10/2).

The law "On Freedom of Conscience and Religious Associations" has—for good
reasons—widely been seen as a step backward in terms of religious freedom in
Russia. It overturns the constitutional guarantee that all religious associations are
equal, and it requires a detailed application for registration, thereby giving the state
ample scope for turning down registration requests. It has also been asserted by a
number of scholars that this law favors the Orthodox Church. For example, an article published in *Post-Soviet Affairs* in 2003 states that: "The law on religion adopted
in 1997 recognizes four 'traditional' religions in the Russian Federation: Russian
Orthodoxy, Islam, Judaism, and Buddhism. Other religious groups must register
and obtain permission to raise funds, own or rent property, and conduct other activities" (Balzer 2003, 199).

There are two errors in this summary. First, the 1997 law does not recognize
four "traditional" religions. The term "traditional" is not used; instead Orthodoxy
is singled out for its special role in Russia's history in the law's nonregulatory
preamble, along with Islam, Judaism, Buddhism, and—vital, but missing from
the above summary—Christianity. Christianity's inclusion, in addition to the acknowledgment of Orthodoxy as of primary importance, implicitly allows for the
contribution made by non-Orthodox Christian denominations in Russia's historical heritage. Second, it is not the case that "other religious groups must register."
All religious organizations, including the Orthodox, must register under the law.
On this latter point, indeed, turns the argument that for many religious organizations the 1997 law might fulfill the function of providing legal recognition and
status *protected* by the state, and in this way, the longer-term future of religious
civil society might be enhanced.

For many who have seen the religion law as negative, including this author, the
view that it might have a role in strengthening religious civil society seems
counterintuitive. However, two developments in support of that hypothesis are worth
noting. First, the 1997 law was crafted in such a way as to make it difficult for small
independent religious groups to register, as registration requirements included matters such as details of history, hierarchy, leadership structures, and administrative
structures, as well as evidence of existence for fifteen years before registration. For
many small, often newly formed, mostly non-Orthodox groups, such requirements
were difficult to fulfill. Their response was to use an option in the legislation that
made registration of religious associations easier if it was done through a registered
"centralized religious organization." For the Orthodox Church and other large hierarchical groups, such a centralized structure already existed. Other denominations—
notably evangelicals of various forms—either established new centralized bodies
to which they could sign up, or signed up to already existing bodies. In this way, the
diverse and dispersed nascent civil society that many religious associations formed
became more coherent, identifiable, and able to work as one, against or around the
demands of the state.

The second development to note with regard to the putative role of the religion law in strengthening religious civil society is that the law has, since its introduction, been used by religious organizations—usually non-Orthodox—to resist attacks from the state, as represented by regional authorities. The cause célèbre with regard to such attacks is probably that of the Moscow city authorities' attempt to close down the Salvation Army, partly on the laughable grounds that it was a militarized organization. In 2002, the Constitutional Court of the Russian Federation issued a ruling on the complaint of the Salvation Army that had been submitted in the name of the organization by the attorneys Riakhovskii and Pchelintsev of the Institute of Religion and Law, a body that devotes itself to fighting such cases. The court ruled that provisions of the federal law "On Freedom of Conscience and Religious Associations" had been applied improperly with regard to the Salvation Army, and it ordered that the decision for liquidation of the Salvation Army was subject to review. This is not the only case where moves against religious groups have been thwarted largely due to the efforts of lawyers using the protection offered by the 1997 religion law. Some will object to this argument, pointing out that the law has been used as often to attack groups as to protect them. Nonetheless, many of these attacks have been aimed at preventing groups from registering, in other words at denying them the protection of the law as religious organizations. This is arguably in itself an implicit recognition that once organizations are registered—and assuming a fair legal system—the law may serve as a shield against interference, particularly at the regional level where such moves are most prevalent. The U.S. State Department's Country Report on Human Rights for Russia in 2003 makes this very point, noting that:

> While isolated difficulties with registration continued to appear in different regions around the country, human rights lawyers and representatives of religious minorities reported that such difficulties related to the 1997 law decreased during the year. Local courts have upheld the right of non-traditional groups to register or reregister in a number of cases (U.S. Department of State 2004).

Conclusions

This chapter has set out four apparent paradoxes with regard to the relationship between the church and civil society in Russia today. The specific historical and cultural context of Russia sheds light on those issues and offers a holistic picture of civil society and religion in contemporary Russia. The stereotype beloved of many Russian patriots, that the Russian people as a whole are somehow more spiritual than their materialistic Western counterparts, may be borne out in terms of self-perception but certainly not in terms of engagement with religious civil society. Nonetheless, although church attendance figures are low in international comparison, for those who do participate, church represents a voluntary organization that provides a communal identity. Many churches not only engage with perceived spiritual needs but also have a charitable function, meeting material and physical needs.

All religious organizations in Russia are formally independent of the state, although contact between church and state may occur at the level of hierarchies locally, regionally, and nationally. Such contact, from the point of view of the religious organizations, can be negative—for example, in attempts by regional authorities to restrict the activities of churches—or positive—for example, President Putin's award of medals to church leaders from various denominations in 2001. The relative closeness to the state of the Russian Orthodox Church—as opposed to all other faiths and denominations—undermines to some extent its place in civil society. Nonetheless, the primacy of the Orthodox Church in the eyes of the people of Russia as a whole is simply a fact. The implicit acknowledgment of this by the state does not amount to state control or state management. Although the Church may be to some extent compromised by its partial reliance on the state's support for turning its cultural precedence into access to opportunities and material benefits, the relationship between church and state is mutually beneficial, with the state seeking to use Orthodoxy as one element in the inculcation of some sense of national identity.

The Russian Orthodox Church's place in civil society might also be seen to be compromised by the fact that it backed the 1997 law on religion, which sought tighter state control on religious activity. The 1997 law on religion has not led though, as at first feared, to the widespread closure of non-Orthodox churches and indeed has at times been used to protect such churches from overzealous prosecution.

None of these conclusions should suggest that Russia's religious scene represents a level playing field where wholly benevolent organizations enjoy equal status and protection before the law. Extreme nationalist views and intolerance remain too prevalent in some wings of the Orthodox Church. Non-Orthodox denominations continue to be more likely to experience harrassment from the authorities, and at any given time since the mid-1990s several such cases can be identified. From the point of view of Russia's weak civil society, the religious sphere remains fraught with difficulties, but nonetheless it represents a clearly identifiable sector where autonomous communal and civic action takes place. It is watched carefully by the state, but not controlled by it.

Notes

1. For discussions of alternative approaches to defining civil society, see Hann (1996, 3) and Howard (2003, 49–50).
2. I refer to the Russian Orthodox Church, the Orthodox Church, and the Church (upper case) to mean the church under the authority of the Moscow Patriarchate.
3. Author interview, anonymous human rights activist, Moscow, October 23, 2002.

References

Bacon, Edwin. 1997. "The Church and Politics in Russia: A Case Study of the 1996 Presidential Election." *Religion, State and Society* 25, no. 3 (September): 253–65.
———. 2002. "Church and State in Contemporary Russia: Conflicting Discourses." *Journal of Communist Studies and Transition Politics* 8, no. 1 (March): 97–116.
———. 2003. "Conceptualising Contemporary Russia." *Slavonic and East European Review* 81, no. 2 (April): 293–301.

Balzer, Harley. 2003. "Managed Pluralism: Vladimir Putin's Emerging Regime." *Post-Soviet Affairs* 19, no. 3 (July–September): 189–228.

Ekho Moskvy News Agency. 2002. "Russian MPs Critical of Putin's Remarks on Religion." August 30.

Emory International Law Review. 1998. "Soul Wars: The Problem of Proselytism in Russia." Special Volume 12, no. 1 (Winter).

Federal'nyi zakon o svobode sovesti i o religioznykh ob"edineniiakh. 1998. Moscow: Os'-89.

Fein, Elke. 2002. "Zivilgesellschaftlicher Paradigmenwechsel oder PR-Aktion? Zum allerersten allrussischen 'Bürgerforum' im Kreml." *Osteuropa* 52, no. 2 (February): 158–80.

Fond Obshchestvennogo Mneniia. 2002. "Religioznost' i votserklovennost'." August 22. bd.fom.ru/report/cat/man/religion/d023309.

Hall, Peter A. 1999. "Social Capital in Britain." *British Journal of Political Science* 29, no. 3 (July): 417–61.

Hann, Chris. 1996. "Introduction: Political Society and Civil Anthropology." In *Civil Society: Challenging Western Models*, ed. Chris Hann and Elizabeth Dunn, 1–26. London: Routledge.

Howard, Marc M. 2000. *Free Not to Participate: The Weakness of Civil Society in Post-Communist Europe*. Studies in Public Policy No. 325. Glasgow: Centre for the Study of Public Policy, University of Strathclyde.

————. 2003. *The Weakness of Civil Society in Postcommunist Europe*. Cambridge: Cambridge University Press.

Knox, Zoe. 2005. *Russian Society and the Orthodox Church: Religion and Society after Communism*. London: RoutledgeCurzon.

Korobov, Pavel. 2003. "Patriarkh Aleksii II: mnogie oblasti tserkovno-gosudarstvennykh otnoshenii nuzhdaiutsia v uregulirovanii." *Kommersant-Daily* (Moscow), January 9.

McFaul, Michael, and Elina Treyger. 2004. "Civil Society." In *Between Dictatorship and Democracy: Russian Postcommunist Political Reform*, ed. Michael McFaul, Nikolai Petrov, and Andrei Ryabov, 135–73. Washington, DC: Carnegie Endowment for International Peace.

Nikitin, Alexander, and Jane Buchanan. 2002. "The Kremlin's Civic Forum: Cooperation or Co-optation for Civil Society in Russia?" *Demokratizatsiya* 10, no. 2 (Spring): 147–65.

Pinsker, Dmitrii. 2001. "Kremlin Tames Civil Society." *Russia Journal*, November 16–22.

Poroskov, Nikolai. 2003. "Voenno-tserkovnyi sbor. V Rossii formiruetsia otriad polkovykh sviashchennikov." *Vremya novostei* (Moscow), June 25.

Pravoslavie v Rossii News Service. 1998. March 18. www.or.ru/news. English translation at www.stetson.edu/~psteeves/relnews/9803b.html.

RFE/RL Newsline. 2002. "(Un)Civil Societies: Two-Thirds of Russians Profess Faith in God." Vol. 3, no. 36 (September 4).

Shevchenko, Maksim. 1998. "Paskhu prazdnovali i v Moskve i v Groznom." *Nezavisimaia gazeta* (Moscow), April 21.

Sluzhba kommunikatsii OVTsS MP. 2001. "Prezident Rossii V.V. Putin vruchil gosudarstvennye nagrady sviashchennosluzhiteliam." www.russian-orthodox-church.org.ru/nr101161.htm, January.

University of Michigan News Release. 1997. "Study of Worldwide Rates of Religiosity, Church Attendance." December 10 (17). umich.edu/~newsinfo/Releases/1997/Dec97/r121097a.htm.

U.S. Department of State. 2004. *Russia Country Report on Human Rights Practices 2003*. February 25. www.state.gov/g/drl/rls/hrrpt/2003/27861pf.htm.

White, Stephen, Richard Rose, and Ian McAllister. 1997. *How Russia Votes*. Chatham, NJ: Chatham House.

8

Civil Society in Rural Russia

Stephen K. Wegren

Theorists of democratization frequently argue that the development of civil society is an integral component of democracy (Linz and Stepan 1996). A strong civil society is an essential element of a healthy democracy, providing a counterweight to state power. A civil society creates a society in general that is more participatory, with citizens who have more community spirit and volunteer more readily. In short, civil society, helps develop "participant" citizens and avoids the consequences of "subject" citizens (Almond and Verba 1965).

Most definitions of civil society draw a distinction between state and society, in that civil society involves the development of autonomous organizations that are able to act with a minimum of state interference. The term "civil society" customarily includes organizations that are created by citizens to achieve common goals, and those organizations are independent and separate from government. Such organizations may include nongovernmental organizations (NGOs), the media, labor unions, advocacy organizations such as human rights groups, and community service nonprofits such as food banks. Civil society organizations range in formality from ad hoc groups to formal organizations that have permanent bureaucratic staffs. In sum, the most common usage of civil society assumes the development of independent, self-governing, and self-organized associations (Fish 1995, 52).

Beyond that very general level of agreement, however, there is considerable debate in the scholarly literature about civil society, as indicated in the introduction to this volume. For example, questions arise from efforts to understand the preconditions of civil society. One such precondition is the presence of modernity, as used by Seymour Lipset in his analysis of necessary elements for democracy (Lipset 1960; 1994). The idea that populations require a certain level of education and other "modern" sociological attributes in order to democratize implicitly suggests that different subcomponents of society democratize at different rates and at different times, with the eventual result of societal democratization once a critical mass is reached. Taking that proposition one step farther, the Lipset argument that "modernity" is a necessary precondition for democratic consolidation suggests that subpopulations in a society that lack the necessary educational levels, urbanity, and modern cultural norms are either unable to participate in democratization or will democratize at much slower rates.

For Russia, about which prognoses for successful democratic consolidation are often negative, questions of civil society and democratization are further complicated by a distinct urban–rural cleavage, which, unfortunately, many scholars overlook in their analysis of the democratization process (see, for example, Eckstein et al. 1998). While some authors choose to ignore the urban–rural divide, the urban–rural cleavage has manifested itself in different voting patterns during national elections and in attitudes toward reform policies during the 1990s (Colton 2000; Colton and McFaul 2003). Urban and rural Russia differ considerably in terms of their respective values, their forms of social organization, their patterns of interaction, and their economic means of survival.

If the Lipset theorem is applied to rural Russia, the logic of this argument yields two contrasting hypotheses of theoretical and policy interest: (1) rural Russia (comprising nearly 30 percent of the population), which lacks characteristics of modernity, is hindering democratic consolidation and therefore lies outside of civil society; and (2) rural Russia, despite lacking many of the modern sociological characteristics presumed necessary for civil society, displays elements of civil society and thus is an important part of the broader democratization process. These two hypotheses raise interesting questions about whether it is more accurate to talk about *a* national civil society, or whether we need to distinguish between civil *societies* that simultaneously exist but may or may not interact, may or may not be developing in the same direction, and may or may not be developing at the same speed.

This chapter investigates the development of civil society in rural Russia.[1] The basic arguments in the paper are threefold: (1) our knowledge about rural civil society is still in its infancy and much more research is necessary; (2) concerning the contrasting hypotheses that derive from Lipset, this chapter favors hypothesis number 2 and suggests that rural civil society may develop independently of urban/national civil society; and (3) the basic prerequisites for the development of civil society appear to be in place in rural Russia, meaning that there are causes for optimism. Intervening variables such as government policy toward nongovernmental organizations and political freedom in general will, of course, affect future developments. In that respect, the primary question concerns the future trajectory of rural civil society.

The approach used in this paper assumes that the development of civil society is multidimensional, comprising organizational, attitudinal, and behavioral aspects. Therefore, the chapter is organized around three main questions: (1) What are the attitudinal attributes of rural Russians and do they contribute to civil society? (2) What organizational developments are occurring in rural Russia that may contribute to civil society? (3) What are the behavioral attributes of rural Russians, and do they contribute to civil society? Each section of the chapter addresses one of these questions. The conclusion assesses the contribution of each aspect and summarizes the prospects for civil society in rural Russia.

Attitudinal Aspects of Civil Society: Political Trust

Attitudinal aspects of rural civil society constitute the beginning point of the analysis. If attitudes are conducive, the likelihood of positive trends toward the development or consolidation of civil society is greater. In particular, this section focuses on feelings of political trust, which is an important component of civil society. This section utilizes national survey data on political trust, showing how rural dwellers are oriented toward leaders, parties, and political institutions. The time period covered is 1993–2002.

Political trust in leaders, parties, and political institutions is an extremely important component of civil society, having the effect of lowering corruption and improving the operation of democratic institutions (Putnam 1993). Among the different dimensions of political trust, two stand out for our purposes: trust toward "outsiders," persons who are outside a network known to an individual; and trust toward "insiders," those who are inside such a network. Another way to characterize the difference is between personal and impersonal relations (see Rose 2000).

It would be perfectly logical to expect that rural dwellers in Russia would have lower levels of political trust toward outsiders and higher levels toward insiders. This hypothesis is based, first, upon the fact that rural dwellers have "denser" (larger) personal networks that are based upon familiarity and trust among members of the network (O'Brien, Patsiorkovski, and Dershem 2000, chap. 6). In other words, trust among rural dwellers might be expected to be stronger within informal networks— that is, personal relations—and relatively weaker vis-à-vis formal networks—that is, impersonal relations with persons unknown to the actor. There is strong evidence of this occurrence when behavioral aspects of social capital are examined later in this chapter. Second, lower levels of trust toward outsiders could be expected because policy makers in Moscow were perceived as largely responsible for the precipitous decline in the rural standard of living and the financial deterioration of farming enterprises during the 1990s (Wegren 2003). Third, voting patterns during national elections during the 1990s showed a clear urban/rural divide, with urban centers, particularly the largest such as Moscow and St. Petersburg, displaying strong support for reformist candidates, while rural areas gave more support to conservative candidates.[2] It is reasonable to expect that underlying electoral support for reform policies and reform candidates is an element of political trust. Finally, it could be argued that political trust would be lower among rural residents given that rural society possesses fewer of the characteristics of "modern" society that are linked to civil society.

Based upon national survey data gathered by the Russian Center for Public Opinion Research, located in Moscow, it is therefore somewhat surprising to see that rural levels of trust not only did not lag behind urban levels but actually were higher than urban levels vis-à-vis many political actors and institutions in 1993–2002. In short, the data indicate that rural levels of trust toward impersonal actors and institutions are higher than in urban areas. These data are shown in Table 8.1 on pages 130–131.

The table displays two sets of data for different population cohorts. For each cohort, there are two rows of data: the first row shows the percentage of the rural sample that "fully" trusted the particular actor/institution. The second row compares the rural level of trust to the level of trust in urban centers, specifically cities but excluding Moscow and St. Petersburg (for which there is a separate category in the survey). The table uses eight time points, selected on the basis of availability of data and when the same questions were asked in different surveys.

Several patterns emerge from the data. The most obvious is that rural trust toward the president increased substantially once Boris Yeltsin left office and Vladimir Putin became president. One wonders, at least in passing, about potential ambiguity in what "political trust" toward the president really means. Does it reflect potential for a civil society that will support democracy, or does it instead reflect submissive respect for a semi-authoritarian leader?[3]

The second pattern is that rural trust toward national political institutions (the parliament and the government) also increased significantly after Yeltsin left office, suggesting that levels of trust are susceptible to rather rapid change depending on policies and perceptions about the leadership in office. If this interpretation is correct, it means that rural "opposition" to reform and reform candidates is more ephemeral and much less visceral than has been believed.

The third pattern is a reversal in levels of trust toward local government and the national government. The data show that rural dwellers trusted the national government more than their local government early in the post-Soviet era, perhaps a result of the belief that the national government could lead the nation to prosperity and democracy in a relatively short time. However, as the 1990s progressed, the level of trust for the national government declined, reaching its nadir in September 1998, following the financial collapse in August 1998. Thus for much of the Yeltsin period, local government was trusted more than national government. Since Putin became president, however, trust in the national government has again surpassed trust in local government. This trend suggests that trust is conditional and perceptual, varying according to perceptions about the leader and conditioned on social and economic trends in society.

The final, and arguably the most important, pattern is that rural levels of trust were often higher than urban levels. As seen in Table 8.1, rural levels of trust were *always* higher toward the parliament, political parties, the army, state security organs, and the Church and religious organizations. Additionally, rural trust was higher than urban trust in six or more of the eight time points toward the national government, regional government, the police, and the press, radio, and television. The fewest number of times rural trust was higher than urban trust was five times—toward the president and local government. Even if the percentage differences are small, this is an important finding because it raises questions about the validity of assumptions that see the rural population as resistant to reform and lacking in trust toward political institutions.

It is not entirely clear why levels of rural trust are higher than levels of urban trust, and this is an issue that requires further investigation. One reason might be due to the

Table 8.1

Rural Feelings of Political Trust (as %)

	October 1993	February 1994	September 1997	September 1998	September 1999	September 2000	September 2001	September 2002
Trust in the president	22.1 (−5.4)	18.6 (−3.4)	11.1 (+0.1)	2.4 (+.5)	2.5 (−0.8)	50.5 (+14.8)	58.5 (+9.6)	62.1 (+0.7)
Trust in the parliament	—	—	7.6 (+0.5)	6.0 (+2.1)	5.4 (+1.3)	13.0 (+7.6)	13.5 (+4.4)	16.2 (+5.5)
Trust in the national government	16.9 (−2.4)	11.3 (+0.6)	11.1 (+0.2)	3.8 (+1.6)	8.0 (+2.6)	24.5 (+9.3)	26.3 (+6.7)	26.1 (+3.9)
Trust in the regional government	13.4 (+2.3)	17.3 (+7.2)	19.5 (−1.5)	15.2 (−0.3)	24.0 (+5.2)	22.1 (+1.8)	26.7 (+8.8)	20.7 (+5.4)
Trust in the local government	15.1 (+1.4)	18.8 (+8.0)	22.9 (+2.7)	19.3 (+4.0)	23.9 (0.0)	19.6 (−2.5)	20.6 (−3.8)	23.1 (+7.5)
Trust in political parties	—	—	4.7 (+1.6)	4.3 (+1.8)	4.5 (+2.5)	9.6 (+5.7)	7.9 (+3.3)	7.9 (+0.6)
Trust in the army	39.6 (+2.7)	34.6 (+0.9)	28.8 (+4.5)	31.4 (+6.2)	37.2 (+6.7)	40.1 (+6.9)	39.0 (+13.7)	33.4 (+10.8)
Trust in the state security organs	20.8 (+2.5)	25.8 (+9.3)	19.1 (+.2)	17.5 (+1.8)	21.7 (+3.3)	23.9 (+4.6)	21.7 (+1.0)	22.5 (+3.7)
Trust in the police and courts	14.8 (−0.1)	24.1 (+9.4)	14.4 (+2.9)	12.9 (+3.1)	13.6 (+3.6)	18.5 (+10.1)	14.2 (+5.4)	11.7 (+1.3)

Trust in the Church, religious organizations	51.1 (+6.0)	53.2 (+2.9)	40.2 (+7.0)	33.2 (+2.5)	43.5 (+13.1)	42.9 (+11.9)	44.9 (+12.8)	41.5 (+3.5)
Trust in the press, radio, television	23.1 (+0.2)	28.7 (+2.1)	26.8 (+2.3)	25.7 (−0.7)	28.2 (+2.3)	27.6 (+3.0)	30.9 (+11.7)	26.0 (+7.2)

Source: Monitoring obshchestvennogo mneniia: ekonomicheskie i sotsial'nye peremeny, 1994, no. 1, 54–55; 1994, no. 3, 69–70: 1997–2002, no. 6, various pages.

The question asked: "To what degree do you trust . . ."

The responses were scaled 1–4:

   1 fully
   2 not fully
   3 not at all
   4 hard to say

The percentages in the table above are for "fully" only. The top row indicates the absolute level of trust among rural respondents. The second row compares rural trust to levels of trust in large cities (*bol' shie goroda*).

rural way of life, which is simpler, less cynical, and therefore inherently more trusting. Another reason might be due to the physical remoteness of rural dwellers from policy makers. Whatever the reason, the finding that rural trust often exceeds levels of urban trust suggests a reason for optimism—that there is an important component of civil society that exists and potentially can be developed. Rural Russia is not significantly more distrustful of political actors or institutions—rather the contrary. Thus a basic precondition of civil society is present in rural Russia that heretofore has not been adequately recognized by analysts. An element of trust among the rural population in turn has important implications for the success of NGOs, some of which operate on the basis of foreign sponsorship and funding. Although NGOs face many obstacles, the data herein suggest that the rural population might be essentially trusting and supportive of their activities. NGOs and some of their activities are surveyed next.

Organizational Aspects of Rural Civil Society: Nongovernmental Organizations

The second part of the analysis focuses on rural organizations and their contribution to the development of civil society. The purpose of this section is to survey NGOs and their activities and to assess their impact on the development of civil society. After some summary comments about the obstacles confronting NGOs in rural Russia, I provide two examples of NGOs and their activities.

Nongovernmental organizations are important to the development of civil society because they stand between the state and the individual. NGOs help bring the needs of the population to the attention of the government, serve as a check on state power, engage in lobbying to promote their causes to policy makers, and offer alternative channels for participation and the representation of interests. The number of NGOs that operate in Russia has increased substantially, from about 8,479 in 1993 to over 270,000 in 2001 (USAID 2001). Despite their numerical growth and legal protections embodied in the Civil Code and elsewhere, NGOs face considerable obstacles. For example, NGOs confront financial and economic obstacles: funding is hard to obtain, needs outstrip resources, and Russians tend not to donate a lot of money to charitable organizations.[4] The three largest donors to NGOs are Russian businesses, foreign foundations, and local administrations. As a result, NGO staffs tend to be small and their facilities and equipment very limited, which constrains their impact.

A second obstacle is that NGOs often have multiple functions, with technical, humanitarian, or economic assistance the most urgent priority. The multidimensional nature of rural organizations' responsibilities is complicated by inadequate resources—underfunding and understaffing—as well as conflicting agendas. For example, the management boards of foreign NGOs often emphasize priorities that are different from those suggested by the humanitarian needs that field workers confront every day.[5] Finally, NGOs confront bureaucratic obstacles in registering, a process that is seldom transparent or easy. Following registration, NGOs are susceptible to bureaucratic arbitrariness (*proizvol*) at the local level.

Despite a legal framework that ostensibly protects the activities of NGOs, relations between the state and NGOs have become more strained. Human rights groups in particular have been very critical of Russia's policies in Chechnya, citing "unabated" human rights violations. In response, the Russian government has cracked down selectively on various groups and individuals (*New York Times,* January 16, 2003). For example, in mid-2002, thirty U.S. Peace Corps workers' visas were not renewed, following the refusal to renew ten visas in 2001 (*New York Times,* August 14, 2002). In late 2002, a little-noticed regulation removed human rights and democratic rights' groups from the list of organizations exempt from taxation on foreign grants they receive. The new rule could allow the government to claim up to 25 percent of grants given to human rights groups and greatly increases state leverage over human rights activities (*Washington Post,* January 26, 2003). In May 2004, President Putin accused some NGOs of working for foreign interests. In July 2004, the government proposed legislation that would regulate the way in which Russian and foreign donors may contribute to NGOs. According to early reports about the draft legislation, foreign donors would be required to register each grant with a special government commission. Russian donors would be required to have their names included on a special list of certified donors or their contributions would be subject to a 24 percent tax (*RFE/RL Newsline,* July 22, 2004).

Before turning to a discussion of rural NGOs, it is worthwhile to clarify what a "rural" NGO is. In this chapter, a rural NGO is defined as an organization that serves the rural population. It may or may not be located in a rural area. Implicit to my argument, then, is the idea that the target audience is more important than the location of an NGO. If we insisted that "rural" NGOs had to be located in "rural" areas, then very few NGOs would qualify. A "rural" NGO is often located in a raion or oblast center, but this has no particular political significance and merely reflects rural social conditions (World Bank 2003, 38–51). Because rural Russia is often quite primitive, it is easier and more convenient to travel to (or call) a raion or oblast center than a remote and obscure rural location. Infrastructure (roads, communications, public transit, etc.) is better developed in oblast centers and thus more accessible to a greater number of people. As a result, "rural" NGOs must be located in local urban centers if they are to survive. With these general comments in mind, an overview of activities of domestic and foreign NGOs is discussed below.

Domestically Funded NGOs

Domestically funded NGOs do not accept money from foreign donors but are funded by domestic donors or sources of financing. A primary domestic NGO in rural Russia that acts to foster cooperation and aid in the development of civil society is the Association of Peasant Farmers and Agricultural Cooperatives of Russia (AKKOR). AKKOR is a good starting place for a discussion because it is the largest, oldest, and best-known organization that was formed to provide wide-ranging assistance to the rural population, in this case, primarily private farmers.

AKKOR is self-financing and receives no financial support from the Russian government or from foreign donors. Instead, members of AKKOR, that is, private farmers, pay dues. The AKKOR organization in each raion decides how much each member farmer owes in dues, but in general " financially strong" farmers pay about twice as much annually as "financially weak" private farmers. Specifically, strong farmers pay, on average, about $200 a year, while weak farmers pay about $100 a year (Morozov 2004).

At first glance, it might appear odd to include AKKOR as an organization that aids in the development of civil society. Steven Fish warned about "concept stretching," whereby state agencies are included in the realm of civil society, and his point is well taken (Fish 1995, 52–53). Although AKKOR was never a state organization per se, it was founded with state backing, and its president used his position in the state and Communist party apparatuses to help create the organization (Van Atta 1993, 20). Following the creation of AKKOR in January 1990, it became the primary rural agent representing rural policies of reformers in Moscow. In return, when the "Russian Farmer" program was introduced in 1992, state subsidies and credits were channeled through local branches of AKKOR offices with the goal of expanding the private farmer movement and increasing the number of private farms (Wegren 1998, 191–93). When the "Russian Farmer" program was in operation, private farmers had an economic interest to join AKKOR in order to be eligible for government loans and credits. As a result, nearly all private farmers were members. Once the "Russian Farmer" program ended, there was less incentive to join, although members were eligible for loans from peasant banks at market rates and could enroll in courses at nearby educational institutes.[6] In addition, while the "Russian Farmer" program was in place, the number of private farms and farmers grew, but it then declined during the second half of the 1990s. (To put potential membership in perspective, in 2000, the total labor force on private farms equaled 919,000, a number that included registered members of private farms, family members who participated in farm production, and hired laborers.)[7]

The early symbiotic relationship between AKKOR and the state led one analyst to warn: "Unless a variety of similar groups rapidly develop to compete with AKKOR, it . . . may become little more than [an] instrument for the same kind of high-pressure reorganization as collectivization was sixty years ago" (Van Atta 1993, 21). This never happened. As the 1990s progressed, the relationship between AKKOR and the Russian government became more distant. State funding for the " Russian Farmer" program ceased in late 1994; and thereafter, state assistance to private farmers, even for production subsidies and the construction of infrastructure, also stopped. AKKOR began to operate based on dues and fees levied by a series of banks started and backed by local peasant associations. From about the mid-1990s onward, therefore, AKKOR was much less a quasi-state agent and much more an independent, self-governing organization that at times allied itself with conservative parties such as the Agrarian Party against various government agrarian policies (Wegren 1996).

The functions of AKKOR facilitate the development of rural civil society, even if that aspect is secondary to economic and technical assistance to private farmers. The impact of AKKOR in rural Russia has probably declined since the mid-1990s, when private farming reached its apex. However, AKKOR's functions remain important, and the organization as a whole is still one of the principal rural NGOs in operation. It is not an exaggeration to claim that AKKOR is an organization of farmers by farmers. The urban bureaucratic apparatus is very small, and most functions are fulfilled by raion offices. AKKOR strives:

(1) to facilitate economic production cooperation among private farmers;
(2) to provide technical assistance to private farmers;
(3) to organize educational seminars on a range of topics from accounting to land laws to how to obtain credit;
(4) to facilitate the formation of marketing cooperatives and farmers' commodity exchanges;
(5) to organize private farmers' banks, which provide credits and loans to members;
(6) to provide information about rural legislation; and
(7) to assist private farmers with knowledge about prices and market conditions in their locality.

Foreign-Funded NGOs

Foreign-funded NGOs receive the bulk of their funding from foreign sources, even though the organization is based and operates in Russia. An example of an NGO that works with the rural population is the Center for Land Reform Support of Vladimir Oblast (Region), which was created in August 1996.[8] For almost two years, until April 1998, the center functioned under the administrative guidance of the Rural Development Institute, located in Seattle, Washington. In April 1998, the center became a legal entity unto itself and was registered as a nonprofit organization, with the purpose of providing free legal assistance to rural citizens. The center in Vladimir is funded with grants from international organizations and is completely independent of the oblast administration financially and operationally.

Similar to many "rural" NGOs, the center is located in the city of Vladimir and provides various services to rural clients. The staff is composed of urbanites who serve the rural population but who live within the city itself. The center's objectives include promoting the development of legal awareness among rural citizens, assisting rural citizens in defending their rights and interests as landowners, promoting the development of private farms, assisting oblast and local authorities in matters related to the regulation of land relations, and promoting the development of a land market in the oblast.

To fulfill its objectives, the center offers the following services.

(1) Informational services. The legal experts in Vladimir prepare informational articles, which are published in the sixteen raion newspapers of Vladimir Oblast. In 2001, the team of experts from the center published twelve articles in Vladimir Oblast, as well as in twenty papers in four neighboring oblast newspapers. Every month, fifteen-minute radio broadcasts are taped and played throughout the oblast and repeated several times throughout the month. Every two months, informational bulletins are published, with printings of fifteen hundred copies. At least once a month, legal experts from the center visit rural population points in the oblast to answer questions or conduct seminars on issues relating to land legislation and rights. In 2001, eleven seminars were held, attended by 212 people. Finally, the center's legal experts publish books on land rights and land relations that are distributed throughout Russia (Pulin 2003).

(2) Consulting activities. Clients may appear in person or submit specific questions in writing. For clients appearing in person, the center's experts not only answer questions but also provide information about land laws, decrees, and resolutions at the national and regional levels. Copies of extracts of the relevant legislation are provided to the client. A client may also obtain legal opinions and recommendations about the client's situation. Clients also receive assistance in preparing claims and appeals to be submitted to various administrative and judicial bodies. It is estimated that in a year the center provides advice and consultation to about 250 clients and to an additional twenty to thirty oblast officials (ibid.).

(3) Work with state organs and officials. The legal experts at the center consult with regional and local officials on questions concerning land rights of citizens and participate in the drafting of legislation concerning land rights.

The center's importance to land reform and civil society is that, although small, it provides a unique service. There is no state organization or agency that works directly with rural dwellers to inform them about their land rights or to assist them with their problems and questions. State organizations concerned with land relations work with and among bureaucrats and state officials, not with citizens. Furthermore, the center in Vladimir is one of only a handful of NGOs that provide the services discussed above. The most similar center to the one in Vladimir operates in Samara Oblast. Other organizations that provide advisory and informational support to the rural population include: the Foundation for Support of Agrarian Reform and Rural Development (city of Moscow); the AgroMir Foundation (Orel); and the Southern Agro Foundation in Rostov-on-Don.

Behavioral Aspects of Rural Civil Society: Social Capital

The third and final aspect of rural civil society considered in this chapter concerns social capital among rural individuals. Social capital, or civic engagement, as it is sometimes called, refers to the idea that "social networks matter," having value for the people who are in them as well as external effects on the larger community. Robert Putnam summarizes the importance of social capital, emphasizing that "networks of social interaction appear to foster sturdy norms of generalized reciprocity. . . . Social interaction, in other words, helps to resolve dilemmas of collective action, encouraging people to act in a trustworthy way when they might not otherwise do so. A society characterized by generalized reciprocity is more efficient than a distrustful society" (Putnam 2002, 7).

To assess social capital in rural Russia, this section uses survey data from a sample of 800 rural households in 5 Russian regions in 2001, funded by the National Council for Eurasian and East European Research. Those five regions are: Belgorod Oblast, Volgograd Oblast, Krasnodar Krai, Novgorod Oblast, and the Chuvash Republic. Within each region, 4 villages were selected, and within each village, 40 households were surveyed, for a total sample of 800 households (160 households in each region). The pretest of the questions was conducted in June 2001 in Riazan Oblast, followed by the full survey in July–October 2001. The regions were selected for their geographical diversity, ethnic component, economic performance, and importance of the agricultural economy.

In selecting villages to be surveyed, a primary objective was to gather data from "real" rural Russians, due to the well-known effects of modernization and urbanization that influence attitudes and behavior. Previously, in surveying rural Russia, it has often been the case that "rural" villages have been selected due to their close proximity to an urban center, for the sake of convenience. The consequence of this selection method is that respondents' views do not capture the real attitudes of rural Russia. The selection method used here purposefully selected remote villages that were located several hours (by bus) from an urban center. Moreover, a cross-section of different types of villages was used: small and middle-sized; economically weak and economically strong.

For each of the selected villages a stratified sample was composed from the household list of permanent residents that is kept by the village administration for all households within its jurisdiction. This list is updated annually and contains demographic and social characteristics of the households on the list. Households on this list included persons working on large farms, private farmers, persons working in food processing or the food trade, and persons engaged in private household agricultural production and/or processing. One person from each household was interviewed. Data were collected about the respondent and the household in which he/she resides, thereby allowing either the individual or the household to be used as the unit of analysis. The survey consisted of more than one hundred questions per respondent. Interviews were conducted person to person by a research team from the Institute of Socioeconomic Problems of the Population (Moscow). The nonresponse rate was less than 5 percent.

These survey data shed light on the socioeconomic characteristics of persons who are more participatory and interactive with others. In particular, this section focuses

Table 8.2

Distribution of Responses Regarding Type of Participation
(as number of respondents)

	Never	Very rarely	Rarely	Some-times	Often	Very often	Total
How often participate in family celebrations and holidays?	98	254	107	118	106	117	800
How often participate in friends/neighbors celebrations and holidays?	113	333	137	110	66	41	800
How often participate in village celebrations and holidays?	290	338	71	54	28	18	800

Source: Author's survey data, 2001.

on social interaction, using location, gender, age, education, and income as independent variables. These independent variables are used to measure interaction with family members, with neighbors and friends, and with the village, which are used as dependent variables.[9] These particular independent variables were used because they have been identified as important factors that influence a person's attitudes toward reform and voting behavior.

Three separate survey questions were asked of respondents:

(1) How often do you participate in family celebrations or holidays (*torzhestva ili prazdniki*)?
(2) How often do you participate in the celebrations or holidays of friends and neighbors?
(3) How often do you participate in village celebrations or holidays?

The distribution of responses for the three forms of participation is indicated in Table 8.2.

As is evident from the data in Table 8.2, most responses are clustered in "never," "very rarely," or "rarely" responses. The ordering of the rates of participation ("often" or "very often") shows that interaction with the family is most prevalent, followed by friends and neighbors, and last is the village. Only 12 percent of respondents never participate in family celebrations and holidays, 44 percent do so rarely or very rarely, and 28 percent do so often or very often. For celebrations and holidays of friends or neighbors, 14 percent never participate, 49 percent do so rarely or very rarely, and 13 percent do so often or very often. Finally, for village celebrations and holidays, 36 percent of respondents never participate, over 51 percent do so rarely or very rarely, and only 6 percent do so often or very often. This pattern of responses is neither surprising nor unexpected, as people would be expected to interact at higher rates within their personal networks than in activities based upon impersonal relations. Thus a definite relationship exists between the degree of interaction and community integration and personal well-being, both physically and mentally.

Turning next to the relationship between regional location and participation, there are regional differences for each of the forms of interaction, although no obvious geographical patterns emerge. That is, one does not discern a notable north–south axis. From the five regions in the survey, respondents in Volgograd Oblast have the highest mean for participation in family celebrations and holidays at 2.64 (the mean for the five regions is 2.29, which essentially equates to "very rarely"). The region with the second highest mean is Krasnodar Krai at 2.56, and the region with the lowest mean is Chuvashia at 1.87. Thus significant regional differences exist, but in none of the regions are respondents highly participatory.

With regard to the celebrations and holidays of friends and neighbors, the mean for the five regions is 1.76, which is lower than for family celebrations and holidays. The two regions with the highest means are Novgorod Oblast at 1.93 and Belgorod Oblast at 1.92; the regions with the lowest means are Chuvashia at 1.56 and Krasnodar at 1.51. These responses equate to "very rarely."

Finally, for village celebrations and holidays, the mean for the five regions is 1.06, the lowest mean of the three types of participation. The mean essentially equates to "never" participating. Respondents are the least likely to participate in village celebrations and holidays, which suggests a low level of social capital in all five regions. Again, there are significant regional differences. Volgograd and Novgorod have the highest means at 1.36 and 1.33; Chuvashia and Krasnodar are significantly below the aggregate mean at 0.95 and 0.54, respectively. These responses equate to "never." An investigation of the factors influencing participation rates would take this chapter in a dramatically different direction, one that space constraints do not permit. This author hopes that future research will illuminate this question more fully.

Differences in participation by gender indicate that men tend to be slightly more participatory than women, perhaps owing to more free time and less burden from the combination of employment, household chores, and child raising. For example, data from the Soviet period show that women spend more time tending the household's private plot (Goskomstat 1989, 27). Since household production has increased during the transition period, it may be surmised that a good portion of the extra time expenditure comes from women. Compared to women, the mean for male participation is higher for each of the three dependent variables: 2.61 to 2.13 for family celebrations and holidays, 1.97 to 1.65 for celebrations and holidays of friends and neighbors, and 1.15 to 1.01 for village celebrations and holidays. However, as noted above, neither gender displays highly participatory behavior for any type of festivity.

Turning to the relationship between age and participation, Pearson correlations

Table 8.3

Mean Participation by Husband's Age

	Family celebrations and holidays	Celebrations and holidays of friends/neignbors	Village celebrations and holidays
18–29	3.12	2.00	1.19
30–39	2.55	2.13	1.36
40–49	2.57	2.06	1.21
50–59	2.64	1.99	1.31
60+	1.86	1.39	0.80
Total mean	2.29	1.76	1.06
F score	13.62	13.14	8.77
Significance	0.000	0.000	0.000

Source: Author's survey data, 2001.

with a two-tailed significance test show that age is negatively correlated with participation in family, friends/neighbors, and village celebrations and holidays, and each correlation is statistically significant at the 100 percent confidence level ($p = .00$). This negative correlation means that the older a person, the less likely he/she is to participate. The distribution of means of participation by age intervals is provided in Table 8.3.

The data in this table confirm the correlation and support the conclusion that younger people have a somewhat greater tendency to participate than older people. The elderly, defined as sixty or above, have the lowest mean participation rates for all three types of festivities. Table 8.3 illustrates a linear descent in the means of participation as age increases, and this finding is statistically significant at the 100 percent level of confidence. The fact that the elderly participate less is somewhat surprising, given that social networks and social interaction have both social and economic functions. It might be expected that with lower monetary incomes, elderly people would have greater incentive to interact at each level. Moreover, it might be expected that the elderly would have more time for interaction, since many would be retired. Finally, it would be expected that the elderly have had more time to establish personal and impersonal networks. The data in the table confirm the previous conclusion that family interaction is most prevalent, followed by interaction with friends and neighbors, and last is village participation.

Turning to education, Pearson correlations with a two-tailed significance test show that education is positively correlated with participation in family, friends/neighbors, and village celebrations and holidays, and each correlation is statistically significant at the 100 percent confidence level ($p = .00$). The correlations are significant for both the husband's and wife's level of education. This positive correlation means that as education levels rise, so, too, do rates of participation. The distribution of mean participation by intervals of education for the husband and wife is shown in Table 8.4.

Table 8.4

Mean Participation by Level of Education

Grade completed	Family celebrations and holidays	Celebrations and holidays of friends/neighbors	Village celebrations and holidays
Husband			
0–6	1.79	0.50	1.25
7–9	2.28	0.94	1.54
10–11	2.60	1.31	2.00
12+	2.18	1.03	1.77
F score	4.61	5.88	7.69
Significance	0.003	0.001	0.000
Wife			
0–6	1.42	0.50	1.03
7–9	2.14	.98	1.51
10–11	2.56	1.15	1.89
12+	2.46	1.21	2.03
F Score	13.53	17.32	10.53
Significance	0.000	0.000	0.000

Source: Author's survey data, 2001.

Both the husband and wife participate in the family celebrations and holidays more often than in other forms of social interaction included in the survey, as would be expected. Neither the husband nor wife could be considered highly participatory in any form of activity, but this applies particularly outside the household. The lowest levels of education also have the lowest mean participation, and this is true for both husbands and wives in the survey.

For family celebrations and holidays, husbands (who are the main income earners in the households) with twelve or more years of education participate at a lower rate than husbands who only completed grades 7–9, which might be explained by the fact those with more education are busy with their jobs, household businesses, or other activities. The highest rate of participation is for husbands who completed ten or eleven years of education. For celebrations of friends and neighbors, there are very low rates of participation, with the highest in the 10–11 grade category, which equates to "very rarely." The same pattern is true for village celebrations and holidays, although the means are somewhat higher than for participation with friends and neighbors. All the findings are statistically significant at the 100 percent level of confidence for the husband.

For wives in the survey, those who only completed up to sixth grade participate in each of the three types of celebrations about one-half as much as a wife with twelve or more years of education. For family celebrations and holidays, wives with ten to eleven years of education have the highest mean, which decreases slightly with twelve or more years. Similar to husbands, mean participation rates decline dramatically outside the home and are lowest for celebrations and holidays of friends and

Table 8 5

Mean Levels of Participation by Income Category

Income as percent of subsistence level	Family celebrations and holidays	Celebrations and holidays of friends/ neighbors	Village celebrations and holidays
0–49	2.20	1.82	1.03
50–75	1.95	1.56	0.88
76–90	2.33	1.69	1.12
91–99	2.43	1.80	0.84
100–110	2.25	1.72	1.19
111–125	2.79	2.05	1.28
126–150	2.73	2.27	1.56
151–175	2.46	1.85	1.12
176–190	2.71	1.00	0.86
191–200	2.83	1.83	1.17
201+	3.09	1.91	1.42
Total mean	2.29	1.76	1.06
F Score	2.87	1.69	2.10
Significance	0.002	0.078	0.022

Source: Author's survey data, 2001.

neighbors. However, wives with twelve or more years of education have the highest mean for celebrations and holidays of friends and neighbors. For celebrations and holidays in the village, the mean participation rates increase, with wives having twelve or more years of education participating the most. However, even with a mean of 2.0, this equates to a response of "very rarely."

Turning to income, two-tailed significance tests show that monthly per capita income is positively correlated with participation in family, friends/neighbors, and village celebrations and holidays. This finding conforms to Putnam's argument that "one's income is determined by the range of his or her social connections, perhaps even more than by educational credentials" (Putnam 2002, 7). However, the correlation between per capita income and participation is statistically significant only for family celebrations and holidays ($p = .003$). The other correlations are signed positively but not statistically significant at the minimum 0.05 level of confidence.

Concerning the distribution of means of participation, an interval of monthly per capita monetary income was created. The intervals represent different percentages of the subsistence level in 2001, when the survey was taken. This allows a view of how economic status affects rates of participation, and the results are shown in Table 8.5.

The first trend to note in Table 8.5 is a confirmation of previous findings that interaction within the household is most prevalent, with a mean of 2.29, followed by participation with friends and neighbors with a mean of 1.76, and then participation in the village, with a mean of 1.06. Once again, this confirms the fact that individuals are not highly participatory, with responses equating to "never" or "very rarely."

A second trend is a general increase in the propensity to participate in family celebrations and holidays as monthly income increases. There is more or less a linear increase in participation as income rises. Individuals with monthly incomes of 201 percent or more of the subsistence level participate the most and are significantly above the mean. The distribution of means is statistically significant, with more than a 99 percent level of confidence, and so we are assured that the findings are real. It should be noted, however, that even the highest-income individuals are not highly participatory, with a response mean that equates to "rarely."

The general trend of rising income equating to rising participation is not true for celebrations and holidays of friends/neighbors or in the village. For these two forms of interaction, rising income does not appear to have much of an impact at all, since no real patterns emerge. For village-level participation, the distribution of means is statistically significant with a 98 percent level of confidence, while for family/friends the mean is at the 93 percent level of confidence, which is very close to the accepted minimum of 95 percent. For celebrations and holidays of friends/neighbors or in the village, the fact that poorer individuals do not interact at significantly lower rates is somewhat surprising, because one might expect that higher rates of interaction would be linked to economic need and the receipt of assistance.

Conclusion

Does a rural civil society exist in Russia? Is a rural civil society emerging? Is there a basis for optimism about the trends in rural civil society? To address these questions, this chapter examined three aspects of rural civil society: attitudes, organizations, and behavior (social capital). The general arguments were threefold. First, our knowledge about rural civil society is fragmentary and incomplete; this chapter serves merely as a starting point for future research and has defined some of the important issues for that research to consider.

Second, in contrast to Lipset's hypothesis about the link between modernization and civil society, although rural Russia is at the lower end of the education and income scale for the nation, there does appear to be at least some evidence that the basic prerequisites for the development of civil society exist. Although a lower level of socioeconomic modernization is found among Russia's rural population, that does not appear to pose an insuperable obstacle to the growth of civil society, especially in terms of attitudes. The discussion here has shown that since 1993, rural Russians have generally been more trusting of political actors and institutions than the urban population. The data in Table 8.1 on political trust indicate considerable variance over time and show sensitivity to policy outcomes and leadership personalities, and therefore the question is whether levels of trust will become more stable and less variable to the outside political environment. In terms of nongovernmental organizations, it has been shown that NGOs are promoting reform and instilling values that are consistent with the development of civil society. The question about organizations is one of scale and impact. Relatively few organizations exist to serve the rural population. The few that do find their capacities restricted by shortages in resources, both human and financial, and therefore their impact is limited. Whether human and financial resources are maintained at current levels, increase, or decrease due to donor fatigue is an open question for the future.

With regard to social behavior and social capital, in contrast, the primary pattern is that personal relations continue to dominate, meaning that social networks among family members are much stronger than with outsiders. In short, the "anti-modern" networks analyzed by Richard Rose (2000) are confirmed by the findings herein. What is surprising is not so much that participation is greater within the household, but that there is very little participation outside the household, showing that impersonal networks are extremely undeveloped. This is likely to be a carryover effect from the Soviet period, during which "outsiders" were not to be trusted. In the contemporary period, however, this legacy has both social and economic effects. Limited social networks affect household welfare and income. Specifically, social networks have demonstrated effects on household food production, food sales, mood, and household business activities (O'Brien, Patsiorkovski, and Dershem 2000).

Within the general pattern of personal networks, relations, and interaction, some variance was discovered in examining different independent variables. In answer to the question of who participates, the following portrait emerged: males tend to participate more, as do persons who are younger, have a higher education, and have higher income levels. Although one would like the number of respondents to be larger for some of the variables, the fact that the results were statistically significant assures us that the findings were real and not merely a statistical aberration.[10]

The general conclusion is that there are reasons for cautious optimism about the development of civil society, as some basic preconditions exist in rural Russia. Lacking longitudinal data, trends in the development of civil society cannot be tracked; and one can only surmise that the level of civil society in 2001 (the time of the survey) was greater than in 1991, although that is not assured. At the same time, there are reasons for cautious optimism, although significant obstacles exist, and Russia is far from having consolidated a civil society as is understood in the West. The crucial question for the future is whether the aspects of civil society described herein represent the apex of rural civil society or a step along the continuum of further development. Only time will tell.

Notes

1. The survey data presented in this chapter are drawn from research funded by a grant from the National Council for Eurasian and East European Research, grant number 816–14g.
2. On voting cleavages, see Berezkin, Myagkov, and Ordeshook 1999, 395–406; and Clem and Craumer 2002, 1–12. On differences in attitudes, see Hough, Davidheiser, and Lehmann 1996; and Colton 2000.
3. I owe this point to the editors of this volume.
4. Sarah Henderson claims that only 2 percent of donations to Russian NGOs come from private contributions. See Henderson 2003, chap. 2, which explores the development of NGOs in Russia and surveys the obstacles they confront.

5. See the postings on NGOs by Sarah Henderson and John Squier in Johnson's Russia List, nos. 7051 and 7053—February 6, 2003, and February 7, 2003, respectively. Available at www.cdi.org/russia/johnson.

6. In the early 1990s, virtually every private farmer was a member of AKKOR, and AKKOR's newspaper published information on the organization. Starting in 1996, the private farmer movement became much more difficult to follow in detail with the closing of its weekly newspaper, *Rossiiskii fermer*. Therefore, it is difficult to quantify national membership in AKKOR after the mid-1990s. I have seen no references to membership in published reports covering AKKOR's annual congresses.

7. A survey found an average of 1.4 members per farm, 0.7 family members per farm, and 1.3 hired workers per farm, for a total of 3.4 persons per farm. That average per farm was then multiplied by the number of registered farms to arrive at a total labor force. See Smirnov 2003, 34. For somewhat lower estimates of the private farm labor force, see Goskomstat 2000, 36.

8. Unless otherwise noted, all information about this center was obtained from Aleksei Pulin, director of the center, through conversations and correspondence. In 2002, the personnel of the center consisted of three legal experts and an accountant.

9. The Alpha reliability of the three dependent variables is 0.73, which is fairly strong, indicating that there is co-linearity and assuring us that we are measuring the same phenomenon across variables.

10. For example, in the sample used in the analysis, only 11 percent (eighty-six people) were aged eighteen to twenty-nine; and of those, only twenty-one were males. This outcome reflects demographic realities of rural Russia, from which the young and males have among the highest out-migration rates. A total of sixty-six persons were males under the age of forty. Only 4.6 percent of the sample had a monthly income level twice or more the subsistence level. Attainment of education, a legacy of the Soviet period, was somewhat better, as 47 percent of husbands and 39 percent of wives had twelve or more years of education.

References

Almond, Gabriel A., and Sidney Verba. 1965. *The Civic Culture: Political Attitudes and Democracy in Five Nations*. Boston: Little, Brown.

Berezkin, Andrei, Mikhail Myagkov, and Peter Ordeshook. 1999. "The Urban–Rural Divide in the Russian Electorate and the Effect of Distance from Urban Centers." *Post-Soviet Geography and Economics* 40, no. 6 (September): 395–406.

Clem, Ralph S., and Peter R. Craumer. 2002. "Urban and Rural Effects on Party Preference in Russia: New Evidence from the Recent Duma Election." *Post-Soviet Geography and Economics* 43, no. 1 (January): 1–12.

Colton, Timothy J. 2000. *Transitional Citizens: Voters and What Influences Them in the New Russia*. Cambridge, MA: Harvard University Press.

Colton, Timothy J., and Michael McFaul. 2003. *Popular Choice and Managed Democracy: The Russian Elections of 1999 and 2000*. Washington, DC: Brookings Institution.

Eckstein, Harry, Frederick J. Fleron, Erik P. Hoffman, and William M. Reisinger. 1998. *Can Democracy Take Root in Post-Soviet Russia: Explorations in State–Society Relations*. Lanham, MD: Rowman and Littlefield.

Fish, M. Steven. 1995. *Democracy from Scratch: Opposition and Regime in the New Russian Revolution*. Princeton, NJ: Princeton University Press.

Goskomstat. 1989. *Biudzhet vremeni naseleniia SSSR*. Moscow.

———. 2000. *Sel'skokhoziaistvennaia deiatel'nost' krest'ianskikh (fermerskikh) khoziaistv v Rossii*. Moscow.

Henderson, Sarah. 2003. *Building Democracy in Contemporary Russia: Western Support for Grassroots Organizations*. Ithaca, NY: Cornell University Press.

Hough, Jerry F., Evelyn Davidheiser, and Susan Goodrich Lehmann. 1996. *The 1996 Russian Presidential Election*. Washington, DC: Brookings Institution.

Linz, Juan J., and Alfred Stepan. 1996. *Problems of Democratic Transition and Consolidation: Southern Europe, South America, and Post-Communist Europe*. Baltimore, MD: Johns Hopkins University Press.

Lipset, Seymour Martin. 1960. *Political Man: The Social Bases of Politics*. Garden City, NY: Doubleday.

———. 1994. "The Social Requisites of Democracy Revisited," *American Sociological Review* 59, no. 1 (February): 1–22.

Morozov, Andrei. 2004. Interview, Moscow, May 24.

O'Brien, David J., Valeri V. Patsiorkovski, and Larry D. Dershem. 2000. *Household Capital and the Agrarian Problem in Russia*. Aldershot, UK: Ashgate.

Pulin, Aleksei. 2003. Correspondence and conversations, February–March.

Putnam, Robert D. 1993. *Making Democracy Work: Civic Traditions in Modern Italy*. Princeton, NJ: Princeton University Press.

Putnam, Robert D., ed. 2002. *Democracies in Flux: The Evolution of Social Capital in Contemporary Society*. Oxford: Oxford University Press.

Rose, Richard. 2000. "Uses of Social Capital in Russia: Modern, Pre-modern, and Anti-modern," *Post-Soviet Affairs* 16, no. 1 (January–March): 33–57.

Smirnov, V. D. 2003. *Fermerstvo v Rossii—chto eto takoe*. Novosibirsk: Russian Academy of Sciences.

USAID annual NGO report. 2001. "2001 NGO Sustainability Index." www.usaid.gov/regions/europe_eurasia/dem_gov/ngoindex/.

Van Atta, Don, ed. 1993. *The Farmer Threat: The Political Economy of Agrarian Reform in Post-Soviet Russia*. Boulder, CO: Westview Press.

Wegren, Stephen K. 1996. "Rural Politics and Agrarian Reform in Russia." *Problems of Post-Communism* 43, no. 1 (January–February): 23–34.

———. 1998. *Agriculture and the State in Soviet and Post-Soviet Russia*. Pittsburgh, PA: Pittsburgh University Press.

———. 2003. "The Rise, Fall, and Transformation of the Rural Social Contract." *Communist and Post-Communist Studies* 36, no. 1 (March): 1–27.

World Bank. 2003. *Local Self-Governance and Civic Engagement in Rural Russia*. Washington, DC.

9

Vladimir Putin's Design for Civil Society

Alfred B. Evans, Jr.

It is often assumed that Russia has had a continuous tradition of authoritarian rule characterized by a strong, dominant state and a weak, submissive society, but the previous chapters in this volume have presented evidence of a more complex pattern of interaction between state and society. Though undoubtedly the successive states that have established their authority in Russia have all been essentially authoritarian, and the country's rare experiments in democracy at the national level have proved to be short-lived, Russian citizens repeatedly have shown the capacity for organizing cooperative endeavors and devising ingenious ways of achieving their objectives. In fact, the relationship between state and society has varied greatly among different periods in the history of Russia. The consensus of a large number of scholars reinforces the conclusion that elements of civil society have emerged with surprising vigor in Russia in those periods when the relaxation of control by the state has given citizens the opportunity to engage in self-organization.

As we have seen, under Gorbachev the extraordinarily rapid proliferation of the "informal" groups dispelled previous impressions of the passivity of Soviet citizens and encouraged the most optimistic observers in the West to predict the imminent appearance of a full-blown civil society in Russia. Despite the disintegration of the USSR and the fall of the power of the Communist Party in Russia, however, by the middle of the 1990s civil society in Russia was weak, and independent social or nongovernmental organizations had been consigned to a marginal status in society and politics. It seemed as if almost everything that could have gone wrong for such organizations had gone wrong in the immediate postcommunist years, as citizens' distrust of such organizations persisted, a deep decline in the economy left most citizens preoccupied with the struggle for survival, and political leaders made deliberate efforts to discourage citizen mobilization and reward insider connections. Mobilizing substantial numbers of people as members of nongovernmental organizations (NGOs) or volunteers in their campaigns seemed impossible to most NGO activists. The apparent boom of civil society in the late 1980s had been followed by a slump in the first decade of postcommunist politics.Though civil society in Russia was weak by the beginning of the twenty-first century, it had survived, in part because the leaders of many groups had displayed considerable resilience and resourcefulness. Hundreds of thousands of NGOs continued to function even under generally adverse conditions, and new organizations appeared each year.

Civil Society under Putin

After Vladimir Putin became president of Russia, scholars debated the nature of his intentions for the Russian political system.[1] Recently a consensus concerning the general character of Putin's administration has formed, as his actions have increasingly made his goals clear. In the words of Michael McFaul (2004), Putin "has undermined every independent source of political power" in Russia during the past few years. For a while, some analysts invented terms such as "managed democracy" or "virtual democracy" to try to capture the complexity of Putin's design. Now more would find Gordon Hahn's (2004) description of Putin's "stealth authoritarianism" or Aleksei Zudin's (2003) concept of Putin's "monocentrism" to be accurate portrayals. The real question is no longer whether Putin wants to decrease the degree of pluralism in the Russian polity, or whether he can successfully manipulate political forces to make that possible, since the answers to both those questions are obviously affirmative; the real challenge for researchers is to discern the contours of the structures that Putin seeks to construct. There is no evidence that Putin has a detailed blueprint of the political system that he wants to shape; he has explicitly disavowed the idea of an official state ideology.

It is clear that Putin is determined to strengthen the Russian state and enhance Russia's status as a respected power, and that he regards economic growth and internal order as necessary means to those ends. Putin's style is to implement his plans cautiously and gradually, often using indirect methods of discouraging independent criticism, while ostensibly endorsing democracy and the rule of law. Hahn is also correct in observing that Putin seeks "a hegemonic rather than a monopolistic centralization of power," so that many groups and institutions that retain token independence, remaining formally outside the vertical executive hierarchy of the state, have become (or will become) part of the base of support for the administrative structures headed by Putin. It is also part of Putin's mode of operation to offer rewards for organizations that are integrated into his pyramid of support, while he makes it clear, usually by deeds rather than words and often in a manner that makes it possible for him to deny responsibility, that there will be penalties for resisting subordination to centralized authority. It should be noted that key features of Boris Yeltsin's system of governance, especially the dominance of the institution of the presidency (Fish 2001) and the premium placed on personal relationships radiating from the president himself (Breslauer 2001), helped set the stage for Putin's moves. Also, popular bitterness toward the privileges of the oligarchs and rampant crime and corruption under Yeltsin created causes that Putin could exploit in order to win support. Within a few years after becoming president, Putin was able to decrease pluralism in the mass media in Russia, curtail the independence of the regional governors, ensure that the national parliament would accept his leadership with docility, and intimidate the "oligarchs" of the business world so that they would not stand in the way of his political moves.

Already during Putin's first term in office it became clear that journalists and environmentalists who were too critical of the government's actions in the most sensitive areas of policy would be subject to harassment or prison sentences. Most recently Putin has stepped up his efforts to integrate nongovernmental organizations into his system of comprehensive support. An early indication of Putin's wishes was the announcement in 2001 that a Civic Forum would be convened in Moscow in November of that year, so that five thousand representatives of NGOs could meet with government officials. The original purpose of that gathering apparently was to integrate "civil society organizations throughout Russia into a single corporatist body that would allow them an official consultative role with the government" (Squier 2002, 177). Social organizations would sacrifice their independence in order to gain institutionalized consultation of their interests and a share of the benefits allocated by the state. After vocal complaints from many social activists, the government backed away from efforts at the immediate implementation of that plan, and while some NGO leaders refused to take part in the conference, others saw it as an opportunity to bring their concerns to the attention of the political leadership. If the results of the Civic Forum were a temporary setback for Putin and his lieutenants, it did not deter them from a patient attempt to use the means at their disposal, including the legal, administrative, and financial tools in the hands of the state, to make it gradually more difficult for existing NGOs to operate independently of government domination. At the same time, while some social organizations resisted co-optation by the state, a growing number of groups that were informally dubbed "government-organized nongovernmental organizations," or GONGOs, appeared (Nikitin and Buchanan 2002, 149). While Putin has made many statements giving token endorsement for the development of civil society, it is now apparent that his vision is of a quasi-civil society (or, some would argue, a pseudo-civil society) in which social organizations are subordinated to the authority of the state and express demands within the parameters of the program of the highest executive leadership. While groups that resist integration into the centralized system may risk prosecution in the courts or denial of registration, for most of them the real penalty will be irrelevance, as they will be consigned to a marginal political status and denied a voice in influencing the shaping of policies (Lipman 2005).

Putin has shown a preference for organizations that share his enthusiasm for a strong state, nationalistic themes, and traditional Russian values. In his state-of-the-nation address to the national parliament in May 2004, though he repeatedly endorsed the idea of civil society (or paid lip service to that term) and acknowledged that "many citizens' associations in Russia are working constructively," Putin complained that for some social organizations the priority is "obtaining funding from influential foreign or domestic foundations," and for others it is "servicing dubious group and commercial interests" (Putin 2004a). His criticism seemed to be aimed at NGOs that are supported by international funding sources and organizations that receive support from oligarchs who have earned the disfavor of the Kremlin. He implicitly linked criticism of the Russian state by domestic human rights groups with the machinations of external forces that allegedly are inimical to Russian national strength. It should be noted that Putin's speech highlighted a previously tacit policy of putting pressure on human rights groups with foreign ties that had been in effect for at least two years before Putin's pronouncement. During the same period, the Russian government had terminated the U.S. Peace Corps program, expelled the head of the AFL/CIO affiliate in Moscow, and pressed dubious charges against Russian researchers and journalists who were accused of having revealed state secrets to foreign governments.

The pressure on groups that were seen by the political leadership as troublemakers was intensified perceptibly after Putin's remarks. Putin's speech was soon followed by a statement from Gleb Pavlovskii (Saenko 2004), an important adviser to the government, in which Pavlovskii accused human rights advocates of a conflict of interests, saying that their striving for Western grants had led them to accept foreign conceptions of rights and forget about protecting the interests of Russian citizens. A few weeks later, in an interview in *Rossiiskaia gazeta*, Pavlovskii (2004) dismissed the notion that civil society should be a force opposing the political regime and characterized Russian human rights groups as "dissident organizations" that are archaic, since in his view they do not form a genuine civil society and do not solve any social problems. The Ministry of Foreign Affairs accused humanitarian organizations in Chechnya of using their missions to cover up anti-Russian activities (Pravda.ru 2004). Ominously, masked men entered the offices of the Human Rights Center in the city of Kazan in central Russia and smashed computers and other equipment (Birch 2004). By September, Catherine Fitzpatrick (2004) reported that Putin's major address in May had been followed "by months of articles placed in pro-government newspapers and various propagandistic interventions at public meetings and abroad attacking the human rights movement as 'unconstructive.'" In late September, Vladislav Surkov, deputy head of the presidential administration, warned of the activities of a shadowy "fifth column of left and right radicals united by a common hatred for 'Putin's Russia,' as they call it, and shared foreign backers," and accused such people of seeking "the defeat of their own country in the war on terror" (RFE/RL 2004a). Surkov's remarks reinforced the impression that xenophobia was being used to direct suspicion toward groups that voiced criticism of the government.

Soon after Putin's state of the nation speech, the regime's ideas for supervising existing social organizations became clearer when the Ministry of the Interior, which commands the regular police, announced a plan to assign police representatives to all rights groups, ostensibly to promote cooperation and prompt responses to citizens' complaints, but in the view of leaders of such groups, with the implicit purpose of placing them under supervision by the government. In June, Russian Foreign Minister Sergei Lavrov met with representatives of forty-eight NGOs, including a number known for their support of the government and none who are highly critical of official policies, to call on them to work with the government to promote Russian interests abroad and "help create a positive image of Russia outside the country" (Mereu 2004). While ostensibly calling for dialogue and cooperation with civil society,

Lavrov clearly suggested that nongovernmental organizations should serve Russia's national interests as interpreted by the Russian state and should refrain from actions that would tarnish Russia's image. In July 2004, the government submitted draft legislation to the lower house of the national parliament that would regulate the process by which domestic and foreign donors may assist nongovernmental organizations (Yablokova 2004). The proposed law would require foreign governments and foundations to register each grant made to a Russian NGO with a special government commission. Russian organizations that want to support NGOs would have to be included on a government list of approved donors or their grants would be subject to a 24 percent tax. Leaders of some Russian NGOs saw the proposed legislation as another step toward tightening the state's control of social organizations, which would narrow the list of approved organizations and give local officials more opportunities to interfere in their work (Il'ichev 2004).

Putin's outlook was epitomized by his speech to federal ministers and regional officials on September 13, 2004, in the wake of a series of terrorist attacks that had climaxed with the tragic events at Beslan in early September (Putin 2004b). He warned that terrorism posed the threat of the disintegration of Russia and that the proper response should be to strengthen the Russian state. Building on his favorite theme, he emphasized even more explicitly than before the imperative of tightening the vertical structuring of power, saying that "the bodies of executive authority in the center and constituent parts of the Russian Federation will be formed by a single system of authority," and that those executive organs "must work as a single integrated organism with a clear structure of subordination." He added another detail of his design for civil society, suggesting that it would be worthwhile to set up a "Public Chamber" (*obshchestvennaia palata*, which also may be translated as "social chamber") "as a platform for extensive dialogue, where citizens' initiatives could be presented and discussed in detail." In December, Putin submitted the bill on the Public Chamber to the Duma. The draft legislation specifies that the president will choose forty-two members of the chamber, who will then pick forty-two more members. The eighty-four members of the chamber who have been chosen in that manner will select the remaining forty-two members (Farizova 2004). The decisions of the Public Chamber will have the status of recommendations to the government. The bill on the Public Chamber was adopted by the Duma on March 16, 2005, and was approved by the Federation Council on March 23. Putin signed the law on April 4. (RIA Novosti 2005). So Putin wants the state to establish an institution for dialogue with society, evidently a controlled forum that will serve as a substitute for the articulation of citizens' demands by independent social groups (and in the absence of meaningful competition among parties or a major role for the parliament in representing competing interests). Ekho Moskvy Radio reported in January 2005, however, that some well-known human rights activists had denounced the proposal to create the Public Chamber as "an attempt to create a dummy of a civil society," as part of Putin's plan of reinforcing "the vertical chain of command" by building civil society from the top down (BBC Monitoring 2005).

Most paradoxically, in his speech of September 13, 2004, Putin proposed that as part of the security services' work in cooperation with citizens, and as a means of helping people "learn how to conduct themselves appropriately in emergencies," the state should "support citizens' initiatives in setting up voluntary structures to maintain public order." It seems implicit from the context of those remarks in his speech that the state, and particularly the security agencies including the Federal Security Service (FSB), would help give direction to the "citizens' initiatives," and that the "voluntary structures" to be formed would operate under the guidance of those state agencies. In addition, in November 2004 the government of Russia announced that it planned to revive the GTO (Ready for Work and Defense) program for young people, with military training, sports, rallies, and clubs (RFE/RL 2004b). The original GTO program had been familiar to citizens of the Soviet Union, since it had been created in the 1930s under Stalin. The revival of the GTO indicates that under Putin the Russian government continues efforts to expand the network of GONGOs. In summary, though the structures of Putin's system are still emerging and many details of that system remain unclear, recent statements and actions by the political leadership have reinforced the evidence that the Putin administration speaks of the need for a vigorous civil society but interprets civil society as a network of organizations that, while remaining technically outside the state, will be co-opted to assist the leadership of the political regime in pursuing the objectives that it has chosen for society. The compliant social organizations envisioned by Putin would constitute not a genuine civil society but a quasi-civil society.

Civil Society in Russia between the Past and the Future

The background provided by the earlier chapters in this volume should help the reader place Putin's machinations in context both in relation to the history of the interaction between state and society in Russian history and in relation to the condition of civil society in contemporary, postcommunist Russia. The relationship between state and society has varied dramatically among distinct periods of Russian history, with society having greater autonomy in some periods, such as the late tsarist decades and the years of the disintegration of Communist Party control, and the state suppressing the independence of social organizations in other periods, with the Stalin era as the most extreme example. A major lesson to be learned from the historical background is that the relationship between state and society has fluctuated periodically in Russia, with a great impact on the opportunities for citizens to form self-governing associations. Another lesson is that in different and widely separated periods Russian citizens have proved themselves as capable as any others in the world of creating and leading the organizations that constitute a vibrant civil society. That is a lesson that has been retained in the historical memory of the people of Russia, and it is not likely that it can be effaced.

Vladimir Putin's outlook on the relationship between state and society must also be placed in historical context. Putin is generally said to be a pragmatist, but as our

PUTIN'S DESIGN FOR CIVIL SOCIETY 153

analysis of his emerging design for Russian society has suggested, when he confronts a policy problem, he instinctively frames the answer in terms of relationships of dominance and subordination. Putin's expectations for the structuring of authority in the state and society are rooted in familiar, deeply ingrained tendencies in Russian history. Lilia Shevtsova (2004) has aptly said that Putin prefers "to remain within the framework of traditionalism," which for him means "returning to a state which stands over society." After 1991, it was widely supposed that Russia had begun a departure from that tradition, so it may be surprising to some observers that Putin has been successful in imposing increasingly authoritarian rule by curtailing the autonomy of a wide range of institutions. The explanation for that change must be found not only in the wide sweep of Russian history but also (and even more) in the conditions that were established by the end of the 1990s.

The trend of the growing concentration of power and the constriction of political pluralism under Vladimir Putin has been possible in part because of the weak institutionalization of civil society in postcommunist Russia. The weakness of civil society and its feeble capacity to check the power of the state help explain Putin's success in brushing aside obstacles to his increasing domination of the political system while encountering little effective resistance. The most prominent theorists of civil society and democracy argue that independent organizations of citizens are important not only for representing the interests of social groups but also for limiting the reach of the government. Russia in this decade would seem to furnish support for that thesis with an example of change in the negative direction, as significant gains in democratization are being reversed by the second administration of postcommunist executive leadership. One reason for the weakness of civil society and the marginal status of most organizations of citizens in Russia at the time that Putin came to power was the "superpresidentialism" that had developed under Yeltsin in the 1990s. As Steven Fish (2001) has emphasized, the extreme dominance of the institution of the presidency and the relative lack of importance of political parties and the parliament under Yeltsin diminished the incentives for groups to mobilize popular support and engage in traditional forms of lobbying, since the only way to achieve significant influence on policy was by cultivating personal connections with insiders in the executive leadership. As Fish has expressed it, "a superpresidential system tends to encourage the formation of small, closed, compact societal organizations that are adept at applying pressure on and currying favor with individuals in ministries and other executive-branch agencies" (ibid., 22).

Thus political factors as well as the economic and cultural factors reviewed in other chapters of this book ensured that by the time Putin took power, most active social organizations in Russia that were committed to democratic values were elite, professionalized structures with tenuous grounding in their natural constituencies. Since groups that are most likely to challenge the tendency toward more authoritarian techniques of governance, such as feminist organizations, environmentalists, and human rights advocates, lack broad popular followings, they have been unable to mobilize popular resistance to Putin's movement toward monocentrism. Moreover, many of those organizations depend heavily on financial assistance from Western sources, which has led them to neglect the need to build a base of domestic support and has left them vulnerable to the charge that they are serving the will of foreign masters. (Laura Henry's chapter [13, note 9] in this collection points out that in 1999, even before coming to power as president, Putin complained that "foreign secret service organizations not only use diplomatic cover but also very actively use all sorts of ecological and public organizations.") Social organizations with active participants consisting almost exclusively of elite activists may rather easily be marginalized by the political regime and replaced with surrogate associations sponsored by the state. One factor that limited the growth of civil society before Putin came to power was the dominance of interest-driven politics by the oligarchs whose close connections with key leaders in government have inhibited the representation of other interests. Peter Rutland's chapter in this volume (chapter 5) makes it apparent that the business elite's reliance on personal relationships with top executive leaders and the oligarchs' emphasis on the pursuit of individual goals rather than the forging of associational linkages for the achievement of common objectives left them vulnerable to being picked off with almost embarrassing ease by Putin, one at a time, when he had consolidated his power sufficiently.

In historical perspective, it is possible to discern significant contrasts between Putin's design for the relationship between state and society and the pattern that was established by the Communists from 1918 to the mid-1930s. The Communists virtually absorbed society into the state, by creating a web of "public" associations that preempted the entire field of formal social organization, were controlled in detail by the Communist Party, and were financed by compulsory membership dues and subsidies from the state. Putin seeks to dominate society but not to absorb it completely, partly because he does not want the state to shoulder full responsibility for providing material resources to all nongovernmental organizations. Also, unlike the Bolsheviks, Putin is not inspired by an ideology that calls for comprehensive social transformation. He has shown a tendency to create some key GONGOs, while manipulating rewards and punishments to ensure compliance from existing groups and marginalizing other groups that attempt to preserve their independence (Lipman 2005). The changes that Putin is introducing are probably not altogether unwelcome to many social organizations. Many organizations that are already dependent on one or another level of government for crucial assistance may not notice much difference in the near future, and some of those probably hope to benefit from slightly more generous allocations of support (Weir 2004).

From the opposite standpoint, organizations that are committed to a role of advocacy that often brings them into an adversarial relationship with the government authorities will face more unfavorable conditions. They are already being subjected to tighter restrictions and are often stigmatized as unpatriotic, especially if they receive funding from abroad or from Russian oligarchs who are not on good terms with the Putin leadership. (Funding for such organizations from Western governments and foundations is already decreasing, and the oligarchs who remain at large are increasingly subservient to the wishes of the central leadership, so support for advocacy organizations will probably continue to dwindle.) There are already signs that advocates of values that are not favored by the government will be consigned to the role of "dissident" groups. If they are not suppressed by the regime, they will play a marginal role in the political system and will have very little impact on the policies of the government. Organizations that have initiated projects evoking substantial support from the public and receiving favorable attention from the government will run the risk of seeing members of the political elite co-opt their causes and impose subtle changes in their objectives, which may divert those groups from the pursuit of some of their original goals. The social organizations that are created by the state and those that come to terms with it will downplay policy advocacy, especially the open expression of controversial positions, and will see their main mission as providing services for the population and mustering mass support for government policies.

Though Putin's emerging design for state–society relations differs in some significant respects from that put in place by the Soviet Communists, it may also be subject to the same fundamental internal contradictions that created chronic problems for mass organizations in the USSR. Putin has proved largely successful in narrowing the boundaries for the expression of competing interests arising from Russian society, but he cannot eliminate the root causes of pluralism in that society. One of the main lessons to be learned from the history of civil society in tsarist Russia and the Soviet Union is that over time, economic modernization, along with higher levels of education and urbanization, ensures the growth of a more complex and diverse social structure, giving rise to a growing pluralism of groups and interests. (It should be noted that contemporary Russia is at a much higher level of economic development and technological complexity than Soviet Russia in the 1920s and 1930s, not to speak of the tsarist empire in its last decades.) Tsarist Russia tolerated and at times encouraged the creation of social organizations that reflected that pluralism, but the leadership of the empire attempted to block the representation of those interests at the national level. The Soviet regime embraced a pattern of multifaceted social organization but sought to direct all groups toward the achievement of common goals set by the political leadership. Both variants ultimately proved to be political failures, despite distinct successes by some social organizations and activists in delivering valuable benefits to citizens. If Putin's government subordinates all nonstate organizations to its domination, as it seems determined to do, it will find that the system that it has structured must encompass social pluralism and build channels for the representation of diverse interests stemming from society.

Thus Putin's quasi-civil society seems fated to face the same inherent contradiction from which the Soviet system suffered, since it is likely that organizations that are manipulated by the national political leadership will lack credibility with their members and will fail to provide adequate mechanisms for voicing the demands of the constituencies whose interests they are supposed to represent. In early 2005, protests by Russian pensioners who were angered by their loss of benefits such as free public transportation served to illustrate the consequences of the withering of political competition under Putin (Corwin 2005). The protestors complained that the increases in cash allowances from the state did not adequately compensate for the cost of services that formerly were provided to them for free. During January and February 2005, protest demonstrations took place in eighty of Russia's eighty-nine regions, persisted for over four weeks, and forced the government to back down from some of the changes that it had introduced. It might have been predicted that the ineffectuality of institutionalized channels of representation of interests and the lack of opportunities for meaningful debate over policy proposals would increase the importance of spontaneous direct action by citizens as a means of expressing popular demands.

That interpretation is supported by assessments from some well-informed Russian observers. Explaining the reasons for the protests in January 2005, Vladimir Lukin, the frustrated human rights ombudsman of the Russian Federation, decried the problem of "an acute shortage of feedback mechanisms between the authorities and the public" (Tsepliaev 2005), while Nikolai Petrov of the Moscow Carnegie Foundation charged that "by usurping all power and eliminating normal channels of opposition in the political system, the Kremlin has lost an important 'safety valve' and cut itself off from public opinion" (Bransten 2005). The probability that current trends will encounter the contradiction between the imperatives of control from the top down and initiative from the bottom up is implied by Putin's own statements, as his words suggest that he wants to have it both ways by combining an integrated system of control with a genuine dialogue between leaders and the public. The comparison of the Soviet experience with the history of democratic political systems teaches that only groups that can bring independent resources to bear in their relationship with political authority can provide genuine representation for diverse social interests to a degree that will satisfy the expectations of a pluralistic society. A crucial question is whether the Putin leadership has the capacity to learn from the problems engendered by its strategy, or whether criticism of its policies will only encourage it to adopt more stringent means of silencing its critics.

In Putin's Russia, if the state distributes valuable assets only to loyal nongovernmental organizations, and if public debate and political competition are restricted by the national leadership, we may be sure that the importance of personal connections with individuals in positions of power will be reinforced. If, in Valerie Sperling's terms, politics in Russia now "center[s] around individual," (chapter 10), that feature is likely to become more pronounced as accountability to the public decreases even further because of a lack of political competition and open criticism. Also, we may confidently predict that if Putin's design is institutionalized, the corruption that he so bitterly decries will continue, since comparative analysis confirms that a high level of corruption is closely associated with the predominance of patron–client ties in politics. Though for understandable reasons most Russians now believe that Putin promises stability and security, if he continues along the path he has taken, in the long run the cynicism concerning the public sphere, the psychological withdrawal into a narrow private sphere, and "the lack of a culture of free collective activity" that Smolar (1996, 33) depicted as the heritage of Communist systems in the Soviet Union and Eastern Europe may be recognized as the ultimate cultural legacy of Putin's attempt to subordinate civil society to the state. Thus the long-term stability of the regime that he is consolidating is still very much open to question. And one can at least see the basis for Lilia Shevtsova's (2004) warning that "modernization by way of reform from above and by subordinating society to the state can do nothing but keep development in stagnation."

Notes

The author would like to thank Blair Ruble, Valerie Sperling, and his fellow editors for their helpful comments on an earlier draft of this chapter.
1. Parts of this section also appear in this author's chapter, "Civil Society in Russia?" in *Developments in Soviet Politics 6*, ed. Stephen White, Zvi Gitelman, and Richard Sakwa, Durham, NC: Duke University Press, 2005).

References

BBC Monitoring. 2005. "Rights Campaigners Blast Moscow's Public Forum Bill." January 12.
Birch, Douglas. 2004. "Putin Criticizes Human Rights Groups. A Day Later, An Attack Smashes the Office of an Activist Group." *Baltimore Sun*, May 29.
Bonnell, Victoria E., and George W. Breslauer. 2001. *Russia in the New Century: Stability or Disorder?* Boulder, CO: Westview Press.
Bransten, Jeremy. 2005. "Is Putin's Magic Wearing Off?" *RFE/RL Russian Political Weekly*. Vol. 5, no. 3, January 20.
Breslauer, George. 2001. "Personalism Versus Proceduralism: Boris Yeltsin and the Institutional Fragility of the Russian System." In Bonnell and Breslauer, 35–58.
Corwin, Julie A. 2005. "Analysis: Pensioner Power." RFE/RL, reprinted in Johnson's Russia List, www.cdi.org/russia/johnson, no. 9016, January 14.
Farizova, Suzanna. 2004. "Vladimir Putin Organizes the Public." *Kommersant*, December 9, reprinted in LexisNexis, web.lexis-nexis.com/cis.
Fish, M. Steven. 2001. "When More Is Less: Superexecutive Power and Political Underdevelopment in Russia." In Bonnell and Breslauer, 15–34.
Fitzpatrick, Catherine A. 2004. "Russian NGOs Slam Putin Reforms as 'Unconstitutional.'" *RFE/RL Political Weekly* 4, no. 37, September 24.
Hahn, Gordon A. 2004. "Putin's Stealth Authoritarianism." *RFE/RL Russian Political Weekly* (www.rferl.org/reports/rpw) 4, nos. 14, 15, and 16 (April 15, 22, and 29).
Il'ichev, Georgii. 2004. "Open Season for Hunting 'Captain Grant.'" *Izvestiia*, October 7, in What the Papers Say, LexisNexis, web.lexis-nexis.com/cis.
Lipman, Masha. 2005. "How Russia Is Not Ukraine: The Closing of Russian Civil Society." *Russian and Eurasian Project Policy Outlook*, Carnegie Endowment for International Peace, January 2005, reprinted in Johnson's Russia List, www.cdi.org/russia/johnson, no. 8362, January 27.
McFaul, Michael. 2004. "Putin's Strong Hand Is Failing Russia." *Washington Post*, September 12, reprinted in Johnson's Russia List, www.cdi.org/russia/johnson, no. 8362, September 12.
Mereu, Francesca. 2004. "Kremlin Looking for Loyal NGOs." *Moscow Times*, June 25.
Nikitin, Alexander, and Jane Buchanan. 2002. "The Kremlin's Civic Forum: Cooperation or Co-optation for Civil Society in Russia?" *Demokratizatsiya* 10, no. 2 (Spring): 147–65.
Pavlovskii, Gleb. 2004. "Russian Civil Society Hampered by Weak 'Grass Roots.'" *Rossiiskaia gazeta*, July 22, BBC Monitoring International Reports, July 26, in LexisNexis, web.lexis-nexis.com/cis.

Pravda.ru. 2004. "NGOs in Chechnya Do Not Pursue Their Declared Humanitarian Mission." Johnson's Russia List, www.cdi.org/russia/johnson, no. 8228, May 28.

Putin, Vladimir. 2004a. "Full Text of Putin's State of the Nation Address to Russian Parliament." RTR Russia TV, BBC Monitoring, May 26.

———. 2004b. "Russia's Rulers and Public Must Unite against Terrorism." RTR Russia TV, BBC Monitoring, September 13.

RFE/RL Newsline. 2004a. "Putin Senior Staffer Details Proposed Political Reforms." Vol. 8, no. 185, part I, September 29.

———. 2004b. "Moscow to Revive Patriotic Youth Movement." Vol. 8, no. 208, part I, November 3.

RIA Novosti. 2005. "Putin Inks Public Chamber Law." April 4.

Saenko, Larisa. 2004. "Financing of NGOs by West Is Not Transparent, Says Russian Political Expert." RIA Novosti, May 27, in Johnson's Russia List, www.cdi.org/russia/johnson, no. 8228, May 28.

Shevtsova, Lilia. 2004. "President Putin Is Shaping His Own Political Regime: What Will Be the Import?" Carnegie Endowment Moscow Center Briefing Paper, vol. 6, issue 1. (January).

Smolar, Aleksander. 1996. "From Opposition to Atomization." *Journal of Democracy* 7, no. 1 (January): 24–38.

Squier, John. 2002. "Civil Society and the Challenge of Russian *Gosudarstvennost'.*" *Demokratizatsiya* 10, no. 2 (Spring): 166–82.

Tsepliaev, Vitalii. 2005. "Vladimir Lukin: Replacing Benefits with a Swindle?" *Argumenty i fakty*, January 19, from WPS Monitoring Agency, www.wps.ru/e_index.html, January 19.

Weir, Fred. 2004. "Russian Civil Rights Groups See Threat in Putin Oversight." *Christian Science Monitor*, August 19.

Yablokova, Oksana. 2004. "New Controls Planned for Funding of NGOs." *Moscow Times*, July 22.

Zudin, Aleksei Iu. 2003. "Rezhim V. Putin: kontury novoi politicheskoi sistemy." *Obshchestvennye nauki i sovremennost'*, 2: 67–83.

Part III

Civil Society in Contemporary Russia: Case Studies

10

Women's Organizations

Institutionalized Interest Groups or Vulnerable Dissidents?

Valerie Sperling

If civil society is defined as the institutionalization of interest groups, acting as established channels between state and society, then how do women's organizations measure up in the post-Soviet era? From the latter days of the Soviet Union up to the present, women's groups have proliferated dramatically. But how strong is this sector of civil society? Have these organizations become institutionalized? Do they have offices, phone numbers, incomes, constituents, and other resources sufficient to enable them to act as a check on state power? Do they successfully promote women's concerns to the state leadership? As actors in Russia's incipient civil society, how effective are these organizations? Do they alter public consciousness about women's issues? Do they base their work on the needs of an explicit constituency? Civil society organizations, by their very existence as loci of citizen interaction, are also supposed to promote social trust, an important element underlying the maintenance of democracy.

Research on the Russian women's movement suggests a mixed evaluation when its organizations are held up to such a rigorous definition of civil society. To some extent, women's groups in Russia, like political parties, center around individuals. Perhaps civic activism in Russia is still closer to dissidence (individual forms of protest and action) than to the mass mobilization and institutionalization characteristic of civil society. In the case of a presidential system largely unresponsive to civic demands, and even repressive of manifestations of societal activism, there may be an incentive for activism in Russia to continue to be closer to dissidence than to large-scale mobilization and well-institutionalized civic organizations.

Some sectors of women's organizing, with the aid of foreign donors, have shown increasing institutionalization over the past fifteen years. This institutionalization, however, raises questions about the role and impact of foreign support for Russian civil society, and its implications for the development of domestic constituencies—a crucial factor in the process of democratization.

While many nonprofit groups attempt to hold the Russian state accountable for upholding its obligations to the citizenry and observing the rule of law, as the Committee of Soldiers' Mothers has attempted to do (Sperling 2003), recent examples of Russian state behavior seem to suggest its movement in the opposite direction. Under Putin, the Russian state ousted the human rights monitoring mission run by the Organization for Security and Cooperation in Europe (OSCE) from Chechnya at the close of 2002, took significant steps toward shutting down independent television media sources, and reined in Russia's most reputable public opinion polling firm, the Russian Center for Public Opinion Research (VTsIOM), apparently with the intention of exercising increasing control over the data released to the public. The state seems intent on isolating itself from public opinion and on narrowing the spectrum of expressed public opinion in general.

The women's movement in Russia provides a lens on the development of civil society over the past fifteen years, since the "beginning of the end" of Soviet rule. While there has been an indisputable increase in the numbers of civic, nonprofit organizations, it is far less obvious how successful these groups have been at making democracy irreversible. This chapter explores changes in the women's movement since the late Gorbachev era, looking at the trends that could suggest the successful institutionalization of civil society, as well as the obstacles that seem to keep grassroots democratic activism at arm's reach in Russia.

Funding, Membership, and Constituency: 1988–2003

How has the women's movement changed over the past fifteen years in Russia? The advent of glasnost and perestroika in the late 1980s provided an undeniable opening for civil society in Soviet Russia. Women's groups, environmental groups, democratic proto-parties, and other nongovernmental organizations (NGOs) formed quickly, catching the attention of scholars and politicians alike. Although the economic and political infrastructure to support civic organizations was weak in late Soviet and post-Soviet Russia, thousands of these organizations emerged and began their work. Political advocacy, professional support, and direct service organizations formed, alongside consciousness-raising groups and groups devoted to raising public awareness on a variety of issues. Lacking domestic economic wherewithal, many organizations turned to Western civic groups, foundations, and governments as sources of support.

The new women's organizations in Russia followed these trends. In the early 1990s, meetings, conferences, and seminars took place, sponsored and attended by women's groups ranging from small women's studies research centers in Moscow and St. Petersburg and other major cities, to political advocacy groups that lobbied on women's issues, to organizations of women journalists and other professionals, to women's employment training organizations, businesswomen's clubs, charities, single mothers' groups, and rape and domestic violence hotlines. These groups, however, were frightfully short of funds and relied on volunteer labor.

By the mid-1990s, many women's groups, particularly advocacy groups based in Moscow, had become the recipients of foreign grants, while in the provinces, women's groups struggled to get by with even less support and were virtually untouched by foreign assistance. There was also a marked tendency for the lion's share of Russia's women's organizations not to engage in domestic fundraising or constituency-building measures (Sperling 1999). Issues that might have mobilized large numbers of women, such as the difficulty women experienced in trying to combine child care with paid work, did not enter into the agenda of most women's organizations as a means to mobilize the female population. Nor were such issues on the agendas of most foreign donors.

Based on interviews in 1994–95 with activists representing 37 women's organizations in Moscow, roughly half of the women's organizations in Russia's capital city were receiving foreign grants. By contrast, in the smaller cities of Ivanovo and Cheboksary, none of the ten women's groups there had benefited from foreign sponsorship. In 1998, Sarah Henderson found that half of the 150 women's organizations she surveyed across the Russian Federation had received foreign grants, suggesting that foreign support had spread beyond Russia's largest cities. This funding helped build "organizational infrastructure" and allowed the groups to engage in networking—two important aspects of organizational institutionalization largely unavailable to groups not receiving foreign grants. According to Henderson's research, charities and service-providing groups received considerably less foreign aid but probably had constituencies of greater size than did the more well-funded "feminist" groups (2001, 256)—a third crucial aspect of institutionalization. By the late 1990s, then, some Russian women's movement groups exhibited some of the virtues of civic society institutionalization, but very few groups were enjoying all the critical aspects of institutionalization themselves.

By the end of the 1990s, women's organizations, particularly those receiving foreign funding, were largely still trapped in a more-or-less professionalized or elitist structure, lacking mass membership, and devoted more to policy-related advocacy (and grant renewal) than to social mobilization (Richter 2002a, 32, 36). Many were reliant on Western funding, which had spread beyond the capital and major cities, as donors grew increasingly interested in the "regions" (ibid., 34). As late as 1995–97, however, more than half of the funding stemming from the Ford Foundation, the MacArthur Foundation, and the U.S. Agency for International Development (USAID) was "channeled through three core organizations [in Moscow]: the Moscow Center for Gender Studies, the Information Center of the Independent Women's Forum, and the Consortium [of Women's Nongovernmental Organizations]" (ibid., 34, 36). According to James Richter, the donor-driven "model of professional civic action" and the channeling of funds through Moscow-based groups were fostering "the creation of hierarchical instrumental ties rather than the horizontal informal ties associated with civil society" (ibid., 37–38). In short, by the late 1990s, foreign aid to women's movement groups had "failed most significantly" in promoting outreach to the broader Russian community (Richter 2002b, 83). Foreign funding was thus reinforcing a "new civic elite" in Russia, rather than fostering the development of a broad-based civil society (Henderson 2000).

Domestic funding plays a lesser but significant role among Russian women's groups. Such sources include local and regional governments as well as wealthy donors. However, although some of Russia's "oligarchs" have begun to provide funding to various charities, they largely support noncontroversial causes (Squier 2002), and cannot be relied upon as a resource for women's movement organizations striving to alter women's status.

Similarly, as of 1999, a number of service-oriented women's groups in the regions were relying on financial support from state bureaucracies, which were "far more willing to give money to organizations providing charitable services than to organizations seeking to change the status quo" (Richter 2002a, 40). Henderson's aforementioned survey found that 32 percent of the responding women's organizations had received some support from government bureaucracies at the local and regional level, and another 32 percent had received "some sort of contribution or donation from Russian businesses" (2000). Henderson also found that 19 percent of the groups received membership fees "to provide them with a little bit of funding" (ibid.). These numbers are not vastly different from those in a smaller sample from a few years earlier, which found that roughly half of the groups in Ivanovo and Cheboksary, and nearly a quarter of the groups in Moscow, had received some amount of "domestic" funding (often in the form of "in kind" donations) (Sperling 1999, 228). Thus, to some extent, women's civic groups had diversified their funding sources over the course of the 1990s, but they were largely not relying on a dues-paying membership and were at risk in several ways.

One critical aspect of civic organizations is their relative independence from state control. Reliance on state funding and support can be dangerous to a civic group, in that it may compromise the group's ability to criticize state policies, while leaving the group at risk of state budget cuts. Almost as problematic, however, is the reliance of civic groups on foreign aid organizations for financial support.

Political scientists Joyce Gelb and Jennifer Leigh Disney (1996) have argued that the success of women's organizations (in the United States) is best guaranteed by a diverse funding base. By the same token, it would follow that the most reliable way to institutionalize a civic organization is to diversify its funding sources. This inevitably involves building a dues-paying constituency and expanding membership in the organization.

The importance of having a constituency as a means toward making civil society a more viable prospect in Russia should not be underestimated. If the purpose of a civil society is to reliably transmit citizen concerns to the state, and then to hold the state accountable for addressing these concerns, then the development of a constituency is a critical piece of the puzzle. Some of Russia's women's organizations clearly have a constituency, if not a mass dues-paying membership. The Committee of Soldiers' Mothers, for instance, draws on an immense constituency: the parents of draft-age sons. Similarly, given the rates of domestic violence and domestic murder in Russia (estimated to be 14,000 women killed per year by their male partners), and the significant number of women—estimated at almost 100,000 in 2002—who contact crisis hotlines and centers across the country, it seems likely that the crisis center movement enjoys a significant (if somewhat hidden) constituency for their services as well (RFE/RL 2003a). A brochure printed by the Russian Association of Crisis Centers for Women (RACCW 2002) cites a 2002 survey showing that, among their 45 crisis centers, they received almost 74,000 calls in that year and had assisted 96,000 people through their hotline, legal advice, and support groups (RACCW brochure 2002). Whether that constituency for service translates into a constituency for advocacy, and whether that constituency could be mobilized or enticed to support crisis centers financially, is more debatable.

Given the difficulties in finding domestic sources of funding, many groups turn to foreign funding. Indeed, there are clear incentives for women activists in Russia to address their English-speaking audiences abroad for support, rather than turning to their potential mass audience at home. Civic organizations need money in order to carry out program work and advertise their services, pay rent on office space, and acquire technology. Yet the pursuit of foreign support can engage a civic organization in a vicious circle. If the focus remains on reaching out to foreigners for funding, then domestic support may never be built.

The women's movement in Russia is sometimes dismissed as being a non-Russian phenomenon, a movement imported from the West, a movement that does not belong. This type of labeling occurs not only in Russia—feminism or any ideology that promises to change the existing balance of power is almost always blamed on outside agitators, irrespective of global geographic location. However, the fact that many women's organizations in Russia are largely detached from a domestic constituency leaves women's groups vulnerable to criticisms of being "foreign."

One result of this foreign rather than domestic outreach strategy is that civic groups may operate on a somewhat Western-driven agenda. Russia's women's crisis center movement provides a good example of this phenomenon. In addition to confronting domestic violence, the crisis center movement has taken up the issue of human trafficking, particularly the trafficking of women into sexual slavery (see Abubikirova 2002). Although trafficking is a horrifying example of human rights abuse, and one that clearly affects thousands of Russian (and other post-Soviet) women (see Stoecker 2000), it may not serve as a successful fundraising cause in a domestic constituency that is likely to view economic issues (unemployment, housing, child care) as more widespread and more critical than trafficking.

Moreover, foreign funding is itself unstable. Not only can it be detrimental in some ways to constituency building (Sperling 1998; 1999, 244–46), but it can also leave civic groups in the lurch when differences of opinion arise between donors and groups as to what issues to fund and when funding is cut in general. One of the major funders of the Russian women's movement (as well as of various human rights initiatives, independent news media, and the like) has been the Soros Foundation, known in Russia as the Open Society Institute. In the late 1990s, the Soros Foundation joined

USAID, the MacArthur Foundation, and the Ford Foundation as the largest funders of women's organizations in Russia, and it went on to supersede the levels of support provided by the other three (Richter 2002a, 31). Then, in June 2003, George Soros, the financier behind the foundation, declared his intention largely to withdraw from his Russian philanthropic efforts, leaving a significant gap in the future funding of numerous nonprofit organizations, including women's groups (Baker 2003). Meanwhile, U.S. government funding for democratization in the post-Soviet region, including funding for civil society initiatives, has declined considerably over the past decade.

The expansion and contraction of funding from foreign governments and foundations is unpredictable. By 2003, many civic groups receiving foreign funding in Russia were experiencing tighter budgets. As donor agendas contract, civic groups are forced to choose what to cut from already minimal organizational budgets and what programs to scale back or eliminate. Donors also change their minds about which kinds of projects to fund over time; Sarah Henderson (2000) writes that funders "often change their own ideas about what constitutes a fundable project over the space of several years, causing groups to chase after various funding projects that have little or nothing to do with their original mission statement." By the mid-1990s, for instance, funders were stressing the need for networking among groups outside Russia's largest cities; this led Moscow- and St. Petersburg-based groups to develop projects involving regional networking, although they were mainly driven to do so by the prospect of receiving a grant (ibid.). In this way, donors hold crucial strings attached to the funding, which may result in civic groups adopting issues that their own potential constituents might readily ignore in lieu of other more pressing concerns.

Finally, funding may not be available to support nonprofit work on certain topics that could make for excellent constituency-building issues. Reproductive choice in Russia is one of these issues. In recent years, in light of the declining population, the Russian state is increasingly paying attention to Russia's demographic "crisis," and therefore to questions of women's reproductive choices, with the intention of finding ways to increase the birthrate among Russians. Putin's envoy to the Central Federal District, for instance, recently asserted his intention to start a campaign against Barbie dolls, believing for some reason that they play a role in the falling birthrate (RFE/RL 2003b).

More significantly, the government has restricted access to abortion over the past several years. In 1998, for example, federal funding for abortion was eliminated by a vote in the Duma, which effectively closed off affordable access to abortion for many Russian women, leaving them with the costly option of turning to a private clinic (Weir 2003). Continuing in this vein, the Health Ministry has recently sought to change Russia's abortion accessibility policy, by restricting (by decree) the conditions under which women can have abortions after the first trimester ends. Religious groups support even further restrictions on abortion, seeking to ban the procedure except in cases where the mother's life is endangered by the continuation of the pregnancy. In August 2003, Russia's prime minister, Mikhail Kas'ianov, signed the new decree, reducing the number of medical and social circumstances under which women could get abortions and outlawing abortion entirely after twenty-two weeks of pregnancy (RFE/RL 2003c).

Against this background, however, Russian public opinion remains solidly in favor of access to abortion, with 62 percent of survey respondents expressing opposition to an abortion ban (Weir 2003). Thus, defending access to abortion would appear to be a good issue for women's groups to adopt as part of a constituency-building strategy. However, because of the supremely controversial nature of the issue, particularly in the United States, it is unlikely that Russian women's organizations adopting this issue would find it fundable. Indeed, under the Bush administration, all USAID funding has been banned for overseas groups that engage in abortion counseling. At least at present, this would render impossible any U.S. government-sponsored support for Russian groups striving to maintain or improve access to abortion.

Achieving Goals

Tracking any social movement's effectiveness—success at achieving its goals—is a difficult process. Changes in state policy and public opinion on any issue could be traced to attempts by civic organizations to lobby politicians to place stories prominently in the media or to public protests intended to raise societal awareness and alter public consciousness. But such changes can also result from individual efforts within the state system or from shifting economic conditions. Disaggregating the causes for changes consistent with those supported by social movement groups is therefore nearly impossible. Still, the presence of civic organizations promoting shifts in policy and public opinion—in however limited a fashion—should not be ignored. Russian women's movement organizations, like other civic groups, have stressed a variety of issues over the past decade or so, articulating goals of improving the status of women in the political, economic, and societal realms. To what extent have these goals been achieved?

One goal set by a number of Russian women's organizations in the early 1990s was to increase the number of women involved in high politics. The quota system applied during the Soviet period quickly gave way in post-Soviet Russia to a significantly lower representation of women in Russia's series of legislatures. In 1991, at the First Independent Women's Forum, a conference bringing together approximately two hundred women activists, the conference slogan addressed the question of women's involvement in politics explicitly: "Democracy without Women Is Not Democracy" (*Demokratiia minus zhenshchina ne demokratiia*). The participants hoped to see their organizing efforts result in a greater voice in the public sphere, where women could raise problems that male politicians seemed content to ignore. Such problems included the dramatic collapse in women's social, economic, and political status in Russia that began in the early 1990s.

Initially, the potential for increasing women's participation in high politics seemed strong. In 1993, with the first elections to Russia's new legislature, in a surprising development, a new party, Women of Russia, entered the public eye. Women of Russia attained roughly 8 percent of the vote and crossed the threshold into the Duma. That success brought the percentage of women in the Duma to just over 11 percent (Sperling 1999, 117). However, the percentage of women in Russia's Duma has declined since then, and was only about 7 percent in 2003. In the upper house of Russia's legislature, only 7 of the 178 members of the Federation Council are women. None of the governors of Russia's regions are women, although one region (the Koriak Autonomous Okrug) elected a female governor in 1996, who served until her electoral defeat in 2000 (RFE/ RL 2003d). Women's representation at the national level is at woefully low levels.

A political gender gap also persists at the regional level in Russia, where parliamentary bodies are still dominated by men. As of the summer of 2000, legislatures in several of Russia's regions contained no women at all. In two of Russia's eighty-nine regions women's representation reached or exceeded 30 percent, but, overall, across Russia's subnational legislatures, as of the summer of 2000, only 9.5 percent of the deputies were female (Nowacki 2003, 174–76). Relatively few women are being elected to Russia's lawmaking bodies, despite the concerns of women's organizations.

Similarly critical for women's organizations in the early and mid-1990s, as unemployment began to affect increasing numbers of women (as well as men), was the question of market-oriented economic reforms and their effects on women specifically. Women's employment-training programs played an important role among women's civic organizations in the 1990s, and the dramatic collapse in women's economic status in the post-Soviet era spurred a great deal of concern within the women's movement. Women's groups participated in legislative hearings and conferences about Russia's proposed new labor code (which contained several problematic points promoting discrimination against women in the labor market). Such organizations found fruitful contact points in the executive branch, such as with Minister of Social Protection Liudmila Beslepkina (Sperling 1999, 129–30). Yet women continued to suffer from increasing poverty and employment discrimination. Although establishing policies sensitive to the gendered results of economic reform has been on the agenda since the early 1990s, and the state's declared intention to improve women's status was reinforced after a Federal Plan of Action was adopted in the wake of the United Nations' Fourth World Conference on Women, held in Beijing in 1995, women's organizations noted little concrete change.

In recent years, a collaborative project on "Women and Labor Market Reform in Russia," between Canadian scholars at Carleton University and the Russian Ministry of Labor (as well as several Employment Services offices) has worked to develop and include gender-related sections in the Russian government's Federal Employment strategy. A conference was held in Moscow in 2002 to address these issues, co-chaired by a Canadian senator and Russian First Deputy Minister Galina Karelova (Canadian International Development Agency 2004). Significantly, Karelova, as the president of the Ekaterinburg-based Confederation of Businesswomen of Russia, has roots in a civic organization. To the extent that this project leads to ongoing awareness of gender-based employment discrimination, and to programs promoting women's increased participation in the labor market, it will reflect women's movement goals. However, it is important to point out that such institutionalization also reflects foreign influence and encouragement. It seems likely, moreover, that Karelova's role has been central to the success of the project to date; the type of civic "institutionalization" that centers around individuals (particularly those individuals who are state government employees) is fragile at best.

The desire to achieve changes or shifts in public opinion on a variety of women's issues also underlies women's organizations' efforts, although little programmatic attention has been paid to public mobilizations such as demonstrations on women's issues. From the blossoming of the women's movement in the early 1990s to the present time, public demonstrations have not been the primary tactic for the women's movement. Henderson found that a mere 6 percent of the Russian women's groups she surveyed in 1998 made use of protest "often or very often" (2000, 114). Lisa McIntosh Sundstrom, studying sixty women's NGOs in seven Russian cities, similarly found that only four of the groups (6.7 percent) had ever conducted demonstrations (2001, 191). This is not to say that demonstrations play no role. There have been several public demonstrations protesting against domestic violence, for example. In 1999, the Psychological Crisis Center for Women held a protest on the main avenue in St. Petersburg (Richter 2002a); and in December 2002, the Women's Alliance Crisis Center in Barnaul held a march under the slogan "For Life without Violence," which achieved local newspaper coverage, and inspired a certain amount of "shock" among onlookers (Shitova, interview 2003). A small demonstration calling attention to sexism and to the paucity of women in government positions took place in St. Petersburg on International Women's Day 2003, sponsored by the St. Petersburg Center for Gender Issues (Tavernise 2003). Such events, even if rare and largely ignored by most media outlets, serve to raise public awareness about the issues and draw attention to the fact that activists concerned with these issues exist.

While various issues like domestic violence are no longer taboo topics for public discussion, in general, Russian society remains highly permeated by gender stereotypes perpetuated by the media, the educational system, and other sources. According to Tat'iana Mel'nikova (2003), head of the Department of Women's Socioeconomic Status at the Ministry of Labor and Social Development, Russia's mass media inculcates gendered stereotypes, such as the "image of the homemaker who is worried about problems in her bathtub, toilet, and kitchen but not about politics." Even in discussing politicians, Mel'nikova argues, Russia's mass media treats male and female politicians differently, devoting "more attention to women's physical appearance and emotions." Consistent with this, for International Women's Day in 2002, Putin presented packages of cosmetics to the female troops in Chechnya (Popeski 2002). The textbooks used in Russia's educational system, too, according to Mel'nikova, are "filled with stereotypes that perpetuate particular cultural-behavioral gender differences" (2003). Perhaps as a result, polls released in time for International Women's Day in 2003 indicated that 40 percent of Russians believed "women's main role was as a mother," and 67 percent thought "men should go out of their way" to engage in chivalrous behavior, such as opening doors and giving women their arm, while only 2 percent thought that politics was a legitimate arena for women's "main role" (Agence-France Press 2003). Similarly, in a 1999 poll, over 70 percent of respondents across Russia agreed that "a woman needs to give birth in order to feel completely fulfilled," and 56 percent agreed that, given a lack of jobs, priority in the labor market should be given to men. On top of such societal stereotypes lies another obstacle to organizing on women's issues, namely, the belief that women and men in the Russian Federation already have equal rights, a statement with which a majority of respondents (55 percent) agreed (ROMIR 1999). Without comparable opinion polls from earlier years, it is difficult to discern whether the women's movement goal of changing public opinion in a less stereotypically sexist direction has met with much success.

Creating shifts in policy at the state level has also been central to a variety of Russian women's organizations devoted to lobbying on women's status issues. These groups have achieved a measure of success, although that success is largely declarative. As one example, in April 2003, a bill on women's rights passed its first reading in the Duma. The bill proclaimed that "men and women should have equal access to the economic resources of society, including property and real estate, land, and financial resources," and promoted the staffing of state bodies at all levels by men and women alike, although apparently the executive branch opposed the bill (RFE/RL 2003e). The Russian government has also continued to present periodic reports to the United Nations in compliance with its obligations as a signatory to the UN Convention on the Elimination of All Forms of Discrimination against Women (CEDAW) (Mel'nikova 2003), and, after the Beijing Conference in 1995, created a Commission on Improving the Status of Women. In 1997, the chair of the Duma Committee on Issues of Women, Family, and Youth introduced a "Legal Framework on Equal Rights and Equal Opportunities" (*Kontseptsiia po obespecheniiu ravnykh prav i ravnykh vozmozhnostei muzhchin i zhenshchin*) to the State Duma, which was subsequently approved, although funding to achieve the equal rights and opportunities envisioned by the framework was not provided (Kochkina 1997). This "framework," developed in consultation with one of the large coalitions of women's organizations in Moscow (the Consortium of Women's Nongovernmental Organizations) was not adopted as a law, but was "sent to all subjects of the Russian Federation as an official document" (Consortium n.d.).

The state is also paying growing attention to issues like domestic violence. Between the mid- and the late 1990s, domestic violence increasingly became an issue adopted by women's groups, even by those, like the aforementioned Consortium, that had not been concerned with it earlier. These concerns were shared with state officials at various events sponsored by women's organizations. In 1997, for instance, round-table discussions on domestic violence were held with Yeltsin's Presidential Committee on Women, Family, and Demographic Issues, as well as with the State Committee on Women, Family, and Youth Issues (Consortium n.d.). In 2001, the Russian Association of Crisis Centers for Women sponsored a "Postcard to the President" drive, where citizens were encouraged to mail in postcards portraying a graveyard cross and flowers, with statistics printed in the background, noting the roughly fourteen thousand women killed by their partners each year in Russia (Shitova, interview 2003). In 2002, the federal government created a working group, within the Ministry of Internal Affairs (MVD), designed to thwart violence against women (ibid.). The RACCW also works with legislators and executive branch administrators to promote cooperation on issues of violence against women, holding educational seminars for MVD specialists and police, as well as for city employees in relevant state agencies (RACCW brochure 2002).

In general, programs countering domestic violence are also enjoying increased support from local governments and police forces. The Women's Alliance crisis center in Barnaul, for instance, works with local police to educate them about domestic violence (Women's Alliance brochure 2002), and it created a working group including representatives of its own organization, along with the heads of local police, health, education, and other administrative departments. Although the local administration was supportive of the conferences and roundtables initiated by the Women's Alliance, this support took the form of "applause" rather than financial support (Shitova, interview 2003). In interviews with crisis center activists, James Richter (2003) similarly found that local government bodies in cities including Tver, Saratov, and Ekaterinburg had consulted crisis centers in a "respectful" fashion. Sundstrom also notes city government support for crisis centers in Ekaterinburg, as well as in Izhevsk (2001, 304, 340). Martina Vandenberg (interview, 2003), an American activist who has worked closely with the Russian crisis center movement, notes that although individual crisis centers may be on shaky ground financially, such interactions among crisis centers, local administrators, and police have made the crisis center movement a "permanent feature of Russia's political terrain."

Institutionalizing Civil Society?

Political and civic life under Putin has in some ways restricted the potential for the institutionalization of civil society, at least in the terms traditionally accepted in political science, namely, as established intermediary organizations that serve as channels to the state but remain uncontrolled by the state. Putin's desire to reassert state power in Russia has been reflected not only in the increasing numbers of state officials with military and state security service backgrounds, but also to some extent in the state's attempts to assert control over civil society groups. One such means has been the convening of "Civic Forums." The first of these took place in Moscow in November 2001, bringing together a large group of NGOs in Moscow, along with various state officials. The NGOs at the Forum varied from quite independent human rights organizations, including a few women's organizations, to "official" NGOs with close ties to the state. Fears arose that this would be an attempt on the part of the Putin administration to co-opt NGOs; these fears were substantiated by proposals (on the part of the "official" NGOs) that the state, in effect, oversee NGO activity in exchange for financial support (Squier 2002).

One outcome of the first Civic Forum was that it provided an opportunity for NGO activists to make contacts with state officials, contacts that were later pursued by state officials in some cases, seeking policy advice from NGO leaders (ibid.). An example of such cooperation that Squier notes is the formation of a working group pulled together by the Ministry of Labor, intended to develop amendments to the Labor Code (ibid.). Similar ties were established between women's movement activists and state officials in the aftermath of the Beijing Conference in 1995, when state officials recognized the level of expertise enjoyed by the NGO leaders; following the conference, for instance, an academic at the Moscow Center for Gender Studies was asked to do a research project by the Russian Ministry of Social Protection (Sperling 1999, 253). Whereas this may appear to "count" as an aspect of civil society institutionalization, in that some civic groups establish channels to the state, in reality, this type of contact usually amounts more to an individual connection with a particular state official, rather than a more traditional representation of civil society, which would take the form of a group representing a constituency's interests to the state in some kind of organized and stable fashion. As Squier (2002) points out, such informal consultative mechanisms between NGO leaders and public officials may provide some influence on policy making, but it is a nontransparent process and does not involve the general citizenry in civic participation.

Another aspect of the Russian state's interaction with civil society has involved the process of registering civic organizations. When in 1999 the state required all non-profit groups to officially register their organizations with the Ministry of Justice (in order to enjoy fundamental rights, such as opening a bank account, hiring employees, and so on), this created problems for some women's groups that lacked either the money or time to go through the somewhat cumbersome bureaucratic process (although others had no difficulty or even believed the registration process to be a good method of weeding out organizations that were functioning only on paper) (Richter, interview 2003). Just as irritating was the fact that organizations that had registered before 1995 had to re-register in 1999, and that the laws governing NGO activity often treat it as commercial activity (to the point where the recipients of free counseling services provided by women's NGOs, like crisis centers, can be theoretically required to declare the services they received as taxable income) (Squier 2002). The Russian state has helped somewhat to institutionalize civil society, setting up rules by which organizations may legally operate and providing a largely benign environment in which civic action could take place—except on sensitive topics, where there is more likelihood of state involvement and infringement on organizations' activities. This type of overt interference has not been a complaint of women's organizations in recent years, although monitoring by the security services was noted by several activists in the early 1990s and some have pointed to the "assistance-as-income" problem as being an obstacle to their work (Shitova, interview 2003).

The crisis center movement in Russia certainly exhibits signs of institutionalization, however tenuous and fragile. According to the RACCW, in 2002 its network included forty-five crisis centers across Russia (RACCW brochure 2002). When the association was founded officially in 1994 (later re-registered in 1999), there were only eleven crisis centers in the network (Abubikirova et al. 1998, 77), which suggests a strengthening of the association over time. Yet individual crisis centers exist on shaky ground. The Barnaul-based Women's Alliance received approximately seventy-five hundred calls from clients between March 1998, when the organization was founded, and March 2003 but has not been able to attain a guaranteed office space. According to the organization's director, Elena Shitova, the group began by paying rent for an office but was forced to give it up when the rent increased. The staff then moved to a smaller office donated by the Barnaul police department, but in early 2003 they were told that they soon would have to leave that office as well. The ramifications for the organization, in addition to being in danger of losing its office, include pressure to "tone down" its message and activities, lest it irritate the authorities at whose pleasure it is housed (Shitova, interview 2003). Moreover, while the number of crisis centers has clearly risen, there are precious few shelters for battered women—only a handful, spread across the entire Russian Federation. Yet, despite the difficulties experienced by her own organization at the local level, Shitova (ibid.) argued that over the past decade, since the crisis center movement was established, such organizations receive "more respect" from local authorities and state officials and the potential for partnership has grown notably.

Institutionalization of the women's movement is also visible in the significant growth of gender studies scholarship and programs in Russian universities over the course of the past fifteen years. As James Richter points out, however, such programs reach an academic elite, rather than a large constituency, and may attract "opportunists" rather than scholars sincerely committed to women's studies (2002b, 79).

The institutionalization of women's movement media also plays a role in the solidification of civil society. While several early women's movement publications enjoyed a brief blossoming and then failed for lack of funds (such as the newspaper *Delovaia zhenshchina*), one example of an ongoing publication is the joint Russian-American magazine, *Vy i My*, now retitled *We/My* with the subheading *Dialog zhenshchin* (Women's Dialogue) and co-edited by the Russian–American team of Nadezhda Azhgikhina and Colette Shulman (see Chances forthcoming). The magazine's first issue was published in 1990, and number 35 has recently been released. Financial support for *We/My* has come largely from individual Western donors and foundation grants; in 2001, the U.S. Embassy in Moscow also secured funding for three issues through the State Department (Shulman, interview 2003). The fact that the magazine receives foreign support (rather than domestic subscriptions) perhaps puts it at risk, but its mere persistence suggests an important degree of institutionalization.

With approximately five thousand copies printed and distributed through women's NGO networks across Russia six times a year (and with selective back translations available in English on the Web), *We/My* serves as a constant in the women's movement, as both an informational resource about women's organizing and a source of analysis and reflection about the movement itself. Interviewed in 2003, Shulman confirmed that *We/My* had contributed significantly to creating closer connections between women's organizations: "The articles in *We/My* give evidence of the growth of these ties between women's groups within a city and region and between cities and regions. They e-mail one another, they get together at conferences, and no longer just in Moscow but in regional centers such as Irkutsk. Perhaps this was one of the most important contributions of our magazine—that in the early post-Soviet stage when women's groups were sprouting like mushrooms all over the country, it helped put them in touch with one another."

Such networking and coalition-building among civic groups may be a sign of institutionalization; the establishment of inter-organizational ties (that go beyond personal relationships) may promote social trust and increase activists' sense of efficacy (since the state and the public tend to pay more attention to issues presented by large groups of complainants than to small gatherings). Several coalition-style groups exist within the Russian women's movement, such as the Consortium of Women's Nongovernmental Organizations, the Information Center of the Independent Women's Forum (ICIWF), and the aforementioned Association of Crisis Centers. The leaderships of the Consortium (see Consortium n.d.) and the ICIWF (see ICIWF n.d.) have both been successful at establishing individual connections with lawmakers, testifying in the State Duma, and having some impact on legislation touching on gender issues. Yet individual contact of this type is not the functional equivalent of institutionalization. Such groups' activity often centers around a single, powerful leader, who leads the organization for a long period of time—a problem sometimes referred to as "founderitis" in Western social movements. The Consortium may provide a particularly clear example of this. Its leader, Elena Ershova, elected to head the organization in 1996, remained in that position seven years later. Indeed, both the Consortium and the ICIWF have existed for roughly a decade, but neither is backed by a mass domestic constituency, and both are fully reliant on foreign funding to support their work.

In general, networking among women's organizations for the purpose of public activism is limited. Nor are Internet resources well distributed across the spectrum of women's organizations (Mel′nikova 2003, 29) in order to facilitate such connections. Henderson (2000) found in 1998 that 83 percent of groups receiving foreign funding, for instance, had a computer, and just over half had access to e-mail, whereas only 27 percent of those groups that relied on domestic funding (or on none at all) had computers and only 12 percent had access to e-mail. (Also see Sundstrom 2001, chapter 5, for extensive data on networking among Russian NGOs.) Ties between women's groups across Russia's vast expanse are not as strong as they could be, and this has a detrimental effect on the collective power and influence of these organizations (Mel′nikova 2003, 29).

Some women's movement activists frankly evaluate the progress and institutionalization of the movement with a certain amount of skepticism. Ol′ga Lipovskaia, a long-time activist, reviewing the decade of women's movement activity in the aftermath of the first independent women's conference, held in 1991 (the Independent Women's Forum), argued that the so-called movement was sorely lacking in "solidarity of action," and that it had failed as yet to make "any serious positive changes" attributable to women's organizing. Instead, Lipovskaia (2002) saw a persistent *nomenklatura* and a "hierarchical mindset," which, in conjunction with the historical repression of Russia's civil society, had brought the movement little in the way of changing women's status or achieving "transparency and accountability from government agencies with regard to their 'programs.'" From her perspective, Russia's women's groups were not living up to a rigorous definition of civil society.

Conclusion

Although women are often excluded from high-level politics, they tend to play a large role in the nongovernmental sector, which is less prestigious and lower paid than the business sector or high politics. But the NGO sector, however flawed, is nonetheless crucial for the eventual development and entrenchment of civil society. Civil society, in turn, is an essential element of any stable, consolidated democracy; it can check state power by encouraging citizen responsibility and activism, thereby promoting civic engagement. The American sociologist Myra Marx Ferree refers to the work of civil society as the "housework" of politics, the unrecognized, largely unrewarded backbone of a democracy that keeps politicians in check, keeps them responsible to the people, and thereby keeps democracy working (Sperling, Ferree, and Risman 2001). Yet public forms of protest, such as demonstrations, which highlight both citizen activism and state accountability, are still quite rare in Russia's women's movement. The director of Barnaul's crisis center, which has led several public demonstrations, explained that her organization was composed largely of young women, because her parents' generation "was not taught to take responsibility for their own lives" (Shitova, interview 2003). Perhaps a generational shift will promote the public checks on politicians that were sorely lacking under the Soviet regime and remain rare afterward.

Women in Russia could clearly benefit from a strong and institutionalized women's movement. From domestic violence and abortion, to unemployment and a lack of affordable child care, there are a number of issues on which to mobilize a potentially large scale constituency. There is little evidence of such a mobilized movement thus far; and without one, it would seem the prospects for creating change on these issues are limited.

It is the establishment of this type of challenge to the state that forms a crucial aspect of building democracy. The more women publicly organize on critical issues, the more citizens will become accustomed to the idea that the state, ultimately, should be accountable to them. This is a concept that was obviously anathema to the Soviet state, and one that is all too distant even from established democracies. Without a strong judicial system to hold executive power in check and absent a media that is able to safely portray the seamy underside of executive actions, it is inevitably up to the people to hold their elected leaders accountable and to overcome whatever hesitations they may have about being actively engaged in the public sphere. This is one of the challenges central to democratization and civil society building in Russia.

References

Abubikirova, Natal'ia. 2002. "Russia: The Main Goal Is to Protect the Victims." *We/My* 18, no. 34: 24–27.
Abubikirova, N. I., T. A. Klimenkova, E. V. Kochkina, M. A. Regentova, and T. G. Troinova. 1998. *Spravochnik: Zhenskie nepravitel'stvennye organizatsii Rossii i SNG.* Moscow: Eslan.
Agence France-Press. 2003. "Russian Woman Belongs in the Home: Poll." March 7.
Baker, Peter. 2003. "Soros's Mission I\in Russia Ends, $1 Billion Later." *Washington Post*, June 10.
Canadian International Development Agency. 2004. "Women and Labour Market Reform in Russia." www.carleton.ca/polisci/rusgen (accessed August 24, 2004).
Chances, Ellen. Forthcoming. "Contemporary Russian Women's Journals: A Case Study of *We/My.*" In *Mapping the Feminine: Russian Women and Cultural Difference*, ed. Cathy Nepomnyashchy and Hilde Hoogenboom.
Consortium of Women's Nongovernmental Organizations (Consortium). n.d. www.wcons .org.ru/about/about.en.shtml#top (accessed October 11, 2003).
Gelb, Joyce, and Jennifer Leigh Disney. 1996. "Feminist Organizational 'Success': The State of the Women's Movement in the 1990s." Paper presented at the American Political Science Association Convention, San Francisco, August 30–September 2.
Henderson, Sarah. 2000. "Importing Civil Society: Foreign Aid and the Women's Movement in Russia." *Demokratizatsiya* 8, no. 1: 65–82.
———. 2001. "Foreign Funding and the Women's Movement in Russia." In *Encyclopedia of Russian Women's Movements*, ed. Norma Corigliano Noonan and Carol Nechemias, 254–57. Westport, CT: Greenwood Press.
Inform Center of the Independent Women's Forum (ICIWF). n.d. www.owl.ru/eng/women/ org001/main.htm (accessed October 19, 2003).
Kochkina, Elena. 1997. "What Will Be the Outcome of the Feminist Revolution in the Russian State Duma?" Informational Update, November 20. Moscow. Received December 5, 1997, on the women.east-west listserv from genderexpert@glas.UUCP.
Lipovskaia, Ol'ga. 2002. "Memories of Dubna: Thoughts on the Seminar: 'Developing Strategies to Help Women's NGOs in Russia and the CIS Defend the Interests of Women.'" *We/My* 19, no. 35. www.we-myi.org/issues/35/lipovskaya.htm (accessed October 11, 2003).
Mel'nikova, Tat'iana. 2003. "Osnovnye podkhody k razrabotke strategii gendernogo razvitiia Rossii." *We/My* 19, no. 35: 26–29.
Nowacki, Dawn. 2003. "Women in Russian Regional Assemblies: Losing Ground." In *Women's Access to Political Power in Post-Communist Europe*, ed. Richard E. Matland and Kathleen A. Montgomery, 173–95. New York: Oxford University Press.
Popeski, Ron. 2002. "Putin Sends Perfume to Female Troops on Women's Day." Reuters, March 8.
Radio Free Europe/ Radio Liberty (RFE/RL). 2003a. "Conference Discusses Horrific Scale of Domestic Violence." *RFE/RL Newsline*, May 14.
———. 2003b. "Envoy Ratchets up Pressure on Barbie." *RFE/RL Newsline*, March 12.
———. 2003c. "State Moves to Limit Late-Term Abortions." *RFE/RL Newsline*, August 19.
———. 2003d. "The Time for Women Politicians in Russia Is Now?" *RFE/RL Newsline*, March 6.
———. 2003e. "Duma Gives Initial Nod to Declarative Law on Women's Rights." *RFE/RL Newsline*, April 17.
Richter, James. 2002a. "Promoting Civil Society? Democracy Assistance and Russian Women's Organizations." *Problems of Post-Communism* 40, no. 1: 30–41.
———. 2002b. "Evaluating Western Assistance to Russian Women's Organizations." In *The Power and Limits of NGOs*, ed. Sarah E. Mendelson and John K. Glenn, 54–90. New York: Columbia University Press.

ROMIR. 1999. "Zhenshchiny Rossii." www.romir.ru/socpolit/socio/october/women.htm (accessed October 10, 2003).
Russian Association of Crisis Centers for Women (RACCW). 2002. "Stop Violence" brochure.
Sperling, Valerie. 1998. "Foreign Funding of Social Movements in Russia." Policy Memo 26. Program on New Approaches to Russian Security (PONARS). www.csis.org/ruseura/PONARS/policymemos/pm_index.cfm#1998 (accessed August 28, 2004).
———. 1999. *Organizing Women in Contemporary Russia: Engendering Transition.* Cambridge: Cambridge University Press.
———. 2003. "The Last Refuge of a Scoundrel: Patriotism, Militarism, and the Russian National Idea." *Nations and Nationalism* 9, no. 2: 235–53.
Sperling, Valerie, Myra Marx Ferree, and Barbara Risman. 2001. "Constructing Global Feminism: Transnational Advocacy Networks and Russian Women's Activism." *Signs: Journal of Women in Culture and Society* 26, no. 4: 1156–86.
Squier, John. 2002. "Civil Society and the Challenge of Russian *Gosudarstvennost'*." *Demokratizatsiya* 10, no. 2: 166–83.
Stoecker, Sally. 2000. "The Rise in Human Trafficking and the Role of Organized Crime." *Demokratizatsiya* 8, no. 1: 129–44.
Sundstrom, Lisa McIntosh. 2001. "Strength from Without? Transnational Influences on NGO Development in Russia." Ph.D. dissertation, Stanford University.
Tavernise, Sabrina. 2003. "Women Redefine Their Roles in New Russia." *New York Times*, March 9.
Verdery, Katherine. 1991. "Theorizing Socialism: a Prologue to the 'Transition.'" *American Ethnologist* 18, no. 3: 419–39.
Weir, Fred. 2003. "Russia Begins to Reconsider Wide Use of Abortion." *Christian Science Monitor*, August 28.
Women's Alliance. 2002. "Women's Alliance" brochure.

Interviews

Richter, James. 2003. Personal communication, October 11.
Shitova, Elena. 2003. Director, Women's Alliance Crisis Center, Barnaul. Cambridge, MA, March 10.
Shulman, Colette. 2003. Co-Editor, *We/My*. E-mail interview, October 16.
Vandenberg, Martina. 2003. Telephone conversation, October 19.

11

Soldiers' Rights Groups in Russia

Civil Society through Russian and Western Eyes

Lisa McIntosh Sundstrom

Soldiers' rights groups, including the famous soldiers' mothers committees, developed in the late 1980s and early 1990s as a response to brutality in the Soviet army. This chapter examines how the networks and activities of soldiers' rights organizations in Russia have developed under formally democratic institutions. By anyone's measure, soldiers' mothers' organizations are a healthy and strong component of contemporary Russian civil society. Yet many other soldiers' rights organizations, not based on mothers as members, remain small and little known; why is this so? I argue that the success of the soldiers' mothers' groups in particular is attributable to their appeal to societally embraced norms regarding the image of mothers and the unacceptability of bodily harm.

In addition, this chapter seeks to generate hypotheses about how well Western theory and experience concerning the role of civil society in democratization apply to Russian civil society, through consideration of the developmental path and political role of the soldiers' rights organizations. The soldiers' mothers, as well as other soldiers' rights groups, have worked to advocate the interests of individuals in a particular sector of society and, by using formal laws to do so, they have begun to teach government officials and citizens at large about the value of the rule of law and the importance of mobilizing to defend one's rights.

Moreover, the soldiers' mothers specifically have tended to work much more cooperatively with Russian military structures and government figures than other soldiers' rights groups have, and this has contributed to their success. Western theory on civil society development and Western organizations that assist Russian nongovernmental organizations (NGOs) have both tended to emphasize that constructive dialogue with the state is an important aspect of a healthy civil society, and the experience of soldiers' rights organizations suggests that this principle is true in Russia as well, as long as government actors are reasonably respectful of the concept of autonomous civil society. The kind of cooperation that the soldiers' rights groups have achieved, while maintaining autonomy from the state, is a balancing act that few Russian NGOs have been able to attain—and is becoming increasingly difficult with a government that despises any opposition—but it indeed appears to be helpful when possible for strengthening civil society.

In one important respect, the experiences of these organizations diverge from Western theory on democratization, practices in foreign democracy promotion, and the experiences of American social movements specifically concerning successful mobilizational strategies in civil society. In contrast to civil society in Western contexts and the tenets of recent works on democratization, Russian soldiers' rights groups have not succeeded best through rights-based argumentation. Instead, they have succeeded by first attracting supporters with images of brutal treatment of soldiers, and only later connecting solutions to soldiers' problems with the language of human rights and the need for political change. Groups like the soldiers' mothers that make emotional appeals to certain basic universal norms tend to experience great success, while those that argue on an exclusively legalistic basis experience much less success.

By analyzing these organizations with reference to theoretical expectations about civil society, we begin to uncover what is distinctive about Russian civil society development and what is shared with civil society in established Western democratic states. The arguments in this chapter are developed from a field research study that was conducted between March 1999 and August 2000 and included interviews with and observation of activists from fourteen soldiers' rights organizations in five Russian cities: Moscow, St. Petersburg, Ekaterinburg, Izhevsk, and Khabarovsk.[1]

Historical Development and Successes of Soldiers' Rights Organizations

Organizations that advocate for the rights of soldiers and military draftees are, if not the strongest, then one of the strongest sectors of civil society existing in Russia today (Caiazza 2002, 138–39; Sundstrom 2001, chap. 3). Soldiers' rights NGOs can be classified under two basic categories: those whose membership consists of mothers of soldiers (present or former); and those that are not based on mothers, which are less widely known, and whose membership is usually primarily male. As will be seen from the discussion below, the two sets of organizations largely engage in different types of activities and strategies in order to achieve their goals.

"Success" in NGOs can be measured on a number of levels. Victories at the policy level (such as through changing legislation on conscription) are one obvious measure. These do not figure prominently among soldiers' rights groups, since they have not yet won many victories of this type, although the soldiers' mothers' groups have been instrumental in changing military procedures in some areas. There are other important measures of success as well: membership size and regional coverage, and awareness and support in the wider public and the mass media.

Soldiers' Mothers

The first committees of soldiers' mothers were formed in Russia in 1989, near the end of the Soviet campaign in Afghanistan, in protest of the Soviet army's decision to draft male students enrolled in postsecondary educational institutions, as well as in protest of the deaths of their sons serving as soldiers during peacetime (Salikhovskaia, interview 2000; Pinnick 1997, 145; CSMR 1999). The approximately three hundred soldiers' mothers who participated in that campaign succeeded in overturning the policy. They held their first national conference in June 1990.

The early history of the original Committee of Soldiers' Mothers of Russia (CSMR) is peppered with surprising policy victories, given the absence of material resources at the group's disposal at the time. They persuaded President Gorbachev to issue a decree in 1990, called "Measures to Implement Proposals from the Committee of Soldiers' Mothers," which ordered the disbanding of military construction battalions (notorious for their inhumane service conditions) and called for a review of the procedures for investigating deaths and injuries among servicemen, among other components. A presidential commission was formed, including CSMR members, to investigate the deaths of soldiers during peacetime, and it resulted in guarantees of pension and insurance policy payouts to deceased soldiers' parents. In 1991, the mothers lobbied successfully for a temporary legal amnesty for army deserters who had fled because of abuse (BBC 1991; UCSMR 2003). During the first war in Chechnya, the CSMR once again successfully pressured the Russian government to proclaim a temporary amnesty for army deserters who fled their military posts to escape physical abuse or to avoid service in Chechnya. As a result, 1,770 of the 5,512 deserters who turned themselves in between June 24 and December 24, 1998, were relieved of all criminal charges (*Kommersant* 1998).

In addition, the CSMR initiated consideration of a draft law on alternative service in the Supreme Soviet; however, this Soviet-era law was never passed (Caiazza 2002, 135–39; Obraztsova 1999, 2). Soldiers' rights organizations continued to be completely confounded in their attempts to secure passage of an alternative service law until the summer of 2002, when a law of questionable improvement finally passed by a slim margin in the Russian State Duma (AFP 2002; Bivens 2003).[2] Other soldiers' rights organizations in addition to the soldiers' mothers' groups have also lobbied for an alternative service law, so "credit" for this dubious victory cannot be attributed to the soldiers' mothers' groups alone.

In 2002, Ida Kuklina, a member of the Coordinating Council of the Union of Committees of Soldiers' Mothers of Russia (UCSMR), the largest association of soldiers' mothers' groups, was invited to join the Russian Presidential Commission on Human Rights. This was an important signal of the presidential administration's understanding of the power of the soldiers' mothers' organizations, and it provided the UCSMR with a high-level forum at which to articulate its complaints on soldiers' rights issues.

Initially, many Russians perceived the soldiers' mothers to be an inconsequential and emotionally unstable group of women (Pinnick 1997, 145). They soon garnered a great deal of popular support, however. The soldiers' mothers' groups are now widely known, receive ample positive media attention, and are respected, if not always liked, by the government. In their 2002–3 Russia-wide survey of 2,408 respondents, Gerber and Mendelson (2003, 5) found that 81 percent of Russian respondents were familiar with the activities of the soldiers' mothers, and the vast majority took a positive view of their activities, while only small minorities of respondents were familiar with the work of other major Russian human rights NGOs. Articles about the soldiers' mothers' work run frequently in regional and national newspapers, and they have appeared numerous times on national television programs discussing topics of military reform. According to the UCSMR, which claims over three hundred member committees across Russia, its members gave over two hundred interviews to Russian and foreign journalists in 2002 alone (UCSMR 2003).[3] A search of a database including newspaper contents and television and radio news summaries for major Russian national publications and stations during the years 2002 and 2003 revealed 180 newspaper, 21 television news, and 26 radio news items mentioning "soldiers' mothers."[4] There are committees of soldiers' mothers in nearly every major Russian city today. They assist thousands of draftees, active soldiers, and families annually in various areas ranging from reestablishing contact between soldiers and their families to walking families through the process of legally avoiding the draft to investigating instances of murder and suicide among active soldiers.

The soldiers' mothers at first did not oppose military conflicts as such; instead they protested the ways in which their sons were treated in the Soviet military and the unreasonable risks to which they were exposed during service. In fact, in the post-Soviet Russian armed forces, unbelievable numbers of conscript soldiers die even during peacetime. According to the UCSMR and other human rights organizations, peacetime deaths among Russian conscripts total between three and five thousand each year (Hall 2001; Obraztsova 1999, 2). The most common reasons for these deaths are beatings, harassment leading to suicide, intolerable living conditions (cold, hunger, and lack of hygiene), denial of needed medical treatment, and excessive labor. Aside from this, the UCSMR estimates that thirty thousand Russian soldiers are beaten by their officers or fellow soldiers every year (RFE/RL 2001b).

Although their early concerns and accomplishments mostly surrounded the mistreatment and deaths of soldiers in peacetime, the soldiers' mothers' organizations have been busiest and have experienced their greatest surges in membership during times of military conflict. Initially, the movement expanded in connection with Soviet-era internal conflicts in locations such as Nagorno-Karabakh, Georgia, North Ossetia, and Tajikistan. But the greatest increase in their activities and popularity occurred surrounding the First Chechen War in 1994–96. They protested both the excessive killing and terrorizing of Chechen civilians, and the involvement of their unprepared sons in the war. They called upon the country's leaders to cease military means of settling the conflict (Kuklina 1997, 101). Among other activities, they expended a great deal of energy arranging for mothers of soldiers being held prisoner in

Chechnya to travel there and beg for the release of their sons. They sought remedies in thousands of cases of active soldiers experiencing problems such as abuse or neglect and those who were drafted illegally despite medical problems. They also defended draftees who were refusing to fight as conscientious objectors, and whom the military formally considered to be criminals evading service. According to UCSMR records, the numbers of appeals for help from soldiers and their families increased fivefold from 1994 to 1995, and the number of draftees seeking assistance in avoiding service more than doubled.[5] It was during the First Chechen War that the soldiers' mothers acquired expertise in defending conscientious objectors in the courts system.

While the least radical soldiers' mothers' organizations merely lobby to ensure that soldiers receive proper food and clothing during service and their legally due social benefits following service, the more radical organizations have openly opposed Russian military operations in Chechnya. Virtually all soldiers' rights organizations call for military reform to a professional army and an end to conscription, although some committees of soldiers' mothers merely passively articulate this position, while other organizations, particularly the groups in Moscow and St. Petersburg, actively lobby politicians and hold occasional public demonstrations on the issue.

Most of the day-to-day work of the soldiers' mothers' committees—especially busy during the spring and fall draft seasons—involves individual consultations for draftees and their parents concerning their rights in the draft process, as well as responding to letters from sons and parents in distant locations concerning these and other questions. Annual numbers of consultations have increased steadily to the point that in 2002, according to the UCSMR, forty thousand soldiers and parents turned to its affiliated committees across Russia (UCSMR 2003).

Organizations of soldiers' mothers are well known not only within Russia; they have also become renowned internationally as human rights advocates and reliable sources of information about violations of soldiers' human rights and crimes against civilians during war. The UCSMR has delivered reports twice to the UN Commission on Human Rights, and in 1996 it received the Right Livelihood Award, which is informally known as the "Alternative Nobel Peace Prize."[6] In June 2004, they testified before the U.S. Helsinki Commission in the U.S. Congress (U.S. Helsinki Commission 2004). The Soldiers' Mothers of St. Petersburg (SMSP) have given reports to the European Commission, the European Parliament, and Amnesty International.

Another organization for soldiers' parents (but not a "committee of soldiers' mothers") deals specifically with the rights of parents whose sons have died in the army in peacetime. This Moscow organization is called "Mother's Right" (*Pravo Materi*). Most of its activities are directed toward investigating the details of soldiers' deaths in peacetime military service, demanding delivery of remains to parents for burial, and securing legally due monies for burial, pensions, and insurance. The idea for the organization developed gradually, beginning in 1985, when its leader, a journalist, Veronika Marchenko, published a story on some terrible instances she had heard of regarding soldiers' peacetime deaths as a result of *dedovshchina,* a widely practiced extreme form of "hazing" in which senior soldiers abuse first-year recruits (Pantiukhina, interview 1999). Marchenko began to receive letters and telephone calls from dozens of parents who had similar stories. In 1990, she invited fifteen mothers of soldiers killed in peacetime to go to Moscow and conduct a demonstration in front of the Central Military Prosecutor's Office (Right to Life and Civil Dignity 1999, 3). Soon afterward, Marchenko decided to create a formal organization to seek legal redress for the military's negligence and refusal to pay benefits that were due to the parents by law. Today, Mother's Right consults with parents, takes their cases to court, and publishes data on the deaths of soldiers.

Other Soldiers' Rights Organizations

There are many other Russian human rights NGOs whose membership is not primarily soldiers' mothers but that also advocate the rights of soldiers and draftees. They are often more radical in their approach than the soldiers' mothers' organizations. Two paradigmatic examples of these non-mother-based organizations encountered during the research study are the Antimilitarist Radical Association (ARA) and the Ekaterinburg Movement against Violence (EMAV).

ARA, based in Moscow, advocates long-term goals that are similar to those of the soldiers' mothers: facilitation of the right to refuse military service, reform to a professional army on a volunteer basis, civilian control over the military, and demilitarization of Russian society more generally. Russian members of the Transnational Radical Party, a UN-accredited transnational political party with headquarters in Italy, formed ARA in 1995. The organization's establishment was partly a result of its leaders' reactions to the First Chechen War in 1994–96. It has set as its main goal the passage of a satisfactory Russian law on alternative service.

ARA's strategy and methods in pursuing its goals serve as an interesting contrast to those of most soldiers' mothers' organizations. It devotes very little attention to individual consultations with draftees and instead focuses most of its activities on political lobbying and mobilizing public opinion in favor of legislation to allow refusal of military service. Nikolai Khramov, ARA's secretary and effectively its leader, described the mandate of his organization in the following way:

> The immediate task we've set ourselves is working toward the final acceptance of a federal law on alternative service. . . . We aren't really a human rights organization in the narrow sense that in this country people generally understand human rights—of which the Committee of Soldiers' Mothers are the most vivid example. Our mandate is not the defense of rights of a concrete person in each concrete situation. Of course, we work on this as needed, but generally we define ourselves as a political organization (Khramov, interview 2000).

The chair of the organization, Valerii Borshchov, a liberal Duma deputy from the Yabloko Party, strongly supported passage of an alternative service law (but did not support the 2002 law that passed). ARA frequently holds public demonstrations at which it distributes materials and petitions related to its campaign. In 1998,

ARA had 238 members in forty-nine cities across Russia. The organization also operates an e-mail listserv, to which it claims over one thousand people subscribe (ARA 2000).

A similar organization, and one that cooperates closely with ARA, is EMAV. EMAV works not only on soldiers' rights but also on ecological and antinuclear issues. The main difference between these organizations is that EMAV does conduct weekly individual consultations with draftees and soldiers and regularly manages court cases for those who have refused military service. Despite this tactical difference between ARA and EMAV concerning work on individual cases, the philosophies of the two organizations are virtually the same. EMAV especially resembles ARA in its frequent use of public demonstrations as a tactic. In fact, since the Second Chechen War began in 1999, EMAV has held small weekly demonstrations in the center of Ekaterinburg. The organization was formed in 1994 to protest the war in Chechnya by a number of activists from the Ekaterinburg Democratic Union—one of the major pro-democratic political coalitions in Ekaterinburg during the late perestroika and early post-Soviet periods. EMAV has only a few dozen active members who participate in protests or help with legal assistance—and only some of these work in the area of soldiers' rights, while others are interested instead in the ecological or antinuclear concerns of the organization.

Across Russia, there are several other organizations of this type (not relying on mothers as members). For example, there is a youth center within the Perm division of the human rights organization Memorial, which since 2000 has worked on an experimental local program of alternative service that has been supported by the Ford Foundation and the oblast administration (Permskoe oblastnoe otdelenie "Memorial" 2004). There is also an organization in Kazan called the Center for Peacebuilding and Human Rights Action (Tsentr mirotvorcheskikh i pravozashchitnykh deistvii), which does conduct consultations for draftees as well as pursue more strategic goals like the passage of an appropriate alternative service law (Center for Peacebuilding and Human Rights Action 2004). These groups tend to be aware of one another's existence and exchange information frequently (Edelev, interview 2000).

The contrast between the soldiers' mothers' organizations and these other soldiers' rights organizations in terms of popular awareness is stunning. Outside the circle of soldiers' and human rights NGOs, and especially beyond Moscow and St. Petersburg, very few people know of soldiers' rights organizations besides the soldiers' mothers (Caiazza 2002; Malyakin and Konnova 1999). Unfortunately, since they are not well known, there are no survey data available concerning public knowledge about them. Caiazza states in her case study of ARA versus the CSMR that "ARA had relatively little political capital. Its public membership and support were minimal" (Caiazza 2002, 151). It is striking that even the secretary of ARA, Nikolai Khramov, noted that "politically, we are marginal" (Khramov, interview 2000).

Explanations for Varying Success

Why has a huge movement grown around the concept of soldiers' mothers in particular, rather than soldiers' fathers or third-party advocates? The outcomes are connected to norms operating in Russian society, some of which are specific to Russia and others more universal in character. There are three norms that play important roles in the issue of soldiers' rights. These concern questions of bodily harm, the role of mothers, and antimilitarism.

Bodily Harm

First, there is a norm at work in the question of soldiers' rights that seems to be virtually universal, rather than specific to Russian society. This is a norm against bodily harm—it is the idea that physical harm to individuals is wrong. Many of Russians' concerns about mandatory service in the contemporary Russian army result from widespread reports of beatings, torture, and neglect of conscript soldiers, especially under the well-known system of *dedovshchina,* an extreme form of hazing. Growing resistance to mandatory military service has been well documented. Gerber and Mendelson found that only 30 percent of respondents believed that Russia should maintain a conscript army (Gerber and Mendelson 2003, 3). In addition, over the past few decades, conscription rates have plummeted: in the spring of 2004, only 9.5 percent of those of draftable age were actually conscripted, compared to 54.6 percent in 1988 (Ministry of Defense of the Russian Federation 2004; Egorov 2000). It is difficult to find surveys that indicate the reasons for citizens' opposition to conscription. However, one of the few existing large surveys found that, among the 72 percent of respondents who would not want one of their relatives to serve in the army, by far the most common reasons were the possibility of death in a conflict (44 percent), *dedovshchina* (35 percent), and poor physical conditions (23 percent). Pacifism or opposition to militarism did not appear as a reason at all (VTsIOM 2002). Recently in the city of Riazan, Memorial organized a focus-group study to design a public relations campaign, which found that "people react badly to posters showing how many schoolbooks one tank shell would buy, because they do not think the army should be kept short of funds, but that they are moved by images of soldiers' suffering" (*Economist* 2004).

Soldiers' mothers' groups have become very popular through voicing their objections to the unwarranted violence to which conscript soldiers are subjected in the Russian military. An example of their rhetorical style is the following statement from the UCSMR, which reflects the position of most soldiers' mothers' organizations: "From the very beginning the soldiers' mothers have said: a degraded, beaten, hungry, and rights-deprived soldier can protect neither the state nor its citizens, since he himself is in need of protection" (Obraztsova 1999, 1). As I argue below, other kinds of soldiers' rights organizations, which focus on a rhetoric of antimilitarism and the right to conscientious objection, are not as successful.

Keck and Sikkink argue that this norm against bodily harm is nearly universal, stating that "not all cultures have beliefs about human rights (as individualistic, universal, and indivisible), but most value human dignity" (1998, 205). Case studies on transnational campaigns in other issue areas, such as antipersonnel landmines, torture of political dissidents, violence against women, and rainforest destruction, have shown how campaigns frequently succeed when they are framed in terms of physical harm to humans, especially vulnerable groups.[7] In contrast, campaigns often fail when they are framed in terms of norms that are not accepted as universally (for example, discussing environmental issues in terms of conservation or biodiversity rather than human suffering), or when the norm against bodily harm competes with strong local norms (such as national pride in the issue of female genital cutting in Africa) (Keck 1995; Keck and Sikkink 1998).

Role of Mothers

In addition, the image of mothers as protectors of their sons resonates strongly in Russia, as well as in other societies. Mothers' groups are more successful than other largely male-based soldiers' rights groups in Russia, in part because of their very invocation of motherhood. When mothers mobilize as mothers to protest some perceived injustice, regular citizens and people in positions of official power alike tend to listen. Amy Caiazza (2002) has linked respect for mothers' protest movements to societal identification with traditional gender ideology (such as the idea that women's major life role is as mother and nurturer) (also Pinnick 1997). Caiazza maintains that this normative identification is significantly stronger in Russia than in many other societies, particularly in the West. It may not in fact be true that the image of mothers is less salient in some countries than others: the success of a movement like Mothers Against Drunk Driving in the United States suggests that mothers' mobilization is just as strongly respected in countries where less traditional gender ideologies have developed. Mothers' movements have certainly also succeeded spectacularly in countries that we would identify as those where traditional gender ideologies reign—such as the Mothers of the Plaza de Mayo in Argentina and Parents Against Silence in Israel (open to all parents but dominated by mothers) (Bayard de Volo 2001; Caiazza 2002, 114–15).

Regardless of whether the norm of respect for mothers' authority is universal or particular to some societies, it certainly exists in Russia in the form of a belief that mothers are capable and duty-bound to take on the responsibility of protecting their children. There seems to be special significance attached to the mother–son relationship in Russia. Men traditionally live at home with their parents until marriage (with the exception of the two years of military service), which encourages a rather strong and lasting dependence on mothers for everyday needs. Kathryn Pinnick (1997, 146) points out that Russia's low birthrate means that conscripted sons are often mothers' only children; hence, there is a mutually strong attachment of mothers to their sons. Literary traditions and frequent contemporary statements by female politicians reinforce the view of women as protectors of families and matronly figures upon whom the country can depend to "clean up the mess" that men have made (Du Plessix Gray 1989; Heldt 1987, 12; Lakhova 1995, 11). A leader of the UCSMR writes that women in particular are less willing to give in to military consciousness "when the discussion is about saving the life and health, honor and dignity of their children; that is, of a completely natural biological instinct that lies at the basis of women's existence" (Obraztsova 1999, 2). Caiazza argues very persuasively that Soviet and post-Soviet Russian political rhetoric and policy approaches to welfare and labor issues have also encouraged a glorification of motherhood (Caiazza 2002, 38–41).

The identification of women as providers of security and sustenance for their families and of mothers as being sources of moral authority leads to a context in which a movement based on mothers demanding certain protections for their sons is highly resonant and has acquired great popularity. In other countries where sons do not typically depend on their mothers for such a long period of their lives, the public might not embrace such a movement so strongly. People might ask, "Why don't these soldiers stand up for themselves rather than have their mothers defend them?"

Antimilitarism

Finally, there is a norm of respect for and even glorification of the military, which is particularly resilient in Russia, despite recent decay in the power and organizational integrity of the Russian armed forces. This widespread lingering sense of respect for the military as an institution means that soldiers' rights groups (typically not soldiers' mothers groups) that espouse clearly pacifist or antimilitarist ideals do not succeed particularly well in Russia. Objection to military service for reasons of conscience is a far less accepted action in Russia than objection on the basis of likely physical abuse.

Both the soldiers' mothers' organizations and other soldiers' rights organizations pursue the same central long-term goal: the end of a conscription-based army. Yet NGOs that focus on the constitutional right to conscientious objection are far less successful in marshaling public support and bringing about changes in government policy and military conduct than those that focus on rampant physical abuse as the basis for demanding an end to conscription. While many soldiers' mothers' organizations in fact oppose militarization in general and, for example, oppose the Russian army's interventions in Chechnya, they pursue their goal of army reform by using a popular tactic: exposing physical abuse and lawlessness in the army.

The enormous number of Russian adults who have undergone military service or are employed by military institutions contributes to a common attitude of strong support for the military, which hinders support for soldiers' rights campaigns framed as antimilitarism. The proportion of the Russian population included at any one time in the armed forces is staggering. According to one widely referenced source on military forces, Russia's active military and paramilitary personnel in 2002 totaled approximately 1.4 million, or 1 percent of Russia's population (International Institute for Strategic Studies 2002; CIA 2002). This is approximately the same absolute size as the forces in the United States, in a country with half the population. These figures make Russia one of the largest per-capita military forces in the world. Other counts by military analysts and soldiers' mothers' groups dispute these official figures, claiming that the real size of the Russian armed forces, including Defense Ministry and other forces, is between five and six million people—approximately 3.2 percent of the Russian population (Felgenhauer 2000; Ivankovskaia 2001; RFE/RL 2001a).

Many eager parents of new draftees, especially those in more remote regions with little access to information, are not aware of the extent of the army's decline in recent years. Thus they enthusiastically expect their children and grandchildren to serve as they and their peers did. Sometimes only after their sons experience serious abuses do they realize the extent of deterioration in the army. During visits to soldiers' mothers' organizations in Moscow, Ekaterinburg, and St. Petersburg, I observed several instances of this shock among fathers of conscripts, with fathers tearfully admitting they had no idea that army service had become so dangerous.

It is difficult to locate surveys that precisely indicate Russians' attitudes toward antimilitarism. However, public opinion on related issues suggests that a large proportion of Russians espouse pro-military ideas. Gerber and Mendelson (2003, 2) found that, while confidence in the Russian military has declined significantly in the post-Soviet era, approximately half of their survey respondents continue to have partial or complete confidence in the army. Over two-thirds of respondents believed that military spending should be increased in Russia (ibid., 6). The ongoing New Russia Barometer surveys find that, consistently throughout the 1990s, the military received higher levels of trust from respondents than any other state institution, despite a campaign in Chechnya that has dragged on miserably since 1995 (Rose 1999, 21). Another example of positive views of military authorities comes from a poll by ROMIR Monitoring in October 2000, in which 31 percent of respondents agreed that military leaders generally (not naming specific candidates) would make better governors than civilians, and only 10.1 percent thought that they would make worse governors (ROMIR 2000). All these data concerning attitudes toward the military suggest that among most Russian citizens, opposition to conscription is based not on a philosophical objection to military values but on concerns about the dangerous conditions of service in the current army.

Applicability of Western Expectations Regarding Civil Society

These norms are important factors in explaining the relative success of various types of soldiers' rights organizations. What do soldiers' rights groups tell us specifically about the applicability of Western theoretical and practical expectations about civil society development to the case of Russia? The outcomes among these organizations indicate some aspects of support for the extension of Western expectations to Russia, and other areas where Western concepts of civil society development do not apply so easily.

In this section, I am referring primarily to expectations about the roles of civil society in democratization that practically oriented transnational actors have adopted in the field of foreign democracy assistance. These practical interpretations are based mostly on recent theoretical literature on the role of civil society in processes of democratization—a literature that has developed over the past twenty years as part of the so-called transitology approach to understanding democratization. This theoretical literature has been adopted and modified by transnational actors that work to promote civil society development in new democracies, including Russia (Carothers 2002). According to the transitology approach, transitions to democracy tend to take place in a somewhat predictable manner, with anticipated stages and roles that various actors and institutions play. In this recent literature, scholars often argue that civil society fulfills particular roles, to some extent during the initial process of transition from authoritarian to democratic rule, but more crucially in the period of "consolidation" of democracy that follows the initial transition. Ideas about the roles of civil society following a transition often come from an understanding of the roles that civil society plays in long-standing democracies, such as the democracies of Western Europe and North America.

Some expectations from this literature apply directly to the case of soldiers' rights organizations in Russia. Many scholarly definitions emphasize the idea that important actors in a democratic civil society are advocacy groups that promote the interests and status of certain groups in society (Diamond 1996, 229; Fish 1996). Certainly Western practitioners of democracy promotion (foreign donors such as official aid agencies and nongovernmental foundations) tend to focus on advocacy groups as the core of civil society, as numerous observers have pointed out (Carothers 1999; Carothers and Ottaway 2000; Van Rooy and Robinson 1998). For example, the U.S. Agency for International Development (USAID) states that "Civil society activities help empower non-governmental organizations to ensure that citizens can articulate their opinions and influence decision-makers through collective action" (USAID 2000). Soldiers' rights organizations constitute exactly this kind of advocacy group.

Indeed, from approximately the mid-1990s, Western donors have financially supported soldiers' rights organizations, constituting their only significant source of funding. In recent years, because of their growing reputation and track record as established organizations, the major soldiers' mothers' organizations (particularly UCSMR, SMSP, and Mother's Right) are becoming increasingly successful at maintaining a constant supply of foreign grants to sustain their work (Kuklina, interview 1999; Pantiukhina, interview 1999; UCSMR 2003; SMSP 2004). The lesser-known soldiers' rights groups receive less foreign funding, but some, such as ARA and the center within Perm Memorial, have received foreign funding in similar amounts to the soldiers' mothers.

In accordance with Western theory, it seems logical that these organizations are promoting further democratization in Russia by increasing contact among citizens and placing pressure upon political and bureaucratic actors to observe the rule of law. The SMSP, for example, insists that parents of soldiers who seek the organization's help must receive training and write their own legal complaint documents for their sons' cases. By so doing, states SMSP Co-Chair Elena Vilenskaia, "those who accompany the soldiers to the organization also learn about their rights and how to defend them, so the results are wider" (Vilenskaia, interview 1999).

It is important to note that not all the soldiers' mothers' organizations are politically active and directly promote the rule of law. Many of these organizations, particularly in remote regions of Russia, act more as service provision organizations, which deal with soldiers' problems on a case-by-case basis and do not lobby actively for changes in the law. Nonetheless, by basing their work on an insistence that the Russian government and military structures fulfill the formal rules on military service that are set out in existing regulations, the soldiers' mothers in effect are always arguing for the rule of law, even if they do not do so with soaring rhetoric or political protest.

Another way in which the record of the soldiers' rights organizations supports recent thought about democratic civil society development is in terms of their relations with state institutions. The organizations that have experienced the greatest success—the soldiers' mothers' organizations—are the ones that have been most willing to cooperate with the state. Some Western works on civil society in democratization suggest that organizations should act as bulwarks against the state, to ensure that the state does not encroach on the rights of citizens. In the simplest Western liberal model of civil society, the two realms of state and civil society must be maintained as clearly distinct from each other (Black 1988, 119). However, not all Western scholars who theorize about civil society development have insisted that organizations should act as adversaries of the state. Instead, they have claimed that, to encourage democratic change, civil society organizations must interact with the state rather than stand in complete defiance of it. Diamond argues vehemently, for example, that "a vigorous civil society gives citizens respect for the state and positive engagement with it" (Diamond 1996, 234). Foreign donors in turn have often suggested that organizations in civil society should be autonomous from the state and receive their material resources for survival chiefly from nonstate sources but should engage in a constructive conversation with the state. As such, foreign donors have tended to promote neither a strictly adversarial model of liberal civil society nor a communitarian model. Thomas Carothers states that "advocacy NGOs are expected to be politically *engaged,* in the sense of tackling issues that concern government policies, but *nonpartisan*—that is to say, not affiliated with or working to advance any particular camp" (1999, 221). As Carothers points out, it is exceedingly difficult for NGOs to avoid crossing the fine line between involvement and nonpartisanship, and it is unrealistic to pretend that in the United States and other Western countries, NGOs have been able to remain outside the fray of partisan politics while engaging in political dialogue. Indeed, for many Russian NGOs, particularly in the more statist Putin era, this balance of "constructive engagement"— neither standing in complete opposition to cooperation with state power, nor falling into a relationship of submission and dependency with state institutions—is extraordinarily difficult to achieve.

Yet in the specific case of soldiers' rights organizations, those organizations that have been most successful have also been most willing to compromise and engage in dialogue with state institutions. Those that have been most adversarial and refused to reach compromises with the state, such as ARA and EMAV, have been least successful. The most successful soldiers' mothers' groups, such as the UCSMR and the SMSP, have in the past found allies within the Ministry of Defense and military operational structures with whom they communicate on a regular basis; yet in most cases, aside from some regional committees of soldiers' mothers, they are not deferential toward these state institutions. Ida Kuklina of the UCSMR in Moscow states:

> We are in constant contact with the presidential administration. . . . We associate with everyone in the military structures. We are even able to work with such a Soviet structure as the "Coordinating Council" under the Ministry of Defense. . . . There is a huge complex of military structures where we have connections; we know whom to write and what to write (Kuklina, interview 1999).

It must be noted that the UCSMR has become much more adversarial since this 1999 quote, due to a lack of support for its demands in the Putin administration and the organization's unwelcome, fervent opposition to the continuing military campaign in Chechnya (U.S. Helsinki Commission 2004). In certain situations, it may be preferable for NGOs to abandon attempts at dialogue with the state rather than compromise their autonomy and become co-opted by the state in an attempt to win favors from a government that dislikes the concept of an open political spectrum.

Despite these aspects in which the soldiers' rights groups' record supports Western expectations about civil society development, there is one key respect in which the their success defies Western theoretical and practical expectations. Recent Western theory on civil society in democratization, as well as practical approaches to encouraging democratization in newly democratic regimes, has stressed the importance of civil society in pressing at the political level for institutionalization of the rights of citizens. That is, there is a posited role of civil society in making rights-based arguments about processes and outcomes to which citizens are entitled in a general way. Diamond states that human rights organizations in particular "continue to play a vital role in . . . greater institutionalized respect for individual liberties and minority rights" (1996, 233). Foreign donors, too, have focused on the importance of NGOs' promoting institutionalization of citizens' rights in newly democratic countries. For example, the European Initiative for Democracy and Human Rights (of the European Commission) named two of its eight granting priorities as "support for education, training and awareness-raising in the area of human rights" and "promoting and protecting the freedom of opinion, expression and conscience, and the right to use one's own language" (Delegation of the European Commission in Russia 2000). The Ford Foundation also, under its "Peace and Social Justice" grants program, has sought to "promote access to justice and the protection of civil, political, economic, social and cultural rights, especially for the most vulnerable individuals and groups in society" (Ford Foundation 2003).

For the most part, the mothers' groups have not engaged in rights-based argumentation in a consistent way as their fundamental approach to resolving soldiers' problems. Most of their efforts certainly have not been devoted to pursuing change in the general observance of human rights at the legal or public policy level. Instead, as mentioned earlier, most of the soldiers' mothers' groups have worked on a case-by-case basis, sifting through chiefly medical, family, and education-related reasons to exempt draftees from service, rather than making general claims about the rights of young men to refuse military service. The Committee of Soldiers' Mothers in the provincial city of Izhevsk, in the Ural region, for example, spends nearly all its energy on a weekly reception to handle specific complaints related to soldiers and draftees. A member of that committee, Liudmila Akatieva, states flatly: "We don't work in politics. . . . There's a lot we don't agree with about what's happening in the army. Our main problem now is that we are trying to get a professional army. But that doesn't depend on us" (Akatieva, interview 2000).

Gleb Edelev of EMAV describes the local Ekaterinburg Committee of Soldiers' Mothers as such: "They work more on humanitarian aid and concrete help in finding concrete individuals and yanking them out of horrible situations. But if there is a legal problem, they send people to us" (Edelev, interview 2000).

Some soldiers' mothers' organizations, such as the Moscow UCSMR and particularly the SMSP, have worked more diligently using human rights-based language in an attempt to persuade politicians of the necessity of reasonable alternative service laws, in addition to their case-by-case work on avoidance of military service for technical reasons. Yet their approach is to first attract supporters—particularly when speaking in public forums—by calling attention to the physical abuses that soldiers endure, and only later to teach citizens that the solution to those problems is through a more legalistic human rights approach.

Other soldiers' rights groups such as ARA and EMAV use the language of human rights and rights of citizens in a democracy more centrally in their work; yet, as noted earlier, their work has achieved very little organizational growth, public resonance, or policy success. ARA focuses on the rights of conscientious objectors and on lobbying for a satisfactory law on alternative service, and it refuses to work on individual cases of soldiers, while EMAV initially tried to focus on conscientious objection alone but found itself dealing with individual legal cases as a result of being inundated with emergency requests from soldiers and draftees in trouble (Khramov, interview 2000; Edelev, interview 2000).

This difference between Western expectations regarding civil society success and Russian realities of NGO development points to the importance of understanding the domestic normative context in which Russian NGOs are operating. Different kinds of approaches will be more or less successful in varying societal contexts. In Russia, discussion of "rights" does not have the same resonance as it does in the United States, a country that was founded and has developed on the principles of individual rights and liberties. Yet since most theorists of democratization and practical promoters of democracy come from the West, and most prominently from the United States, literature on democratic civil society promotion often places great emphasis on the role of NGOs in promoting individual rights of citizens. Although in several respects, Russian soldiers' rights organizations provide support for Western theoretical and practical expectations regarding the route to successful civil society development, these organizations also provide an important cautionary note to such sweeping generalizations.

Notes

The author wishes to thank Kelly McMann, Masha Lipman, Laura Henry, and Alfred Evans for their helpful comments on drafts of this chapter and ideas expressed in it. She also thanks the Social Sciences and Humanities Research Council of Canada for their generous funding of the research.

1. The research also included a detailed study of women's organizations in seven Russian cities. For the full analysis from the study, see Sundstrom 2001.

2. The 2002 law was greeted as only a half-measure by soldiers' rights groups and liberal politicians, since its provisions included an exceedingly long alternative service term (ranging from thirty-six to forty-two months depending on type of service), discretion to military commissions in deciding whether to grant alternative service in each draftee's case, and unclear (and potentially exceedingly onerous) service conditions (AFP 2002).

3. Numbers of committees associated with the UCSMR are reported in U.S. Helsinki Commission 2004 and Caiazza 2002, 124. There is also another umbrella association of Committees of Soldiers' Mothers, called the Russian Committee of Soldiers' Mothers, headed by Mariia Kirbasova. Until the late 1990s, the two organizations were united as a single organization, the Committee of Soldiers' Mothers of Russia (CSMR). The CSMR split apart due to leadership rivalries and disputes over how to spend the prize money, amounting to over $80,000, that accompanied the Right Livelihood Award it received in 1996 (Salikhovskaia, interview 2000; UCSMR, interview 1999). The UCSMR is now the better-known and larger of the two associations.

4. The search was conducted on the ISI Emerging Markets Web site database (www.securities.com).

5. UCSMR records show an increase in soldiers' appeals (*obrashcheniia*) to them from 1,400 in 1994 to 7,000 in 1995, and an increase in the number of consultations given to draftees and their parents from 5,200 in 1994 to 11,000 in 1995. By 1998, the number of appeals had settled to 2,600, and the number of consultations to 10,000 (UCSMR, interview 1999). In 2001, the numbers increased again as a result of the second Chechen campaign: the UCSMR reported that over fifteen thousand soldiers and parents had appealed to them for assistance (RFE/RL 2001b).

6. The Right Livelihood Award is granted by a foundation that Jakob von Uexkull, a writer and former European Parliament member, created in 1980. The award is intended to spread the recipients' knowledge and to show that small numbers of mobilized people can confront difficult problems (Right Livelihood Foundation 2000).

7. On the landmines campaign, see Cameron, Lawson, and Tomlin 1998; Price 1998. On torture, see Keck and Sikkink 1998; Risse and Sikkink 1999. On the issues of violence against women and rainforest destruction, see Keck and Sikkink 1998.

References

AFP. 2002. "Russian Parliament Approves Alternative Military Service Bill." June 28. Reprinted June 28, 2002 in Johnson's Russia List #6327, www.cdi.org/russia/johnson.

Antimilitary Radical Association (ARA). 2000. "Chto takoe ARA?" Retrieved from www.ara.ru/whatsara.html.

Bayard de Volo, Lorraine. 2001. *Mothers of Heroes and Martyrs: Gender Identity Politics in Nicaragua.* Baltimore, MD: Johns Hopkins University Press.

Bivens, Matt. 2003. "A Glum Report Card on Russia." *Moscow Times,* June 2.

Black, Antony. 1988. *State, Community and Human Desire: A Group-Centred Account of Political Values.* New York: Harvester Wheatsheaf.

British Broadcasting Corporation (BBC). 1991. "Interview with Head of Commission for Servicemen's Welfare." *BBC Summary of World Broadcasts,* October 3. Retrieved July 13, 2004, from LexisNexis.

Caiazza, Amy. 2002. *Mothers and Soldiers: Gender, Citizenship, and Civil Society in Contemporary Russia.* New York: Routledge.

Cameron, Maxwell A., Robert J. Lawson, and Brian W. Tomlin, eds. 1998. *To Walk without Fear: The Global Movement to Ban Landmines.* Toronto: Oxford University Press.

Carothers, Thomas. 1999. *Aiding Democracy Abroad: The Learning Curve.* Washington, DC: Carnegie Endowment for International Peace.

———. 2002. "The End of the Transition Paradigm." *Journal of Democracy* 13, no. 1 (January): 5–21.

Carothers, Thomas, and Marina Ottaway. 2000. "The Burgeoning World of Civil Society Aid." In *Funding Virtue: Civil Society Aid and Democracy Promotion,* ed. Thomas Carothers and Marina Ottaway, pp. 3–17. Washington, DC: Carnegie Endowment for International Peace.

Center for Peacebuilding and Human Rights Action (Tsentr mirotvorcheskikh i pravozashchitnykh deistvii). 2004. Web site. Retrieved July 12, 2004, antimil.narod.ru.

Central Intelligence Agency (CIA). 2002. *The World Factbook 2002.* Retrieved June 24, 2003, from www.cia.gov/cia/publications/factbook/geos/kn.html.

Committee of Soldiers' Mothers of Russia (CSMR). 1999. "Glavnoe—ne opozdat'! Molodye soldaty 'golosuiut nogami' za voennuiu reformu." Press release distributed at press conference of Committee of Soldiers' Mothers of Russia and the Moscow Solidarity Movement, National Press Institute, Moscow.

Delegation of the European Commission in Russia, European Initiative for Democracy and Human Rights. 2000. "Democracy and Human Rights Protection." Retrieved June 6, 2003, from www.eur.ru/eng/neweur/user_eng.php?func=coopspec&id=22.

Diamond, Larry. 1996. "Toward Democratic Consolidation." In Diamond and Plattner 1996, 227–40.

Diamond, Larry, and Marc F. Plattner, eds. 1996. *The Global Resurgence of Democracy.* 2d ed. Baltimore, MD: Johns Hopkins University Press.

Du Plessix Gray, Francine. 1989. *Soviet Women: Walking the Tightrope.* Toronto: Doubleday.

Egorov, Ivan. 2000. "Shortage of Draftees." *Vremia novosti,* April 12.

Economist. 2004. "Russia: Who Needs Democracy?" *Economist* (UK), May 22–28.

Felgenhauer, Pavel. 2000. "Defense Dossier: True Numbers, No Reform." *Moscow Times,* October 5.

Fish, M. Steven. 1996. "Russia's Fourth Transition." In Diamond and Plattner 1996, 264–75.

Ford Foundation. 2003. "Peace and Social Justice." Retrieved June 6, 2003, from www.fordfound.org/program/peace_units.cfm?unit_name=human_rights.

Gerber, Theodore P., and Sarah E. Mendelson. 2003. "Strong Public Support for Military Reform in Russia." Program on New Approaches to Russian Security Policy Memo no. 288 (May). Retrieved June 30, 2003, from www.csis.org/ruseura/ponars.

Hall, Macer. 2001. "Russians Call in Our Army over Suicides." *Telegraph* (London), August 5. Retrieved September 17, 2001, from www.psan.org.

Heldt, Barbara. 1987. *Terrible Perfection: Women and Russian Literature.* Bloomington: Indiana University Press.

International Institute for Strategic Studies. 2002. *The Military Balance 2002–2003.* London: Oxford University Press.

Ivankovskaia, Svetlana. 2001. "Soldaty—zhertvy nasiliia v Rossiiskoi armii." Retrieved May 16, 2001, from Soldiers' Mothers of St. Petersburg Web site: www.hro.org/docs/reps/spbmoth.htm.

Keck, Margaret. 1995. "Social Equity and Environmental Politics in Brazil: Lessons from the Rubber Tappers of Acre." *Comparative Politics* 27, no. 1 (July): 409–24.

Keck, Margaret, and Kathryn Sikkink. 1998. *Activists beyond Borders: Advocacy Networks in International Politics.* Ithaca, NY: Cornell University Press.
Kommersant. 1998. "Results of Six Month Amnesty." December 24.
Kuklina, Ida N. 1997. "Soldatskie materi: uroki Chechenskoi voiny." In *Mezhdunarodnaia konferentsiia. Zhenshchiny v ekstremal'nykh situatsiiakh: zashchita prav i interesov zhenshchin,* Vol. 2, pp. 98–105. Moscow: Ekonomika i informatika.
Lakhova, Ekaterina. 1995. *Moi put' v politiku.* Moscow: Aurika.
Malyakin, Ilya, and Marina Konnova. 1999. "Voluntary Organizations in Russia: Three Obstacle Courses." *Jamestown Foundation Prism* #8, April 23. Retrieved December 15, 1999, from www.psan.org.
Ministry of Defense of the Russian Federation. 2004. "Osobennosti prizyva grazhdan na voennuiu sluzhbu vesnoi 2004 goda." Retrieved May 25, 2004, from www.mil.ru/articles/article5379.shtml.
Obraztsova, Liudmila. 1999. "Stat'ia." Photocopy, Moscow.
Permskoe oblastnoe otdelenie "Memorial." 2004. "Permskii eksperiment po otrabotke modeli al'ternativnoi grazhdanskoi sluzhby v Permskoi oblasti." Retrieved July 12, 2004, from www.memo.perm.ru/prog_10b.htm.
Pinnick, Kathryn. 1997. "When the Fighting Is Over: The Soldiers' Mothers and the Afghan Madonnas." In *Post-Soviet Women: From the Baltic to Central Asia,* ed. Mary Buckley, 143–56. Cambridge: Cambridge University Press.
Price, Richard. 1998. "Reversing the Gun Sights: Transnational Civil Society Targets Land Mines." *International Organization* 52, no. 3 (Summer): 613–44.
RFE/RL. 2001a. "5.9 Million Still in Uniform." *RFE/RL (Un)Civil Societies,* May 23.
RFE/RL. 2001b. "30,000 Russian Soldiers Said Beaten Each Year." *RFE/RL (Un)Civil Societies,* September 13.
Right Livelihood Foundation. 2000. "About the Award." Retrieved December 18, 2000, from www.rightlivelihood.se/about.html.
Right to Life and Civil Dignity. 1999. *Za mirnuiu Rossiiu,* no. 1 (19), Moscow (January).
Risse, Thomas, and Kathryn Sikkink. 1999. "The Socialization of International Human Rights Norms into Domestic Practices: Introduction." In *The Power of Human Rights: International Norms and Domestic Change,* ed. Thomas Risse, Stephen C. Ropp, and Kathryn Sikkink, 1–38. Cambridge: Cambridge University Press.
Rose, Richard. 1999. "New Russia Barometer: Trends since 1992." *Studies in Public Policy,* no. 320. Glasgow: Centre for the Study of Public Policy, University of Strathclyde.
ROMIR Monitoring. 2000. *Otnoshenie Rossiian k voennym vo vlasti.* Retrieved May 24, 2001, from www.romir.ru/socpolit/vvps/11_2000/power-military.htm.
Soldiers' Mothers of St. Petersburg (SMSP). 2004. "Finansirovanie organizatsii." Retrieved July 13, 2004, from www.soldiersmothers.spb.org/rus/Finanse_rus.htm.
Sundstrom, Lisa McIntosh. 2001. "Strength from Without? Transnational Actors and NGO Development in Russia." Ph.D. Dissertation. Department of Political Science, Stanford University, Stanford, CA.
Union of Committees of Soldiers' Mothers (UCSMR). 2003. *Annual Report 2002.* Retrieved April 6, 2004, from www.ucsmr.ru/english/ucsmr/report/report2002.htm.
U.S. Agency for International Development (USAID). 2000. "Russia: FY 2001 Program Description and Activity Data Sheets." Washington, DC.
U.S. Helsinki Commission. 2004. "Briefing: The War in Chechnya and Russian Civil Society." Washington, DC, June 17. Transcript available at www.csce.gov/briefings.cfm?briefing_id=281.
Van Rooy, Alison, and Mark Robinson. 1998. "Out of the Ivory Tower: Civil Society and the Aid System." In *Civil Society and the Aid Industry: The Politics and Promise,* ed. Alison Van Rooy, 31–70. London: Earthscan.

Vserossiiskii tsentr izucheniia obshchestvennogo mneniia (VTsIOM). 2002. Press-vypusk no. 4: 21 (February). Retrieved May 25, 2004, from www.wciom.ru.

Interviews

Akatieva, Liudmila. 2000. Member, Committee of Soldiers' Mothers. Izhevsk, April 13.
Edelev, Gleb. 2000. Ekaterinburg Movement against Violence. Ekaterinburg, April 18.
Khramov, Nikolai. 2000. Secretary, Antimilitarist Radical Association. Moscow, August 9.
Kuklina, Ida. 1999. Member of Coordinating Council, Union of Committees of Soldiers' Mothers of Russia. Moscow, March 29.
Pantiukhina, Valeriia. 1999. Press Secretary, Mother's Right Foundation, Moscow, March 23.
Russian Committee of Soldiers' Mothers. 2000. Various leaders. Moscow, August 10.
Salikhovskaia, Fliora. 2000. Deputy Chair, Committee of Soldiers' Mothers of Russia. Moscow, August 10.
Union of Committees of Soldiers' Mothers. 1999. Various leaders. Moscow, May 27.
Vilenskaia, Elena. 1999. Co-Chair, Soldiers' Mothers of St. Petersburg. St. Petersburg, August 12.

12

Russian Trade Unions

Where Are They in the Former Workers' State?

Sue Davis

The average worker is one of the big losers in the political transition from Communism to whatever we call the current Russian system. Under Communism, the workers were the putative kings who were glorified in art, song, and story. After the collapse of the Soviet system, however, the Communist truism of "we pretend to work, you pretend to pay us" has morphed into a capitalist truism of "we work hard with no social protections and lots of insecurity, and sometimes—maybe—you'll pay us." Despite the fact that the exalted status of workers was mostly an ideological fiction and reality never lived up to that fiction, this myth was part of the lore of Communism and even today, workers will tell you that they feel wronged by the changes from Soviet times until now. Today in Russia, workers have less vacation time, longer working hours, less freedom, more job insecurity, fewer perks, and worse access to health care than they did fifteen years ago. Wage arrears are rampant. Unemployment and underemployment are common. Yet we rarely hear complaints from Russian labor.

Most Russian workers belong to a trade union. As a matter of fact, most Russian workers still belong to the same trade union to which they belonged under the Soviet system, or at least to its successor. However, strikes are few and localized. Trade unions do not have a real political party or any real political power. Even when wages have been in arrears for many months, protest is still muted. So one may wonder what trade unions do in Russia today. Trade unions are the single largest membership organization in the Russian Federation, though their membership is smaller than it was ten years ago. They have great potential and could exercise substantial economic power as well, but they have not done so. As a part of civil society, they have the capacity (because of sheer numbers) to be either disruptive or supportive of liberal reforms and movement toward capitalism and democracy. Yet in reality, trade unions have not been able to do much of anything. In this chapter, I argue that Russian trade unions today are generally weak and do not contribute substantially to civil society in the country. That does not mean that trade unions have had no successes; it just means that their potential power outweighs their actual influence, many of the trade unions lack legitimacy, and their memberships lack the feelings of efficacy to create and sustain the kind of labor movement that is needed to adequately articulate and aggregate the demands of workers in Russia. To support this argument, we need to take a closer look at the history of Soviet and Russian trade unions as well as the situation of Russian trade unions today.

History

In the Soviet Union there were no "unions" in the accepted Western sense of the word. Trade unions primarily performed a variety of management functions, including encouraging workers to fulfill the Plan, distributing social benefits, and exhorting increased worker productivity. Trade unions also carried the Communist Party's message to the workers and helped indoctrinate workers into the ideology and expectations of the system as a form of social control. Hence, worker protection was not an overriding goal in the Communist system. Since theoretically the state was run by and for the workers, higher productivity benefited everyone, including workers; thus state rulers considered protection of workers from arbitrary management practices to be secondary (Ruble 1981, 9).

One of the ways in which Soviet trade unions did serve worker interests was through their concern with the material welfare of workers. The trade unions performed three functions that are the province of government or company management in the West: (1) administration of Social Insurance Funds (SIF), or what we term short-term cash benefits such as sick pay and maternity benefits; (2) administration of pension funds; and (3) provision of housing and other goods and services. Trade unions and enterprises often distributed scarce goods and provided services to members, ranging from sausage and cheese to day care and vacation spots. Trade unions ran media outlets, set up clubs and palaces of sport and culture, established libraries and "red corners," showed films, ran tourist jaunts (especially pilgrimages to Lenin's Mausoleum), offered art classes and musical performances, and supported schools and universities. Trade unions also had the right of "legislative initiative" and used it on a regular basis. They drafted laws, statutes, and rules and led public discussions once such laws were published. Those "rights and privileges" of trade unions actually constituted control of governmental resources. Thus, trade union power stemmed not from working-class support but from being allocated control and disbursal privileges over important and scarce goods and resources (Davis 2001).

Membership in a trade union was technically voluntary, but workers had 1 percent of their pay automatically withheld as dues whether they joined or not and were subject to union-negotiated labor agreements regardless of membership. Under the Soviet regime, there was no provision for quitting or opting out of the system.

Because the Communist Party of the Soviet Union had a monopoly on interest representation, independent parties or social movements were strictly forbidden, and thus independent trade unions were prohibited. There was no independent political action by workers, and the unions were one means of ensuring that. Officially, unions fell between party and government, though in practice, unions were part of the government and party. Trade unions functioned as a branch of government—their main duty was ensuring plan fulfillment.

The Official Union: The All-Union Central Committee of Trade Unions (AUCCTU)

The trade unions described above were actually a single system of roughly thirty trade unions organized on the basis of industrial branches that culminated in the peak association called the All-Union Central Committee of Trade Unions (AUCCTU, in Russian, Vsesoiuznyi tsentral'nyi sovet professional'nykh soiuzov, VTsSPS). As part of the Soviet system, the AUCCTU operated on the principle of democratic centralism. Union membership consisted of all employees within an industry, so doctors, lawyers, electricians, enterprise management, janitors, and underground miners were all members of the Coal Miners' Union if they were all employed in a coal-mining enterprise. This arrangement reinforced the belief that, under Communism, the interests of management and workers were synonymous. The unions had a state-granted monopoly in their respective industries and were part of the decision-making structure of the enterprise. The troika of enterprise director, party chief, and trade union leader defined the peak of power in most enterprises under the Soviet system. This type of organization allowed for maximum party control and great efficiency in decision making. It did not make much allowance for the protection of workers' rights.

The official trade unions functioned as administrative cogs designed to hand out benefits and transmit information from the state and enterprise to the worker. Trade unions controlled much property and many perks, as mentioned above. They were part of management and a pillar of the state.

The Gorbachev Era

When Mikhail Sergeevich Gorbachev took power in March 1985, the AUCCTU claimed a membership equal to 98 percent of the workforce and was considered a close partner with the state and party in the ruling structures. The first years of Gorbachev's rule were quiet on the labor front, little different from previous years. He introduced rhetoric about greater worker involvement in production and management, enterprise autonomy, and restructuring. But he did little with respect to workers and trade unions in his first three years in office. The AUCCTU remained the conservative, politically inert, public organization it had been since its inception. By the end of Gorbachev's rule, the party no longer had a leading role, was eventually made illegal, and the workers' state was no longer part of the political vocabulary. New trade unions, independent of the state, began to spring up in some industrial sectors and strikes suddenly became far more common.

The Beginnings of "Independent Trade Unions"

Beginning in 1987, the official unions had competition. In March 1987, a workers' club called Workers (Rabochie) was founded in Sverdlovsk. In February 1988, the Committee of Democratic Trade Unions was formed in Leningrad and the first Congress of the Trade Union of Independent Journalists was held in Riga, Latvia. The Association of Socialist Trade Unions of the USSR (Sotsprof) was founded on April 1, 1989, by intellectuals and cooperative workers and held its first conference in February 1990 in Moscow. Sotsprof referred to the AUCCTU as "totally unrepresentative" and said that workers in the Soviet Union were without "rights and defenses" and needed independent trade unions and a new labor code to protect them (Davis 2001, 55). They favored grassroots initiative and protection of individual rights. Sotsprof established a "social fund" for legal defense as well as a strike fund, and rendered aid to pensioners, invalids, and those unjustly fired. To finance this fund and other projects, Sotsprof charged dues that were 3 percent of workers' incomes (three times higher than the dues of the official union, and they had to be paid out of a worker's pay packet instead of being automatically withheld). Estimates in November 1991 counted membership at between twenty and thirty thousand.

However, 1989 was the year in which the labor movement really began to develop. The coal miners began to strike in opposition to the official trade unions. The first waves of strikes in July were spontaneous, without any real institution building, although strike committees formed the basis and provided the leaders for a new trade union later on, once the real organizational work began. In September 1989, the official trade union plenum tried but failed to co-opt the looming radicalization of labor. Its condemnation of the inactivity of trade union leaders during the strikes did not appear genuine to members of the strike committees. A second coal miners' congress was held in October 1990. Some members demanded a truly independent union and walked out of the meeting. Thus, the NPG (Nezavisimii profsoiuz gorniakov, or Independent Miners' Trade Union) was finally formed in October 1990, over a full year after the 1989 strikes. The air traffic controllers and flight personnel established unions, and many independent trade unions and workers' clubs were formed in 1990. Many were small; some were highly militant, and others did little.

Despite these new organizations, the government showed no signs of weakening AUCCTU control of social funds and other state resources. Automatic membership and withholding of dues were still firmly entrenched, making it a very difficult and time-consuming process to quit the AUCCTU, and it was impossible to get one's dues refunded. So joining a new trade union meant double payment of dues for fewer benefits and, in many cases, being cut off from the contacts and perks of the enterprise, without which life became much more difficult. Among the benefits that were provided by the enterprise, usually through the trade union apparatus, were day care for children, vacation vouchers for free travel, recreational camps for children, sick care, disability pay, access to apartments, waiting lists for the purchase of cars, and in-kind payments of food and other deficit items. Although many who joined free trade unions remained formal members of the AUCCTU, enterprise management and the official trade union leaders would cut them off from access to the social benefits provided by the enterprise. Without the prospect of dues-paying members, it was difficult for new unions to develop, so the independents remained few, small, and relatively weak.

In October 1990, at the Nineteenth Congress of Trade Unions, the AUCCTU liquidated itself and adopted a new name: the General Confederation of Trade Unions (VKP, for Vseobshchaia konfederatsiia profsoiuzov). In addition, a Russian branch was created, called the Federation of Independent Trade Unions of Russia (FNPR, Federatsiia nezavisimykh profsoiuzov Rossii).[1] The VKP and the FNPR retained the vast majority of their members despite the name change.

The main reason that the official unions retained membership was due to their continuing control over the distribution of state social benefits, including social insurance funds, housing, day care, and other necessities of life (Davis 2001). This control of government funds greatly increased the risks to both trade union leaders and members who wanted to leave the official union. A survey conducted in 1991 by the Academy of the National Economy found a very low level of trust in the official trade unions. Only 7 percent rated trust in the unions as very high or fairly high, the lowest of all institutions rated in the poll (*Narkhoz* 1991). Trust in many other institutions has been higher. For example, in 1994, 10 percent of the population trusted the trade unions, while 41 percent fully trusted the president, 35 percent the parliament, and 31 percent the government.[2]

By the end of the Soviet era, there were independent trade unions in several sectors, most notably coal mining and aviation. They remained small both in terms of their overall numbers and in terms of the percentage of workers within the industry and enterprise that they represented. Even at the height of the coal strikes, the Independent Union of Miners represented only a small fraction of those at each coal face and enterprise. In 1992, some of the independent unions formed a confederation to strengthen their voices in dealing with the wage arrears crisis. This confederation was the Labor Confederation of Russia (KTR, Konfederatsiia truda Rossii) with the NPG among its founding members.

The Situation Today

In the first years of Russian independence, many scholars thought that the old Communist-era trade unions would collapse completely or be forced to change into more Western-style organizations that promoted the rights of workers. That did not really happen. Instead, there are two types of trade unions in Russia today: successor unions under the umbrella of the Federation of Independent Trade Unions of Russia (FNPR), and independent or free trade unions. We look briefly at the basic characteristics of each of these trade union types and then discuss more broadly how each fits into the system of labor relations in Russia today.

Successor Unions

The FNPR left the Soviet era with an organization, a membership, and an incredibly good financial situation. However, the legitimacy of the FNPR is problematic due to its history and its actions. It has the stigma of being a Soviet-era institution (this has had both pluses and minuses). Its members have not freely chosen to join. Membership was inherited or inflicted upon workers by historical occurrence, but the leaders of the FNPR have not been too worried about the low levels of trust in unions or by their apparent lack of legitimacy among many of their members. The wealth they inherited and managed as well as the perks they continue to distribute insulate them against their memberships. As a matter of fact, some believe that the vast majority of funds at the disposal of unions in the FNPR come from their commercial interests, not member dues, so members are important solely for the trade unions' ability to claim a large membership in hopes of boosting their political power. However, most observers would agree that the FNPR has not effectively translated its membership into usable political power.

In fact, the FNPR owns billions of dollars in property and receives an annual income of around $300 million from those properties (*Kommersant* 2001). Mikhail Shmakov, the chair of the FNPR, is the chief shareholder in the holding company that controls all those assets, the Rofoprim Closed Corporation. In many ways, this arrangement makes the FNPR independent of its dues-paying members. However, the political power the FNPR wishes to exert is contingent upon its numbers. If it can get two or three million Russians into the street to protest, as it did on May Day 2002, it has the potential to exercise leverage over political actors in the country. The FNPR has not been able to mobilize workers consistently, however, despite calls for "annual days of protest" and the like. Even when the FNPR can rally over a million in protest, that is still only a small percentage of its membership.

The structure of the FNPR is virtually identical to that of the AUCCTU. It is still organized on the basis of branches of industry. It still lumps managers and workers into a single trade union for each branch. While the regional unions within the FNPR have managed to gain some power, the FNPR is still quite centralized and autocratic. Since 1993, the tension between the demands of the regional unions and the desires of the central bureaucracy has meant that the FNPR is spending a lot of time on internal battles. This has decreased its effectiveness even more.

In general, dues still are withheld automatically for the FNPR in many enterprises, even though this practice was declared illegal in the mid-1990s The procedure for leaving the union is often extremely cumbersome and time-consuming. Access to scarce goods, access to mortgage or car loans, vacation housing, and other benefits all still come from trade unions in many firms. Social insurance (sick pay, disability benefits, pensions, maternity benefits, and so on) has been removed from the official control of the FNPR, as have pensions, but the FNPR still exerts substantial power over the social insurance funds. In 1992 and 1993, the FNPR played a role in selecting and overseeing the board of directors for social insurance. The first chairman of the board for the independent social funds was Igor Klochkov, the former president of the AUCCTU and the FNPR. In the events of October 1993, the FNPR sided with Aleksandr Rutskoi, Ruslan Khasbulatov, and the Russian parliament in the executive–legislative conflict that ended with pro-Yeltsin forces bombarding parliament with tanks and arresting the plotters. As a result, the government froze FNPR assets, took away its control of social insurance, and abolished the automatic dues deduction. The FNPR was saved from oblivion by a combination of a rapid leadership change to a more acceptable leader, Mikhail Shmakov, and a lack of government follow-through. The FNPR was quiescent for quite awhile after these events due to its leaders' fear of once again incurring the wrath of Yeltsin's administration. Under Putin, the FNPR is once again in favor and appears to have regained its prior role in allocating the social insurance funds. Cities and villages often have official control over apartments now. But the FNPR *owns* a lot of those apartments and so still has some control. For example, the FNPR can still deny housing, kindergarten spaces, and deficit goods to anyone belonging to a rival trade union or simply offer better perks to its members than to nonmembers.

In 1992, the Russian labor force was 72.1 million (Goskomstat 2000), and the AUCCTU claimed to have 66 million members or 92 percent of the workforce. This was a decline from the high Soviet period when it claimed that 98 percent of all workers belonged to its unions. However, in 1992, three years after the creation of the miners' and air traffic controllers' unions, that was still quite a substantial percentage of the labor force. In 2001, Russia had 64.6 million people in the labor force (Goskomstat 2002). The FNPR claimed 38 million members, or roughly 60 percent of the labor force. However, that decline cannot be attributed to workers leaving the FNPR for independent unions. Most of the decrease was due to the changing structure of the Russian economy. New small and medium-sized businesses that are not unionized at all account for most of the exodus from the FNPR.

During the first years of Russian independence, privatization opened up opportunities for labor to gain economic and perhaps political power. Since independent trade unions remained small, the FNPR took the greatest advantage of privatization. Many trade union leaders and managers cooperated in enterprises to ensure that their workplace was not purchased by any outsiders, resulting in many of the plants becoming collectively owned by the workers or labor collective. This insider privatization required management and workers to work closely together toward a common goal. Unfortunately, once privatization was complete, most of the decision-making power was squarely in the hands of management. The FNPR seemed unable, or unwilling, to translate workers' shares into any power or influence at all. Instead, the FNPR reemphasized ties with management and continued to act as if it were an administrative and managerial entity instead of a representative of the workers.

At the policy level, the FNPR generally does not operate as the defender of the worker but as the defender of its own substantial organizational interests, which entails walking a thin line between supporting enterprise directors and state interests and opposing those interests. However, on "big-ticket items" like wage arrears or welfare policy, the FNPR will usually side with the workers' interests. Like other societal groups, the FNPR does this through straightforward lobbying as well as connections (*sviazi*). Generally, self-preservation explains the FNPR's policies and alliance better than any alternative explanation.

Under President Vladimir Putin, the FNPR has been hewing a line much closer to state interests as Putin labors to bring control (the power hierarchy or *vertikal'*) back to Russia. The best example of Putin's rising influence on the FNPR is the battle for the new Labor Code—significant not so much for its content (it is quite pro-business) but for its political backers and its implications for trade unions. The new Labor Code replaced the 1971 version in February 2002. The old code included such perks for workers as regional pay differentials, guaranteed employment, and payment to workers for "public duties" like Komsomol work. Obviously some of these, if not all, are no longer appropriate, given the political changes in the thirty-some years since the last labor code was passed under Brezhnev. The FNPR is granted sweeping new powers in the new Labor Code that could potentially revive it as a monolithic Soviet-type union. The code grants special privileges to the union that represents "most" of the workers in an enterprise. This seriously disadvantages the new trade unions, which very rarely constitute a majority. This provision of the new code is widely thought to be payment to the FNPR for its support in passing a generally very pro-business Labor Code through the Duma.[3]

Putin and the party in power also courted the FNPR for support in the 2003 Duma and 2004 presidential elections. Due to the FNPR's large official membership numbers (around 38 million), it is a logical constituency for politicians to court. President Putin himself attended the last FNPR Congress in September 2001, as did Moscow Mayor Yuri Luzhkov. The FNPR has used this opportunity to support Putin in ways important to the administration, but it also has asked for Putin's help. For example, on a recent call-in show in Krasnoiarsk that featured Putin as a guest, a call came in from a local FNPR leader about wage arrears at an enterprise.[4] Putin made a quick phone call on the air and "fixed" the problem. FNPR representatives have been repeating this success story to everyone who will listen to improve its legitimacy with its members, which is very low. The FNPR has also claimed credit for the recent increase in the minimum wage and claimed to be a strong participant in gaining a 33 percent pay increase for state workers, effective October 1, 2003. However, it is difficult to attribute policies like the increase in the minimum wage solely to the FNPR, since many groups and members of the administration favored such increases regardless of lobbying efforts by the trade unions.

The FNPR was also an active participant in forcing Moscow Mayor Yuri Luzhkov to rescind dramatic rent hikes for Moscow businesses. The difference between the market rate for rentals and what the city was charging for city-owned properties had become quite large. The Luzhkov administration allowed the rates to equalize in January 2003. It also withdrew special discounts for small businesses. Therefore, rental rates rose between ten and five hundred times. After the FNPR organized protests, Luzhkov backed down and promised that no one's rent would more than double. Though the FNPR claims this success story, it was not alone in protesting, and Luzhkov was more likely to be swayed by the large number of his constituents who protested and complained in a variety of ways.

The FNPR has been courting its members and trying to enhance its legitimacy in a number of ways in order to bolster its appeal to those in political power. The larger FNPR's membership is, the more leverage it can exert on the state and other actors in Russia. It still has vast patronage networks and wealth that it uses to strategic advantage. For example, the FNPR donated funds to Unity and other parties and supported Andrei Isaev's Duma campaign in 1999. In addition, the FNPR publicly favors policies that benefit workers, including opposition to wage arrears, and it sponsors national "days of protest" to help workers articulate their problems to the state. However, it is also highly compliant with and supportive of the administration.

So the FNPR seems to be a mixed bag. It seems to be drawing ever closer to the Putin administration and yet has attained some autonomy as well. It is working hard on raising its legitimacy with its own members, but polls do not show much improvement. As with much in Russia, we are left without a firm conclusion about the state of the successor unions. The FNPR, the main Russian trade union, is not a state institution, but neither is it truly independent. However, I would predict that the "independence" of the FNPR will be ever more limited as Putin constructs his *vertikal'* of power and tightens control by the state organs. The successes of which the FNPR boasts have not been individual or institutional successes, but points on which the FNPR happened to agree with the administration.

Independent Unions

Independent unions were formed mostly during the late Soviet period, and most of them are in extractive or transportation branches of industry. These are strategic sectors of the economy in which most workers are either well educated or difficult to replace. This has given them additional bargaining power vis-à-vis the state. Estimates of their membership range from 300,000 to around 600,000 (Cook 1997). That is roughly 1 percent of the labor force. They have not achieved much growth in membership since their initial founding. This is due in part to the apathy and inertia of the workers, as well as continuing state support for the FNPR (and the perks it controls) and the difficulty inherent in quitting the FNPR and joining a new union.

The independent unions are rank-and-file workers' unions; that is, they do not accept management as members. Generally, leaders are elected in free and fair elections. The independent trade unions see their mission as protecting workers against the demands and abuse of management and participate in (or advocate) collective bargaining. In other words, they aim to be trade unions in the Western style.

None of the independent unions has a truly statewide structure, though Sotsprof claims to have a national association, and most have a fairly narrow range of action. They are either regional in scope or deal only with a small segment of industry like air traffic controllers. Some, though, despite small numbers, have had a substantial impact and have succeeded in forcing government concessions on wages and work rules.

The largest of the independents is Sotsprof. Sotsprof is an umbrella organization of unions in a variety of industries that favor social democracy and "responsible" unionism. In general, those unions view strikes as negative phenomena and prefer to negotiate about problems rather than call for work stoppages. Sotsprof is often at odds with the FNPR and seeks to claim the same prerogatives as the former official unions. It demands representation at state-sponsored events, it seeks a portion of the FNPR's inherited wealth, and it has lobbied in the Duma for the same state favors granted the FNPR. Sotsprof generally follows the same policies it did during the late Soviet era, discussed above. Its membership is under dispute. The union itself claims 500,000 members, but others say it has a membership of around 250,000 (Cook 1997).

Perhaps the best-known independent union is the Independent Union of Miners. This union eventually arose out of the coal strikes in 1989. It has roughly 100,000 members. In 1994, the NPG liberalized its membership rules to allow all non-management personnel in the coal-mining industry to join, not just workers at the coal face (Christensen 1999, 112).

Politically, the NPG has been a strong supporter of democracy and market economics. During the August 1991 coup, the NPG openly sided with the Yeltsin forces while the FNPR did nothing. During the October events of 1993, it again sided with Yeltsin against his enemies. Unfortunately, its loyalty did not lead to concomitant political gains. While the FNPR was weakened due to its political choices at these critical junctures, it still represented far more workers than the NPG both in society at large and within the coal-mining industry (The FNPR has over 1,000,000 members in coal mining compared to the NPG's 100,000.)

Of the independents, the NPG is by far the most strike-prone. It has called numerous strikes. The NPG can count on its own members as well as FNPR miners to join in strikes aimed at increasing wages and benefits or fixing serious problems in the industry. Thus it would be a mistake to discount the NPG solely on the basis of its official membership numbers, as its influence is broader than that.

Other independent unions include those of the air traffic controllers, pilots, longshoremen, and railroad engineers. All are small unions with restrictive memberships. However, like the NPG, most can claim to have the allegiance of more workers in their industry than membership numbers alone convey.

A slightly different kind of "independent" is represented by those previously existing unions that broke from the FNPR. The Mining and Metallurgical Workers' Union (Gorno-metallurgicheskii profsoiuz Rossii—GMPR) broke with the FNPR in 1992, shortly after Boris Misnik was elected chair of the branch union. Misnik had been arguing for reform of the FNPR's decision-making structures for several years. He advocated including workers in decision making and thought that trade union leaders should be autonomous from enterprise directors. Misnik also favored economic and democratic reforms in Russia and generally supported Yeltsin, while the FNPR did not. When the FNPR formally allied itself with the Russian Union of Industrialists, Misnik decided to make his union independent. The GMPR reaffiliated with the FNPR in late 2000. However, the structural openness and membership policies remain quite different in the two organizations, so the GMPR still belongs in the "independent" category.[5] The GMPR's Web site states that it is "developing cooperation" with the FNPR (GMPR n.d.).

The structure of the GMPR changed when it split from the FNPR. Voting was opened up to all members, and workers became active in the union's decision-making bodies. Secret ballot voting was introduced and at the GMPR's first trade union congress, there were open microphones, and about 20 percent of all members were official representatives to the congress. Power was devolved to regional and enterprise-level unions. Dues and decision-making power were retained at the lower levels.

Boris Misnik has been prominent in the pro-reform party Yabloko. He was high on the electoral party list in 1995 and was elected to the Duma. He also represents Yabloko on the leadership council that is trying to form a coalition of democratic forces in the wake of the 2003 Duma elections, in which none of the democratically oriented parties crossed the 5–percent threshold to attain seats in the Duma. He was replaced by Mikhail Tarassenko after Misnik took up his parliamentary duties.

Conclusion: Labor in Russia Today

In answer to the questions posed in the beginning of the chapter, the successor unions have managed little true reform. They remain authoritarian in decision-making structure, still allow management and regular workers to belong to the same union, and continue to receive substantial state preference in the Russian system. The FNPR, with its constituent branch unions, remains the single dominant union organization in Russia, though regional affiliates have shown autonomy and even ignored the peak organization at times.

A substantial number of Russians still belong to trade unions, though the number is falling. Yet membership is neither voluntary nor meaningful. In general, trade unions—and labor broadly speaking—are quite weak in Russia today. However, they remain an important focus for study because they have a significant amount of potential power. Massive strikes could disrupt the economy or destabilize politics. But this potential power has not been realized.

There are several reasons that the potential and actual power of trade unions differ dramatically. First, all trade unions have weak legitimacy in the eyes of society. On the individual level, most Russians will tell you when queried, "We have no trade unions" (*u nas net profsoiuzov*).[6] Most Russians firmly seem to believe that all trade unions are sham organizations created solely to make the leadership rich and the average person poor. According to research conducted by the Russian labor scholar Leonid Gordon, only 12 percent of Russians see unions as playing a positive role, and 64 percent claim that unions play no serious role in society at all (Gordon 1997, 38).

In addition, many Russian trade unions have serious legitimacy problems with their own memberships; over 55 percent of Russians interviewed in one study stated that trade unions could not be trusted at all (Zaslavsky 2001, 215). They are no longer "transmission belts" for the Communist Party; however, they are also not staunch defenders of the embattled worker. Over 66 percent of Russians interviewed in Gordon's study stated that unions do not defend the interests of ordinary persons (1997, 38). Even those few unions that do try to defend workers are often lambasted when they fail to make workers' lives better or easier. Lastly, trade unions in Russia are not united. They fight one another in numerous ways and in numerous venues, from the State Duma and the Tripartite Commission to the International Labor Organization and the AFL/CIO. This is because of the odd post-Soviet politics of the trade unions.

The operation within the Tripartite Commission is a good example of the lack of unity within the Russian labor community. Established in 1992, the Tripartite Commission for the Regulation of Social and Labor Relations has representatives from labor, management, and government. The FNPR has most of the seats given to labor, nine of fourteen. Sotsprof and the Labor Confederation of Russia (a confederation of various independent unions) have five seats. Thus the FNPR was recognized by the Russian state as the main labor organization. On the Tripartite Commission, unions generally side with management to pressure government to agree to more state subsidies, state investment, tax cuts, and high tariffs for imports. Since the state is by far the most powerful actor of the three, it is not surprising that unions and management must opt to work together in pursuit of these common interests. However, the independents squabble with the FNPR, which reduces their bargaining power, and the state seems to veto much of what labor and management would like to accomplish. Each year the Tripartite Commission negotiates the General Agreement on wages, unemployment, welfare issues, and more. The state usually wins against labor and management, due in part to the structure of the commission, but aided by the lack of unity among the labor representatives. In the Tripartite Commission, each side has fourteen members, but the state side members are almost all of ministerial level, and the state side chairs the meetings and controls the agenda.

With the collapse of Communism, the old way of running trade unions vanished. But instead of changing into defenders of the workers, the former official unions worked to enrich themselves by leveraging the property inherited in the Soviet collapse, protect trade union property (and privatize it when they could), and work on maintaining their government-sponsored perks of automatic dues withholding and control of numerous benefits that trade unions traditionally distributed. Independent unions have remained small and without substantial, or sustainable, political power, largely due to the systematic advantages of the successor unions. The development of independent unions has also been hindered by other factors .

While unions are obviously part of civil society, the FNPR, the largest of Russian unions, tends to favor statist, paternalistic policies and retains significant ties to the state. The workers, however, do not reliably follow the FNPR since their membership is neither voluntary nor deeply rooted. The independent unions' autonomy from the state makes them part of civil society, but they remain quite small and exist primarily in a few specific industries. The ties the FNPR still has to state structures make its autonomy more problematic and thus its place in civil society questionable.

Notes

1. As was also true of the Communist Party and the KGB, Russia—the RSFSR—had not had a trade union of its own during most of Soviet rule. The Soviet institutions represented Russian interests.
2. Unpublished survey by the Institute of Applied Politics with a sample of 1,509 respondents, cited in Wyman 1997, 118.
3. The new Labor Code has a number of pro-business characteristics, including easier standards allowing businesses to fire workers, significant limitations on the right to strike, limitations on the collective bargaining process at the enterprise level by restricting the number of unions with which management must negotiate, removal of mandatory consultation with trade unions over workplace rule changes, and abolition of a forty-hour work week limitation.
4. This occurred during Putin's third annual national call-in show on December 18, 2003 (BBC Monitoring 2003).
5. Report of the President, Mikhail V. Tarassenko, to the Fifth Congress of the GMPR (February 4, 2004).
6. I received this response from innumerable interviews I conducted with Russians in the 1993–97 period.

References

Aduev, A. N. 1987. *Spravochnik profsoiuznogo rabotnika.* Moscow: Profizdat.
Ashwin, Sarah. 1998. "Endless Patience: Explaining Soviet and Post-Soviet Social Stability." *Communist and Post Communist Studies* 31, no. 2 (June): 187–98.
Baglai, Marat V. 1987. "Perestroika i profsoiuzy." *Kommunist* 12: 80–90.
Baglione, Lisa A., and Carol L. Clark. 1994. "New Trade Unions and Democratic Development in Russia." Paper presented at the Annual Convention of the American Association for the Advancement of Slavic Studies, Philadelphia, PA, November.
BBC Monitoring. 2003. "Putin Says Russia Had a Good Year in National Live Phone-in" (December 24).
Christensen, Paul T. 1999a. "The Noncommunist Left, Social Constituencies, and Political Strategies in Russia." *Demokratizatsiya* 7, no. 1 (Winter): 135–46.
———. 1999b. *Russia's Workers in Transition: Labor, Management, and the State under Gorbachev and Yeltsin.* DeKalb: Northern Illinois University Press.
Cook, Linda J. 1997. *Labor and Liberalization: Trade Unions in the New Russia.* Washington, DC: The Brookings Institution.
Crowley, Stephen, and David Ost, eds. 2001. *Workers after Workers' States: Labor and Politics in Postcommunist Europe.* Lanham, MD: Rowman and Littlefield.
Davis, Sue. 2001. *Trade Unions in Russia and Ukraine: 1985–1995.* London: Palgrave.
Dokumenty politicheskikh partii i rabochego dvizheniia Rossii 1987–1991. 1991. Moscow: Moscow Independent Press Publishers.
Dowley, Kathleen M., and Brian D. Silver. 2002. "Social Capital, Ethnicity, and Support for Democracy in the Post-Communist States." *Europe–Asia Studies* 54, no. 4 (June): 505–28.
Fish, M. Steven. 1994. "Russia's Fourth Transition." *Journal of Democracy* 5, no. 3 (July): 31–42.
Frege, Carola M. 1999. "The Illusion of Union–Management Cooperation in Postcommunist Central Eastern Europe." *East European Politics and Society* 14, no. 3 (Winter): 636–60.
Gordon, Leonid A. 1993. *Ocherki rabochego dvizheniia v poslesotsialisticheskoi Rossii.* Moscow: Institut mirovoi ekonomiki i mezhdunarodnikh otnoshenii RAN.
———. 1995. *Nadezhda ili ugroza? Rabochee dvizhenie i profsoiuzy v perekhodnoi Rossii.* Moscow: RAFPROFIO.

Gordon, Leonid A. 1997. "Polozhenie naemnykh rabotnikov v Rossii 90–kh godov." *Sotsial'no-trudovye issledovaniia*, no. 7.

Gorno-metallurgicheskii profsoiuz Rossii (GMPR). n.d. www.gmpr.ru (accessed August 25, 2004).

Goskomstat Rossii. 2000, 2002. www.gks.ru (accessed March and April 2004).

Green, Andrew T. 2002. "Comparative Development of Post-Communist Civil Societies." *Europe–Asia Studies* 54, no. 3 (May): 455–72.

Hauslohner, Peter. 1987. "Gorbachev's Social Contract." *Soviet Economy* 3, no. 1: 54–89.

———. 1988. "Democratization 'From the Middle Out': Soviet Trade Unions and Perestroika." *The Harriman Institute Forum* 1, no. 10 (October): 161–80.

Healey, Nigel M., Vladimir Leksin, and Aleksandr Svetsov. 1999. "The Municipalization of Enterprise-Owned 'Social Assets' in Russia." *Post-Soviet Affairs* 15, no. 3 (July–September): 262–80.

Karatnycky, Adrian. "The Battle of the Trade Unions." *Journal of Democracy* 3, no. 2 (April): 43–54.

Kommersant. Various.

Kubicek, Paul. 2002. "Civil Society, Trade Unions, and Post-Soviet Democratization: Evidence from Russia and Ukraine." *Europe–Asia Studies* 54, no. 4 (June): 603–24.

Lomax, Bill. 1997. "The Strange Death of Civil Society in Post-Communist Hungary." *The Journal of Communist and Transition Politics* 13, no. 1 (March): 41–63.

Manning, Nick, Ovsey Shkaratan, and Nataliya Tikhonova. 2000. *Work and Welfare in the New Russia.* Aldershot, UK: Ashgate.

Marsh, Christopher, and Nikolas Gvosdev, eds. 2002. *Civil Society and the Search for Justice in Russia.* Lanham, MD: Lexington Books.

Narodnoe khoziastvo SSSR (Narkhoz). 1989, 1990, 1991.

Ost, David. 1999. "Unionists against Unions: Toward Hierarchical Management in Post-Communist Poland." *East European Politics and Society* 14, no. 3 (Winter): 1–33.

*Profsoiuzy i ekonomika.*1989, 1990, 1991, 1993, 1995.

Profsoiuzy Rossii v internete. www.trud.org (accessed March and April 2004.)

Robinson, Neil, ed. 2000. *Institutions and Political Change in Russia.* London: Macmillan Press.

Rossiia v tsifrakh. Moscow: Goskomstat. 1989, 1990, 1993, 1995.

Ruble, Blair. 1981. *Soviet Trade Unions.* Cambridge: Cambridge University Press.

Rudik, E. N., Ia. N. Keremetskii, and L. A. Bulavka. 2000. *Rabochii protest v Rossii: opyt i problemy.* Moscow (mimeo).

Rutland, Peter. 1990. "Labor Unrest and Movements in 1989 and 1990." *Soviet Economy* 6, no. 4 (October–December): 345–84.

Weigle, Marcia, and Jim Butterfield. 1992. "Civil Society in Reforming Communist Regimes: The Logic of Emergence." *Comparative Politics* 25, no. 1 (October): 1–23.

Wyman, Matthew. 1997. *Public Opinion in Postcommunist Russia.* London: Macmillan Press.

Zaslavsky, Victor. 2001. "The Russian Working Class in Times of Transition." In *Russia in the New Century: Stability or Disorder?* ed. Victoria Bonnell and George Breslauer, 201–30. Boulder, CO: Westview Press.

13

Russian Environmentalists and Civil Society

Laura A. Henry

The Russian environmental movement presents several puzzles to scholars interested in the development of civil society in post-Soviet Russia. Although environmental issues mobilized thousands of citizens during the perestroika era and environmental conditions in Russia remain dire, environmental protest has declined. In spite of the decline in protest events, however, the number of Russian environmental organizations increased steadily during the 1990s, and thousands of green groups now exist throughout Russia. Contemporary Russian environmentalists have previously unimagined levels of organizational capacity, access to technology, and partnerships and funding from transnational actors. The overall number of environmental organizations, their geographical dispersal throughout Russia, and their increasing professionalism all seem to signify the development of a vibrant sector within civil society.

The mere establishment of nongovernmental organizations (NGOs), however, is not an indicator of civil society development. This chapter adopts two strategies for assessing Russian environmentalists' contribution to civil society and, in doing so, highlights elements of change and continuity. First, informed by Western theories of civil society development, this chapter asks whether Russian environmental organizations are able to act as intermediaries between state and society. Second, the chapter uses interview data to explore the goals and activities of Russian environmentalists and to ask how activists relate to state and societal actors, thereby revealing unique features of the country's social transformation.

A close examination of the Russian environmental movement reveals that greens have a mixed record of effectiveness in acting as intermediaries between the state and society. They have struggled to present policy alternatives and monitor the government, encountering hostility from government officials and largely failing to mobilize the population. Yet a narrow assessment of environmental organizations' relative strength or weakness along the standard criteria for civil society development overlooks an increasingly diverse sector of green activism. In fact, we see different types of organizations emerging from within the environmental movement that are broadly related to their leaders' professional backgrounds. Environmental leaders influence their organizations' activities, strategies, and partners; and these choices have different consequences for how civil society develops. A blanket charge of NGO ineffectiveness also obscures the way in which the Soviet legacy continues to affect the development of the green movement, both as an enabling and constraining factor. Indeed, environmentalists are able to "recycle" norms, institutions, and networks from the Soviet era, thereby identifying a usable past on which to base social change.

Environmentalists as Intermediaries: Measuring Up Theoretically

Although a small number of scientific and student organizations devoted to ecology survived during the Soviet period, the Russian environmental movement did not take on a mass character until the perestroika era of the late 1980s (Weiner 1999, 429). Unleashed by Gorbachev's policies of openness and restructuring, environmental activists coordinated some of the first truly nationwide protests and brought thousands of people out into the streets to demonstrate against nuclear power plants, water diversion projects, and industrial expansion (Ianitskii 1996; Dawson 1996). Environmentalists became influential critics of the Soviet regime and gained widespread support for the cause of strengthening environmental protection in the country.

The collapse of the Communist regime and the economic upheaval that followed the country's disintegration threw the environmental movement into disarray. Some movement participants felt that they had achieved their primary goal—the end of the Soviet regime. Broad coalitions fell apart in the rhetorical shift from early declarations of "freedom from" state-sponsored destruction to "freedom to" carry out diverse environmental projects and work toward conflicting goals. Finally, hyperinflation and economic instability led many citizens to retreat from public activism, returning to the security of personal survival networks.

In spite of the end of mass protest and the shift in public attention away from green issues, by the mid-1990s the number of environmental organizations in Russia was again increasing steadily. This increase was part of an overall rise in Russia's NGO population, and it can be attributed in part to a dedicated cadre of environmental activists who have worked tirelessly to build organizations on meager resources and in part to an influx of foreign assistance designed to support the country's democratization.[1] Now, little more than a decade after Russia's regime change, thousands of environmental NGOs inhabit the Russian Federation, working on issues from tree planting to sustainable development. The Socio-Ecological Union (SEU), an umbrella group of environmental NGOs based in Moscow, claims more than 250 organizations in Russia as members. By the late 1990s, according to NGO directories, St. Petersburg hosted more than 160 environmental groups, Vladivostok had more than 40, and even smaller cities such as Vladimir could boast 12 green organizations.[2] These numbers likely understate the actual population of green NGOs since they generally do not include smaller unregistered groups. Given that only a handful of environmental organizations existed in Russia in the late 1980s, these numbers are striking. The Russian green movement has developed a stable organizational base, seemingly a sign of the movement's institutionalization and ability to act as a routine player in the political process.

Do these environmental organizations in fact contribute to the development of civil society in Russia, however? The literature on transitions to democracy defines civil society as comprising "self-organizing groups, movements, and individuals, relatively autonomous from the state" that "articulate values, create associations and solidarities, and advance their interests" (Linz and Stepan 1996, 7–9). Civic organizations are thought to contribute to the consolidation of democracy through their ability to serve as intermediary organizations between the state and society, a role that includes representing public opinion, stimulating participation, presenting policy alternatives, and monitoring and holding the government accountable (Diamond 1999, 239–44; Carothers 1999, 211–14; Van Rooy and Robinson 1998, 43–51). Considering NGOs' role as intermediaries by examining two broad categories of their behavior—engagement with citizens and engagement with the state—it becomes clear that Russian environmentalists have struggled with both halves of the equation.

First, consider environmentalists' engagement with citizens. The Russian public's awareness of the severity of the country's environmental problems remains quite high. For example, a 1993 poll showed that approximately 65 percent of Russians evaluated their local environmental quality, and 85 percent rated their national environment, as fairly or very bad (Dunlap, Gallup, and Gallup 1993). More recent surveys indicate that less than a third of Russians are "satisfied with the environment," and more than 20 percent think that the environmental situation poses a danger to their health (Petrova 1999; Public Opinion Foundation 2002). The degree to which environmental organizations can take credit for this awareness is difficult to assess. Certainly during the past five years, transnational environmental organizations such as Greenpeace and the World Wide Fund for Nature have sponsored advertising campaigns to highlight the country's environmental problems, further raising the profile of environmental issues, and other green organizations have worked to publicize local problems. Awareness of environmental problems has not necessarily led to support for new environmental policies or environmental organizations, however. Survey data show that the willingness of Russians to pay the costs of environmental improvement declined by 20 percent, from 58.5 percent to 38.1 percent between 1993 and 2001 (Whitefield 2003, 101). This decline appears to be relatively consistent across all social categories and may be a result of citizens' anxiety about economic instability. Knowledge of environmental organizations also appears to be generally low: in a 2001 survey, only 30 percent of respondents were aware of environmental groups working in their region and respondents familiar with environmental organizations were almost evenly divided over whether environmentalists' activities are positive (31 percent) or negative (32 percent) (Public Opinion Foundation 2001).

Environmentalists also have not been particularly successful at encouraging public participation in their organizations and projects, a common measure of the effectiveness of civic organizations. Across the postcommunist region, only 4 percent of the public claims to be a member of an environmental organization, as compared to 13 percent in more established democracies.[3] My research on Russian green organizations found that most groups remain quite small, with active memberships ranging between five and thirteen individuals. In fact, most Russian environmental groups are not membership-based—in other words, they do not rely on membership fees for their continued development, and recruiting new members is often not a high priority. The lack of importance environmentalists assign to members is due to several factors: most Russians are not able to pay even modest membership fees; those that do pay contribute so little that it is practically impossible to carry out projects on that basis; and finally, finding new members is a difficult and time-consuming task. One experienced organization in Novosibirsk, Ekoklub—a group founded a decade ago and based upon a Druzhina student environmental group—concluded after much experimentation that "membership fees are not possible in Russia right now" (Dubinin, interview 1999). Greenpeace Russia makes the strongest claim to membership support. As of 2000, the organization had 4,680 members—an impressive number in post-Soviet Russia—yet these members do not necessarily pay dues and some members of the Russian organization are citizens of other countries such as Germany and Sweden (Tsyplenkov, interview 2000). Given the difficulties in attracting members and collecting dues, many environmental organizations have found it easier to rely on foreign grant funding or manage to survive without financial resources.

Another possible route to representing public opinion and encouraging participation is through the development of green parties. While parties are not usually considered part of civil society since they aspire to control the elected offices of government, the emergence of successful green parties in many European countries has been a sign of environmentalists' widespread public support. The largest Russian green political party is known as KEDR (an acronym that means Cedar in Russian).[4] The party—formed in 1993 by representatives from two state agencies, the State Epidemiological Authority (Gossanepidemnadzor) and the Ministry of Ecology—is not supported by most environmental activists. On the contrary, many environmentalists charge that KEDR is a government organization or "a party organized from above." The former head of the State Committee on Ecology, Viktor Danilov-Danil'ian, even discouraged environmentalists from supporting KEDR in the 1999 parliamentary elections (Center for Russian Environmental Policy 1999, 4).[5] Smaller green parties also have proliferated in post-Soviet Russia. St. Petersburg alone has five parties focused on ecology. Few of these parties have had any electoral success, however, and many have not yet gathered enough signatures to allow their participation in elections. Instead they currently act more as small debating clubs for politically minded intellectuals or proto-think tank organizations.[6]

Greens charge that the Russian state has neglected environmental protection in favor of economic development, yet activists have found it difficult to influence policy making and enforcement (Whiteley 1999; Newell and Wilson 1996). In particular, environmentalists have struggled with the privatization of natural resource extraction industries, necessitating a shift in attention from one big opponent—the state—to many new adversaries, including new industrial and natural resource conglomerates that have proved even more difficult for activists to challenge due to their vastly disproportionate resource bases. Environmentalists have made an effort to propose alternative environmental policies to the government, in particular at two meetings of the All-Russian Congress on Environmental Protection in 1995 and 1999, where environmentalists promoted a sustainable development plan.[7] At the 1999 Congress, greens pressured the government to sign the UN European Economic Commission's convention "On Access to Information, Participation of the Public in Decision-Making, and Access to Justice in Issues Pertaining to Protection of the Environment," also known as the Aarhus convention. Activists also reminded government officials that existing rights to public participation in environmental decision making based on the federal law "On Ecological Expertise" still lack enabling legislation that would permit a meaningful policy-making role for NGOs.

Relations between environmentalists and the Russian state have been quite contentious since the mid-1990s. Far from responding positively to green activism, the Yeltsin and Putin administrations have deemphasized environmental protection. As of 2000, the government budget allocation for environmental protection had not exceeded 0.3 percent of the federal budget, although the government's statements suggested that 3 percent was a more reasonable funding level (Peterson and Bielke 2001, 68). In 1996, the Yeltsin administration demoted the Ministry of Ecology to the State Committee on Ecology (Goskomekologiia). Then, in May 2001, in the most significant blow faced by the green movement, President Putin dissolved Goskomekologiia entirely and passed its functions on to the Ministry of Natural Resources, the agency charged with the economic exploitation of the country's resource wealth. Hard on the heels of the dissolution of Goskomekologiia, the Ministry of Atomic Energy proposed that Russia begin importing nuclear waste from other countries for storage and reprocessing in exchange for valuable hard currency (Felgenhauer 2001).

Environmentalists have been most successful at monitoring environmental violations by private actors and chronicling the state's lack of enforcement of its own environmental laws. NGOs have taken a leading role as watchdogs. For example, Green World of St. Petersburg has protested construction of a petroleum port in the Finnish Gulf and chronicled lax safety practices at the Leningrad Atomic Energy Station; Scholars for Global Responsibility of Novosibirsk has publicized the government's failure to clean up areas contaminated by radioactive waste around the city; and Phoenix of Vladivostok has demanded protection for endangered species in the Russian Far East.[8] In general, the Russian state has not looked kindly upon these activities. President Putin and other political officials have painted this type of environmental monitoring as threatening to the state and the economy, accusing environmentalists of corporate espionage and representing the interests of the West.[9] The government's response to this activism has taken several forms. Environmental organizations, along with other NGOs, were required to go through an occasionally politicized reregistration process (Grishina and Dzhibladze 2000). Several environmental groups, including Green World and Greenpeace, have been subjected to tax audits or security investigations that they charge are politically motivated.[10] Prominent whistle-blowers Aleksandr Nikitin and Grigorii Pas'ko were arrested and charged with treason when they revealed illegal dumping of nuclear waste by the military. Supported by Western environmental organizations, Nikitin was eventually cleared of the charges and Pas'ko is out on parole awaiting a review of the guilty verdict against him.

In spite of the government's hostile reaction, greens have had some success holding the state accountable to its own laws. For example, Ecojuris, a public interest legal organization, charged the Russian state with violating citizens' environmental rights and demanded enforcement of environmental regulations on several different issues. In 1998, the Russian Supreme Court ruled in the organization's favor and against the government for its failure to carry out environmental impact assessments of forest management projects as required by law. Also, despite the government's noncooperation with environmentalists, most Russian political figures appear to have tacitly accepted the need to engage in "green talk," expressing their own concern for the environment as a source of Russia's national heritage, even if their rhetoric is not accompanied by action. Indeed, President Putin has even expressed interest in becoming an environmental activist when he leaves government service.[11]

Measured against the criteria for civic organizations articulated by theories of civil society development, it appears that Russia's environmentalists are not yet very effective intermediaries. While surveys demonstrate that citizens are extremely dissatisfied with the quality of Russia's environment, the environmental movement has been unable to tap into those grievances to gain public support for its organizations and encourage participation. State officials also remain unreceptive to Russian activism, and activists are left to publicize environmental degradation rather than prevent it.

How is it, then, that the number of environmental NGOs has grown, but seemingly without a corresponding increase in their effectiveness at acting as intermediaries between state and society? Does this then mean that these organizations have little significance for civil society development? Answering in the affirmative misses an important realm of citizen activism with great significance for the country's future development. The increasing transnationalization of the Russian environmental movement and its effort to mimic its Western counterparts is an interesting aspect of civil society development, but not the entire story. Most of Russia's voluntary organizations are barely a decade old and are developing in the midst of an unprecedented political and economic transformation. Because of these unique conditions, I advocate undertaking an inductive approach to the study of civil society development—in other words, taking a closer look at what these organizations actually do—to complement a theoretical assessment of these groups. Examining these organizations from the ground up reveals the continuing obstacles environmentalists face, as well as their ability to "recycle" the norms, institutions, and networks of the Soviet period to support their activism. In this way, we shift our focus from what is new and innovative in Russian society to consider aspects of continuity with the Soviet period as well.

The Practice of Russian Environmentalism: Recycling the Soviet Past

What does environmental activism in contemporary Russia look like? Field research in five Russian regions reveals three distinct types of environmental organization populating the post-Soviet landscape. I refer to these types as (1) grassroots organizations, (2) professionalized organizations, and (3) government affiliates. As I have argued in the past, these three organizational types are differentiated by their primary funding sources and their sponsorship by other social and political actors.[12] In addition, as demonstrated below, these three types of organizations also pursue different activities and exhibit different orientations toward state and society—in effect, different visions of what civil society organizations should do and can do in the context of Russia today.

What are the broad differences among these three organizational types? Grassroots environmental groups tend to be based on domestic, and usually local, resources. They most often rely on the enthusiasm and unpaid labor of their leaders and small donations in kind from local businesses and government institutions. Professionalized environmental organizations, in contrast, tend to be grant-based groups modeled after Western NGOs. As registered nongovernmental, nonprofit organizations, they represent a fundamentally new institutional form in Russian society.[13] Their activism frequently mirrors the goals, language, and strategies of the transnational environmental movement. As their name implies, government affiliates, the third and smallest category, are closely linked to the state administration and rely on government sponsors and funds for organizational survival. Their mission is often to support the government in its environmental protection role.

To discover the role played by environmental organizations in civil society development, I interviewed the leaders of eighty-four groups in the regional capitals of St. Petersburg, Vladivostok, Novosibirsk, Vladimir, and Briansk.[14] Classification of those groups revealed forty-two grassroots organizations, thirty-three professionalized organizations, and nine government affiliates. Environmental leaders were asked to describe their organization's main activities and projects and recount their own professional background before becoming involved in the NGO. Their responses suggest that variation in the activities pursued by green organizations is correlated to the professional experience of the organization's leader.[15] To a great degree, environmental leaders within each organizational type have a similar professional background—grassroots groups tend to be led by educators, professionalized groups by scientists and scholars, and government affiliates by bureaucrats or political officials. A leader's preexisting preferences and experience, based on that leader's professional background, result in similar assessments of appropriate and inappropriate behavior for the environmental movement and suggest certain relationships with state officials and citizens. In this way, environmental leaders' socialization in their pre-NGO profession often serves as a signifier for the way in which Soviet-era attitudes and resources continue to influence contemporary social activism. While all environmentalists appear to reuse or re-cycle Soviet norms, networks, and organizations, they do so in different ways and with different effects on civil society development.

Grassroots organizations

By far the most common activity of Russian green organizations is conducting environmental education programs for children. These programs appear in many forms: they may be developed as part of a school curriculum or after-school program or be organized around summer camps and nature expeditions. For example, the Radimichi organization of Briansk hosts an environmental program for children called Novocamp each summer and leads expeditions along the Desna River to pick up litter and publicize environmental issues. Some green organizations also support environmental education by offering training seminars for teachers, publishing journals on environmental education, or housing small libraries made available to teachers. The Vladivostok organization Krug (Circle) gathers primary-school teachers in seminars to show them how to integrate information about the environment into their lesson plans. Environmental education programs are offered by all three NGO types, but grassroots organizations are the most likely to pursue this type of activity. Of the twenty-nine environmental education programs mentioned in interviews, twenty of them were coordinated by grassroots groups, as compared with six by professionalized organizations and three by government affiliates.

In addition to environmental education programs, grassroots organizations also engage in other local projects. Of the forty-two grassroots organizations represented in interviews, four groups work on environmental health issues; six lobby the government to preserve local parks, trees, or rivers; and more than a dozen disseminate information about local endangered species and natural sites. A handful of other grassroots organizations work on issues such as protecting stray animal populations and developing environmental tourism. Six grassroots organizations promote environmental spirituality, encouraging the public to improve the quality of their lives through contact with nature. What these projects sponsored by grassroots organizations have in common is their largely apolitical nature and, with the exception of the spiritual groups, an effort to resolve local problems through pragmatic activism.

Grassroots organizations most frequently are led by educators, usually elementary-school teachers but also occasionally teachers from pedagogical institutes or universities, directors of kindergartens, and administrators of after-school programs. Seventeen grassroots environmental leaders interviewed currently work as teachers or had worked as teachers in the past. Four grassroots organizations are led by current students from postsecondary institutes. Other grassroots leaders are employees of the local government administration, journalists, small business owners, or pensioners. The majority (twenty-four out of forty-two) of leaders of grassroots environmental organizations are women, in part reflecting the high number of women who work in the educational sector.

For these educators, students, and others, environmentalism is a means for reforming and revitalizing the school curricula and reviving self-confidence among the general public. In a sentiment echoed by many grassroots leaders, Valerii Solov'ev of the Briansk Ecological Union argues that the most important challenge faced by the environmental movement is to "raise children with a civilized relationship toward nature" (Solov'ev, interview 2000). Natalia Smetanina, the leader of the Laboratory for Environmental Education in Vladivostok, describes the role of her organization thus: "It's a difficult situation in Russia because nobody believes in anything, the joy is gone . . . they need to see good examples and to believe that the changes can be made by individuals" (Smetanina, interview 1999). Grassroots leaders are the more likely than other environmentalists to offer a mixed assessment of the post-Soviet period, lamenting the loss of services for children and the orderliness of Soviet society, while not advocating a return to Communist rule. They tend to have great faith in the regenerative power of society, in particular the potential of the next generation. Recalling the Soviet tradition of *subbotniki*, or voluntary weekend labor, they are likely to express the opinion that it is just a matter of rolling up their sleeves and getting to work, regardless of government policies and societal apathy, in order to get things done.

To carry out their projects, grassroots leaders generally rely on like-minded networks of family, friends, colleagues, or parents of children enrolled in their programs. Many of these networks have persisted since the Soviet era. While reliance on these personal survival networks has been seen as a sign of weakness in civil society (Howard 2002, 162–63), for grassroots environmentalists these networks, however limited, provide one of the few resources available for generating community change. For example, the Kukushkin Pond group of Vladimir and the Krestovskii Island group of St. Petersburg have drawn on networks of neighbors to preserve green spaces in both cities. The spiritual group Mir (Peace) of St. Petersburg has been organized by a group of friends who spend their summers on the island of Valaam. In fact, grassroots organizations are more likely to draw community members into their activities than the other two types of green organizations.

Grassroots environmentalists frequently use Soviet-era educational or cultural institutions—such as schools, libraries, small museums, dormitories, kindergartens, houses of children's creativity, former Pioneer summer camps, or nature preserves (*zapovedniki*)—as the site for their group's activities. These institutions provide office space and access to a telephone. As the leader of Ladushka, a Briansk environmental educational program formed within one of the city's kindergartens, comments, building an organization on an established community institution "makes it easier to attract attention and publicity, to survive" (Vasil'eva, interview 2000). Most grassroots groups relate to the government only peripherally, through educational and cultural institutions. They tend to have a nonconfrontational or neutral attitude toward the government, preferring to address pragmatic rather than political issues. Due to the apolitical nature of their projects, dealing with issues of child development, health, self-esteem, and citizenship, it is relatively easy for grassroots groups to gain support from other societal actors or to go unnoticed.

Professionalized Organizations

Professionalized organizations are most likely to address transnational environmental problems and become involved in international projects on issues such as preserving the Siberian tiger, European bison, or migratory bird populations; improving water quality in the Baltic Sea; and pursuing sustainable development. In addition, sixteen out of thirty-five professionalized groups engage in scientific research on endangered species and habitats or scientific monitoring of polluted areas. For example, scientists from Ekolog of Vladivostok study the Pacific gray whale population. Fifteen professionalized groups, including ISAR-Siberia of Novosibirsk and Ecologos of Vladivostok, offer support for other NGOs or seminars for environmental activists, and sixteen disseminate environmental information. Finally, fifteen professionalized organizations lobby the local or regional government for the enforcement of environmental regulations, increased funding for environmental issues, or simply more transparency in the policy-making process. For example, the St. Petersburg Agenda 21 working group has pressured the city government to include NGOs in its urban planning process.

The leaders of professionalized organizations tend to come from the scientific intelligentsia. Nineteen out of thirty-three professionalized organizations have leaders who have advanced degrees in the natural or social sciences, most of whom have worked at universities or research institutes. Other professionalized leaders were attracted to environmental activism by earlier contact with transnational NGOs, such as the World Wide Fund for Nature. The leaders of professionalized green groups frequently have ties to Soviet-era scientific organizations that promoted nature protection—in particular, the Society of Naturalists (Obshchestvo estestvoispytatelei) and Druzhina, a university student movement started in the 1960s to promote enforcement of nature protection laws.[16]

Professionalized organizations are more distant from the general public than grassroots groups. Most professionalized environmental leaders, socialized in the institutes of higher education during the Soviet era, place great faith in the objectivity of science and tend to believe that those with the proper training "know best" and should play a dominant role in environmental protection. Vladimir Aramilev from Vladivostok's Institute of Sustainable Development notes that he and his colleagues "do not have much in common with teachers' organizations . . . teachers' organizations don't need the kind of advanced information we provide" (Aramilev, interview 1999). Evgenii Sobolevskii of Ekolog speaks for many professionalized leaders when he extols the virtues of having a "team of experts" leading his environmental organization (Sobolevskii, interview 1999). This attitude has roots in the history of scientific dissidence in the Soviet period. Throughout the Communist regime, a vocal minority of natural scientists asserted their right to represent an autonomous public opinion to the state based on their scholarly expertise (Weiner 1999, 31–32). Environmentalists from professionalized organizations tend to have an ambivalent attitude toward the state. They frequently oppose state polices and often are critical of the government's efforts at environmental protection, but their skepticism coexists with a desire to work with and through the state—arguably the only institution that can achieve comprehensive nature protection and other environmental goals.

Leaders of professionalized organizations also tend to have a more cosmopolitan outlook than other environmental activists based on their membership in the international community of scientists. They are more comfortable communicating with environmentalists from other countries and participating in grant competitions. Not surprisingly, professionalized groups have been the most successful in winning foreign funding. This external funding has been something of a double-edged sword, however, sustaining green groups through a difficult period yet also further lessening their need for ties to their domestic constituency. Thus professionalized groups draw up preexisting networks of scholars and resources from outside the domestic political arena and justify their projects based on the importance of expert opinion.

Government Affiliates

In contrast to grassroots and professionalized organizations, government affiliates tend to be closely aligned with political officials or the bureaucracy. Six out of nine government-affiliated organizations stated that one of their primary activities was either to enforce government regulation or to help the government pursue environmental protection. For example, the leader of Novomir, a group from Novosibirsk, states that the organization's goal is "to support the local government by carrying out projects that contribute to a green city" (Rakhno, interview 1999). Specific projects undertaken by government affiliates include evaluating the environmental significance of natural monuments and preserves, working with industrial enterprises to meet current environmental standards, researching urban environmental issues such as waste disposal, and publishing a newspaper that highlights the local administration's ecology-related projects. Two government affiliates interviewed were green political parties that campaigned on platforms supportive of the government and fielded candidates drawn from the bureaucracy.

Not surprisingly, six out of ten leaders of government-affiliated organizations have experience working in political or administrative posts. Their backgrounds range from experience as an oblast first secretary to an administrator at a state university to bureaucratic positions in the public health and ecology ministries. Government-affiliated leaders are also more likely than other environmentalists to occupy positions in the state administration at the same time that they conduct their nongovernmental work. For example, the leader of the All-Russian Nature Protection Society in Vladimir simultaneously holds a seat on the government's Ecology Commission. Most leaders of government affiliates have adopted a supportive relationship with government officials, continue to use government-friendly rhetoric, and argue that environmental protection is a state function that society should support, not challenge. Ilias Gadzhiev, the leader of Novosibirsk's All-Russia Nature Protection Society, argues that "the environmental movement lessened in scope and intensity [after the perestroika era] because the government established a committee to deal with those questions" (Gadzhiev, interview 1999). In his opinion, social organizations no longer need to oppose the state and therefore have moved into other areas of activity, such as education. This statement represents a fairly common belief among the leaders of government affiliates that the current Russian government can now be relied upon to act in the interests of the public without the need for oversight or criticism from societal groups. Government affiliates often have collective members, such as firms from a certain economic sector, or large formal memberships—all the schoolchildren in the city, for example. These memberships do not extend much beyond a list of names. Government affiliates also tend to discount the work of other green NGOs. The leader of the All-Russia Nature Protection Society in Vladimir argues that her group is "the only serious nature protection organization besides the government" (Esiakova, interview 2000). Government affiliates thus maintain Soviet-era environmental protection societies that had been co-opted by the state, maintain professional positions in the state administration, and most important, continue to espouse the value of loyalty to the state itself.[17]

Environmentalists Unite: The Issue of Nuclear Waste

One of the greatest challenges recently faced by the environmental movement occurred in the summer of 2000, when the Russian government proposed legislation allowing Russia to import twenty-one thousand tons of radioactive waste from countries such as the United States, Japan, France, and Bulgaria for reprocessing and long-term storage in the Urals and Siberia. This scheme would allow the country to earn approximately $20 billion of valuable hard currency over ten years. Russian environmentalists were outraged and made an enormous effort to publicize the potential negative environmental and health effects of this plan. Public opinion was clearly on the environmentalists' side: polls showed that the plan was opposed by more than 93 percent of Russians. In June, hundreds of environmental activists from fifty-eight regions in Russia gathered together in Moscow to oppose the plan (Peterson and Bielke 2001, 69). They decided to organize a petition drive to collect signatures to demand a national referendum on the issue. In response to the referendum initiative, government officials expressed skepticism about the role green NGOs should play in determining policy and once again charged environmental NGOs with espionage.

In spite of these charges, a coalition of several hundred professionalized and grassroots environmental organizations successfully gathered almost 2.5 million signatures in support of a referendum. Gathering signatures is no small task, since signing a petition requires citizens to give their address and passport number as well, offering the authorities a specific record of citizen protest. Russian environmentalists were supported in this effort by a number of European environmental organizations that channeled funding to the Russian groups and publicized the issue in their own countries.

Although environmental NGOs overcame their earlier divisions to work together, their campaign was not successful. The Central Election Commission ruled that only three-quarters (or 1,873,000) of the signatures were authentic, causing the campaign to fall short of the 2 million signatures required. Russian environmentalists have vowed to pursue the issue in the courts. While greens did not succeed in forcing a referendum, their petition drive demonstrated an unprecedented level of public support for an environmental issue in the post-Soviet period and reinvigorated their ties with local communities. In fact, adversity seems to have brought environmentalists together in a spirit of cooperation that the movement lacked in the mid-1990s and may presage a new era of growth and strategic adaptation.

Conclusion

The contemporary Russian environmental movement exhibits elements of change and continuity. While the existence of a sector of environmental nongovernmental organizations is new for Russia, the country's green NGOs, with few exceptions, are based upon preexisting institutions, networks of individuals, and norms. In reaching back to the past to facilitate current activism, all green organizations draw upon the resources of the state. Even many professionalized environmental groups, arguably the most similar to Western NGOs, rely on state scientific institutes to sponsor their organizations informally. This raises two interesting points. First, one legacy of the Soviet era appears to be greater state involvement in the development of Russian civil society, evident through NGOs' continuing reliance on state resources, even if the transfer of those resources is often indirect. Russian civil society organizations' ongoing reliance on the state is a logical outgrowth of the state's monopoly on organizational resources during the Soviet era. Second, analyzing the role of the state in early civil society development in Russia draws attention to the fact that the role played by state agencies, actors, and resources in supporting American and European NGOs is poorly understood. For the most part, scholars have relied on conventional wisdom about the purported autonomy of Western NGOs, a claim that may not stand up to greater scrutiny.

Certainly some of the activities that Russian environmental organizations engage in do not fall clearly into the role of acting as intermediaries between citizens and the state. Instead, these activities represent efforts to provide services related to environmental protection or recreation that were once the responsibility of the state. Grassroots groups in particular have leapt in to fill the loss of recreation opportunities for children and public maintenance of city parks. Public safety and public health information, as well as information about local recreation opportunities, are also frequently distributed by environmental NGOs. Professionalized environmental groups have adopted tasks previously carried out by the state's scientific research institutions and environmental inspectorate, including monitoring, antipoaching efforts, and the development of green technology. Government affiliates are well positioned to take on some of the functions of the former State Committee on Ecology. In part, then, instead of state–society engagement, environmental organizations are filling in for partially dismantled state bureaucracy and services.

Concerning the institutions, networks, and norms employed by Russian green NGOs, each of these "legacies of the past" has characteristics that may be more or less beneficial for generating social mobilization and contributing to civil society. Grassroots organizations emphasize the norms of voluntary labor and collective responsibility in caring for the community, but do so in a way that avoids politicized issues. Professionalized groups act self-confidently, in part based on the history of scientific autonomy and dissidence, yet they do so largely without contact with the general public. Finally, government affiliates eschew criticism in favor of supporting the government, and yet from their position as insiders they are able to promote environmental protection within local and regional administrations. Each of these three types of organization positions itself in relation to the state and society in part because of its orientation toward the Soviet past, a perspective that tends to be symbolized by the leader's professional background. The decision of whether to oppose, cooperate with, or avoid the state, and whether to interact with members of society, depends on how each leader envisions the goals and strategies of environmental activism.

While the impact of these divergent patterns of activism on future civil society development in Russia remains to be seen, this diversity within the environmental movement suggests that we cannot simply assume that the impact of Soviet-era social structures is monolithic or entirely undemocratic. Instead, each organization finds elements of a "usable past" within the Soviet legacy on which to base its activism. In fact, organizations that combine elements of Soviet-era mobilization with new practices may be the most in tune with their potential constituents, as Russian citizens are also learning to blend new and old survival strategies. These findings suggest that some features of postcommunist society, such as the persistence of friendship and personal survival networks, do not necessarily have a deleterious effect on civil society development, as has been previously thought (Howard 2003, 107–9).[18] If civic organizations are facilitated by social trust and norms of reciprocity, then Soviet-era networks, for example, may provide a basic building block for future civil society development. This demonstrates that measuring social organizations against an idealized template of Western groups may not be the best way of understanding what sort of foundation is being built for future activism. Instead, Russian civil society may have a distinct developmental trajectory that differs from that in the West.

For now, the diversity of orientations, activities, and organizational types bodes well for the sustainability of the Russian environmental movement even as the country's political and economic fortunes continue to shift in unpredictable ways. The question remains, however: how adaptable are these organizations, and how will they respond to new challenges? When environmentalists are confronted with obstacles in the future, will they persist in their current strategies of organization and activism, or will they be able to adjust to changing conditions? Thus far, environmentalists have been able to take advantage of the legacy of the past, but their ability to contribute to the development of civil society and to act as intermediary organizations will depend on their capacity to adapt and innovate.

Notes

1. Works that chart the increase of foreign assistance and its effect on NGOs include Sperling 1999, Mendelson and Glenn 2000, and Henry 2001. As for the number of NGOs in Russia, in her introductory remarks at the Kremlin-sponsored Civic Forum in 2001, Liudmila Alekseeva, leader of the Moscow Helsinki Group, noted that forum attendees represented more than 350,000 nongovernmental organizations (Zolotov 2001).

2. Information about many of these groups can be found in NGO handbooks such as *Obshchestvennye ob"edineniia sibirskogo regiona: Novosibirskaia Oblast'* (Sibirskii tsentr podderzhki obshchestvennykh initsiativ, 1998), *Spravochnik proektov i programm* (TACIS, 1995); and *Obshchestvennye ob"edineniia dal'nego vostoka: informatsionyi spravochnik* (ISAR-Dal'nii Vostok and USAID, 1998).

3. Howard (2002, 160) cites these statistics drawn from the 1995–97 World Values Survey. In this survey, membership in environmental groups in postcommunist countries lags behind nine other types of social associations, including political parties, professional associations, and educational, cultural, or artistic organizations.

4. In St. Petersburg alone, KEDR has 221 dues-paying members (Shemetov, interview 1999).

5. The party ultimately did not participate in the election. The Central Election Commission removed KEDR from the electoral list because a number of the party's candidates withdrew their names (See *RFE/RL Newsline*, December 13, 1999, www.rferl.org/newsline/1999/12/1–rus/rus–131299.html).

6. In general, parties from across the ideological spectrum have failed to thrive in Russia's executive-dominated political system. Russia's "superpresidential" system limits the importance of legislative and electoral politics as political officials recognize that access to power is not dependent upon policy platforms or accountability to citizen demands (Fish 2000).

7. The two congresses were primarily attended by independent ecologists. NGO participation reportedly was low. For example, at the 1999 meeting NGO representatives only accounted for 25 percent of attendees (Zakharov 1999).

8. Information gathered in author interviews. See also Green World's *Baltic News* (www.greenworld.org.ru/eng/gwnews/bn/bngw046.htm), Carpenter 2001 on Scholars for Global Responsibility, and Elliot 1998 on Phoenix.

9. President Putin was quoted as stating that "foreign secret service organizations not only use diplomatic cover but also very actively use all sorts of ecological and public organizations" in *Komsomol'skaia pravda* in July 1999 (*RFE/RL Newsline*, July 20, 1999).

10. *RFE/RL Newsline*, March 3, 2000; and *Baltic News*, no. 53, February 22, 2000.

11. President Putin was quoted by Canadian journalists as saying, "I've often thought what I should do when my term expires. . . . It is a noble task to support the ecological movement. At least I wouldn't be sorry to spend time on it" (Hoffman 2000).

12. I have argued that an organization's primary source of funding (foreign or domestic) and sponsorship (by societal actors or state actors) can influence its behavior in civil society (Henry 2002). I develop this argument further in my dissertation, "Changing Environments: Russia's Green Movement, Civil Society, and Political Transformation," University of California, Berkeley, 2004.

13. Most professionalized environmental groups are registered according to the 1995 Law "On Social Associations" and the 1996 Law "On Noncommercial Organizations."

14. All interviews were conducted by the author from March 1999 to June 2000. The interview questions were open-ended, and leaders of environmental organizations were allowed to give as many responses to the question as they wished.

15. Scholars working within the social movement literature have also recognized that leaders' backgrounds shape organizations, strategies, and outcomes (Morris and Staggenborg 2004).

16. Professionalized activists are less likely to have been previously affiliated with the All-Russian Society of Nature Protection, generally considered to be a "tame" organization by the late Soviet period (Weiner 1999, 195–200).

17. Given this status, one could question whether they are really self-organized groups within civil society. Their official status as independently registered organizations and their persistent advocacy of environmental issues within an indifferent government administration, however, makes government affiliates potential sites of association and debate in the public sphere.

18. For an argument that the persistence of survival networks may, in fact, support the development of social trust and civil society in Russia, see Gibson 2001.

References

Carothers, Thomas. 1999. *Aiding Democracy Abroad: The Learning Curve*. Washington, DC: Carnegie Endowment for International Peace.

Carpenter, Tom. 2001. "Blowing the Whistle on Russia's Nuclear Roulette." *Give and Take* 4, nos. 1 and 2 (Spring/Summer): 45.

Center for Russian Environmental Policy. 1999. "Notes." *Towards Sustainable Development* 1, no. 12 (September): 44.

Dawson, Jane. 1996. *Eco-Nationalism: Anti-Nuclear Activism and National Identity in Russia, Lithuania, and Ukraine*. Durham, NC: Duke University Press.

Diamond, Larry. 1999. *Developing Democracy: Toward Consolidation*. Baltimore, MD: Johns Hopkins University Press.

Dunlap, Riley E., George H. Gallup, and Alec M. Gallup. 1993. "Of Global Concern: Results of the Health of the Planet Survey." *Environment* 35 (November): 7–15, 33–39.

Elliot, Karin V. 1998. "The Evolution of an NGO: "Phoenix" Rises Out of Government Effort to Stop Poaching," *Give and Take* 1, no. 1 (Summer): 11.

Felgenhauer, Pavel. 2001. "Why Russia Wants Waste." *Moscow Times*, January 4.

Fish, M. Steven. 2000. "The Executive Deception: Superpresidentialism and the Degradation of Russian Politics." 2000. In *Building the Russian State: Institutional Crisis and the Quest for Democratic Governance*, ed. Valerie Sperling, 177–92. Boulder, CO: Westview Press.

Gibson, James L. 2001. "Social Networks, Civil Society, and the Prospects for Consolidating Russia's Democratic Transition," *American Journal of Political Science* 45, no. 1 (January): 51–68.

Grishina, Elena, and Iurii Dzhibladze. 2000. "Report: On the Violations Committed in the Course of Registration and Re-Registration on Public Associations in the Russian Federation in 1999." Information Center of the Human Rights Movement and Center for the Development of Democracy and Human Rights, Moscow (February 15).

Henry, Laura A. 2001. "Social Movements, Transnational Actors, and Democratization: The Case of the Russian Environmental Movement." 2001. In *The Paradoxes of Progress: Globalization and Post-Socialist Cultures*, ed. Rachael Stryker and Jennifer Patico, 69–92. Kroeber Anthropological Society Papers, no. 86.

———. 2002. "Two Paths to a Greener Future." *Demokratizatsiya* 10, no. 2 (Spring): 184–206.

Hoffman, David. 2000. "Putin's Words to Media Abroad Contrast with Actions at Home." *Washington Post* (December 17).

Howard, Marc Morjé. 2002. "The Weakness of Postcommunist Civil Society." *Journal of Democracy* 13, no. 1 (January): 157–69.

———. 2003. *The Weakness of Civil Society in Postcommunist Europe*. Cambridge: Cambridge University Press, 2003.

Ianitskii, Oleg. 1996. *Ekologicheskoe dvizhenie Rossii: kriticheskii analiz*. Moscow: Russian Academy of Sciences, Institute of Sociology.

Linz, Juan J., and Alfred Stepan. 1996. *Problems of Democratic Transition and Consolidation: Southern Europe, South America, and Postcommunist Europe*. Baltimore, MD: Johns Hopkins University Press.

Mendelson, Sarah E., and John K. Glenn. 2000. *Democracy Assistance and NGO Strategies in Postcommunist Societies*. Democracy and Rule of Law Project Working Paper no. 8. Washington, DC: Carnegie Endowment for International Peace (February).

Morris, Aldon, and Suzanne Staggenborg. 2004. "Leadership in Social Movements." In *The Blackwell Companion to Social Movements*, ed. David A. Snow, Sarah A. Soule, and Hanspeter Kriesi, 171–98. Malden, MA: Blackwell.

Newell, Josh, and Emma Wilson. 1996. *The Russian Far East: Forests, Biodiversity Hotspots and Industrial Development*. Tokyo: Friends of the Earth.

Ottaway, Marina, and Thomas Carothers, eds. 2000. *Funding Virtue: Civil Society Aid and Democracy Promotion*. Washington, DC: Carnegie Endowment for International Peace.

Peterson, D. J., and Eric K. Bielke. 2001. "The Reorganization of Russia's Environmental Bureaucracy: Implications and Prospects." *Post-Soviet Geography and Economics* 42, no. 1 (January–February): 65–76.

Petrova, A. 1999. "Only One-Third of Russians Are Satisfied with the Environment." Public Opinion Foundation (FOM). english.fom.ru/reports/frames/eof992405.html (accessed June 14, 1999).

Public Opinion Foundation (Fond Obshchestvennogo Mneniia). 2002. "Polluted Water Is Worse for People's Health than Beer." english.fom.ru/reports/frames/short/eof022107.html (accessed July 13, 2002).

———. 2001. "Problemy Ekologii." www.fom.ru/reports/frames/short/do14406.html (accessed November 22, 2001).

Putnam, Robert D. 1993. *Making Democracy Work*. Princeton, NJ: Princeton University Press.

Sperling, Valerie. 1999. *Organizing Women in Contemporary Russia: Engendering Transition*. Cambridge: Cambridge University Press.

Van Rooy, Alison, and Mark Robinson, eds. 1998. *Civil Society and the Aid Industry*. London: Earthscan Publications.

Weiner, Douglas R. 1999. *A Little Corner of Freedom: Russian Nature Protection from Stalin to Gorbachev*. Berkeley: University of California Press.

Whitefield, Stephen. 2003. "Russian Mass Attitudes toward the Environment, 1993–2001." *Post-Soviet Affairs* 19, no. 2 (April–June): 95–113.

Whiteley, John M. 1999. "Still Tilting against the Environment." 1999. In *Critical Masses: Citizens, Nuclear Weapons Production, and Environmental Destruction in the United States and Russia*, ed. Russell J. Dalton et al., 333–77. Cambridge, MA: MIT Press.

Zakharov, Vladimir M. 1999. "First Congress, Second Congress. . . ," *Towards a Sustainable Russia* 1, no. 12 (September): 6.

Zolotov, Andrei. 2001. "Civic Activists Storm the Kremlin." *Moscow Times*, November 22.

Interviews

Aramilev, Vladimir. 1999. Institute of Sustainable Development. Vladivostok, November 17.

Dubinin, Aleksandr. 1999. Ekoklub. Novosibirsk, December 9.

Esiakova, Galina. 2000. All-Russian Nature Protection Society. Vladimir, May 22.

Gadzhiev, Ilias. 1999. All-Russian Nature Protection Society. Novosibirsk, December 3.

Rakhno, Tat´iana. 1999. Novomir. Novosibirsk, December 2.

Shemetov, Vladimir. 1999. KEDR. St. Petersburg, April 22.
Smetanina, Natalia. 1999. Laboratory for Environmental Education. Vladivostok, October 29.
Sobolevskii, Evgenii. 1999. Ekolog. Vladivostok, October 28.
Solov'ev, Valerii. 2000. Briansk Ecological Union. Briansk, April 24.
Tsyplenkov, Sergei. 2000. Greenpeace. Moscow, May 31.
Vasil'eva, Tat'iana. 2000. Detskii sad "Ladushka." Briansk, April 23.

14

Disability Organizations in the Regions

Kate Thomson

The literature indicates that the development of civil society can have an empowering effect on citizens and promote change. Within the realm of welfare, proponents of welfare pluralism point out that the involvement of voluntary sector organizations may have a positive impact on service delivery and policy across the sector (Mayo 1994, 22; Green 1996). This chapter describes the activities of nongovernmental organizations concerned with disabled children in two Russian cities. Following the conceptualization of civil society outlined in the introduction—that is, civil society as a space of collective activity by citizens that can promote political change or continuity—the chapter explores the extent to which disability organizations have the potential to promote "bottom-up" change in the local welfare sphere.

Theoretical Context

State–Voluntary Sector Relationships

Interest in and analysis of voluntary sector involvement in welfare takes a number of approaches, outlined and categorized by Salamon and Anheier (1998). What they term "government failure" approaches (alternatively named the "vacuum hypothesis" by Westlund and Westerdahl 1996, cited in Sätre-Åhlander 2000, 446) indicate that the voluntary sector can contribute to the overall welfare sphere by "gap filling"— that is, providing goods and services that state welfare structures fail to provide. In the case of Russia, glaring "gaps" in Soviet state welfare provision had been exposed over the years preceding the end of Communist Party rule (McAuley 1991, 207). Any agency acting to plug some of those gaps might be welcomed as a positive force. A slightly different perspective on "government failure" would assert that voluntary involvement in welfare is preferable to state involvement in and of itself: that voluntary sector welfare provision is morally superior to that of the state (Green 1993; Kidd 2002, 330). In cases where the state has been indubitably discredited as a provider of welfare services, as happened in Russia from the glasnost period of the late 1980s, this view holds an element of potency for writers from across the political spectrum. This can be combined with a more general sense that the voluntary sector is a desirable element of "civil society," a building block of truly democratic societies, which needs to be nurtured in both West and East (Keane 1988; Powell and Guerin 1997; Salamon 1995).

It is not essential to take a moralistic, either/or position on voluntary versus state welfare provision, however. Many writers, rather than assuming conflict and competition, expect cooperation and partnership between state and voluntary sectors—an interdependence approach (Salamon and Anheier 1998, 224–25). In practice, empirical studies worldwide have tended to demonstrate that state–voluntary sector relationships in this sphere are often of a cooperative, interdependent nature.

This chapter explores concepts around state–voluntary sector relationships in the welfare sphere in relation to four case study organizations working in the area of disability in Russia. The organizations' role as "gap fillers" is assessed in the local context of relevant state service provision. Relationships between the organizations and state structures are explored in some detail. Although the study revealed a variety of relationships between state and voluntary sector organizations, the chapter ultimately concludes that "interdependence" provides the best descriptive and normative base from which to analyze such organizations' development. State structures were found to have an ambiguous but often facilitative role in the development of effective civil society organizations in this sphere, even where those organizations' role included challenging state policies and provision.

Disability

In addition to the concepts around state–voluntary sector relationships, a second theoretical strand running through the evaluation of service provision is provided by the social model of disability (sometimes termed the "civil rights model"). This is an approach that draws a distinction between impairment (a defect in the biological mechanism of the body or mind) and disability (a disadvantage created by social organization and attitudes) (Oliver 1990, 11). The focus is on social structures that serve to effectively disable people who have mental or physical impairments.

The social model is in opposition to the individualized models of disability prevalent in industrialized cultures. One indication of the individual approach is medicalization (ibid., 43), which focuses only on the impaired or "abnormal" body or mind as the source of disablement: "to be defined as a 'flawed' body is simultaneously to be defined as incapable of adequate social participation" (Hughes 2002, 60). Segregation from "normal" social structures has often been a consequence of being labeled disabled or defective; treatment and "repair" of the flawed organism is also emphasized above all else. "Personal tragedy" theory is another aspect of the individualization of disability, emphasizing charity, pity, and "compensation" as appropriate responses (Oliver 1990, 1–3).

The social model approach is a critical one that seeks to expose and challenge the way that those individualized accounts inform social attitudes and institutions. Analyses based on this approach are human rights-based and assume the need for material change to social structures in order to reduce or eliminate oppression. Disabled people are presented as an oppressed minority, aligning the approach with feminist and antiracist standpoints: "as in the cases of women and black people, oppressive theories of disability systematically distort and stereotype the identities of their putative subjects, restricting their full humanity by constituting them only in their 'problem' aspects" (Abberley 1997). Civil society organizations that potentially are effective in terms of this approach therefore parallel movements of other oppressed groups in presenting a "politics of difference" that challenges structural inequities (Young 2000, 81–120).

One aspect of challenging social constructions of disability—including those maintained by state structures—might be the articulation of new and more positive identities for what was a previously hidden and stigmatized group. In the context of this chapter, therefore, the social model approach forms a background for identifying "gaps" or injustices in state services that might be filled or challenged by civil society organizations and for assessing how effective existing organizations have been in meeting those aims. In so doing, however, the chapter also highlights the difficulties of applying this inherently "Western" political and analytic approach in the given context.

Background

The Study

The empirical research on which the chapter is based was carried out in 1998 in the cities of Samara and Saratov, both large regional centers in European Russia. Exploration of voluntary sector activities took place within the wider framework of a project investigating the range of services and support across all sectors for people with learning difficulties (mental retardation). The study indicated from an early stage that state provision of services for this group was lacking, both in its scope and its approach: there were definite gaps that required filling. As well as state activity, the activities of the voluntary and informal sectors (i.e., care provided by family and friends) were examined to provide a fuller picture of the welfare sphere.

All the material presented here was collected through interviews with organization heads, and sometimes with other members or officials.[1] It was supported in most cases with documentary data such as publicity materials and organizational records. There were also opportunities to observe the workings of the organizations by attending meetings or other events. The chapter is informed as well by the other elements of the study— that is, by interviews, documentary data, and observations from state sector institutions and professionals and by parents or other informal caretakers of disabled people.

Local Welfare Context

To identify a possible need for civil society organizations in the case study areas to fill gaps or challenge injustices, a brief outline of state structures and services relevant to people with learning difficulties is required.

The most relevant state services inherited from the Soviet era targeted at children with learning difficulties were the special schools system and long-stay residential institutions. Special, or auxiliary (*vspomogatel'nye*), schools represented a part of the Soviet educational and welfare system in which there was much pride (see McCagg 1989; Foreman 1997; Thomson 2002a). One category of school was for children with mild to moderate learning difficulties who were regarded as "educable." This school system was still in place in both the cities studied, and there was a mix of day schools and those with boarding facilities within the cities.[2] The system had changed very little, despite evidence of professional engagement with "Western" models of special education—for example, the ideal of integrated education (see Thomson 2002a).

The social model of disability regards any form of "special" education as oppressive. Such systems set disabled children apart from others, thereby locating the "problem" within the children rather than considering that the mainstream education system needs to be challenged to become inclusive of children who have impairments (Oliver 1996, 78). The Russian system was distinguished by its very high degree of segregation or differentiation between children based on the perceived type and degree of impairment (Thomson 2002a). Service provision was driven by an apparently "scientific" system of defining what kind of organic impairment children had. It therefore presented a child-deficit, medicalized understanding of impairment and disability. Furthermore, the system was very much geared toward those children deemed most intellectually able; those who had mild or moderate learning difficulties were relatively well served in the special schools system. Children with more severe impairments were explicitly excluded even from the special education system—the only provision for them was in the form of long-stay residential institutions.

Residential institutions for children with more severe impairments (those regarded as "uneducable") were usually located outside the cities, in rural or semirural areas. These provided varying educational input depending on the residents' perceived degree of impairment. Young adults often moved on from these facilities to adult "psychoneurological" institutions. The system often therefore involved disabled people being effectively segregated and institutionalized for their entire lives. Many parent informants in this study regarded the institutions as a dreaded last resort, although many also reported being advised by medical professionals to place their children in this system from infancy. The institutional and educational systems therefore separated disabled people both from nondisabled people and from one another on the basis of impairment category. This kind of segregation, or "fragmentation" (Vernon and Swain 2002, 92), has formed the cornerstone of analyses of disablist oppression.

Although the old state services had changed little, there had been some development of new state services in both Samara and Saratov in the post-perestroika period. This reflected national directives regarding service provision for disabled children and other vulnerable groups. New community-based social services (Thomson 2002b) included "rehabilitation centers" for disabled children. In Saratov the main new rehabilitation center was primarily a residential facility used by children from all over the oblast. Samara had four relatively new centers offering a variety of services: one operated mainly as a preschool facility for disabled children; another provided recreational activities as a kind of after-school club, as well as therapeutic interventions; and yet another was set to operate as a preschool facility as well as offering residential periods for other children.[3] Overall, Samara's rehabilitation center network was more diverse, covering a greater number of children with diverse needs, and was therefore more inclusive in the broad sense.

The rehabilitation centers offered a more inclusive, integrated approach to services for disabled children than that offered by the special schools or residential systems. Those children living in the community (rather than in institutions) who could not access schooling due to being regarded as too severely disabled could make some use of the centers. However, such contact was not always regular or frequent. Perhaps inevitably, since they called on the same pool of professionals and had to complement the system in some way, the centers drew on the terminology and practices of the special education field in defining their work and the type of children they served. They increased the scope of state services, filling certain systemic gaps and addressing previously unmet needs, without challenging radically the approach to children with learning difficulties.

Another part of the community-based social services initiative was the social service centers that were provided at the level of city district. They offered access to social workers and other relevant professionals able to dispense advice and in some cases material support. One of the vulnerable groups catered for by the centers was disabled children. The centers represented a sphere of activity and an accessibility that was lacking in the Soviet welfare system, although their direct contribution to the welfare of most families and children who participated in this study was marginal.

In both sites of study, the main gaps or injustices in state welfare provision for children with learning difficulties involved access to education for more severely disabled children and availability of longer-term services that did not entail separation from the family and community. State authorities were not entirely unaware of these problems, as can be seen from the service developments that had happened in the years leading up to this study. These developments were contingent upon local decision making and resources; in Samara the expansion of community-based services for disabled children had occurred more rapidly and in a more diverse way than in Saratov. This provides an interesting backdrop against which to assess the gap-filling or interdependence theses of voluntary sector activity: were organizations more active or effective in Saratov, where gaps were greater, or in Samara, where state institutions had more obviously committed themselves to making changes and were therefore, perhaps, more cooperative with civil society efforts?

Case Study Organizations

Voluntary organizations were identified through personal contacts (for example, with people working in state services) and publicity materials. Overall, three relevant organizations were identified in Saratov and four in Samara. There were few nongovernmental bodies in Saratov and Samara currently offering "services" per se to people with learning difficulties. This reflected, more than anything, existing voluntary organizations' operational capabilities; it also accorded with the national pattern of voluntary sector development, in that indigenous service organizations are relatively rare (Pestrikova 1998). The present study found only one case of direct service provision for people with learning difficulties by the voluntary sector, and this was an international rather than an indigenous body.[4] With this one exception, the organizations did not form part of the dynamic, new, internationally funded third sector: their activities were small-scale and chiefly of a charitable or advocacy nature. I have selected two organizations from each city as case studies. Although the study as a whole explored the position of children and adults with learning difficulties, the four voluntary sector organizations selected as case studies here were all involved with disabled children. This is a fair reflection of the emphasis on children within state policies and provision and of the lack of organizations that focused on people with learning difficulties as opposed to disability in the generic sense. In each city, the local organization most active in the relevant sphere was selected for case study. The other two case studies are provided by the respective local branches of a national network of organizations, which provide interest because of the contrasting fortunes of the two branches.

Saratov

The two case-study organizations from Saratov are the Children's Fund and First Step (Pervyi shag). The Children's Fund was the regional branch of a national charitable organization that had been established in the late 1980s as an official initiative to tackle child-related social problems, of which there was a growing awareness at the time. Its projects concerned children in general, primarily those from disadvantaged families or living in state institutions. In the past, the Saratov branch had carried out a number of projects involving disabled children, including those with learning difficulties. First, it provided material assistance and social and cultural outings for children living in residential institutions and for children with severe learning difficulties. It also offered more community-based projects such as a drop-in advice service for families, a "parents' school" for those whose children had disabilities, and a parallel social club for their children. The Fund frequently hosted social functions for disadvantaged children and their families, usually in partnership with the state social service centers. Local children registered as disabled and those attending special schools would be invited.

Modest forms of material support for the Fund's activities came from the state and local businesses. For example, local government waived rental fees on the office accommodation. Support for specific activities was often sought through established contacts in the business world (Children's Fund [Saratov], interview 1998a). Effectively, methods of extracting charitable donations had changed little since Soviet times when enterprises were expected to fulfill their duty to the local community by supporting schools or other institutions. Such "donations" rarely took a monetary form; many social and economic institutions at this time were running on a virtually cash-free basis, or what Woodruff (1999) calls the "barter of the bankrupt." Instead, donors would offer the use of facilities or materials that they did have available. Although it cannot be regarded as resource-rich, the Fund was able to make extensive use of established personal and institutional networks to provide some support for its activities. This included links with local media. For example, at the time of the study an appeal for books was being presented on local television for the Children's Fund project of stocking libraries for child residential facilities.

First Step was a self-help association of families with disabled children. It provided a supportive forum for discussion and advice on services and many other areas of life; it did not provide direct services or charitable assistance. Despite its profile, First Step was not a grassroots organization in the true sense. Its creation was not the initiative of parents but of the social worker responsible for disability issues in the city's central social service center. She had made the initial links between parents and organized the first meetings (Central Social Service Center, interview 1998). This relationship continued as the center informed eligible parents about the organization's existence, and some meetings were held in a room provided by the center. Members were also gained through the city's rehabilitation center where the chair of the association worked as the chief doctor.

Samara

The two Samara case study organizations are the Samara branch of the Children's Fund and the Association for Disabled Children. Samara's Children's Fund was far less active than its counterpart in Saratov; while practically every interviewee in Saratov referred me to the Fund, several in Samara claimed that it was defunct. The resources—both material and human—at its disposal appeared to be far more limited, and its activities by 1998 were mainly restricted to the relief of material hardship, such as distributing donated clothing and other goods (Children's Fund [Samara], interview 1998b).

The Samara Association for Disabled Children was made up of parents and professionals, and its chief activities focused on support and services for children who were deaf or hearing-impaired. It was included in this study, however, because it spoke out on all disability-related issues, and because its services were not exclusive to hearing-impaired children. It was created in the same period as the national Children's Fund and was similarly formed by "official," although not governmental, figures—health and welfare service professionals and journalists. In 1991, the association had set up and run the city's first children's rehabilitation center. After a year, the operation of the center was transferred to local government, which matched it with three more rehabilitation centers in the city (Association for Disabled Children, interview 1998). The association had a lay membership of parents, mainly recruited through the rehabilitation center with which the organization was still closely associated.

Voluntary Organizations as Agents of Change

Shaping the Welfare Sphere?

One of the aims of this chapter is to assess the success or potential of the voluntary sector organizations to act as agents of change in the local welfare sphere—could they plug gaps or address injustices created by state structures? All four case study organizations had close historical or ongoing relationships with state bodies, although this relationship was sometimes bound up with problems. Despite operational and structural limitations, some of the organizations could be seen as effecting change.

The most "active" organizations were active chiefly in a social and advocacy sense, rather than providing services in the usual sense. They offered meeting places for families who had disabled children and alerted the relevant state authorities to particular problems faced by young disabled people and their families. In this latter sense, and in some more concrete examples, it is possible to pick out examples of organizations that had acted as change agents in the local service provision sphere. Where this had happened, the nature of relationships with state structures can be seen as crucial.

As an "official" charity in the 1980s, the Children's Fund's origins were in the "ambiguous zone" between the worlds of government ("bureaucracy") and the voluntary sector ("associational" world) (Billis 1989). In its early period, the Fund was instrumental in persuading state agencies to make policy and provision changes to address children's issues (White 1995, 169). Some important, even radical, initiatives were produced that became established parts of governmental welfare provision—for example, the community social service centers mentioned above. The Fund's development might be seen as a good example of the potential for civil society institutions to shape and facilitate change to state systems through a relationship of interdependence. However, this very lack of definite autonomy from the state reduced the integrity of the Fund in certain quarters at a time when state provision for disabled children in particular had been discredited. At the national level, even in the Fund's early years, criticism in the press focused on this ambiguous role (Waters 1992; Harwin 1996). There is a credibility dilemma here, raising the question of whether an organization can meaningfully challenge state structures while relying on them to maintain its own status.

In both Saratov and Samara, the Children's Fund began the advice-related and charitable assistance work that had largely been taken over by state community social service centers. Historically, then, these organizations had shaped the welfare sphere, albeit as part of a national project. The head of the Saratov Children's Fund explicitly stated in an interview that it was still their role to innovate, and that the state was expected to take over the administration of successful projects (Children's Fund, interview 1998a). As Salamon and Anheier (1998) point out, in running services taken over from the voluntary sector, the state is to some extent dependent on that sector for its knowledge and expertise—an aspect of interdependence. The Saratov branch's innovations were on a much smaller scale than in the past, but its expertise was still recognized and valued by local state structures. By contrast, at the time of the study the Samara Children's Fund had a much less productive relationship with the state. The director stated that there was currently no cooperation between the Fund and the committee now in charge of social services development in the region, citing a lack of will on the part of the committee (Children's Fund, interview 1998b). Its involvement and influence in state welfare service provision and even in charitable provision generally had waned significantly. This role, particularly in the area of disabled children, had been assumed by another organization—the Association for Disabled Children (ADC).

All four case study organizations were to a large extent dependent on the favor of the local governmental sector for accessing resources, even though there was no direct funding relationship. Three of the organizations had permanent administrative accommodation that was subsidized or provided by the state: rental was waived for the Children's Fund in both cities, and the Samara ADC used as its base the state rehabilitation center of which the association head was director. Organizations were able to use state links to access additional resources. Close relations to state bodies gave organizations some cachet and opened the door to material support—albeit limited—from local benefactors and commercial organizations. Those with the strongest links were able to pass on this advantage to smaller organizations. First Step, for example, maintained a good relationship with the Children's Fund in Saratov: one of its most active board members was involved with the work of the Fund on a voluntary basis. This relationship was instrumental for First Step, because the recommendation or intervention of the Fund head could open doors to support from commercial bodies and from the state (First Step, interview 1998).

First Step also had more direct links with the state sector, which facilitated one of its chief aims, to represent the interests of parents within the local state welfare authorities. For example, the social service center's disability co-coordinator (who set up the group) took an active part in some meetings. This offered the opportunity for information sharing and discussion of services and benefits, about which she had expert knowledge. Observation of meetings with and without this official indicated, however, that her presence as an "expert" inhibited the discussion somewhat. For example, decision making processes in the commissions, which made recommendations for educational provision based on assessments of individual children, were discussed at length in a private meeting (April 1998). When concerns about favoritism and "political" judgments affecting commissions' decisions were raised at a meeting held in the state facility (May 1998), the official quashed them as not meriting discussion. Another direct state connection for First Step was that the association chairperson was head doctor at the oblast rehabilitation center. He was a true member in that he had a disabled son, and his status must have given the association credibility with other professionals. However, this affiliation clearly limited the organization's inclination to push for change in the rehabilitation service. Thus, while affiliation with state bodies lends credibility to an organization, this very affiliation potentially inhibits its effectiveness, allowing for some control from state bureaucracy. White (1995, 168) neatly sums up this difficult balancing act: "the desirable situation was of course to be simultaneously immune to pressure from the party-state authorities while being able to influence the latter."

Reliance upon state relationships for resources, including private donations, can in theory compromise the self-determination of voluntary organizations, producing what Salamon and Anheier (1998, 225) term "philanthropic paternalism." Furthermore, for theorists who regard the voluntary sector as necessarily superior to state welfare provision, such a lack of real autonomy from the state might be regarded as problematic. In context, however, this genuine interdependence between the sectors with regard to credibility and resources is very understandable. The Russian voluntary sector had been marred by corruption scandals; from the perspective of donors, official connections guaranteed that donations and sponsorship agreements were "safe."

What determined the closeness and effectiveness of organizations' relationships with the state? How could organizations play a key role in the local welfare sphere? For the case studies, personal connections appeared to be very important. A "family connection" between the Saratov Children's Fund and the local administration was claimed by one respondent to explain the relative inactivity of Samara's Children's Fund compared to Saratov's (Anonymous interviewee 1998). This is certainly a very plausible explanation for the degree of cooperation with administration and the authority that the Fund enjoyed in Saratov: family and life history links are ones that may still be appealed to in order to make things happen in the "new" Russia (Lonkila 1997; Ledeneva 1998). Similarly, the head of the Samara Association for Disabled Children was able to utilize her presence within local networks as the director of a state rehabilitation center to maximize the ADC's profile. These connections served the respective organizations well. However, the fact that they were based on existing relationships does not bode well for the development of a truly diverse voluntary sector.

The nature of the state structures themselves, providing the local institutional background against which voluntary organizations were attempting to work, was another important factor determining the degree of mutual influence. In Saratov, there was a State Committee for Cooperation with Voluntary Organizations, which appeared to make a real difference to the way that the two sectors cooperated, even if this applied only to certain state-approved organizations—important in this context, the Children's Fund. Conversely, the different administrative structures in welfare services in Samara—the existence of a single new body, spearheading changes to disability services—may have had an impact on the perceived need for action from the voluntary sector. Although there were calls for change in state disability services from voluntary sector organizations, parent and professional interviewees in Samara generally appeared to feel rather more satisfied with services available than those in Saratov: while still full of gaps and bureaucratic obstacles, by comparison they offered a significant amount of variety.

Shaping Responses to Disability?

The previous section discussed the organizations' presence within and practical impact upon the local welfare sphere. The chapter now turns to an exploration of their ideological impact. Did they challenge dominant constructions of disability/learning difficulties? Were they offering a "politics of difference" or articulating new identities?

Addressing Injustices

The earlier discussion highlighted certain gaps and inequities in the operation of the state welfare system for children with learning difficulties. Did the voluntary organizations recognize these injustices, and in which ways did they address or draw attention to them? A key area of concern was the special education system, which was highly differentiated, or segregated, on the basis of impairment and effectively excluded or disadvantaged a significant number of children. Only one of the case-study organizations—First Step—was closely concerned with, and vocal in its criticisms of, special education. This largely reflected the parent membership's concerns. However, the members were challenging not the fundamental principles of the system, but its shoddy, arbitrary administration. Specifically, there were protests against the erroneous, sometimes apparently malicious, categorization of certain children and the consequential detrimental effect on their access to educational provision (First Step Organization Meeting, interview 1998). First Step was suggesting a way of addressing some of the problems in the system, advocating the development of a new school for children labeled as having severe learning difficulties. Some children excluded from existing schools on the basis of severe impairment would therefore be able to remain in the system (First Step, interview 1998).

In Samara, the Association for Disabled Children also proposed a new kind of special education institution: a training institute incorporating a sheltered enterprise for young people graduating from special schools. It did so in the context of a November 1998 conference on vocational and professional education for disabled young people, attended by statutory and voluntary sector representatives. The "problem" in this case had therefore already been recognized by those in the local state sector, and the organization's position was suggestive rather than confrontational. In neither of these examples were the organizations radically challenging the special education system. Rather, they were demanding the system's expansion to include more categories and types of institution. This is a position that could be criticized from a Western social model perspective, which regards any form of segregation as oppressive.

These suggestions can in their context, however, be regarded as significant and reflective of immediate, legitimate concerns of parents and professionals. Parents in First Step, for example, were challenging the "oppression" of some children's total exclusion from the education system. The urgent priority, understandably, was that these children should have access to education. In this context, demanding the dismantling of the special education system in itself can be seen as a rather distant luxury. The Samara ADC's proposals for postschool provision were a response to the general socioeconomic situation of the time. Those already disadvantaged by impairment were more likely to be exposed to unemployment and other forms of material hardship. Given the lack of an effective social safety net for any members of society, the creation of structures to protect a particularly vulnerable group of young people cannot be seen, except in the most rigid social model analysis, as a continuation of oppression.

The organizations were also in a small way addressing gaps and injustices for disabled children in the medical sphere. By and large, in so doing they complied with and even encouraged a "medicalized" approach. For example, the Saratov Children's Fund's work with disabled children was placed within its "Health" stream. The emphasis of services it offered for disabled children and their families was on cure and treatment: tutelage for parents on their children's conditions and help for children within the psychiatric hospital children's ward (Children's Fund [Saratov], interview 1998a). First Step, the parents' organization, included in its aims and objectives the "restoration of impaired functioning and skills" for disabled children (First Step 1997). Much of its supportive work with families involved providing information about treatments for certain conditions; the concerns of many of the members appeared to revolve around medical issues, such as obtaining medicines (First Step Organization Meeting, interview 1998).

In their criticism of the medical model, social model analysts tend to assume that appropriate medical treatments will be provided for disabled people when necessary; their concern is that disability should not be seen *primarily* as a medical problem (Oliver 1990, 48). The background to this study involve a health infrastructure that was truly in crisis; where access to appropriate interventions, such as drug therapies or physical rehabilitation, was severely restricted. Regarding children with learning difficulties as "sick" (*bol'nye*) can be unhelpful in shaping perceptions of the kind of support they might need. However, in their context, organizations that provoke discussion about access to necessary medical interventions or seek merely to improve experiences and understanding of medical treatment should be seen as representing legitimate and even challenging voices.

These examples highlight the tension inherent in applying an apparently universal, human-rights based model such as the social model of disability to a rather different economic, political, and cultural setting from that within which it was first conceptualized. Although useful in highlighting and exploring injustices or possible gaps in services, the very simplicity of the model renders it somewhat insensitive to different contexts and situationally appropriate responses.[5]

A Politics of Difference?

Voluntary organizations working in the area of disability clearly have positive potential to promote the rights of their members or "client" groups, and to articulate new and positive identities. The case study organizations were resisting professional definitions of disability (for example, in the medical and educational spheres) only in a very limited way. These groups did not regard themselves as having a "disability politics" agenda. However, we can identify some ways in which organizations were successfully empowering or promoting the rights of their target groups.

First Step, the Saratov parents' association, offers the most obvious example of limited "empowerment." By observing meetings (April–May 1998) and interviewing members, I could identify the association as having three distinct functions: *emotional support*, an *information and advice* service, and *advocacy*. The organization's very existence promoted the sense that parents of disabled children could have a collective identity and voice. Encountering commonalities of experience was especially important—and potentially empowering—for parents, as the recent history of families of disabled children was one of isolation, silence, and stigma.

The meetings' role as an information and advice source was met through exchange of experiences. Group members were able to arm each other with knowledge about rights and entitlements and on where to go (or sometimes, which person to speak to) to have them upheld. For example, one member would be aware of a strategy for avoiding a particular problem—such as a particular pharmacy that was willing to dispense free medicines to disabled children. In other instances, members would be able to clear up a point of procedure or entitlement about which others were confused. The importance of mutual support and information should not be underestimated; a developing awareness of "rights" in itself cannot be seen as anything other than a political perspective. Although advocacy was not regarded as a prime aim of the association, it did not shy away from bringing particular issues to the attention of the appropriate authorities—for example, the need for educational provision for children labeled "uneducable" and for transparent procedures to access certain benefits.

First Step was "empowering" parents of disabled children by providing a collective voice and a basic sense of solidarity. Creation of a legitimate and assertive voice for this group was particularly important in a context where some professionals still asserted in interviews for this study that parents of children with learning difficulties were themselves usually "sick" or dissolute. The coming into being of all four case study organizations, and their involvement in the sphere of child disability, indicates and encourages social recognition of the existence and rights of disabled children. In this sense the organizations might be credited with *enabling* the articulation of new and more positive identities by challenging, albeit indirectly, cultural constructions of childhood disability—including learning difficulties—as tragic and shameful.

Conclusion

The focus of the chapter has been regional and local. Indeed, these case studies from two separate localities indicate that local factors were paramount in determining the extent of voluntary sector activities and influence. National factors, which were significant in stimulating the original emergence of certain of the organizations, had become less important. Even the Children's Fund, a supposedly national organization, had fragmented and was dependent on local sponsorship and cooperation. It is difficult, therefore, to generalize confidently on the extent to which this picture reflects a national one. It is by necessity a snapshot of the situation in the late 1990s that cannot alone form the basis of a prediction of the current and future situation for these disability organizations. Nonetheless, through comparison of the fortunes of the organizations in two localities some generalizations can be made about the emergence of such bodies and their relation to, and impact upon, the state welfare sphere.

This chapter has assessed voluntary organizations' willingness and potential to change attitudes and practice on disability issues and to empower disabled people or their supporters. There had been changes in the state approach to, and resources available for, disabled children, and behind these changes some "civil society" pressure was identifiable. While a fully politicized approach to disability (in the Western sense) was lacking, there were signs that certain professional practices and social structures were continuing to be challenged. The organizations highlighted in this discussion acted as agents of change in the following ways:

- initiating welfare services later developed by the state sector;
- increasing the visibility of disability issues and disabled people;
- destigmatizing disability ("respectabilization"); and
- acting as bases for social support network growth.

As forms of change, these essentially move disability from the private into the public sphere, creating a space for disability issues in civil society.

Broad comparison of the two sites would point to the support of "government failure" or gap-filling theories of voluntary sector welfare involvement. That the profiled organizations in Saratov were more active and, sometimes, confrontational toward state bodies might be partly explained by the fact that fewer substantive changes had been made to state welfare provision in that city. By contrast, in Samara, the scope and availability of community-based state services for disabled children had expanded quite significantly over a small number of years. There was thus less of a sense of government failure—or the need for gap filling—in Samara than in Saratov.

However, in these cases, the notion of state–voluntary sector interdependence is perhaps even more compelling. One aspect of this is that key figures in the voluntary sector in both sites were "embedded" in enabling networks that centered around state structures. Moreover, the multidirectional nature of influences between the state and voluntary sector must be noted. The idea that the voluntary organizations (as aspects of civil society) might be able to effect change "from below" is, based on these examples, rather problematic. The case studies offered clear examples of organizations being mobilized on the basis of discontent with the status quo (in this case, concerning gaps or injustices in welfare provision for disabled children) and of this form of association having a direct impact on that provision. However, this mobilization had not typically taken place in an arena that can be truly distinguished from "the state." Even First Step, the self-help organization profiled here, cannot be seen simply as a grassroots activist group rising in opposition to the state. It provides an interesting example of the apparently paradoxical tendency for state structures to consciously facilitate "activism" in the form of user groups, which is present in Western societies also (Acheson and Williamson 2001). That is, the state actively participates in what might be termed consciousness raising, kick-starting the transformation of individuals' views of their own situation, and generating a more politicized perspective that seeks change "from below."

State structures and relationships appear to have been deeply implicated in the development of the organizations profiled here, both in the origins of associations themselves and in their ability to act. To an extent this reflects "Soviet" patterns of enabling relationships and social action. Historically, certain of these organizations had been directly involved in important and undoubtedly positive developments in state provision for disabled children, and they continued to pursue this aim. However, this very closeness—and the apparent importance of that closeness for action and presence on the local scene—raises questions about these and similar organizations' ability to effectively provide a voice for excluded groups. Relations (or a lack of them) to state structures and professionals could restrict or compromise that voice.

Care must be taken however not to overemphasize the distinctiveness of these features of the Russian voluntary sphere; after all, the notion of "interdependence" of the state and voluntary sectors appears to resonate cross-nationally (Salamon and Anheier 1998, 224–25). Furthermore, the focus of this study on disability issues carries with it some expectation that civil society organizations will focus their activity on state provision. The very concept of "disability" is one that is essentially a category created and upheld by state structures and policies (Stone 1985). In the Russian case, organizations have had a natural orientation toward drawing attention to huge gaps and injustices in state policies and provision that could only be addressed through some interaction with relevant state bodies. Perhaps, serious improvements in the scope and inclusiveness of that provision, and the material resources available, would facilitate organizations' greater autonomy to focus on consciousness raising or "political" activities. To conclude, these organizations acted in a limited way as a force for change, albeit one that, paradoxically, could be traced back to state structures themselves.

Notes

1. The organizations' real names are used here; this is in accordance with the organizations' own wishes. However, individual interviewees and contacts within the organizations have not been named. Although organization heads' identities would be difficult to conceal, interviews and information were also provided by rank-and-file members or associates of the organizations. All interviews are therefore cited anonymously.

2. There were six "auxiliary" schools (now known officially as "special correctional" schools) for children with learning difficulties in Saratov and eight in Samara. A few other schools within the special education system in the cities—for example, schools for children with hearing impairment, or for children with cerebral palsy—also accepted children with learning difficulties in special units. All these schools catered only for the more able children with learning difficulties; those regarded as more severely disabled remained largely uncatered for within the educational system. Special schools for children with learning difficulties were provided on a residential and a day basis within both cities. The balance of residential versus

day schools was different in the two cities, with just one school in Saratov and six out of eight schools in Samara being primarily residential. Most of these residential schools also had day pupils. Both cities are administrative centers for large provinces, and all special schools elsewhere in the provinces were also residential.

3. One center opened in Samara in the early 1990s was a less recent development and effectively a pioneer in this area. It was associated with one of the case study organizations, the Samara Association for Disabled Children. The three other centers mentioned had been founded relatively recently prior to the study in 1998; one of them had not yet officially opened, although it was operational.

4. This was a project supported by the Soros Foundation, which involved an integrated kindergarten for children with a specific type of learning difficulty regarded as mild and curable through training (ZPR: zaderzhka psikhicheskogo razvitiia or developmental delay) together with nondisabled children. This project does not form part of the body of analysis in this chapter, primarily because I have favored a focus on "indigenous" organizations as opposed to Western-funded projects.

5. This is a point recognized by other cross-national researchers with a commitment to the social model of disability. For example, reflecting on research in China, Stone (1997) points to the difficulty of striking a balance between the "oppression" of colluding with or condoning practices regarded by social model theorists as unjust, and the "oppression" of dismissing local research participants' genuine concerns.

References

Abberley, Paul. 1997. "The Concept of Oppression and the Development of a Social Theory of Disability." In *Disability Studies: Past, Present and Future*, ed. L. Barton and M. Oliver, 160–78. Leeds: Disability Press.

Acheson, Nicolas, and Arthur Williamson. 2001. "The Ambiguous Role of Welfare Structures in Relation to the Emergence of Activism among Disabled People: Research Evidence from Northern Ireland." *Disability and Society* 16, no. 1: 87–102.

Billis, David. 1989. *A Theory of the Voluntary Sector.* London: London School of Economics , Centre for Voluntary Organisations.

Foreman, Nigel. 1997. "What Is Special about Russian Special Needs Education? Implications for Educational Integration." *Education in Russia, the Independent States and Eastern Europe* 15: 2–11.

First Step. 1997. "Ustav saratovskoi gorodskoi obshchestvennoi organizatsii semei, imeiushchikh detei-invalidov 'Pervyi shag.'" Saratov, May 1997.

Green, David. 1993. *Reinventing Civil Society: The Rediscovery of Welfare without Politics.* London: Institute of Economic Affairs.

———. 1996. *Community without Politics: A Market Approach to Welfare Reform.* London: Institute of Economic Affairs.

Harwin, Judith. 1996. *Children of the Russian State 1917–1995.* Aldershot, UK: Avebury.

Hughes, Bob. 2002. "Disability and the Body." In *Disability Studies Today*, ed. C. Barnes, M. Oliver, and L. Barton, 58–76. Cambridge: Polity Press.

Keane, John. 1988. *Democracy and Civil Society.* London: Verso.

Kidd, Alan. 2002. "Civil Society or the State? Recent Approaches to the History of Voluntary Welfare." *Journal of Historical Sociology* 15, no. 3: 328–42.

Ledeneva, Alena. 1998. *Russia's Economy of Favours: Blat, Networking and Informal Exchange.* Cambridge: Cambridge University Press.

Lonkila, Markku. 1997. "Informal Exchange Relations in Post-Soviet Russia: A Comparative Perspective." *Sociological Research Online* 2, no. 2. Available from www.socresonline .org.uk/2/2/9.html.

Mayo, Marjorie. 1994. *Communities and Caring: The Mixed Economy of Welfare*. London: St. Martin's Press.

McAuley, Alistair. 1991. "The Welfare State in the USSR." In *The State and Social Welfare: The Objectives of Policy*, ed. T. Wilson and D. Wilson, 191–213. London: Longman.

McCagg, William O. 1989. "The Origins of Defectology." In *The Disabled in the Soviet Union: Past and Present, Theory and Practice*, ed. L. McCagg and L. Siegelbaum, 39–61. Pittsburgh, PA: University of Pittsburgh Press.

Oliver, Mike. 1990. *The Politics of Disablement*. Basingstoke, UK: Macmillan.

———. 1996. *Understanding Disability: From Theory to Practice*. Basingstoke, UK: Macmillan.

Pestrikova, V. I. 1998. *Sovermennoe sostoianie i dinamika razvitiia nekommercheskogo sektora Samarskoi oblasti: sotsiologicheskoe issledovanie*. Samara, Russia: IEKA Povolzh'e.

Powell, Fred, and Donal Guerin. 1997. *Civil Society and Social Policy*. Dublin: A. and A. Farmar.

Salamon, Lester M. 1995. *The Global Associational Revolution: The Rise of the Third Sector on the World Scene*. London: DEMOS.

Salamon, Lester M., and Helmut K. Anheier. 1998. "Social Origins of Civil Society: Explaining the Nonprofit Sector Cross-nationally." *Voluntas* 9, no. 3: 213–48.

Sätre-Åhlander, Ann-Mari. 2000. "Women and the Social Economy in Transitional Russia." *Annals of Public and Cooperative Economics* 71, no. 3: 441–65.

Stone, Deborah. 1985. *The Disabled State*. Basingstoke, UK: Macmillan

Stone, Emma. 1997. "From the Research Notes of a Foreign Devil: Disability Research in China." In *Doing Disability Research*, ed. C. Barnes and G. Mercer, 207–26. Leeds, UK: Disability Press.

Thomson, Kate. 2002a. "Differentiating Integration: Special Education in the Russian Federation." *European Journal of Special Needs Education* 17, no. 1: 33–47.

———. 2002b. "Regional Welfare System Developments in Russia: Community Social Services." *Social Policy and Administration* 36, no. 2: 105–22.

Vernon, Ayesha, and John Swain. 2002. "Theorizing Divisions and Hierarchies: Towards a Commonality or Diversity?" In *Disability Studies Today*, ed. C. Barnes, M. Oliver and L. Barton, 77–97. Cambridge, UK: Polity Press.

Waters, Elizabeth. 1992 "'Cuckoo-mothers' and 'Apparatchiks': Glasnost and Children's Homes." In *Perestroika and Soviet Women*, ed. M. Buckley, 123–41. Cambridge: Cambridge University Press.

Westlund, Hans, and Stig Westerdahl. 1996. *Contribution of the Social Economy to Local Employment*. Östersund, Sweden: Institute for Social Economy.

White, Anne. 1995. *Democratization in Russia under Gorbachev 1985–91*. Basingstoke, UK: Macmillan.

Woodruff, David. 1999. "Barter of the Bankrupt: The Politics of Demonetization in Russia's Federal State." In *Uncertain Transition: Ethnographies of Change in the Postsocialist World*, ed. M. Burawoy and K. Verdery, 83–124. Lanham: Rowman and Littlefield.

Young, Iris Marion. 2000. *Inclusion and Democracy*. New York: Oxford University Press.

Interviews

Anonymous organization. 1998. Author interview. Samara, October.

Association for Disabled Children. 1998. Author interview. Samara, November.

Central Social Service Center. 1998. Author interview. Saratov, April.

Children's Fund. 1998a. Author interview. Saratov, April.

Children's Fund. 1998b. Author interview. Samara, October.

First Step. 1998. Author interview. Saratov, May.

First Step Organization Meeting. 1998. Saratov, April.

15

Formal and Informal Strategies of Migrant Populations

Migrant Activity in Post-Soviet Russia

Moya Flynn

The widespread social, economic, and political upheaval brought about by the collapse of the Soviet Union in 1991 initiated the large-scale migrations of peoples that continue up to the present day. One of the major population movements taking place is that of ethnic Russians and Russian-speaking migrants "returning" from the former Soviet Republics to the Russian Federation.[1] Upon their "return," migrants face difficulties both in terms of practical resettlement (status, jobs, and housing) and social and cultural adaptation. The previous absence of government structures to deal with this mass movement of people required the rapid development of legislative and administrative frameworks in the field of migration. However, due to a lack of resources, inexperience, and conflicting political concerns, government service provision has been limited. One of the responses to this gap in resettlement provision has been the growth of a nongovernmental migrant sector, which has become an increasingly important actor within the international, national, and regional "migration regimes" of post-Soviet Russia.[2]

This chapter explores the regional development of nongovernmental migrant organizations in the Russian Federation and the role they play in facilitating migrant acceptance, resettlement, and integration as an example of an emerging space of civil society in post-Soviet Russia.[3] Such an exploration provides an insight into the development of nonstate activity in a relatively new area of social concern, activity that has emerged from within the affected communities themselves. The chapter focuses upon the emergence of migrant-initiated organizations in three regions of the Russian Federation: Saratov, Samara, and Novosibirsk Oblasts. Drawing on empirical data gathered in the three regions over the 1997–2002 period, the chapter shows how organizations are negotiating, with varying degrees of success, relationships with government and nongovernmental structures in the region and beyond and with the migrant communities resident in the regions.[4] By taking the level of analysis to a very immediate level, and by drawing upon the narratives of individuals involved, the chapter provides empirical evidence of one sphere of civil society in post-Soviet Russia. Through the investigation of migrant organizations, the valuable personal and societal role that more informal networks of family and friends play in migrants' everyday lives is revealed. These networks, which often reflect and are rooted in Soviet-era connections, practices, and strategies, are frequently the most effective facilitators of resettlement and integration. The role of these networks is not dealt with in any detail in the chapter; however, their significance and centrality to, in this case, migrants' lives suggest that rather than their being excluded from broader analyses of civil society as some authors suggest (Howard 2003, 49),[5] they need to be included if we are to achieve a better understanding of how post-Soviet Russian civil society is developing and why it operates in the way that it does (Hann 1996, 3).

Federal Contexts: Framing the Migration and Resettlement Process

Government Frameworks

The response of the Russian government to the large-scale, "forced" migration movements that began in the early 1990s was fairly liberal and humanitarian in character. In December 1992, the Russian Federation acceded to the 1951 UN Convention and 1967 Protocol Relating to the Status of Refugees. An institutional body, the Federal Migration Service (FMS), was established by presidential decree in July 1992 and mandated to protect the rights of refugees and forced migrants and help in their resettlement. Relevant legislation, primarily Russian Federation laws on forced migration and refugees, was passed in February 1993.[6] In 1992, the initial nature of official discourse and policy was receptive to those wishing to move to Russia from the former republics, indicating not only Russia's acceptance of the obligations of having become the "successor" to the Soviet Union on the international scene but also a readiness to downplay Russia's political interests in the former republics.

However, from 1993 on, the difficulties of an inexperienced migration service that lacked practical legislative support and suffered from severe financial constraints were compounded by the increasing politicization of the question of the Russian communities in the "near abroad"[7] and the economic and social crisis being faced on the territory of the Russian Federation. By the end of 1995, an increasing "securitization" of all forms of migration and the prioritization of immigration control had replaced the previous "liberal" approach. With respect to the returning Russian communities, the shift reflected a consensus between different factions of the Russian parliament and government apparatus over the need to protect the Russian communities in the near abroad, to encompass them as part of the Russian nation's sphere of influence, and to encourage them to remain in the former republics. Although their return was still accepted, this was framed firmly within a discourse of forced migration.

The 1995–2002 period marked a continuation of this policy line and was accompanied by a corresponding change in the Federal Migration Service. The service moved away from its initial role as provider of resettlement assistance to migrants as it placed first priority on the wider management and regulation of migration flows. The shift was rooted in the service's severe lack of resources to enable comprehensive provision for returnees to take place, but equally mirrored the wider policy shifts at the higher levels of political power in Moscow (Pilkington 1998, 53–89; Codagnone 1998a, 37, 46). In addition, changes to the law on forced migrants, introduced in November 1995, tightened the definition of who could qualify for forced migrant status and reduced the levels of social provision available. Finally, in October 2001, the Russian Ministry of Internal Affairs (MVD) took over responsibility for migration issues, a decision that was met with outrage by human rights and migrant groups and certain government deputies. Giving a power structure like the MVD responsibility for migration affairs indicates a tendency to rely increasingly on force to manage Russia's complex migration scenario—a scenario in which vulnerable migrants, such as forced migrants and refugees, are in danger of being forgotten (Heleniak 2002).

Nongovernmental Response

In response to the arrival of large numbers of ethnic Russian and Russian-speaking migrants on Russian territory, and in reaction to emerging state discourse and policy, nongovernmental migrant organizations appeared at the federal and regional levels during the 1990s to become key actors in the Russian migration regime. At the federal level, organizations evolved completely independently of, and in opposition to, the state and developed a dual role: that of filling a gap left by the ineffectiveness and inadequacy of state action through the provision of legal advice, practical information, and material aid to refugees and forced migrants; and that of challenging and influencing state discourse and policy.

The development of the three main Moscow-based nongovernmental organizations— the Civic Assistance Committee (CAC), the Coordinating Council for Aid to Refugees and Forced Migrants (CCARFM), and the Forum of Migrant Organizations —is closely linked.[8] Furthermore, all three organizations demonstrate a similar attitude toward the return of Russian communities; that of actively supporting and encouraging their "repatriation" and insisting on the need for comprehensive resettlement assistance. Following the outbreak of violence in Baku, Azerbaijan, in 1989 and the arrival of the first refugees in Moscow, Svetlana Gannushkina, an academic and legal expert, set up CAC. CCARFM evolved from CAC to unite other Moscow organizations involved in providing assistance to refugees and forced migrants, and it was officially formed in March 1993 by the journalist Lidiia Grafova. In 1996, the Forum of Migrant Associations was created on the basis of these two organizations, as an umbrella organization for the widespread network of regional migrant organizations in the Russian Federation. The CCARFM operates now as the permanently functioning working apparatus for the Forum in Moscow.[9] Initially hostile relations between those nongovernmental organizations (NGOs) and the FMS and other government bodies improved during the 1990s as a result of the inclusion of NGO representatives within joint-institutional structures that allowed limited participation in legislative development.[10] In 1994 and 1995, the organizations took part in discussions regarding amendments to the laws on "forced migrants" and "refugees,"[11] and they are constant advocates for the introduction of alternative repatriation legislation to allow the voluntary return of the Russian communities to the Russian Federation.[12] However, the decision to transfer responsibility for migration affairs to the MVD led to a deterioration of relations between nongovernmental organizations and the government.

At the core of the federal-level organizations' philosophy is an attempt to provide an alternative construction of the return and resettlement of Russian communities than that developed by the state: primarily one of welcoming the repatriates, recognizing their potential (demographic, economic, cultural) value for the Russian state, and emphasizing adequate service provision and viable policies to foster successful resettlement. Their work, which extends beyond the federal level, provides essential practical and legal assistance to migrant organizations and individual migrants and creates a wider space within which migrants' voices are heard. Furthermore, the influence of the organizations extends beyond the borders of the Russian Federation. All three organizations were involved in the CIS Conference on Refugees and Forced Migrants held in Geneva in May 1996, and the subsequent "Program of Action." Those initiatives stimulated NGO development in the migration sphere throughout the post-Soviet space and facilitated the development of links between international, national, and regional government and nongovernmental structures (Codagnone 1998b, 32; Gannushkina 1999; Vitkovskaia 1999).

Regional Developments: Saratov, Samara, and Novosibirsk Oblasts

The development of federal-level activity has been accompanied by the emergence of self-initiated migrant organizations at the regional level. Regional organizations are often more pragmatic than those at the federal level, with a greater socioeconomic focus. They are not always strictly "NGOs" but can be informal self-help groups or commercial legal entities involved in entrepreneurial or industrial activities or attached to a rural compact settlement site (Codagnone 1998b, 31). However, their parallel concern for migrants' rights often means they develop into effective lobbying bodies at the regional level. This chapter explores the origins and activity of five of these regional migrant organizations that are active in Saratov, Samara, and Novosibirsk Oblasts. The five organizations are: Saratov Spring (Saratovskii istochnik), Return (Vozvrashchenie), and the Committee of Refugees from Chechnya (Komitet bezhentsev iz Chechni) in Saratov Oblast, the Samara Migrant/Resettler (Samarskii pereselenets) in Samara Oblast, and Helping Hand (Ruka pomoshchi) in Novosibirsk Oblast.[13]

The Organizations: Origins and Initiatives

> I received forced migrant status in 1993, but since then, despite all my efforts, I don't feel settled. Saratov hasn't become a place that I can call home. Maybe I haven't done something. Perhaps the state system provides some sort of support, but for me, it has not worked in the way that it should. And I needed assistance. So, I came to the conclusion that we [migrants] must help ourselves (Saratov, 1999).[14]

The inadequacy of state assistance and the realization among migrants that they have to depend upon themselves are common reasons for the formation of migrant initiatives. That motivation is also apparent when individual migrants speak of their own resettlement experience (see below). All the regional organizations cited here originated from an initial small group of migrants, who either had moved together from the same republic or had met upon arrival. The essential functions of the organizations are: the provision of general and legal information that is either unavailable or difficult to access from state structures; minimal material support in the form of small monetary payments, clothes, or food vouchers; limited direct help regarding employment and housing; and information about resettlement opportunities in the regions to potential migrants in the former Soviet republics and to individuals investigating possibilities for settlement. The organizations also perceive their role as providing migrants with a vital source of moral and psychological support. Their ability to perform this role is attributed (both by the leaders of the organizations and by individual migrants) to the fact that the organizations are run by migrants who are able to understand what their "client group" is experiencing. Employees in state services, in contrast, are seen as lacking the necessary skills or comprehension:

> The most important thing is that they [migrants] do not feel that they are alone here. They need to feel that they can talk to someone. State structures cannot help with this. Perhaps if a psychologist or sociologist worked there, then they could help—a person who would listen and give advice. Personal, family problems arise, not always just to do with migration. At the moment, social organizations fulfill this role. A person comes to a social organization and knows that the people there are like them, that they will listen, try to help, provide support. Sometimes, you cannot give them anything, you can only listen and sympathize, but they feel better. Because people understand that there is support, that it actually exists. They can come at any time to be given support, to be listened to, advised on what to do (Saratov, 1999).

The organizations' activity extends beyond that of providing material, informational, and moral support, however. They also attempt to raise the level of awareness of migrant issues within state structures, to direct state attention to areas of concern, and ultimately to affect regional state policy and practice. Like NGOs at the federal level, regional organizations endeavor to reframe the arrival of migrants as positive for Russia as a whole, and for the particular region to which they arrived:

Initially, refugees and forced migrants were perceived very negatively, as strangers, as people who were not needed. But now, because of the work of social organizations, the opinions of these people have changed. We have shown that although we are people who have been forced to flee, we have come here prepared to work, to help, to offer our knowledge. If we are needed, that we will be useful. But for this to happen, they [the regional administration] need to know who has come, what they can offer, what is their potential, how can they be used for the good of Saratov Oblast. We can provide this information to the heads of different state departments; it will be useful for them. They will see us as a solution to their problems (Saratov, 1999).

Relations with the State

Representatives of regional migrant organizations are clear about the role they wish to fulfill in relation to migrant communities and within the wider migration regime, and they recognize the need to engage actively with state actors. However, they are often constrained precisely by the nature of the official regional migration regime in which they are operating. Although in the three regions the types and levels of in-migration are similar, the arrival of migrants has evoked different responses on the side of both the regional administrations and territorial migration services due to differing regional political and economic agendas. In Saratov and Novosibirsk Oblasts a generally receptive policy toward in-migration has been encouraged, while in Samara Oblast, the dominant tendency has been to discourage in-migration (Flynn 2004). The nature of the regional migration regime is one factor that has an impact upon the migrant organizations' relationship with the regional branch of the Federal Migration Service: a relationship that is key to the organizations' development. In Saratov Oblast, representatives of the migrant organizations are willing to work with the migration service rather than in opposition to it, although they also see their role as correcting migration service practice. Meanwhile, the migration service recognizes the need to work "in a consolidated way" with the organizations, accepts that they provide additional help to specific categories of migrants, and sees the potential for the social organizations to obtain extra resources from external sponsors, such as international bodies (Pudina 1999). However, the service also perceives the organizations as supplementary, unprofessional, and insufficiently informed (Saratov Migration Service 1999a; 1999b).

The situation in Samara Oblast provides a stark contrast. In 1999, a representative of the organization Samara Migrant identified the lack of cooperation and support from the migration service as one of the most serious problems the organization faced (Samara Migrant 1999), although by 2002 she conceded that they had found a "working compromise" with the migration service (ibid. 2002). However, the attitude of the migration service has served to undermine the legitimacy of the organization's activity within the region and restricts its access to the wider migrant community. For example, the Samara migration service forbids the advertising of the migrant organization at the service's premises, in contrast to Saratov and Novosibirsk migration services.

In Novosibirsk Oblast, although the organization Helping Hand is making efforts to establish a working relationship with the migration service, its efforts are met with hostility. The migration service claims that social organizations do not offer "real help" to migrants and are concerned only with making money, and it maintains that migration is an area of "state concern" (Novosibirsk Migration Service 2002). The difficult nature of the relationship in this case appears to stem from the migration service's perception that the organization is a competitor and not qualified to provide reliable advice or real support, rather than being rooted in a restrictive approach to migration at a regional level. This negative evaluation of migrant organizations by state structures is apparent in all the regions under study and stems from a suspicion of, and reluctance to embrace, nongovernmental actors as viable partners in the solution of specific social issues.

The opportunity to contribute to regional migration debates also varies among the regions. Migrant Coordinating Councils were set up across the Russian Federation during 1999 to foster government–nongovernmental debate, and were an important indication of state recognition of the role of the nongovernmental actors in the migrant sphere. In Saratov Oblast all the migrant organizations were invited to participate in the operation of the council. However, two of the organizations, Saratov Spring and the Committee of Refugees from Chechnya, excluded themselves from this state-led initiative, objecting to the fact that the "elected" head of the Coordinating Council was the director of the migration service, a state representative (Saratov Spring 1999; Committee of Refugees 1999). In contrast, the head of a third organization, Return, believed that having the director of the migration service as chairman of the council brought state and nonstate structures into close cooperation and ensured migrants an influential voice (Return 1999). However, despite their misgivings about the Coordinating Council, all the migrant organizations in Saratov Oblast participated in the development of a regional migration program during 1999. Such participation is unusual and has not occurred in many other regions (*Materialy mezhdunarodnogo seminara* 1999, 6). The openness of debate is reflective of a wider tolerance toward in-migration at the level of the Saratov regional administration. However, with shifts in federal migration discourse and policy in recent years, and growing regional concerns about the socioeconomic impacts of in-migration, this tolerance has lessened (Flynn 2004).

The situation in Samara Oblast again serves as an interesting contrast. A Cooordinating Council was established in May 1999, but, in contrast to Saratov, it was created under the migration service rather than the regional parliament, which limited its influence at the regional government level. While representatives of the migration service claimed that the meetings had increased understanding of their work among the migrant organizations, a representative of the organization Samara Migrant saw the meetings as just for "men in suits" (Samara Migration Service 1999; Samara Migrant 1999). The ineffective operation of this joint-sector institution and the exclusion of the organization from any regional government debate concerning migrant issues severely constrain the scope of the organization's activity and restrict the representation of a wider migrant voice at the regional level. The exclusion of NGOs in this case is a product of the more restrictive attitude toward in-migration practiced by the Samara regional administration, whose priorities feed down to the regional migration service (Flynn 2004).

In both regions, however, it is sometimes the migrant organizations that choose *not* to engage directly with the state, preferring to retain a more independent position. Instead, they often find other means of representation—for example, by using the electoral potential of the migrant population to gain the support of regional Duma deputies.[15] As a representative of an organization in Saratov stated: "We must act in the political arena, we must participate in elections . . . as a result, the situation alters, people's opinions change. It is essential that we show them that we are important" (Saratov, 1999).

Nongovernmental Connections

In addition to relations with regional government structures, connections within the nonstate sector—at the regional, federal, and international levels—are vital for the development, visibility, and legitimization of the migrant organizations. However, inclusion cannot be assumed and depends upon the organizations' ability and capacity to build relationships with both state and nonstate actors. In Samara Oblast, the hostile relations that exist with regional state structures, and the migration service in particular, constrain the wider involvement of migrant organizations in government–nongovernmental debate. For example, Samara Migrant is excluded from the network of "official" social organizations that receive support and some funding from the regional administration.[16] Nevertheless, the organization developed productive links with the Western-funded NGO resource center Volga Region (Povol'zhe), which has provided an alternative means of strengthening the organization's position within the nonstate regional sector.[17] In contrast, Helping Hand in Novosibirsk and Return in Saratov are both active members of the Regional Committee of Social Organizations. However, the Saratov organizations Saratov Spring and the Committee of Refugees from Chechnya tend to exclude themselves from the wider nongovernmental sphere, preferring to concentrate on their own particular issues and to maintain a sense of distance and independence. The different levels of inclusion across the three regions indicate the influence of government institutions but also demonstrate how the organizations might find alternative means to gain a voice within the sphere, or may choose to distance themselves from the sphere to pursue their own priorities independently.

The nongovernmental organizations see connections that extend beyond the region, both federal and international, as a way of securing material resources and as an important source of recognition and legitimization. The following quotation demonstrates the central importance of a Western grant for the development of one of the migrant organizations, an importance that was echoed by all:

> The first push we received toward the possibility of independent development was from the grant we managed to get from UNHCR. It was to strengthen the potential of the organization. Now we have our own computers, our own equipment ... it played a very significant role, it gave us some authority. We could attract the attention of a wider circle of people. It gave us the chance for an independent life (Saratov, 1999).

As is the case for NGOs across Russia, securing funding to keep organizations running is a problematic issue. Kay (2000, 190, 194) notes in her study of grassroots women's organizations that Western grants are seen as the principal solution to an organization's financial problems and that securing such a grant becomes an absolute imperative and grant application writing an art. For all the migrant organizations involved in this study there appeared to be no other option to ensure their survival. To varying extents, all the organizations have been successful in securing international grants and material assistance, and they are consistently filing further applications. No resources are available from the state at the regional level; and alternative sources of funding (i.e., local commercial or business enterprises) are limited. When asked about the future of the organization, a migrant representative stated: "Well, [we will] carry on with what we are doing at the moment, and of course, write grant applications, sit and write grant applications. Every organization must find its own niche, and the ability to pay its way" (Novosibirsk, 2002).

Connections with international organizations, however, are not just seen as a way of securing material resources. In Saratov Oblast the assistance received from, and long-term presence of, international connections furthered recognition of the organizations by the regional state sector. In Samara Oblast, prior international involvement was limited, which may have impeded the development of more positive relations between the state sector and migrant nongovernmental structures. It was noticeable that when Samara Migrant established productive relationships with international and federal nongovernmental actors, there was some improvement in their relationship with regional state structures.

The Saratov case reflects the preferred practice of international organizations in the migration field in choosing the regions on which to focus their activities. The presence of cooperative and receptive local government structures (which, in the migration sphere, existed in Saratov but were lacking in Samara) is preferred; their absence discourages international interest. In turn, international organizations favor NGOs that have productive links with these "cooperative" local government structures.[18] This reflects the wider dominance of a "multi-agency working" strategy, where Western bodies prefer to work in regions where well-established and effective state–nonstate relationships have been developed (Richardson 2001). Although a successful state–nonstate relationship may generate productive results, this study suggests that in some cases international organizations need to look beyond the state structures in a region, and equally beyond the same regularly funded regions, to the efforts of alternative and independent group initiatives that are not, as yet, included within the wider system.

The activity of the federal-level Russian organizations discussed above reflects such a willingness to establish contact with regional organizations that are not necessarily privileged by local government structures. Their willingness may stem from the indirect nature of the working relationship the federal organizations have with the Russian state, and their frequent criticism of and opposition to state migration institutions. For the regional organizations, links with Moscow-based organizations provide essential information and direct access to the wider federal and international migration regimes, which, in turn, facilitate recognition at the regional level. Representatives of the regional migrant organizations highlight the importance of connections to the federal level, both for their own development and for the wider advancement of migrant influence at the regional and federal levels:

> I have been a member of the executive committee of the Forum [of Migrant Associations] for a year already. Being able to turn to people there, to visit, to be involved in joint projects and programs, it has widened our horizons and has meant that we are included in activities not only at the regional but also at the federal level. Because of that we have grown (Saratov, 1999).

> When they [the Russian government] see that social organizations are coming together at the federal level, solving their own problems—then we gain more power. When we are discussing things, working out solutions—the state structures are forced to listen, because they see our strength; it is very significant (Saratov, 1999).

Despite the constraints placed upon their activity, all the regional migrant organizations are emerging as important actors within the regional migration regimes. Although the practical help that is offered by regional migrant organizations to the migrant population is limited, they are making important contributions with minimal material and experiential resources and must be seen as sites of further potential. The organizations directly represent the interests and concerns of some of the migrants arriving from the former republics, and they demonstrate one strategy that these communities are using to negotiate for inclusion within the Russian "homeland." For the involved migrants the organizations have become an important site of resistance and identity as they, as individuals, adapt to new roles, learn new skills, and engage with actors and issues that extend well beyond the borders of the region to which they have arrived. However, the organizations do not represent all the arriving migrants; the vertical links extending down into the migrant community are limited, and, as shown below, many migrants choose not to engage directly with regional NGO structures.

Migrant Organizations and the Individual

> I am insulted by our government, the state, for the way they have handled us (2, Saratov, 1997).[19]

This statement is indicative of the sense of disillusionment with the Russian state that many individual migrants expressed in interviews. Although the majority of respondents had applied for and received forced migrant status, they see it as little more than a piece of paper, and any concrete help—for example, with finding employment or housing—is extremely limited.[20] The lack of state concern and the very real need for assistance in resettlement is clearly a central factor that encourages individual migrants to approach, and become involved with, migrant organizations: "If the government does not care, then we must come together in a group, what other way is there?" (37, Saratov, 1999). Migrants therefore see the organizations as an essential response to state indifference and lack of assistance, and as a source of potential help. In the face of the confusing array of state structures and legislation concerned with migrant resettlement, the organizations are identified as a mediating structure between the individual and the state, which makes any interaction with official departments easier. The organizations are a source of information that is unavailable elsewhere:

> I think that they [migrant organizations] are very important. After all, people are coming from different places. They do not know the laws, they do not know who to turn to, they do not know how to get jobs or find housing. Many do not know because they have not had to do this before, they do not know their rights, and the laws are unclear. Here [at the migrant organization] they are given everything, full information; therefore, I think they are very important. If people know what is going on, they are able to get themselves sorted out more quickly (21, Saratov, 1999).

Moreover, although often identified as a formal structure, migrant organizations are considered, unlike official government structures, to approach migrants with understanding and empathy. The reason for this is that the organizations are run by migrants who both have a similar experience of displacement and may have come from the individual's previous homeland:

> If people have gone through it themselves, they understand that it is very difficult. All the people try to support you with warm words, to provide help in some way, to do something. At the migration service it is more difficult: you go there and it is like a "deaf wall," a wall that doesn't understand, and people who do not understand— that a person has come with nothing, has to start again, and that adaptation is very difficult. Here [in the migrant organization] it is easier, you can always run to the organization with any question (50, Samara, 1999).

The organizations play an important role in facilitating a sense of sociocultural belonging and security at the new place of residence. Russians who are returning from the former republics of the Soviet Union are experiencing not only the problems of physical displacement and subsequent resettlement but also of cultural displacement. They are moving from a familiar environment to one that, because it is their historical motherland (*rodina*), is often expected to feel like home, but that in many ways is unknown and unfamiliar.[21] The process of migration and resettlement foster a sense of difference among Russians returning to the Russian Federation, grounded both in the experience of life in the former republic and in confrontation with Russia and local Russians upon return. However, both for those migrants who are actively involved in the migrant organizations and for those who come within the sphere of their activity, spaces are created where migrants discover and foster feelings of common identity and where, to an extent, they momentarily overcome the complex feelings of cultural displacement and isolation:

> Here, we are all together, we are all a group . . . we can communicate, we have a great deal in common—our way of life, for example. We even have the same dishes, if you go to that extent. We prepare dishes in the same way. It means a great deal. And to have left there, to have lost everything . . . such little things give you joy. We have common recollections, a common outlook. It is something important for us (27, Saratov, 1999).

Migrant organizations, however, were sometimes identified as not beneficial or relevant to facilitating resettlement. Many migrants, after experiencing government indifference, identified a migrant organization as yet another "official" structure in which one should have little faith as a source of help. Often migrants refused to distinguish between official, state bodies and unofficial, nongovernmental bodies, claiming that the migrant organizations had to be either commercial or linked to state structures:[22] "I do not believe in any of these associations, or in this [migration] service; I have no faith in them" (54, Samara, 1999).

Equally, the migrant organizations are sometimes criticized precisely because they are not official structures, and so lack the real power to effect any change or to offer substantial help. Out of the seventy-two migrants interviewed across the three regions, forty-two had not received any help from a migrant organization. The help received by the other migrants was predominantly legal or general consultation, moral support, and material help (clothes or food). Only five migrants received help with finding accommodation, and two with finding employment: "I know about them, but cannot say anything because I did not get anything from them, from this organization. All I got was from the migration service, because the migration service—it is a state department. The organization, it is just a social organization, it exists just for itself, in principle I did not get anything from it" (23, Saratov, 1999).

In other instances, migrants saw the value of migrant organizations only for those who lacked other networks, such as family or friendship ties. If migrants possessed these other ties they did not recognize the organizations as relevant for them: "I did not turn to it [the association] because I had other possibilities. I only found out about its existence recently. I think that it is important for people who do not have any other connections, no sort of acquaintances here at all. It is important for them" (20, Saratov, 1999).

Other Connections: Family and Friendship Networks

The possession of other connections explains, to an extent, the fairly low levels of engagement with the regional migrant NGOs among the individuals interviewed as a part of this study. For some migrants, the organizations provide concrete help and support and the beginnings of a social network that makes it easier to cope with the experiences of displacement and dislocation. However, for the majority of migrants, family and friendship networks are central to migration and resettlement: in the decision to move; as the structure that moved; as an important factor in influencing the choice of settlement region;[23] and in providing initial support upon return.

Upon arrival at the new place of residence, the presence of relatives and friends provides the most effective way of solving some of the immediate problems of resettlement, such as registration (gaining a *propiska*) and finding accommodation or employment. Respondents often move to be close to family or friends who were recent migrants, having resided in the same city or town in the former republic prior to migration, and who had established themselves in the new place of residence. Those relatives or friends can provide information about possibilities of employment and accommodation in the region, which is essential in the absence of official information. In other cases, members of a family or group of friends act as scouts (*razvedchiki*) and conduct scouting missions to Russia to explore the possibilities for resettlement, particularly regarding accommodation and employment, after which they return to the former place of residence to collect the rest of the group:

> We came to some acquaintances of ours . . . we used to live across the hallway in a block of flats. They moved here . . . yes, Lena rang me herself. She said, "it's boring, it's awful here, we are alone, why don't you come?" So I came. We had a very good relationship there, and here we've kept it up. Everyone who we have come across from our old town, we all pass things on to one another by phone, we all support one another. Yes, if someone finds something out, they phone someone else straight away and tell them, it reassures you, gives you hope (68, Novosibirsk, 2002).

> I came here because I have relatives here. My grandmother lives here. That solves a lot of problems . . . I didn't go anywhere to register, because, simply, I have somewhere to live here. My grandmother has an apartment. We have such an institution called the *propiska*. I have the opportunity to receive a *propiska* because I have relatives here. Therefore I didn't turn to the migration service (20, Saratov, 1999).

Another important role that connections with family and friends play in the region of arrival is facilitating the creation of feelings of familiarity, security, and belonging that are lost with displacement. Upon return, migrant statements suggest that such connections recreate a sense of community that they have temporarily lost and allow the continuation of familiar habits, customs and traditions:

> "We are both from Samarkand. We are fellow countrywomen (*zemliachki*). We grew up on one street as friends. We grew up together. I lived with her for two weeks, then we were given the neighboring room [in a hostel]" (41, Saratov, 1999).
> "He [her brother] lives in Novosibirsk; he doesn't live in this district, he lives on Karl Marx Street. As you see, I live here, so we mostly talk on the telephone. But we get together for all celebrations—New Year's, birthdays, 8th March [International Women's Day]—always together. He helps so much morally" (69, Novosibirsk, 2002).

Similarly, new friendships with "other" migrants, or relationships with old acquaintances that become closer due to the experience of migration, help foster feelings of familiarity and security, not yet achieved with the local Russian community: "Of course, we are closer to those who have also moved. Those friends, who have moved, we can turn to each other for help. We met some of them here. Even when you hear a familiar word, you want to go up to someone and ask them 'where have you come from?' And straight away we understand one another. We have the same problems" (63, Novosibirsk, 2002). "Who helped most of all? Of course, close ones, our friends, with whom we moved . . . the locals, those who live here, it's all the same to them who is living nearby, they don't understand how hard it is for us" (64, Novosibirsk, 2002).

The use of friendship and family networks reveals a desire among migrants to maintain or restore a framework of security that has been destroyed. Their importance points to how, in conditions of displacement, uncertainty, and upheaval, lives may become highly localized (Gupta and Ferguson 1992, 11; Castells 1997, 41; Castells 1998, 68). However, these ties equally reflect the continued reliance upon, or adaptation of, trusted and functioning networks inherited from the Soviet past.[24] The use of family and friendship networks among migrants represents a basic survival strategy where, in the absence of state assistance, personal information and assistance channels are crucial to facilitate migration and to begin the reconstruction of a new life at the site of resettlement. Yet migrants' narratives demonstrate that the reliance upon known personal networks is not only due to state inaction or the wider environment of insecurity and upheaval. Rather, such reliance must equally be recognized as a positive and preferred choice of a social network that best meets migrants' practical needs; facilitates the revival of essential feelings of trust, belonging, and inclusion in the new society and state; and ultimately contributes to the "myriad of social relationships that mediate between self and society" (Hann 1996, 21).

Conclusion

This chapter explores two levels of social organization that emerged from migrants' experiences of resettlement in the Russian Federation. One form, the nongovernmental organization, is new; the other, the informal network, is rooted strongly in the Soviet past. Both meet the different needs of migrants in specific ways; therefore their value and meaning must be read through the eyes of the individuals concerned. The development and activity of regional and federal migrant organizations demonstrate the very real advances that have been made over the past decade in a social sphere that was not an issue, and never saw "informal" activity, during the Soviet period. Although engagement of the migrant community with organizations at a regional level is sometimes limited, it should be remembered that the organizations are themselves migrant initiatives and from the evidence of those individuals who are involved, they are a vital source of practical and psychological support. Furthermore, at both the regional and federal level, migrant organizations have had some input into policy making and legislative development and, to varying extents, are influencing the nature of the migration regime developing in the Russian Federation. Thus, where possible, the organizations are actively engaging with state structures, but they are also choosing other paths when this is beneficial for the community they set out to help. In addition, the work of the migrant organizations must be understood within the context in which they are operating. This chapter has shown how state and other international and federal actors can be responsible for fostering the growth of non-governmental organizations but also how their actions, whether consciously or unconsciously, may impede development. At both a regional and federal level in Russia, the state's changing attitude toward migration clearly affects its receptivity to migrant nongovernmental organizations and the assessment of the role they are able to play in migrant resettlement provision and legislative development.

The chapter also reveals how many individual migrants choose not to engage with nongovernmental organizations at the site of settlement. This choice may well be rooted in a mistrust of formal organization inherited from the Soviet period. However, the choice is also a positive and rational one, made in favor of a better option at the time. The trust and support offered by more informal networks of family and friends points to a thriving, responsible, and moral community that provides very real assistance to its members, rather than to isolated, atomized individuals and households, which would more likely impede the building of civil society (White 1996). The existence of strong informal networks cannot be assumed to prevent interaction with more formal NGOs, although it does lessen the need for such interaction. Some migrants justifiably see the concerns of their individual everyday lives as best managed through informal networks, not by an organization that represents them as migrants. Furthermore, in some cases, informal networks of family and friends may choose to adopt a more formal, although temporary, participatory public role when the need arises. In Saratov Oblast, a number of migrants resident in a hostel came together as a group on a short-term basis to organize a protest and petition to prevent their eviction from their hostel, an action that was successful.

Dependence upon personal networks of family and friends also occurs as a result of disillusionment with the Russian state's treatment of the individual as a migrant, and it can lead migrants to distance themselves from state structures. However, informal networks indirectly foster interaction and the building of connections with the state, contributing to the regeneration of social, economic, and political life through the real and practical help they provide. Perhaps such strategies and paths of negotiation are not consistent with traditional Western ideas of civil society that center on individual responsibility; equally they cannot be contained by the equation that measures civil society by assessing the number and viability of NGOs. However, if civil society is understood as a grounded concept that tries "to explain what binds people together in modern state societies in a civic life beyond their individual interests" (White 1996, 146), then both the informal networks of family and friends and the migrant organizations focused upon in the present study are concerned in a very real sense with building their own civil societies in post-Soviet Russia. Although informal networks and migrant organizations may prioritize everyday individual concerns such as housing, employment, and status acquisition, the resolution of these issues must be seen as crucial to contributing to any wider sense of civic inclusion at the site of settlement. In addition, they undeniably foster a sense of a community united in the face of common problems, where individuals resolutely support one another. More active "civic" participation can occur, such as policy input, when it is possible and/or preferable for the involved individuals and communities. To ignore the relevance of insights such as these for understanding the nature of civil society in Russia falls into the trap of ignoring or marginalizing the experiences and voices of members of the society we are trying to understand.

Notes

1. Over the 1991–2002 period, approximately 1.5 million individuals from these populations were officially registered as "forced migrants" or "refugees" by the Russian government. However, it is estimated that up to 8–10 million individuals have come to reside within the borders of the Russian Federation (International Organization of Migration 2002, 5). The term "return" is initially placed in quotation marks to stress the contested nature of the migration movement, which for many migrants is far from a "return" to a "homeland."

2. "Migration regimes" are multilayered structures that are made up of political and non-political agencies concerned with migration at the local, national, transnational, and international level.

3. In this chapter, the concept of "civil society" is used, as Hann (1996, 22) suggests, in an inclusive way, to encompass the development of more formal structures and organizations of civil society and the "ideas and practices through which cooperation and trust are established in social life."

4. The empirical study formed part of doctoral and postdoctoral research carried out by the author into the migration of ethnic Russian and Russian-speaking migrants from the other former Soviet republics to the Russian Federation and their subsequent resettlement. The doctoral research was partly funded by the UK Economic and Social Research Council (ESRC). The postdoctoral research was funded by an ESRC postdoctoral fellowship, Award No. T026 27 1017.

5. Howard (2003, 49) does not dispute the necessity of shifting debates away from formal structures and organizations to acknowledge the importance of other social practices and patterns (such as informal networks) in studying civil society in "non-Western" countries. However, he disagrees that the concept of civil society itself should be expanded or diluted to incorporate such practices.

6. Forced migrant status is awarded to those individuals who are entitled to Russian citizenship and have been forced to leave their former place of residence due to persecution or violence on the grounds of race, nationality, religion, affiliation with a particular social group, or political conviction. In theory, it guarantees greater assistance with resettlement than "refugee" status. Refugee status was originally available to those Russian returnees who did not hold Russian citizenship at the time of arrival. Amendments that were introduced to the Russian law on refugees in June 1997 made refugee status more difficult to acquire, and in practice it was no longer awarded to those returnees who did not possess, but were entitled to, Russian citizenship. The February 1992 Law on Citizenship stated that any resident of the former Soviet Union was entitled to Russian citizenship if he or she applied before the end of the year 2000. This deadline was extended to May 2002 when a new citizenship law was introduced. The new law does not include any special conditions for former residents of the Soviet Union arriving in Russia, apart

from those individuals born on the territory of the Russian Federation, for whom the period of required residence prior to making an application is one year rather than five years.

7. The "near abroad" is a term used to refer to the territory beyond the borders of the present-day Russian Federation that was part of the former Soviet Union.

8. A fourth organization, the Compatriots Fund (Sootechestvenniki), is also active at the federal and regional levels. However, its origins as a semistate organ and later close association with the state set it apart from the other Moscow-based organizations.

9. The member organizations of the Forum now number more than 198 in 50 regions of Russia, together with 3 organizations located in the former republics of Uzbekistan, Kazakstan, and Tajikistan (www.migrant.ru/forum, 15 July 2003).

10. Lidiia Grafova, the founder of CCARFM, is a member of the Governmental Commission on Affairs of Compatriots Abroad, and together with Svetlana Gannushkina, founder of CAC, of the Governmental Commission on Migration Policy. They have also worked with the Parliamentary Committee on CIS Affairs and Relations with Compatriots and in its Subcommittee on Refugee and Forced Migrant Affairs.

11. Initial amendments to both the forced migrant law and the refugee law were presented to the State Duma in the summer of 1994. Both documents were condemned for being "anti-refugee," which led to the formation of the Parliamentary Commission on Refugee and Forced Migrant Affairs, which included parliamentary deputies and representatives of the FMS, the presidential apparatus, the Federation Council, international organizations, and Russian NGOs (Pilkington 1998, 54; Memorial 1997, 8). The discussions led to a thorough reworking of the amendments to the Law on Forced Migrants, which were adopted by the State Duma on November 22, 1995. A new refugee law came into force on 11 June 1997. Although this law was commended by human rights organizations due to its greater clarity and exactness, it was more restrictive than the earlier law and reflected tendencies in West European migration legislative practice of the early 1990s.

12. For a more detailed discussion of NGO involvement in the repatriation debate in the 1996–97 period, see Pilkington and Flynn 1999, 179–80. Repatriation has reemerged as a mainstream debate both within government and nongovernmental circles in recent years due to fears of a demographic crisis in post-Soviet Russia.

13. The author interviewed representatives of the organizations and spent time observing the work of the organizations in Samara and Saratov Oblasts on repeated occasions in 1997–99. The research was continued in Novosibirsk Oblast during 2002 but was not as extensive as that carried out in the other two regions. Apart from those organizations, there were no other associations of migrants in the two urban centers of Samara and Saratov. Interviews were conducted with an organization in the urban center of Engel's, situated across the Volga River from Saratov, but that group was not studied in detail. An organization operating in Novosibirsk city that had been set up to help "environmental" migrants from the Semipalatinsk region of Kazakhstan was also interviewed. In the regional districts a number of more commercially based organizations, or organizations centered on compact settlement sites, were visited during fieldwork periods.

14. The quotations in this part of the chapter are taken from interviews conducted with representatives of the five organizations. The place and year of the interview are indicated in parentheses.

15. It has been suggested that Russian migrants could become a source of nationalist support (Brubaker 1995, 213), or a willing target of nationalist or Communist groups due to their possible marginal position within Russian society. As yet, this has not proved to be a reality. The migrant organizations in this study chose which political factions to approach and lobby, and they did not tend to support nationalist political groups.

16. In 1999, these "official" social organizations numbered twenty-five. They received funding from the regional budget to fulfill certain tasks. The official organizations had frequently functioned in some form during the Soviet era.

17. Volga Region, formed in 1991, became a registered resource center in 1995 to facilitate the development of a strong regional NGO sector. It offers help through the provision of resources and training. It receives funding from Western organizations, primarily the U.S. Agency for International Development (USAID), the Eurasia Foundation, and the BEARR Trust (UK).

18. Kay (2000, 191, 194) notes the tendency of donor organizations to allocate repeat funding either to individuals who have had experience running projects or to areas that have already been established as "useful." Representatives of the International Organization of Migration and the United Nations High Commissioner for Refugees (UNHCR) stressed the importance of already knowing a region and having established connections and a positive working relationship with the regional administrations and regional migration services. The newness of the organization Helping Hand (established in 1999) makes a judgment in this case difficult to make, although there was little evidence of international involvement in the local migration sphere and the organization was not in receipt of any Western funding.

19. In the interests of anonymity, individual migrant respondents are referred to only by the identification number assigned to them by the author in a database of sociodemographic details, the region of resettlement, and year of interview. During the empirical study, seventy-two migrant respondents were interviewed across the three regions. Migrant communities were visited in both the regional centers and in villages and compact-type settlements located in the rural districts of the regions. All but a handful of the respondents (who had been displaced upon the territory of the Russian Federation due to the conflict in Chechnya) had left the former republics—primarily Uzbekistan, Tajikistan, Kazakhstan, as well as Azerbaijan, Georgia, and Turkmenistan—between 1991 and 2002. Eighty-two percent of the respondents stated their nationality to be Russian. The respondents were accessed through migrant associations and the migration service and by using snowballing techniques beginning with migrant contacts.

20. Out of seventy-two migrant respondents, forty-eight individuals received forced migrant status, four individuals received refugee status, and twenty individuals were in possession of neither. Of the fifty-two respondents granted official status, twenty-seven had received a one-time payment of emergency monetary help, and seven had received a loan for the acquisition, construction, or renovation of housing.

21. For an in-depth account of the sociocultural adaptation of Russian returnees on the territory of the Russian Federation, see Pilkington 1998; Pilkington and Flynn 2001; and Flynn 2004.

22. This "mistrust" could be related to previous experiences of social organizations. Howard (2003, 26–27), in his study of "civil society" in postcommunist societies, attributes a lack of participation and suspicion of new social organizations to the legacy of the Communist period, when citizens were often forced to join formal mass organizations. He suggests that a certain mistrust of social organizations continues; and citizens, now free to choose whether or not to join, decide not to.

23. Other factors that are influential in the choice of the region of settlement include the geographical location of the region in relation to the place of departure (including direct transport links connecting the two regions), knowledge of possible sources of assistance in the region, climatic conditions in the region, and the socioeconomic conditions existing in the region of arrival. When migrants speak of these other factors, they are often mentioned in the context of the absence of family or friends in Russia.

24. A significant body of recent research has pointed to the importance of personal social networks in post-Soviet Russian society. Instead of dismissing practices such as a dependence upon personal networks as outdated legacies of the Communist past, these authors suggest that attention should be paid to the ways in which these practices are both surviving and being adapted to new environments (see, for example, Alapuro 2001; Ledeneva 1998; Lonkila 1999a, 1999b).

References

Alapuro, Risto. 2001. "Reflections on Social Networks and Collective Action in Russia." In *Education and Civic Culture in Post-Communist Countries,* ed. Stephen Webber and Ilkka Liikanen, 13–27. Hampshire, NY: Palgrave.

Brubaker, Rogers. 1995. "Aftermaths of Empire and the Unmixing of Peoples: Historical and Comparative Perspectives." *Ethnic and Racial Studies* 18, no. 2 (April): 189–218.

Castells, Manuel. 1997. *The Power of Identity.* Malden UK: Blackwell.

———. 1998. *End of Millennium.* Malden, UK: Blackwell.

Codagnone, Christiano. 1998a. "The New Migration in Russia in the 1990s." In *The New Migration in Europe,* ed. Khalid Koser and Helma Lutz, 30–59. Basingstoke, UK: Macmillan.

———. 1998b. "New Migration and Migration Politics in Post-Soviet Russia." *CEMES Ethnobarometer Working Paper,* no. 2.

Committee of Refugees from Chechnya. 1999. Interview conducted by the author with the organization, Saratov, August 19.

Flynn, Moya. 2004. *Migrant Resettlement in the Russian Federation: Reconstructing "Homes" and "Homelands."* London: Anthem Press.

Forum of Migrant Associations. www.migrant.ru/forum (July 15, 2003).

Gannushkina, Svetlana. 1999. Interview conducted by the author, Moscow, September 13.

Gupta, Akhil, and Ferguson, James. 1992. "Space, Identity and the Politics of Difference." *Cultural Anthropology* 7, no. 1 (February): 6–23.

Hann, Chris. 1996. "Introduction." In *Civil Society: Challenging Western Models,* ed. Chris Hann and Elizabeth Dunn, 1–26. London: Routledge.

Heleniak, Tim. 2002. "Migration Dilemmas Haunt Post-Soviet Russia." *Migration Information Source,* Migration Policy Institute, October.

Howard, Mark Morjé. 2003. *The Weakness of Civil Society in Post-Communist Europe.* Cambridge: Cambridge University Press.

International Organization of Migration (IOM). 2002. "Management of Migration in the CIS Countries." *IOM Open Forum Information Series,* Issue 3 (January).

Kay, Rebecca. 2000. *Russian Women and Their Organizations: Gender, Discrimination and Grassroots Women's Organizations.* Basingstoke, UK: Macmillan.

Ledeneva, Alena. 1998. *Russia's Economy of Favours.* Cambridge: Cambridge University Press.

Lonkila, Markku. 1999a. *Social Networks in Post-Soviet Russia. Continuity and Change in the Everyday Life of St. Petersburg Teachers.* Helsinki: Kikimora.

———. 1999b. "Post-Soviet Russia: A Society of Networks." In *Russia: More Different than Most,* ed. Markku Kangasporo, 99–112. Helsinki: Kikimora.

Materialy mezhdunarodnogo seminara. Razrabotka i realizatsiia regional'nykh migratsionnykh program. 1999. Saratov: Saratovskii istochnik.

Memorial. 1997. *Bezhentsi i vynuzhdennye pereselentsy na territorii Rossiiskoi Federatsii,* Moscow: Zven'ia.

Novosibirsk Migration Service. 2002. Interview conducted by the author with the deputy-director of the migration service, Novosibirsk, July 15.

Pilkington, Hilary. 1998. *Migration, Displacement and Identity in Post-Soviet Russia.* London: Routledge.

Pilkington, Hilary, and Moya Flynn. 1999. "From 'Refugee' to 'Repatriate': Russian Repatriation Discourse in the Making." In *The End of the Refugee Cycle,* ed. Richard Black and Khalid Koser, 171–97. Oxford: Berghahn Books.

———. 2001. "Chuzhie na rodine? Issledovanie 'diasporal'noi identichnosti' russkikh vynuzhdennykh pereselentsev." *Diaspory,* no. 2–3: 8–34.

Pudina, Liudmilla. 1999. "Mir vashemu domu." *Saratovskie vesti,* March 12, 2.

Return. 1999. Interview conducted by the author with the organization, Saratov, August 24.

Richardson, Erica. 2001. "Health Promotion and the 'Third Sector' in Russia." Unpublished conference paper presented at the BASEES Conference, Cambridge.

Samara Migrant. 1999. Interview conducted by the author with the organization, Samara, November 5.

———. 2002. Interview conducted by the author with the organization, Samara, August 24.

Samara Migration Service. 1999. Interview conducted by the author with a representative of the migration service, Samara, September 30.

———. 1999a. Interview conducted by the author with the director of the migration service, Saratov, 16 August.

———. 1999b. Interview conducted by the author with the head of the department for forced migrant and refugee registration, Saratov, August 16.

Saratov Spring. 1999. Interview conducted by the author with the organization, Saratov, August 20.

Vitkovskaia, Galina. 1999. Interview conducted by the author, Moscow, September 23.

White, Jenny. 1996. "Civic Culture and Islam in Urban Turkey." In *Civil Society: Challenging Western Models,* ed. Chris Hann and Elizabeth Dunn, 143–54. London: Routledge.

16

Public–Private Permutations

Domestic Violence Crisis Centers in Barnaul

Janet Elise Johnson

In the midst of the stunted development of post-Soviet Russian civil society, a small independent women's crisis center movement has emerged, addressing the issue of violence against women. Since the early 1990s, the number of these organizations has grown from none to perhaps over one hundred, scattered across Russian cities. Many of these women's crisis centers balance service provision, consciousness raising, policy advocacy, and social movement nourishment. In some ways, the development of this autonomous women's crisis center movement resembles the liberal model of state–society relations (Hale 2002) imagined by many Western political theorists and most international donors. In contrast to much of the Russian third sector, this segment of civil society is beginning to hold the state accountable to respond to its citizens' needs, a crucial step in deepening democracy.

At the same time, domestic violence politics in Russia is also developing along the lines of a more "statist model" of civil society in which there is a blurring of the lines between state institutions and nongovernmental organizations (NGOs). For example, state social services and state university departments have created parallel NGO crisis centers so that they exist as both state institutions and societal organizations. As imagined by the advocates of this statist model, this public–private permutation may facilitate collaboration between state agencies and the autonomous women's crisis center movement, leading to more responsiveness to the problem of violence against women. As proponents of the Western model argue, however, there are also risks associated with this more "statist model" of state–society relations (Hale 2002), especially because of Putin's relegitimation of the strong tradition of *gosudarstvennost'* (statism).

Through a detailed study of domestic violence politics in postcommunist Russia, this chapter examines these two different models of civil society, shedding light on the ongoing debate about what constitutes civil society and what kind of civil society is good for Russia (e.g., in two issues of *Demokratizatsiya* in 2002; Mendelson and Glenn 2002). In contrast to this more abstract and more general debate, I emphasize one zone of civil society, domestic violence politics, in one particular geographic location, Barnaul, a southwestern Siberian city a few hundred miles from Kazakhstan, China, and Mongolia. My belief is that such "thick description" (Geertz 1973) is "an opportunity to learn more about the complexity of the problem studied, to develop further the existing explanatory framework, and to refine and elaborate the initially available theory" (George 1979, 51–52). I argue that this kind of "heuristic" case study is especially important for studying postcommunist civil society, as Western theories and expectations contrast with Russian theories, expectation, and lived experiences (Hemment 2004). I chose to emphasize Barnaul because it represents fairly typical post-Soviet Russian urban life,[1] and because, having both an independent women's crisis center and several examples of public–private permutations, it is a microcosm of domestic violence politics in Russia.[2]

The chapter first examines the Women's Alliance organization in Barnaul within the context of the larger women's crisis center movement. I argue that these organizations approximate a liberal model of civil society in the way imagined by Western political scientists, but also in the way imagined by feminist political theorists. The chapter then describes two hybrids—part state institution, part NGO—that also address domestic violence in Barnaul, assessing the opportunities and risks of these public–private permutations. Next, I describe a working group on domestic violence that links these organizations directly with the state to address domestic violence. In conclusion, I suggest that this kind of multidisciplinary working group, advocated by domestic violence advocates in the United States, represents a "third way" and that, at least in some sectors of postcommunist civil society, this kind of public–private permutation may be a potentially healthier approach to state–society relations.

The Women's Alliance and the Women's Crisis Center Movement

The Women's Alliance (Nekommercheskoe partnerstvo "Zhenskii Al'ians"), founded by Natalia Sereda in 1998, was the result of the restructuring of a women's organization first founded in 1993 in Barnaul. Modeled after autonomous women's crisis centers in Moscow and Nizhnyi Tagil, the primary activity of the Women's Alliance is a hotline, a fairly inexpensive way to reach out to women and provide emotional support, empowerment, and medical and legal referrals. Other services include on-site counseling and support groups as well as escorting of victims to the police and court, a tortuous process for most women victims of violence (Human Rights Watch 1997; Johnson 2001, 2004a).[3] In 1998–2002, the center helped "6,500 victims—most of them female victims of violence" (Shitova 2002, 7). Not a large NGO relative to American nonprofits, the organization is typical of many crisis centers in Russia: there was only a handful of paid staff plus perhaps up to a dozen volunteers loosely affiliated with the center.

The Women's Alliance is part of the larger women's crisis center movement (Johnson 2001, 2004b). As Sereda describes it, the Women's Alliance is a second-generation women's crisis center. The first generation of women's crisis centers emerged following the August 1991 First Independent Women's Forum, inspired by the British and American women's movements and the international discussion of violence against women in preparation for the 1995 Beijing UN Conference on Women. Crisis centers for women victims of violence were founded in both Moscow and St. Petersburg in 1993. By the mid-1990s, in a second generation, more crisis centers were founded in these two megacities, and the movement spread northward and eastward.

By 1998, researchers in Moscow found twenty-four organizations that worked in the sphere of "prevention and elimination of violence against women" within the Russian Federation, from Murmansk to Irkutsk (Abubikirova et al. 1998, 9). Following a September 1998 Russian–American conference on domestic violence attended by Hillary Clinton, the U.S. Agency for International Development (USAID) disbursed approximately $1 million in small grants to crisis centers; and crisis centers proliferated, creating a second generation. By 2001, there were between 60 and 80 organizations. In the summer of 2002, the director of the Russian Association of Crisis Centers for Women (RACCW), an umbrella organization of 40 members, estimated that there were some 120 organizations involved in the issue of violence against women (Regentova, interview 2002).

As a whole, these women's crisis centers constitute a social movement: "collective challenges by people with common purposes and solidarity in sustained interaction with elites, opponents, and authorities" (Tarrow 1994). The Women's Alliance, founded as part of the RACCW, has continually worked to foster networks between crisis centers and with other NGOs. In the summer of 2002, Sereda emerged as the vice president and president elect in a newly restructured RACCW, a restructuring encouraged by USAID and with the purpose of decreasing the centralization of the organization around certain personalities and Moscow.

The Liberal Model of State–Society Relations

As recognized in two recent critiques of Russian civil society (Richter 2002; Henderson 2003), this independent women's crisis center movement is an exception. In contrast to most NGOs that populate the post-Soviet third sector, the movement meets the criteria of civil society as imagined by many Western political theorists and donors of democracy assistance. As Henry Hale (2002) explains in his characterization of the two dominant viewpoints in the ongoing debate about state–society relations, the liberal model "envisions society as a set of associations standing between the private sphere (encompassing individual and family activities) and the state, acting independently of the state" (307).[4] In this model, social organizations provide the link between citizens and the state, creating the political opportunity for the collective expression of needs, interests, and preferences (308). Social organizations are also understood to create the social capital required to make democracy work (Putnam 1993), because these organizations are organized more "horizontally" than hierarchically.

In a context where foreign assistance has helped "a small elite stratum of NGO professionals or career feminists" (Hemment 2004, 234), the Women's Alliance is distinguished by its attempts to develop links with the larger society. In addition to providing services, the center reaches out to the population to try to change the behavior of citizens. This goal is recognized by volunteers and implemented in practice.[5] At their office, and around town, I found a variety of stickers, bulletins, and pamphlets designed to bring attention to the issue and a myriad of photos and news articles on events that the Alliance had coordinated. The Women's Alliance succeeded in getting articles about their work and the problem of domestic violence in a variety of regional news publications. The Alliance also participated in the larger movement's media campaigns, negotiating a discussion of domestic violence on a regional television talk show.

The Women's Alliance also makes claims upon the state, creating new space for political or public action and deeper relationships between the state and society. The Alliance's leaders, like the leaders of all the strong Russian crisis centers, hold the state accountable for dealing with domestic violence as promised, explicitly or implicitly, by the Constitution, international treaties, and statutes.[6] This process began in July 1999 when Sereda co-organized a domestic violence workshop with the gender project of the American Bar Association's Central and East European Legal Initiative (ABA-CEELI) and invited regional administrators involved in education and health care and the police (Post 2002). Following this workshop, Sereda has repeatedly argued—in press and at meetings with government, administrative, and law-enforcement officials—that the criminal-legal system and state social services have a responsibility to address domestic violence.

Since 1998, the director has sought increased response by the police to victims of domestic and sexual violence and has facilitated training for law-enforcement officers. This call for responsiveness has extended to the problem of sexual harassment, a problem that remains much more obscure in Russia than domestic violence. In 2000, the Alliance supported more than a dozen women employees at a regional hospital in their attempts to hold the head doctor accountable for quid pro quo sexual harassment. Using legal counseling available for free from the Women's Alliance, the women pursued a criminal case (which was dismissed); unsuccessfully sued for moral harm; and, finally, persuaded the relevant trade union to dismiss the perpetrator. In addition to calling for legal responsiveness, the Alliance calls for increased social services for women victims of violence. By getting involved in these issues autonomously from the state, they are deepening and broadening concepts of citizenship.

The foreign assistance that is almost the only source of financial support for the Women's Alliance (and the other women's crisis centers) establishes its independence from the state, a point clearly recognized by President Putin, who has decried these type of organizations for their "foreign influence." The reliance on foreign assistance also contributes to the biggest weakness of the Women's Alliance and other crisis centers, a problem typical of NGOs in post-Soviet society: the inadequate attention to recruiting constituents for their organizations. Although gathering financial resources from the relatively poor Russian society is challenging, the failure to recruit constituents leaves more distance from the larger society. What makes the women's crisis centers more connected to society than most Russian NGOs is that they provide real services for a fairly large target population, women living with violence.

Politicizing Public–Private Boundaries

More than just serving as the intermediary between the state and citizens, the independent women's crisis center movement, as the example of the Women's Alliance illustrates, has politicized the boundaries between the public and private. The movement has challenged the neoliberal privatization project, calling for the state not only to maintain certain responsibilities but also to assume new responsibilities that are required for the protection of women's rights. The leadership has contested the inadequate responses from the criminal-legal system and state social services (Human Rights Watch 1997).

This critique of public–private boundaries embodied in the work of the women's crisis center movement is linked to a broader critique by feminist political theorists. Mainstream political theory locates civil society between nebulous (gender-neutral) individuals or the family and the state. With no recognition of the gendered power in the family, these definitions suggest that the family can be bracketed off as outside of politics, implying that all individuals within the family have the same access and opportunities within the civil and political societies (Pateman 1989). The prevalence of violence against women within the home combined with almost all governments' legal tradition of ignoring violence against women (Armatta 1997) shatters this myth (Pateman 1988). Second wave women's movements, especially those protesting violence against women, often contest the way that the boundary between the public (where the state intervenes) and the private (where the state does not, e.g., the family) reinforces gendered power. They do this by bringing into view typically unseen problems or renegotiating the particulars of the problems (Fraser 1990).

The women's crisis center movement in Russia also politicizes the boundaries between the public and the private in this second way, challenging the new gendered drawing of the public and private, which privileges male power in the home (Johnson 2001). By challenging domestic violence and calling for more state intervention to counter male violence, they challenge male power. They assert that the boundaries between the public and the private should be based on consent: the state should intervene in the family when women give consent for it to happen or when women's consent to get involved with an intimate partner has been violated by violence. Furthermore, the project of the Women's Alliance has been about shedding new light on a problem that has often been hidden from public view or misunderstood as women's fault. Their educational campaigns seek to uncover the often-misunderstood problem of domestic violence and link it to the violation of human rights and establish it as crime. They work to counter societal misconceptions about women's culpability in "provoking" domestic violence. This case of domestic violence in Russia is not unique:

politicization of the boundaries between public and private has been implicit in the postcommunist gender politics across Central and Eastern Europe (Watson 1993; Gal and Kligman 2000).

As the thinking about civil society in this region has been characterized by the simplistic, tripartite construction of social life—the state, the market, and civil society as the "Third Sector" (Hemment 2004, 221)—the women's crisis center movement highlights the gendered and contested nature of these categories. As I expand upon later, the case of domestic violence politics in Russia illustrates that some civic organizations do not fit simply into this third category; they undermine the categorization, raising questions about the ways in which social scientists examine postcommunist societies.

At the same time, women activists' assumption of responsibility for this problem that predominantly faces women reaffirms a gender-based division of labor and power (see also Ishkanian 2004). It suggests that men and men's problems are the subject of formal (real) politics and women and women's problems are relegated to the less powerful civic sphere. This gendered division, in turn, reinforces the idea that civil society (which is now feminine) is less important and powerful than formal politics (which is now masculine). Gender stratification leads to gender segregation in the new political life, which, in a vicious cycle, reinforces what advocates of civil society do not want, the minimization of civil society. At the same time, it legitimates the neoliberal privatization project, allowing domestic violence to be privatized into NGOs.

The Altai Krai Crisis Center for Men and Men's Conversation

In the early 1990s, the women's crisis center movement attempted to appropriate the concept of a "crisis center" (*krizisnyi tsentr*) for its own. However, the concept resonated (Hemment 1999)—many Russians understand themselves as living in crisis (Ries 1997)—and by the late 1990s, many social organizations and state institutions, providing a myriad of social services, employed the term.

One of these other crisis centers in Barnaul is the Altai Krai Crisis Center for Men (KCCM), the only men's crisis center in Russia (Regentova, interview 2002), which was founded in the late 1990s (Altai is the *krai*, or region, of which Barnaul is the capital). According to its 2002 brochure, the mission of the organization is "the prevention and rehabilitation of the physical, psychological, and social health of working-age men in the region."[7] Activity, as with the women's crisis centers, centers around a crisis hotline. In this case, the hotline is specifically designed to provide psychological consultations twenty-four hours a day, and most of the calls are from men concerned about health and financial problems. In addition to social workers, there are also psychologists, psychiatrists, various medical doctors specializing in men's sexuality and addiction, an attorney, and a "social pedagogue." In addition to the hotline, the center runs various groups for men and youth facing a variety of different life situations. In 2002, branch offices were being established in three other cities in the krai.

By 1999, the KCCM was also focusing on domestic violence and gender research. According to its brochure, the center provides "psychological help in the situation of domestic violence for men offenders," and Maksim Kostenko, the director of the program since 1998, reports that approximately 10 percent of male callers to the center are concerned about "conflicts in the family" (V Altaiskom krae sklonnost'). One of their group projects is on the prevention of violence for those who employ violent behavior and the development among youths of nonviolent ways of interacting. In addition, Kostenko expresses an intellectual interest in domestic violence and the broader anti–domestic violence movement in Russia.[8]

In contrast to the Women's Alliance, which is clearly autonomous from the state, the KCCM is a state institution. It was founded by the regional government within the structure of the krai administration's Committee on the Social Defense of the Population, at least partially as placement for social work students who needed to do a practicum. The specialists in the center are faculty, researchers, and advanced graduate students from the sociology department of the Altai State University.

Housed in the same space, with many of the same staff, is an NGO called Men's Conversation (*Muzhskoi razgovor*). The existence of Men's Conversation became obvious in conversation with foreign donors at a round table on men's rights to reproductive health held in July 2002. Even though we were meeting in the space of the KCCM—and the meeting was understood to be with the KCCM by my Russian colleagues—Kostenko represented himself on the round-table agenda as the executive director of the Altai nongovernmental organization Men's Conversation. This was crucial, as the round table had been funded through a democracy assistance program.[9] According to a local informational bulletin, this NGO, Men's Conversation, was founded in 1999 to address the problems of domestic violence in collaboration with KCCM and staffed by Kostenko and Natal'ia Kostenko, his wife (Young Altai Journalists 2002).

The creation of this parallel NGO lays bare the incentive structure for NGOs created by Western donors (Henderson 2003). As Sarah Henderson describes in more detail (Henderson 2003, chap. 4), in the 1990s several key donors—including USAID, the Ford Foundation, the John D. and Catherine T. MacArthur Foundation, and the Open Society Institute—decided to promote women's organizations and women's rights in Russia, leading the sector to become relatively well funded (in comparison to other sectors of Russian civil society) (92). By the late 1990s, the new funding fad—exemplified by the USAID distribution described above but also by Ford and the European Union—was women's crisis centers and the issue of domestic violence.[10] Some grants were small, but some—for example, from the Ford Foundation to the Moscow-based crisis center ANNA and to the Irkutsk Crisis Center—were significant ($200,000 and $150,000, respectively, in 1999). As they receive no direct support from the Russian government or from constituents for their day-to-day existence, women's crisis centers have been created and sustained by both heroic efforts of NGO staff and foreign assistance.[11] The availability of these grants—in a context where domestic funds remained in short supply—created a powerful incentive for state institutions such as the KCCM to repackage themselves as NGOs.

Otklik

The Women's Alliance is not the only women's organization in Barnaul. A directory of women's organizations in Altai Krai published in 2002 (Belousova et al. 2001) describes the emergence of women's organizations. In 1991–94, seven women's organizations were registered in the krai, though four of them quickly collapsed (9–10). Between 1995 and 1998, eight were registered (10); nineteen more appeared in 1999 and 2000 (11). Some of these organizations were Altai branches of national organizations such as the political movement Women of Russia. Nineteen of the thirty-four organizations that were registered only in the krai described a major focus to be the defense of women's rights, while others focused on children, more generically on people's rights, or the environment (12).

One of these women's organizations—and the third organization that acts like a crisis center—in Barnaul is Otklik ("Response" in English, but I am using the Russian name for clarity), founded in 1997. While the original purpose was described as the defense of citizens' rights, especially those of women (Bolsko 1999), since 1999 one of their many educational, legal, and social service projects has addressed the problem of violence against women. In 2001–2, one of their two main projects involved "innovative forms of help to survivors of violence" against women. Although not officially associated with the women's crisis center movement, Otklik frames itself as dealing with violence against women and as a women's crisis center.[12]

Like KCCM, Otklik has a complicated status, even though it is clearly registered as an NGO and has received funds from a range of organizations, such as the Canadian Fund for the Support of Russian Women, the NIS–US Consortium of Women's Organizations, and the MacArthur Foundation, which tend to support women's crisis centers as well as other women's organizations. Like almost all organizations in Altai (Belousova et al. 2001), Otklik was apparently founded with support from the state. In 2002, the director of the organization, Svetlana Chudova, was a lecturer at the Altai State University's Faculty of Sociology, where the center is located. Her business card from the university lists both her university position and her position with Otklik. The university also allows the center virtual space on its Web server. Furthermore, much of the center's work is academic in nature. Finally, the center helps train students from the university, much like the KCCM.

Of course, this overlap of state academic institution and NGO does not mean an organization is a tool of the state. In the United States, many academics are employed at public institutions while being critical of the government, and even domestic violence shelters in the United States, which remain relatively autonomous, have almost all received some funding from the government (Elman 1996, 38). In the Russian women's movement, a similar strategy was employed by the Moscow Center for Gender Studies (MCGS). After suffering financial problems as part of the Institute of Socioeconomic Studies of the Population within the Academy of Sciences, the MCGS restructured itself as a nongovernmental organization in 1994 and was sustained through the 1990s by an institutional grant from the MacArthur Foundation (Sperling 1999).[13]

Otklik highlights another part of the puzzle in understanding Russian civil society. As described by Janine Wedel (2001), the Soviet legacy of patronage and influence combined with large-scale economic reform and privatization led to "flex organizing," chameleon-like organizing in which actors shift their organizations between public and private spheres as a tactic to maneuver between constraints of both spheres (Wedel 2004, 5). Although this tactic depends on the legal constitution of the separate spheres of public and private—each subject to different rules and little or no rules to regulate the border crossing—the tactical shifting blurs the boundaries between public and private. As explained by Wedel (ibid., 4), "[i]n postcommunist societies, political–economic influence has accrued to those who skillfully blend, equivocate, mediate, and otherwise work the spheres of state and private, bureaucracy and market, and legal and illegal."

The creation of Otklik—as well as Men's Conversation—illustrates that what Wedel (ibid.) found for the bigger game of foreign aid, by the end of the 1990s was being played by smaller players in regions as far away as Barnaul.[14] The leaders of these organizations, who both have close ties to the state university and the krai ministry of social protection, were doing their own kind of flex organizing, seeking resources from the university, state social services, and international donors.

The Opportunities of the Statist Model of State–Society Relations

The emergence of these two flex organizations suggests that in Barnual domestic violence politics is also developing along the lines of a second, more statist model of state–society relations. According to Hale (2002), who builds his model based on Russian theorists such as Domrin (2003) as well as Western theorists including Hobbes, the statist model views the relationship between the state and society as complementary parts of an integrated whole (Hale 2002, 309). Social organizations, instead of existing autonomously and in opposition to the state, are fostered by the state, and sometimes even created by the state, which, in turn, both protects and restricts these organizations in pursuit of the interests of the state and nonstate society. Under this vision, the expression of needs, interests, and preferences is best facilitated by cooperation between the state and social organizations.

Both the KCCM and Otklik, as part state institution and part NGO, can work as this kind of "two-way transmission" belt (ibid.). Staff in these organizations move in both circles, relating to the state as state employees and to the autonomous women's crisis center movement in conferences and seminars as NGO activists. That some of their funding comes from the state illustrates that the state is taking new responsibility for domestic violence, recognizing the needs of the population that is suffering from domestic violence and adopting some of the preferences of the women's crisis center movement for the increased availability of crisis social services.

In contrast to the women's crisis center movement, which has been at odds with the state, for example, by contributing to a Human Rights Watch (1997) report that condemned the post-Soviet criminal-legal (lack of) response to domestic violence, these two organizations illustrate the potential for "constructive cooperation" between civil society and the state, as called for by participants in the Civic Forum's July 2001 press conference (Domrin 2003). As argued by Alexander Domrin, there is a need for "civil society in Russia . . . [to] develop in tandem with the strengthening of Russian statehood" and for civil society to evolve from simply criticizing the state to constituting post-Soviet politics. As a result of the focus on the problem of domestic violence by KCCM and Otklik, even the Women's Alliance has taken a more conciliatory stand toward the state.

The existence of the men's crisis center, unique to Altai, is also remarkable for another reason. In contrast to most services for domestic violence across Russia— and around the world—it is a men's organization, approximately half staffed by men and focused on men clients. Since it is men who perpetrate most of the severe domestic violence in Russia (Sillaste, interview 1997), men taking responsibility for combating violence signals a shift in gender relations.

The Risks of the Statist Model of State–Society Relationships

On the other hand, exceedingly close ties between social organizations and state institutions may be dangerous, especially in post-Soviet Russia. Russia remains a "transitional government," combining characteristics of authoritarianism and democracy (Karatnycky, Motyl, and Schnetzer 2002). Its Soviet history of etatization of all elements of society, including the co-optation by the state of ostensibly social organizations, raises concerns that the post-Soviet state may seek to control the activities of NGOs and limit the institutionalized channels linking NGOs and the state. This was one of the concerns raised by NGOs concerning Putin's 2001 NGO forum and proposal to establish a Civic Chamber attached to the Office of the President. According to the liberal model of state–society relations, the protection from tyranny is one of the key functions of autonomous social organizations (Hale 2002, 308).

The emergence of KCCM and Otklik may threaten the very existence of the Women's Alliance in Barnaul. The precedent for this threat is a domestic violence bill that was discussed in the national Duma Committee on Women, Family, and Youth in the mid-1990s.[15] The bill was drafted without consultation with the women's crisis centers, and later parliamentary hearings on the draft bill excluded almost all activists. As a result of not including crisis centers' expertise, the bill proposed the elimination of NGO crisis centers (which were portrayed as brothels) and their replacement with state crisis centers. Although the bill was flatly rejected by the Duma in 1997— primarily because of the money involved—the ties that KCCM and Otklik have to the state may give them the power to marginalize the Women's Alliance.

The hybrid organizations pose additional problems for state–society relations. One is that such flex organizing allows for the continuation of elites, especially in regions like Barnaul where the productive economy has collapsed and the region must rely on subsidies from the central government. Those close to the regional government have reaped many benefits, and now these same reapers benefit from democracy assistance. Second, unsurprisingly, following the legacy of Communist rule, civil society in post-Soviet Russia has been plagued by a lack of trust (Rose 1994). A 2001 poll found that 73 percent of respondents said that they would not like to work in an NGO, perhaps because of a lack of trust in these NGOs (Domrin 2003).[16] By not being fully honest with the funding organizations, KCCM/Men's Conversation contributes to the lack of trust in society.

These problems with KCCM/Men's Conversation and Otklik affirm the findings of several arguments about the distortions in civil society in Russia (e.g., Mendelson and Glenn 2002; Sundstrom 2002; Henderson 2003; Hemment 2004). Although much of this research holds democracy assistance responsible, the fact that these distortions happen in Barnaul where less has changed (many of the former Communist leaders remained in power through the 1990s) and where there has been less, and more belated, foreign aid indicates that the Soviet legacy and the failure of reforms have also played a crucial role. These tactics resemble the patronage networks—what has been called the "personalized-public" (Yurchak 2002)—that virtually ran many regions of the Soviet Union (Wedel 2004).

These troubles urge caution in response to an otherwise potentially promising 2004 development in Altai's domestic violence politics. On June 25, the Altai governor announced the establishment of a state crisis center for women designed to provide "specialized social assistance to women," especially those living with violence ("V Altaiskom krae sozdano"). Like the other crisis centers, there will be a hotline, but the state also plans a short-term shelter. This would be a remarkable achievement. Yet this announcement, published on an Altai online news service, provoked controversy as several readers raised legitimate questions about patronage. For example, the new vice governor who has been appointed to direct the founding of this organization happens to be the academic who directed Kostenko's dissertation, and it seems that Kostenko was also the leading candidate to head this new women's crisis center. The allegation from several readers was that this crisis center was simply another avenue for supporting the vice governor's "people." At the same time, some resistance to the center clearly reflects the view that the state should not respond to domestic violence at all.

A Working Group on Violence in the Family

In 2001, relations between the state and society over the issue of domestic violence shifted in Barnaul. The Women's Alliance found an ally in the krai government sympathetic to its claims for more state responsiveness. N. S. Remneva, the director of the Department of Medical-Social and Family-Demographic Problems, had been a member of a national commission on women (Sereda, interview 2002). That experience transformed her thinking, leading her to champion a working group linking the Altai Krai administration, the Women's Alliance, and the KCCM to address problems of violence in the family. Founded in March 2001, the group is officially titled a "working group of specialists-coordinators for solving the problem connected with the growth of violence in the family against women and children, an organization for the systematic struggle with violence in the krai."[17] In addition to Sereda of the Women's Alliance and Kostenko of KCCM, the working group includes social workers, administrative officials, health officials, educators, the head doctor of a private hospital, the head of the youth commission, and the deputy director of the krai administration of internal affairs.

One goal of the organization was to facilitate a common understanding of the problem of violence in the family (Sereda, interview 2002). The hope was that a shared understanding would facilitate better coordination among state institutions, the police, social services, and the women's crisis center. The group also planned to facilitate the training of psychologists, doctors, and police to respond to the problem of domestic violence. They want to spread this training from the capital, Barnaul, out to the other nineteen krai municipalities. The plan is to develop a regional law on the prevention of violence in the family that will institutionalize collaboration.

By May 2004, this group had led ten round tables on "Safety in the Family: Time for Action," attracting a wide variety of both civic leaders and state officials from social services, education, and law enforcement. According to a journalist at the leading Altai newspaper, *Altaiskaia pravda*, "The participants in the conversation [at the tenth round table] were unanimous that departmental segregation strongly hindered the war against domestic violence" (Pol'shchikova 2004). This multidisplinary, multisphere collaboration has apparently been institutionalized, but it has also achieved some changes. For example, police in at least one krai precinct had been convinced to collect statistics on domestic violence, something incredibly rare in Russia. According to the journalist, this collaboration had raised the issue of domestic violence from a private problem to being a problem worthy of state response.

Whereas many women's organizations as well as other NGOs have been thwarted by the state's closed political opportunity structure (Sperling 1999), the working group is an illustration of how women's crisis centers are beginning to make headway in getting their voices heard. The working group is specifically designed for creating new channels as well as a new space for coordination across different disciplines within the state and society, a public–private permutation advocated by feminist activists and scholars.

It resembles the groundwork needed to establish a "coordinated community response" advocated by American domestic violence advocates. As described by Donna Coker,

> In a coordinated response, criminal sanctions are accompanied by strong supports for battered women. Prosecutors craft their strategies so as to maximize victim safety; police provide victims with information about rights as well as referrals to services including shelters; courts routinely order victims compensation; and detectives and prosecutors follow up with victims to monitor threats or intimidation tactics of the batterer. In addition, the justice system works closely with service providers to assist women in safety planning and advocacy with other systems, such as public assistance, child protective services, and employers, and also to encourage support from victims' family and friends (quoted in Schneider 2002).

278 JANET ELISE JOHNSON

This kind of model is advocated because it takes into account the particularities of the problem of domestic violence—the intimate relationship between the perpetrator and the victim, the increased danger when a woman tries to leave this kind of relationship, and the need to empower a victim who has been systematically disempowered over years—while retaining the focus on the similarity of the violence to criminal assault. By keeping women's agency in the process, this model creates a higher standard for invading the privacy of domestic life while continuing to demand state response to domestic violence.

In a comparison of domestic violence policy in thirty-six countries, Weldon (2002) found that the most responsive policies existed in places where there was a similar type of coordination between women's activists and state institutions charged with women's issues. As such coordination—and domestic violence policies—remain limited throughout the world, even imagining this kind of collaboration in Russia signals a dramatic transformation in the way the state and society relate, especially in the inclusion of the clearly autonomous Women's Alliance in this process.

A Third Way

In addition to illustrating the complexity found across civil society in postcommunist Russia, the array of NGOs, state institutions, and flex organizations on domestic violence in Barnaul demonstrates the obstacles to deepening democracy. As I have argued above, relegating many issues to NGOs in Russia allows the state to abrogate its responsibilities and, if this relegation is gendered, it can reinforce both gender stratification and the undervaluation of civil society. Yet leaving state institutions, many of which remain weak and relatively unreformed, to address crucial problems in society has little promise. Flex organizing, the tactic employed by state institutions seeking survival, undermines the transparency and accountability that is essential to moving beyond Russia's "managed democracy."

In contrast, the working group in Barnaul—which resembles developments in domestic violence politics in some other cities such as Saratov[18] and which is called for by most women's crisis centers—suggests a healthier "third way" between the statist and liberal models of state–society relations in post-Soviet Russia. Similar to flex organizing, this kind of multidisciplinary state and society coalition allows for crossing the boundaries between public and private. However, instead of the implicit and opaque boundary crossing involved in flex organizing, this kind of coordination does not necessarily eliminate the boundaries. The boundaries still matter—e.g., the autonomy of the Women's Alliance matters—but problems are not simply relegated to NGOs. The state and society collaborate in sharing responsibilities.

The success of domestic violence politics in Barnaul, although unusual, suggests a model that may work for other segments of civil society. It may be possible and advantageous to balance autonomous organizations with state institutions in other segments of civil society by means of a boundary-crossing structure for communicating among organizations and state institutions. Independent organizations can continue to hold the state accountable for its promises of human rights while new institutionalized channels to power—such as the hybrids and the working group—can facilitate better communication. This delicate balance may be more conducive to the development of a civil society in a Russia that is wary of a lack of order, while simultaneously providing some buffers to tyranny.

Instead of continuing to think of more oppositional, liberal theories of civil society versus more conciliatory, statist models, this case study suggests that social scientists and policy makers consider what might constitute a middle ground when they analyze and advocate. This is especially relevant in thinking about foreign assistance, which can be designated to facilitate this kind of state–society collaboration, especially as Putin works to further institutionalize the state's power.

Postscript

In January 2005, the krai crisis center for women officially opened in Barnaul, and not with Kostenko as director, but Sereda (Sereda, personal communication 2005). As foreign donors pulled out of the region or switched away from the issue of domestic violence, the Women's Alliance could no longer secure sufficient resources. The new center receives limited government funding for a few specialists and the rent but is built upon the experience and staff of the Women's Alliance. Sereda's decision to create this kind of flex organization reflects the fragility of autonomous civil society during Putin's second term, but as a condition for accepting the job, Sereda insisted that she be able to continue her connection with the autonomous women's movement.

Notes

1. Since the collapse of Soviet rule, Barnaul—and Altai Krai, of which Barnaul is the capital—has been transformed from a military-industrial center to an economically depressed region that must rely on financial subsidies from the federal government. This is typical of most subnational units in Russia and is in contrast to Moscow.

2, The field data on domestic violence come primarily from a research trip to Barnaul in July 2002, during which I lived and worked with the leaders of the Women's Alliance, the independent women's crisis center in Barnaul. I employed the method of participant observation, observing and taking part in their everyday activities, as well as conducting interviews with several members of the three organizations concerned with domestic violence. In addition, I have collected and analyzed discourse and literature from the organizations and regional news stories. All this research is bolstered by long-term research on women's crisis centers in Russia.

3. In addition to the crisis center, the Women's Alliance has a parenting training program and a women's resource center that includes a library and runs various programs to advocate for women's rights and aid other women's NGOs.

4. Hale (2002) attributes this understanding of civil society to a variety of scholars, including Mendelson and Glenn (2002), Fish (1994), and Rose (1994).

5. For example, as summarized by one volunteer at the center, "[c]enter specialists conduct informational and educational campaigns against violence in . . . society through publications in mass media, as well as training and seminars for government employees such as

law enforcement officials, social workers, doctors, teachers, and elected officials" (Shitova 2002, 7).

6. The 1993 Constitution, while not directly addressing domestic violence, promises equal rights and liberties (Art. 19) and the right to live free from violence (Art. 21.2). Relevant international documents include the Convention on the Elimination of Violence against Women. The criminal and civil codes include a variety of statutes for assault, battery, and moral harm. For a discussion of all the legal obligations, see Zabelina (2002, chap. 2) and Johnson (2001).

7. The brochure, simply titled "Altai Krai Crisis Center for Men," was given to me by the director, Maksim Kostenko, on July 2, 2002.

8. For example, Kostenko presented a paper on domestic violence offenders at a November 2001 conference of the Network for Crisis Centers for Women in the Barents Region attended by activists and academics studying domestic violence in Russia. In my interview with him, Kostenko spoke of American feminist theories of masculinity and demonstrated familiarity with American and Swedish batterer treatment programs.

9. The donor representative did not speak Russian and did not know of the KCCM, only of the NGO Men's Conversation.

10. For a discussion of the effect of foreign assistance on domestic violence politics in other post-Soviet and postsocialist societies, see Johnson (2004b) and Brunell and Johnson (2004).

11. The Women's Alliance has been sustained by Sereda and her family's hard work—ten-hour days for both Sereda and her husband while I was in Barnaul—plus foreign assistance from various sources such as USAID and UNICEF.

12. Evidence of their focus on violence against women was that I first encountered Otklik at a workshop on fundraising for crisis centers held by one of the first generation of women's crisis centers, ANNA in Moscow. The Otklik staff at the workshop told me that they had a crisis center.

13. Unlike KCCM, MCGS ceased being a state institution.

14. Wedel focused on the game being played between the so-called Chubais Clan and advisers associated with the Harvard Institute for International Development and Harvard University.

15. The bill, under consideration from 1994 until 1997, was finally titled "On the Fundamentals of the Social–Legal Defense from Violence in the Family" ("Ob osnovakh sotsial'no-pravovoi zashchity ot nasiliia v sem'e").

16. Although, as Hale (2002) points out, people may not want to get involved because in some regions, the government has been quite hostile to these organizations.

17. This is from the official list of the participants of the working group signed by the deputy head of the administration of the krai, Ia. N. Shoichet, given to me by Natalia Sereda, Barnaul, July 1, 2002.

18. In Petrozavodsk and Volgograd, Project Harmony reports similar developments as a result of their Domestic Violence Community Partnership Program (for more information, see dv.projectharmony.ru/english/oprogr/coalition.html).

References

Abubikirova, N. I., et al. 1998. *Directory of Women's Non-Governmental Organizations in Russia and the NIS.* Moscow: Aslan Publishers.
Armatta, Judith. 1997. "Getting Beyond the Law's Complicity in Intimate Violence against Women." *Willamette Law Review* 33 (Fall): 773–845.

Belousova, L. G., et al. 2001. *Gender: Obshchedostupnyi slovar'-spravochnik*. Barnaul, Russia: AKZhOO "Otklik."

Bolsko, Ekaterina. 1999. "Altai Krai Women's Organization 'Otklik.'" infohome.dcn-asu.ru/ngo-altai/otklik/index.html (accessed November 15, 2002).

Brunell, Laura, and Janet Elise Johnson, 2004. "The Emergence of Domestic Violence Regimes in Postcommunist Europe." Unpublished manuscript.

Demokratizatsiya, 2002. "Russian Civil Society," Parts 1 & 2, Vol. 10, no. 2 (Spring) no. 3 (Summer) Special issues.

Domrin, Alexander N. 2003. "Ten Years Later: Society, 'Civil Society,' and the Russian State." *Russian Review* 62, no. 2 (April): 193–211.

Elman, R. Amy. 1996. *Sexual Subordination and State Intervention: Comparing Sweden and the United States*. Providence, RI: Berghahn Books.

Fish, M. Steven. 1994. "Russia's Fourth Transition." *Journal of Democracy* 5, no. 3 (July): 31–42.

Fraser, Nancy. 1990. "Struggle over Needs: Outline of a Socialist-Feminist Critical Theory of Late-Capitalist Political Culture." In *Women, the State, and Welfare*, ed. Linda Gordon, 199–215. Madison: University of Wisconsin Press.

Gal, Susan, and Gail Kligman. 2000. *The Politics of Gender after Socialism*. Princeton, NJ: Princeton University Press.

Geertz, Clifford. 1973. *The Interpretation of Cultures*. New York: Basic Books.

George, Alexander. 1979. "Case Studies and Theory Development." In *Diplomacy: New Approaches in History, Theory, and Policy*, ed. Paul G. Lauren, 43–68. New York: Free Press.

Hale, Henry. 2002. "Civil Society from Above? Statist and Liberal Models of State-Building in Russia." *Demokratizatsiya* 10, no. 3 (Summer): 306–21.

Hemment, Julie. 1999. "Gendered Violence in Crisis: Russian NGOs Help Themselves to Liberal Feminist Discourse." *Anthropology of East Europe Review* 17, no.1 (Spring): 35–38.

———. 2004. "The Riddle of the Third Sector: Civil Society, International Aid, and NGOs in Russia." *Anthropological Quarterly* 77, no. 2 (Spring): 215–41.

Henderson, Sarah. 2000. "Importing Civil Society." *Demokratizatsiya* 8, no. 1 (Winter): 65–82.

———. 2003. *Building Democracy in Contemporary Russia: Western Support for Grassroots Organizations*. Ithaca, NY: Cornell University Press.

Human Rights Watch. 1997. "Russia—Too Little, Too Late: State Response to Violence against Women." *Human Rights Watch Report* 9, no. 13 (December): 1–51.

Ishkanian, Armine. 2004. "Working at the Local–Global Intersection: The Challenges Facing Women in Armenia's Nongovernmental Sector." In Kuenhast and Nechemias, pp. 262–87.

Johnson, Janet Elise. 2001. "Privatizing Pain: The Problem of Woman Battery in Russia." *NWSA Journal* 13, no. 3 (Fall): 153–68.

———. 2004a. "Domestic Violence Politics in Post-Soviet States." Unpublished manuscript.

———. 2004b. "Sisterhood vs. the 'Moral' Russian State: The Postcommunist Politics of Rape." in Nechemias, 217–38.

Karatnycky, Adrian, Alexander Motyl, and Amanda Schnetzer, eds. 2002. "Nations in Transit 2001: Civil Society, Democracy, and Markets in East Central Europe and the Newly Independent States," Freedom House. Available online: www.freedomhouse.org.

Kuenhast, Kathleen and Carol Nechemias, eds. 2004. *Post-Soviet Encountering Transition: Nation-Building, Economic Survival, and Civic Activism*. Washington, DC, and Baltimore, MD: Woodrow Wilson Center Press and Johns Hopkins University Press.

Mendelson, Sarah E., and John K. Glenn, eds. 2002. *The Power and Limits of NGOs: A Critical Look at Building Democracy in Eastern Europe and Eurasia*. New York: Columbia University Press.

Pateman, Carole. 1988. *The Sexual Contract*. Stanford, CA: Stanford University Press.
————. 1989. *The Disorder of Women*. Stanford, CA: Stanford University Press.
Pol'shchikova, Ol'ga. 2004. *Mir na zemle nachinaetsia doma*. Barnaul, Russia. Available online through Eastview Universal Databases (accessed June 28, 2004).
Post, Dianne, 2002. "Russian Women, American Eyes: The Rebirth of Feminism in Russia." Paper prepared for the Kennan Workshop on Women in the Former Soviet Union, Washington, DC.
Putnam, Robert. 1993. *Making Democracy Work*. Princeton, NJ: Princeton University Press.
Richter, James. 2002. "Evaluating Western Assistance to Russian Women's Organizations." In Mendelson and Glenn, 2002, 54–90.
Ries, Nancy. 1997. *Russian Talk: Culture and Conversation during Perestroika*. Ithaca, NY: Cornell University Press.
Rose, Richard. 1994. "Rethinking Civil Society: Postcommunism and the Problem of Trust." *Journal of Democracy* 5 no. 3 (July): 19.
Schneider, Elizabeth M. 2002. *Battered Women and Feminist Lawmaking*. New Haven: Yale University Press.
Shitova, Elena, 2002. "Women's Alliance," *Bradley Herald*. Washington, DC: Bureau of Education and Cultural Affairs, U.S. State Department 28 (Spring): 1, 7.
Sperling, Valerie. 1999. *Organizing Women in Contemporary Russia: Engendering Transition*. Cambridge: Cambridge University Press.
Sundstrom, Lisa McIntosh. 2002. "Women's NGOs in Russia: Struggling from the Margins." *Demokratizatsiya* 10, no. 2 (Spring): 207–29.
Tarrow, Sidney. 1994. *Power in Movement: Social Movements, Collective Action and Politics*. Cambridge: Cambridge University Press.
"V Altaiskom krae sklonnost' k suitsidu muzhchin v 12 raz bol'she, chem u zhenshchin." 2001. Online news service: Altaiskii Krai: ofitsial'nyi sait organov vlasti. Available online at www.altairegion.ru/data/2001/12/19/news/13500.shtml (accessed June 24, 2004).
"V Altaiskom krae sozdano novoe gosudartvennoe uchrezhdenie sotsial'nogo obsluzhivaniia— 'kraevoi krizisnyi tsentr dlia zhenshchin.' " 2004. Online news service: Altai Daily Review. Available online at www.bankfax.ru/page.php?pg=24301 (accessed June 28, 2004).
Watson, Peggy. 1993. "Eastern Europe's Silent Revolution: Gender." *Sociology* 27, no. 3 (August): 471–87.
Wedel, Janine R. 2001. *Collision and Collusion: The Strange Case of Western Aid to Eastern Europe*. New York: Palgrave.
————. 2004. "Flex Organizing and the Clan State: Perspectives on Crime and Corruption." Unpublished manuscript presented at the Harvard University Davis Center for Russian and Eurasian Studies Symposium on Crime, Law, and Justice in Post-Soviet Russia, February 13.
Weldon, S. Laurel. 2002. *Protest, Policy, and the Problem of Violence against Women: A Cross-National Comparison*. Pittsburgh, PA: University of Pittsburgh Press.
Women's/Gender Studies Association of Countries in Transition. 1999. www.wgasact.net/map.html (accessed April 15, 2002).
Young Altai Journalists. 2002. " 'Muzhskoi razgovor' planiruet reshat' problemu domashnego nasiliia vmeste s 'Krizisnym tsentrom dlia zhenshchin.' " www.yaj.ru/bulletin/1999/bull_40.ru.shtml (accessed November 16, 2002).
Yurchak, Alexei. 2002. "Entrepreneurial Governmentality in Postsocialist Russia." In *The New Entrepreneurs of Europe and Asia*, ed. Victoria Bonnell and Thomas Gold, 278–317. Armonk, NY: M. E. Sharpe.
Zabelina, Tat'iana, ed. 2002. Rossia: nasilie v sem'e – nasilie v obshchestve. UNIFEM. Available online at www.owl.ru/win/books/camp/book_camp.pdf (accessed August 17, 2004).

Interviews

Sereda, Natalia. 2002. Founder, Women's Alliance. Barnaul, July 1.
———. 2005. Founder, Women's Alliance. Personal communication, June 30.
Sillaste, Galina. 1997. Sociologist and consultant on the domestic violence bill. Moscow.
Regentova, Marina. 2002. Director, Russian Association of Crisis Centers for Women. Moscow, July 8.

17

Is Civil Society Stronger
in Small Towns?

Anne White

It may seem absurd to ask whether civil society is stronger in small towns in Russia, since small towns almost certainly have fewer nongovernmental organizations (NGOs) per capita than do cities, particularly Moscow (see Shomina, Kolossov, and Shukhat 2002, 268). Nonetheless, civil society does not consist only of NGOs. Definitions of civil society that concentrate on organizations and exclude informal networks are particularly unhelpful in a country like Russia, where official channels are often bypassed. If we are seeking evidence of "democratic" mindsets and behavior in contemporary Russia (perhaps the main point of employing the concept of civil society), we need to look beyond NGOs and widen the definition of civil society to include areas such as civic engagement and trust.

Small towns are traditionally regarded as places where "everyone knows everyone." For example, a local newspaper in one such town, Achit, was able to run a competition over several issues where readers identified different well-known local people from photographs of parts of their faces. While familiarity may have its drawbacks, it is often assumed that it does promote trust. Robert Putnam, for example, although labeling such assertions "hoary stereotypes," admits that American small towns have slightly higher levels of trust and civic engagement than larger settlements, according to his measures (1995, 670). In Russia, where small towns are very different indeed from cities, it might be expected that civil society would be rather different, too, and possibly better developed in terms of civic engagement and trust.[1]

This chapter argues that to understand Russian civil society it is important to look not just at Moscow, which is very different from other Russian cities, but also to the provinces—and not only at the regional capitals but also at small and medium-sized towns. The chapter investigates the question of whether civil society is stronger in small towns, measuring civil society by levels of civic engagement (defined as participation in organized activities for the benefit of the local community) and trust. To do so, this chapter looks at small-town civil societies by "rippling" outward, beginning with a consideration of civil society very narrowly defined, then gradually widening the definition. It considers, in turn, NGOs, the media, religious institutions, cultural events and volunteerism, informal networks, and trust. The evidence for this chapter is drawn largely from local newspapers and from 141 interviews with professional people in Achit (population 5,400, Sverdlovsk Oblast), Bednodemianovsk (population 8,200, Penza Oblast), and Zubtsov (population 7,900, Tver Oblast).[2] The interviews were conducted in 1999 and 2000.[3]

I argue that, in the small towns studied, it would be wrong to see a clear trajectory from "bad Soviet" to "good Western" practice. Former Soviet organizations can acquire popularity and authenticity in the hands of enthusiastic local activists, although the Soviet habits of local officials can still be a problem for the development of civil society in the small towns. Moreover, I suggest that, if one looks beyond the stereotypical "civil society organizations" and adopts a wider definition of civil society, the towns in this study did have a kind of civic culture, in the sense of social responsibility and a commitment to the well-being of the community. Again, this culture had strong Soviet roots, and it could in some respects be quite promising for democratization.

Although this chapter draws some distinctions between small towns and cities, this is by no means meant to imply that small towns are the same all over Russia. Civil societies in small towns, as in cities, do, of course, vary from one another. Such differences may stem from the town's location in a particular region or its degree of proximity to a big city. They may also derive from the agency of individual civil society actors and the self-confidence or lack of the same of the local intelligentsia. A factor contributing to this mood of confidence in the three towns studied proved to be the influx, during the 1990s, of talented Russians from large cities in Central Asia and Azerbaijan. Other prominent local activists, however, had been sent from different parts of Russia to work in the small towns under the Soviet system of graduate job placements. The attitude of the local administration was also an important variable: the local administration most zealously attempted to control community life in Bednodemianovsk and was least interventionist in Achit.

Definitions of Civil Society

Definitions of civil society can be categorized according to various criteria.

A range of functions is attributed to civil society, creating perhaps the most important point of difference among the various definitions. Although there seems to be general agreement that a strong civil society promotes democracy, democracy is a term with multiple definitions. Are democracy and civil society more about social solidarity and the building of trust and cooperation within society, or about the rights of the individual and the fortification of these against a potentially hostile state (Seligman 1992; Keane 1988)?

Scope is another criterion that could be used to categorize different definitions of civil society; it is closely linked to function. Very crudely, one can distinguish between "narrow" definitions such as those offered by the editors of this book, which tend to go hand-in-hand with liberal individualist approaches to civil society, and "wide" definitions that include informal networks and families and stress concepts such as trust, civic engagement, and social capital. At the extreme, civil society is defined as "an informal network of relationships" (Zubaida 1992, 4–5, as quoted in Rabo 1996, 158).

There are various arguments against including informal networks and families as part of civil society. "Informality" may be seen as evidence of a weak or embryonic civil society (for example, in Africa, see J. White 1996, 145). There may be a desire to avoid conceptual fuzziness, since civil society, if stretched to the private sphere, includes aspects of life that, at least at first sight, seem to be based purely on personal interests and remote from citizenship. Furthermore, families and kin networks may be viewed as closed, exclusionary groups working for their own ends and may even be places of oppression, of women in particular. Therefore, so the argument goes, they do not promote "democracy." In the Russian context, there is a further worry that "pre-modern networks" may be subverting the creation of a rule-bound society with modern bureaucratic practices and a market economy (Rose 1999).

However, there are good reasons for adopting a wider definition. Although it is understandable that aid organizations, for practical purposes, need to deal with clearly defined associations, it seems odd, for scholarly purposes, to stress the need for formal organization in civil society. After all, civil society is often most powerful during transitions to democracy when it is unorganized, not to say disorganized. To take the Russian example, civil society during perestroika consisted largely of so-called informal organizations, unregistered and in many cases eschewing formal characteristics such as membership lists (A. White 1999). Ostentatiously nonviolent "people power" helped topple potentially violent and highly organized Communist regimes in East Central Europe in 1989. Moreover, many long-established NGOs in developed democracies contain disorganized elements, especially if they depend on volunteers. This all suggests the need to include at least some informal groups inside the concept of civil society. Indeed, perhaps we also need to exclude some groups for being overly organized. Putnam suggests that in the United States, "most prominent nonprofits . . . are bureaucracies, not secondary associations, so the growth of the Third Sector is not tantamount to a growth in social connectedness" (Putnam 1995, 666).

In consolidating or consolidated democracies, other criticisms can be made of narrow definitions of civil society. These include feminist arguments—men are more active and visible in the public sphere, while for women, citizenship may have little to do with what is normally construed as civil society. The concept must therefore take on board power relationships in the "private" sphere (Pateman 1988). Furthermore, "relativists" accuse the propagators of civil society of ethnocentrism. Western governments and donors, acting on the "universalist" assumption that civil society is good everywhere in the world, are forcing postcommunist and developing countries to develop Western-style NGOs without regard for very different local political and other cultures (Hann 1996, 18). Hann, a social anthropologist, suggests that "there is a need to shift the debates about civil society away from formal structures and towards an investigation of beliefs, values and everyday practices" (Hann 1996, 14).

Small Towns in Russia

One reason for studying civil society in small towns is that it is very difficult to generalize about Russia as a whole. Parts of Russia have come to resemble Western Europe in certain respects; other places, especially outside the regional capitals and other large cities, have very different lifestyles and standards of living. In 2001, for example, the average Muscovite had a personal money income 5.6 times the level of the official local poverty line; the average inhabitant of Marii El (a republic northwest of Tatarstan) had an income that was only 87 percent of the local poverty line (*Rossiiskii statisticheskii ezhegodnik* 2002, 189–90). Interviewees in small towns described Moscow as "another planet." The feeling of foreignness is reciprocated, as when, for example, a Moscow-based national newspaper, describing Putin's descent on a small town in the summer of 2003, reported him to be visiting the "aborigines" (Kolesnikov 2003). Even within Moscow, in fact, there are very different neighborhoods: a recent study of civil society in the city found that "social activism is certainly higher in . . . privileged [especially central] neighborhoods, with richer and better-educated people having a greater sense of optimism about the prospects for participatory democracy" (Shomina, Kolossov, and Shukhat 2001, 268).

Small towns in Britain or the United States are in many respects miniature cities, often with similar architecture, the same chain stores, a similar number of automobiles per head of population, and so on. Small towns in Russia (usually defined as towns with populations of under twenty thousand) are very different from cities in all these, and many other, respects. Even in the postcommunist period, they bear little resemblence to Western towns. One is almost as likely to meet a goat or a cow on the street as a car, and rather than the high-rise apartment blocks that tend to characterize Russian cities, the housing consists largely of small wooden farmsteads surrounded by outhouses, vegetable plots, and piles of firewood; this is true for the homes of surgeons, school principals, laborers, and factory workers alike. Almost everyone, in fact, grows vegetables and fruit, in many cases supplying most of their family's diet from their own livestock, gardens, and potato fields and from the local forest. The private sector is small: the market, some grocery stores, and construction and timber-cutting companies—not all operating within the official economy. In 1999–2000, there was an acute shortage of cash both among state institutions, which engaged in complicated barter deals with one another, and among their employees, who had not only lost their savings in 1992 and 1998 but also often experienced delayed payment of wages, sometimes for more than six months at a time (hence the significance of growing and gathering one's own food). All three towns had heads of administration who, even if not officially labelling themselves "Communist," were widely identified as such by local inhabitants.

Foreigners are rare birds in the small towns, and it is not surprising that the international community has had no impact on civil society in these particular three towns. This prompts some intriguing questions. Steven Sampson suggests that "the transition in Eastern Europe is a world of projects" (Sampson 1996, 121). Western governments and aid organizations are sometimes charged with creating artificial "civil societies" in postcommunist and developing countries, financing "elite-dominated groups with limited support in society" (Sabatini 2002, 8). It is interesting, therefore, to study places ,where there are no Western-funded projects, to see if no projects equals no transition. If civil society is nonetheless developing, how is it resourced?

On the one hand, the environment of small towns seems unpromising for civil society development, given the acute money shortage described above. On the other hand, NGOs may operate with state support. Even in wealthy Western countries, many voluntary organizations are dependent, not on foreign charity but on government grants. An important theoretical requirement for civil society is that it should be independent of the state, and in Communist-era Poland, for example, critics of the regime would draw a sharp line between "authentic" and "inauthentic" institutions, "ours" and "theirs." In practice, in mature democracies, civil society organizations may be able to cope with a certain degree of dependency. This often prompts soul-searching but does not necessarily invalidate the usefulness of the subsidized NGO. Can the same be said about contemporary Russia, however, with its authoritarian political culture and recent experience of the totalizing, if not quite "totalitarian," party-state? Is any link with the state, in Russia, an insuperable obstacle to civil society status?

NGOs in the Small Towns

Although new organizations appeared sporadically in the small towns of Achit, Bednodemianovsk, and Zubtsov, they often vanished soon afterward. At the time of my fieldwork, in 1999–2000, there seemed to be just one completely independent organization, a group of painters in Bednodemianovsk, led by a prominent member of the local intelligentsia, a former college lecturer and Komsomol official turned gas station manager. The painters' organization persisted through 1999 and 2000 in trying to gain official registration, organized an exhibition visited by fifteen hundred people, and planned to give educational talks to schoolchildren (Zhupikov 1999; Zhupikov, interview 2000).

The small towns had lost a number of their Soviet-era organizations, including branches of the Knowledge, Booklovers', and Automobile Associations; women's councils (except in Bednodemianovsk); and even football teams. Remaining organizations were linked to the local authorities and/or local Communist parties. These included veterans' councils, composed of retired people, and branches of the Russian Society of Disabled People, often barely distinguishable from the "veterans." The veterans were numerous, with, for example, 6,476 members in Achit District (population 21,200) (Salnikova 1999). These were quite active groups, who were involved in a range of activities that were well publicized in the local press. In Zubtsov, for example, pensioners had staged a large demonstration in the town square against late payment of pensions, marching to one of the bridges over the Vazuza River and blocking it to traffic. In Achit, disabled people organized a gardening club and charitable events such as sales of secondhand clothes, and they lobbied the local council to provide proper premises for the town's voluntary organizations (Trofimov 2000).

The liveliest organization in Achit seems to have been a club and choir for retired women, Sudarushka, formed in late 1998 and still going strong two years later. The members of Sudarushka (Young Lady) were mostly former teachers and doctors who sang for their own pleasure, made concert tours in the local district (including in return for money as election propaganda for a candidate they apparently did not intend to support), did aerobics, and went on rambles (author interviews and *Nash put'* 1999). Despite being housed in the local government offices, this was clearly an authentic organization, to use the Polish term mentioned above. Sudarushka appeared to be genuinely voluntary and meaningful to its participants.

By contrast, the administration in Bednodemianovsk had created a very inauthentic, Soviet-style women's organization, in the form of a women's council, run by a college lecturer whose son had served in Chechnya. The administration used it when it needed a female face—for example, to distribute food aid from the Red Cross to poor families or, most important, to publish articles in the newspaper encouraging a positive attitude toward conscription. Because of this latter role, the council was often referred to by local residents as the "Soldiers' Mothers' Committee." It had nothing in common with the genuine and militant network of NGOs that went under the same name in cities throughout Russia but was probably not dissimilar to other small-town women's councils.

The Moscow-based Union of Soldiers' Mothers' Committees believes, however, that even such dependent and powerless groups are to be encouraged as potential future authentic civil society organizations (Men'shikova, interview 2001). The council was created as a front organization for the local administration, but this did not mean that it had no value for local citizens. It did some useful work, for example, giving emotional support to conscripts and their parents and advice about how to write and send parcels to those serving in the armed forces (Surovatkina, interview 2000). Its members visited the barracks where local conscripts would be sent and reassured readers of the Bednodemianovsk newspaper that they were neat and tidy (Nechaeva, Volkina, and Nozhkina 2000). The council also, according to the local newspaper, interceded with the local administration on behalf of mothers who complained about nonpayment of child benefits. The situation was an ambiguous one, however, and perhaps the council's role could be understood as shielding the administration from having to deal with mothers directly (*Vestnik* 1999b).

In none of the three towns was the local adminstration a rich patron to social organizations. Even the Bednodemianovsk women's council operated on a shoestring and had no premises. Achit, however, had the advantage of being in a relatively rich region, Sverdlovsk. This meant that organizations could attract funding from the regional capital, Ekaterinburg, and specifically from Governor Rossel in his attempt to build up loyal social organizations outside the capital city. For example, Rossel sponsored both Tatar and women's organizations. Achit District boasted an active NGO, Tatar National Cultural Autonomy, funded by the governor. In 1999, with regional funding, a Tatar cultural center opened in one of villages, and the governor attended the opening (Timkanova 1999). Also in 1999, the Association of Achit District Women was created by a kindergarten director in a village near Achit. It intended to help women set up businesses, provide family planning advice, and support families and young people (Andreeva 1999). After a few months, the association seems to have transformed itself into a branch of the Ekaterinburg-based Association of Urals Women, patronized by Rossel, which aimed to promote women's employment and especially female entrepreneurship, health, culture, and political skills (Aleksandrova 1999).

In summary, the largest and most active organizations in all three towns are veterans' organizations with Soviet roots. Local inhabitants sometimes lament the loss of other Soviet organizations and sports teams; and Soviet-style organizations are sometimes revived, such as the women's council in Bednodemianovsk. New NGOs do also emerge occasionally, particularly, it would seem, in Achit, a fact that may be linked to its location in relatively rich Sverdlovsk Oblast, with access to regional funding. It is hard for NGOs to be genuinely independent of regional and/or local authorities.

The Media

A free media is an essential ingredient of any civil society. However, like NGOs, so, too, the media find it hard to be truly independent in small towns. All local newspapers in the three towns studied lacked advertising revenue and were short of money. (Indeed, in Achit the newspaper had temporarily suspended publication in 1999 because it had no paper.) Newspapers were therefore vulnerable to pressure from local administrations on whom they depended financially, although this pressure seems to have been least in Achit, perhaps because there was competition from a rival newspaper published in a neighboring city, and most in Bednodemianovsk, where the deputy head of administration with responsibility for social affairs was particularly interventionist.

In Zubtsov, the editor of *Zubtsovskaia zhizn'* was a Yabloko supporter who tried to make the newspaper lively and even occasionally critical. He was proud that he had published articles criticizing the local administration. A well-respected local figure, he gave advice to citizens on a range of matters. He tried to encourage people to vote and believed that high turnouts in local elections might be partly thanks to his influence (Kotkin, interview 1999). In Bednodemianovsk, *Vestnik,* the local newspaper, was very Soviet by comparison, often appearing to act as a propaganda vehicle for the local administration. The editor did not appear to play an independent public role, unlike her Zubtsov equivalent. *Vestnik*'s lack of connection to local realities was revealed, for example, by the fact that, apart from listing candidates, it hardly mentioned the election campaign for the local council in the fall of 2000, and it failed to describe a struggle for the mayorship.

Achit had two newspapers. *Nash put'* was the official district newspaper, while *Gorodok* was published in a larger neighboring town but had an editorial office in Achit and special pages devoted to Achit news. *Nash put'* was edited by a former member of the district Communist Party committee. It sometimes criticized the local council—for example, questioning the deputy head of administration about reports that he had illegally felled timber from the forest and exported it out of the district, and publicizing the drunken and violent behavior of another local council official (*Nash put'* 2000; Vorob'eva 1999). *Gorodok*'s offices were the Yabloko campaign headquarters in 1999–2000; and this underlined its role as offering an alternative voice, although neither newspaper adopted an explicitly political stance. Some readers, however, did draw a clear distinction between the two publications, perhaps basing their judgments to some extent on their impressions of the personalities and backgrounds of the editors. Some interviewees accused *Gorodok* of being shoddily researched and superficial; others felt that *Nash put'* was "Communist" and hence not always objective. Given that many local people could not afford to buy two newspapers, the existence of a competitor could be seen as threatening to the future of *Nash put'*, the smaller paper. If two newspapers can survive, however, the element of choice and competitiveness could be viewed as an advantage for civil society.

Many professional people, particularly teachers and doctors, wrote for the newspapers, giving advice about matters such as child rearing and health care. As in Soviet times, this seemed to be viewed as a duty of prominent members of the intelligentsia. In March 2000, for example, particularly notable figures in both Achit and Bednodemianovsk contributed articles praising Putin as a presidential candidate, presumably because it was supposed that their advice would carry weight with the electorate; in at least one case there was pressure from the local administration to do so (interview evidence).

The newspapers did not normally carry letters from ordinary readers, however. There has been a similar decline in letter writing to city and national newspapers. In a curious way, public opinion was better developed in Soviet days when newspapers printed many readers' letters, even if these were censored or concocted by party officials. It seems odd that, unlike in some other Russian towns, the newspapers in these particular postcommunist small towns did not serve as a forum for local debate, even on relatively trivial topics, and this would appear to indicate a weakness of civil society.

Almost every respondent in the study read a local newspaper. Although they criticized the press—for example, because it was too subservient to the local administration (in Bednodemianovsk) or not always accurate—they also emphasized how important the paper was to their identity and that of the community, saying, for instance, "It's my own (*rodnaia*): how could I not read it?" They seemed to agree with *Zubtsovskaia zhizn'*'s claim that "without a district newspaper a district isn't a district, just a territory with an atomized population" (*Zubtsovskaia zhizn'* 1999b). It was hard to tell how many people in total read the newspapers, since many seemed to borrow the newspaper from friends or the library. In all towns, the print run had fallen below 2,000 (from between 3,600 and 6,900 in 1990).

Religious Institutions

Religious institutions are sometimes excluded from definitions of civil society, but in the Russian context it seems sensible to include them as arenas of nonstate activity that could gather together the local population and strengthen community morale. Respondents said that religious services in all three towns were well attended, and some also stressed the social diversity of church congregations. The churches all have Sunday schools, so they also reach out to the local community. The local newspapers can also be used for dialogue between priests and congregations, printing sermons and answering readers' questions about Orthodoxy.

However, given the shortage of resources to support community activities in small towns, gains for the Church may be at the expense of other community institutions. In Achit, there was a continuing struggle over premises between the Church and the local government officials responsible for the children's after-school clubs, which occupied most of the former church building. Opinion in the local community was divided as to whether the church should be fully restored and the children evicted. In the second settlement of Zubtsov District, Pogoreloe Gorodishche, the community debated whether the ruined church should be used as a cinema or restored as a place of worship; the Church found more support (Kuteinikov 1999).

Cultural Events and Volunteerism

Civic engagement also included volunteering and participation in cultural events. Given what has been said about the old-fashioned quality of small-town life, it would not be surprising to find that many Soviet practices persist in the area of participation in state-sponsored community activities. As Theodore Friedgut pointed out in his study of Soviet participation, citizens could feel motivated to participate in "voluntary work" on behalf of the local community even when they were being used instrumentally by local authorities if there was an obvious practical purpose to these activities (Friedgut 1979). Small-town communities had revived the *subbotnik,* a day when Soviet citizens were expected to contribute their unpaid labor to coincide with Lenin's birthday on April 22, but which was now just the occasion for tidying up all the garbage that had collected under the snow, painting outside woodwork, and general spring cleaning. There were still some "apartment block councils" and "street committees" where activists nagged their neighbors to remove logs from the pavement and keep public spaces in order. Schoolchildren in Zubtsov were responsible for keeping the war memorial tidy. Achit had even revived its people's militia, responsible for patrolling the streets and maintaining public order; in 1999, it had eighty-eight members who worked a total of 1,617 hours. By March 2000, however, only four members remained (Vatolin 1999; Salnikova 1999).

Soviet citizens were also expected to attend official festivals, such as May Day parades, and participate in other organized leisure activities. Such "cultural enlightenment" was an important plank of the Communist Party's socialization program (A. White 1990). The social control function was probably uppermost in the authorities' minds, but the teachers, librarians, and house of culture employees who organized events and clubs could nonetheless be driven partly by an idealistic conviction that access to high culture makes people better human beings, and events could be enjoyable in their own right as well as occasions for people to get together with their workmates, friends, and neighbors. Hence, as an unintended consequence of state-sponsored mobilization, communities could be strengthened and the content of cultural enlightenment be regarded as acceptable by its recipients, as long as the local authorities did not force too much crude propaganda down citizens' throats.

In the postcommunist period, the three towns were very different from one another in the extent of control that the local government tried to exert over cultural enlightenment. Achit, while keeping some old traditions, such as a big Victory Day celebration, did not aspire to Soviet-type influence on citizens' leisure. For example, at the Town Day celebrations in 2000, the program was quite devoid of propaganda—some sports events were followed by accordion playing and flower arranging competitions, the latter won by journalists from *Nash put'* with some compositions, made from gladioli, satirizing pompous government officials and Duma deputies.

In keeping with their more watchful eye over the local press, local authorities continued to play a more active role in cultural events in Bednodemianovsk and Zubtsov. In Bednodemianovsk, in particular, the deputy head of administration kept a close eye on librarians and House of Culture employees. (As second in command, he was responsible for "social affairs," just as the second secretary on Communist Party committees had been in charge of ideology.) In January 1999, for example, before the Kosovo War, during a time of heightened anti-Western feeling, the administration tried to make houses of culture focus more on Russian folk art. Responding to the administration's urging, a conference of arts employees penned an appeal to the local population, written in entirely Soviet rhetoric, stating: "Nowadays our young people, submerged by a wave of imitation Western culture, hardly ever sing folksongs. . . . Only by opposing this alien ideology will we be able to return to our ancient Russian roots" (*Vestnik* 1999a). In Zubtsov, in 1999, cultural events focused largely on World War II and Pushkin—themes that had both national and local significance. Although they could be seen as meaningful to ordinary people, the quantity of events required by the local authorities could seem excessive to those responsible for organizing them. One librarian complained that such programs were "voluntary but still somehow compulsory."

However, despite and perhaps to some extent in reaction to the unfavorable political environment, Zubtsov and Bednodemianovsk had a livelier cultural scene than did Achit. This was connected to the state of the intelligentsia in general; in Achit, teachers and arts workers seemed to be less well qualified, more overworked, and less self-confident. The flourishing cultural life in the other towns can be attributed to the impact of particularly talented individuals, who were able to some extent to bypass the local administration and put on their own, parallel events. In a number of cases these were not local people but Russian migrants from Central Asia or people who had, in Soviet days, been sent after graduation to work in the small towns and had developed a genuine commitment to the local community.

Particular centers of activity for these individuals were the music and art schools, which provided children with extracurricular instruction but actually also targeted the adult population. The influence of the music and art school in Zubtsov was illustrated by the fact that, after intensive lobbying, it had been able to move into the former CPSU district committee building. The Dushanbe artists who expanded the activities of the old music school were praised in the local press for their "high level of professionalism, morality, intellect, and talent" (Burdina 1999a). They recruited writers and performing artists from Moscow, who had dachas near Zubtsov, and persuaded them to perform and give lectures. The director's husband, a professional artist, put on an exhibition that drew many visitors. In Bednodemianovsk, music teachers put on their own shows once a week, driven partly by the feeling that because it was now so expensive to travel to Penza or Moscow for access to culture, it had become necessary for the local community to entertain itself. Although only a few dozen adults, perhaps up to fifty, came to such performances, those who did felt that the programs were important, not just because they were entertaining but also because they brought local people together. In both towns, members of the intelligentsia used the word "salon" to refer to these events, and in interviews they commented on how they served as a lifeline, lifting respondents out of the everyday world of growing potatoes and relieving their sense that they were turning into peasants. Also in Bednodemianovsk, a kebab seller on the Moscow road opened a computer club with Internet access (possibly the first in the town) aimed at young people. He explained his motivation as the desire to do something useful by linking Bednodemianovsk to the rest of the world, commenting, "I got fed up with living on a desert island" (Sedov 2000).

To conclude: despite the efforts of local administrators in Zubtsov and Bednodemianovsk to imbue local entertainments with ideological (chiefly patriotic) content, in all three towns Soviet forms of participation had been revived because of their practical usefulness and, in Zubtsov and Bednodemianovsk, local people, especially artists and musicians, organized successful, less ideologized events.

Changing Levels of Participation

Zubtsov respondents in the pilot survey, when asked about their own activism as members of the intelligentsia, sometimes contrasted their behavior with the perceived passivity of much of the ordinary population. Respondents in Achit and Bednodemianovsk were therefore asked directly whether they thought people participated less in community life than they had done in the past: 80 percent agreed in Achit, and 50 percent in Bednodemianovsk (see Figure 17.1). In Achit the most common reason given for thinking that participation had declined was not demand but supply (26 percent blamed a shortage of worthwhile events), which, as has already been suggested,

Figure 17.1 **"Do People Participate Less in Community Life?"**
(percentages giving each response)

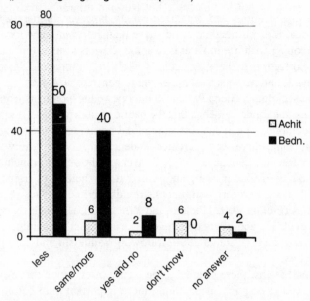

was a particular problem in Achit, with its overworked and passive intelligentsia. According to the interviewees, local citizens *would* go to concerts and festivals if they were properly organized and financed, as had been done in the past. People still went eagerly if good performers came to town. In Bednodemianovsk, by contrast, only three people criticized the supply of events, which does seem to have been plentiful. Respondents were more prone to attribute lack of participation to lack of interest among the public, blaming partly television (as does Putnam 1995), but mostly overwork, apathy, and depression. Comments included: "people are too engrossed in survival"; "people go straight home after work to tend their gardens"; and "people think only about their families—they don't think about their neighbors anymore."

Naturally the intelligentsia respondents, who often had responsibility for organizing events, were likely to be depressed by perceived poor turnouts and perhaps therefore pessimistic about participation levels, although the fact that they cared is in itself indicative of persistent community spirit. In the absence of other survey evidence, it is impossible to draw hard and fast conclusions about how much participation had declined, if at all; moreover, it may well be that more "authentic" events were more popular than those organized by the local administration. For example, in Zubtsov, although the newspaper reported a disappointing turnout for the official Victory Day celebrations in 1999, it also carried stories about how people sat for hours in the unheated library and cinema, with snow whirling outside, to listen to local poets and singer-songwriters (Aleksandrov 1999; Burdina 1999b; *Zubtsovskaia zhizn'* 1999a).

Informal Networks

To describe organizations and organized events, however, is merely to scratch the surface of local life. All neighborhoods have their informal networks, but the complexities of coping with life in what is in some respects a subsistence economy with acute cash shortages is perhaps particularly likely to reinforce old Soviet networks in the small towns, and perhaps to some extent to generate new ones.

When the sociologist Alena Ledeneva interviewed respondents from a number of Russian cities, she found evidence that the nature of informal networking was changing. "Considerations of self-interest and mutual profit" were replacing the "rhetoric of friendship," and there was a greater tendency to rely on family members, not neighbors or friends (Ledeneva 1998). Conversely, however, Francine Pickup's research in the city of Ekaterinburg suggests that the rhetoric of friendship was still strong and that, furthermore, neighbors, friends, and colleagues remained important resources (Pickup 2002; Pickup and White 2003). Hence there seems to be conflicting evidence about whether "particularized trust" is gaining at the expense of "generalized trust" (Uslaner 1999, following Yamigishi and Yamigishi 1994) in the Russian city.

In the small towns, there seemed to be plenty of evidence that Soviet-style networks were still strong and, if anything, more important than before. As in larger cities, these ties could involve the swapping or sale between friends and neighbors of various small goods and services, such as tutoring or home repairs. However, there was also a big difference from the city in that home food production was the small-town residents' chief livelihood strategy, an even more significant one than it had been in Soviet days, according to a number of respondents. Numerous networks revolved around food. Family and kin played an especially significant role in these networks, but neighbors, friends, and colleagues were also involved. For example, in Achit, where the local dairy had closed, people who were too busy to keep their own cows often depended on relatives or neighbors for milk and cream, and people with a surplus had no means of selling it through official channels. Colleagues in small towns gave each other seedlings and covered for one another at work if someone had to gather their potato harvest or go to feed their livestock. Many colleagues still made each other small cash loans, as was accepted practice in Soviet days. Friends and colleagues went fishing or mushroom and berry picking; the top brass in the Bednodemianovsk administration, for example, picked strawberries together. In Zubtsov, the only town with a substantial estate of modern apartment blocks, little communities of dacha neighbors evolved, socializing, for instance, in the bathhouse, as well as laboring over their potatoes. As the "dacha community" was just a strip of land outside the town boundary, neighbors could maintain and exploit their networks in their everyday life within the small town.

In a society where relatives and friends are particularly important, hospitality is crucial. A well-heeled respondent, married to a shopkeeper, said, "I have about thirty friends and we always have guests in the house." If one could afford to do so, it was desirable to participate in the celebration of birthdays and weddings and in wakes and the various mourning ceremonies at the appropriate intervals after a death. This was the course followed by one not particularly wealthy couple with a large extended family. They had a car and frequently visited their relatives, supplying their many urban kinfolk with food or digging their potato patch in an in-law's village. They would borrow money if necessary to go to a wedding.

However, very poor households in the sample had stopped seeing friends and relations, condemning themselves to a downward spiral of deprivation: if they cannot give, they will not receive. The poorest and most depressed respondents increasingly identified themselves only with members of their immediate families and their thoughts were focused largely on their garden plot. Such involution was not total, however: in a small town it is difficult to avoid being at least to some extent engaged in the life of the local community, so even the very poorest respondents were not completely isolated (as their urban counterparts might well have been).

Trust in Small Towns

High levels of interpersonal trust would seem to characterize the local community in all three towns. When asked "How is your town different from other towns?" although many respondents focused on poverty, about a quarter of interviewees in both Achit and Bednodemianovsk chose to describe their towns as quiet, safe, or friendly. The small handful of interviewees who described the towns as "unfriendly" were recent arrivals who were not yet well integrated into the community. In Bednodemianovsk, where only one woman said "unfriendly," the same respondent also described the town as "a little island [of security] in a hard world." Respondents in Zubtsov, the location of the pilot survey, were asked only if they were proud of Zubtsov; most said they were. They characterized Zubtsov as attractive, possessing friendly people, being of historic significance, and unpolluted, quiet, and safe. Interviewees in all three towns often described at length how friendly people were, that they greeted each other on the street, had time to chat, and so forth. Observation suggested that this was true. It was hard to take a quick walk across any of the towns. Moreover, very small children walked around unsupervised, and livestock were left to roam the streets. Judging by the interviewees' comments and behavior, crime was not seen as a major problem in the small towns, despite the fact that the local newspapers regularly published details of crimes. Recorded crime rates in the small towns remained below regional and national levels. Once again, the fact that people knew one another personally was significant. A lecturer in Achit, for example, said that she had no reason to fear rowdy young men on the street at night, because they would be her own students. A sense of "connectedness" was also manifest in respondents' answers to questions about social class. The general opinion seemed to be that the mass of the population was poor but respectable, and respondents identified themselves with this group.

It was true that not everyone in the small town was seen as trustworthy. Most interviewees, however, felt that only a handful of families were rich and to some extent therefore to be mistrusted; they also identified a group of "unemployed" people living in deep poverty, who were sometimes also seen as untrustworthy and characterized as alcoholics and potato stealers. In Zubtsov respondents seemed particularly mistrustful of this underclass, partly because they were also identified with former prisoners (barred from settling inside the Moscow area and therefore living in Zubtsov, which borders Moscow Oblast).

If interpersonal trust was generally strong, "institutional trust" (Mishler and Rose 2003) was weak, although respondents in smaller towns and cities may be more supportive of Putin than their big city counterparts, who may be more cynical ("Informatsiia: Rezul'taty oprosov" 2003). Putin is perhaps, however, seen as a distant potential "friend," the understanding "good tsar," rather than a typical politician. With most individuals in the small town engaged in subsistence farming and highly dependent on family and friendship networks, and a restricted range of local government services, there was a strong sense that the community had been left by central and regional authorities to "stew in its own juice." Although surveys in Russia regularly show that respondents trust people they know more than they do officials, whom they blame for corruptly siphoning off public resources, in the small town there is also a spatial dimension to weak institutional trust. Moscow and the regional capital were often viewed as grasping and uncaring, keeping all resources to invest in the city, and a sense of spatial injustice was keenly felt (A. White 2004).

In reaction, respondents displayed a high level of sentimental attachment to their local area and a tendency to retreat into local identities. This did not necessarily imply trust and involvement in their local administration, although members of the intelligentsia did stand in local elections (see ibid.). The local identification was stronger with regard to nature, churches, and the family. The phrase "Mother Russia," for example, was identified with the small town [A. White 2003]). It would be untrue to suggest that the interviewees had lost all sense of connectedness with "Russia"; they were merely relocating it to Achit, Zubtsov, and Bednodemianovsk.

Conclusion

In conclusion, if "civil society" is defined narrowly as formal organizations and institutions—chiefly NGOs and the media—it seems, predictably, rather weak in the small towns, particularly if one looks for signs of new organizations emerging as proof of a healthily growing civil society. Achit had the strongest record in this respect, perhaps partly because this is the most politicized and best-resourced region (Sverdlovsk). Achit also had the least interventionist local administration, and its cultural life had a less "planned" and patriotic quality, so it was overall less Soviet. However, it would be misleading to suggest that civil society was weak in the other two towns—Bednodemianovsk and Zubtsov. Both seemed less favorable for the emergence of independent NGOs and staged more Soviet events in their libraries and houses of culture. However, intelligentsia activists breathed meaning into some of these traditional events and organized parallel ones, which were genuinely popular.

The intelligentsia here seemed to be more highly educated and confident than that of Achit, with a more diverse and urban background. They displayed a strong sense of duty toward the community and interest in adding something to local life beyond tending the potato patch. They were able to build on Soviet frameworks to maintain a certain sense of connectedness and solidarity in the small towns. To some extent the same tendency was visible also in Achit. Furthermore, all three towns were distinguished by high levels of trust among fellow citizens, and not, it seemed, just the intelligentsia respondents. Atomization did exist, perhaps particularly among those living in extreme poverty, but it seemed to be less marked than the post-1991 impoverishment and isolation of the three towns might lead one to expect.

Although Putnam and others suggest that neighborly trust is important in promoting a working democracy, the links between interpersonal and institutional trust are complex and contested (Mishler and Rose 2003). Russians, including the respondents in these three small towns, clearly do mistrust institutions; however, it is not so clear that the resulting tendency to focus inward on informal networks of Soviet origin is an insuperable obstacle to the creation of civil society and the development of Russian democracy more generally. As we have seen, in the small town these smaller networks, based on "particularized trust," are not so very "particular," if they encompass the majority of local society. Moreover, just because local activism builds on Soviet intelligentsia attitudes and practices does not make it unsuitable for democratic development; quite the reverse, since such activism has genuine roots.

Finally, as the sociologist Petukhov suggests, it may be misplaced to lament that "the assertion of local values and interests is gradually eroding overall civic identity, and the understanding of the importance and significance of participating in the affairs of the country as a whole" (Petukhov 2003, 13). This is, first, because, as we have seen, a sense of Russian identity is not lost and may even be strengthened because Russia is identified with the small town rather than Moscow and the Kremlin. Second, as, for example, both Petukhov (ibid.) and Rose and Mishler suggest, a weakening of links between Russian citizens and their government may be only temporary: "improvements in political and economic performance will enhance both trust and political support" (Mishler and Rose 2003, 28). This may restore a wider understanding of what it means to be a Russian citizen.

In Poland, by analogy, the immediate postcommunist period was characterized by high levels of mistrust, but Piotr Sztompka argues that by the end of the 1990s "the vicious loop of deepening distrust in Poland [had] been overcome, and the virtuous self-amplifying loop of trust culture [had] finally been started on its way" (Sztompka 1999, 190). Explaining the revival of trust in postcommunist Poland, Sztompka identifies as one of the component factors "strong personal networks of friendships, acquaintances and partnerships inherited from the communist period" (189). It is just such networks in the three towns analyzed in this chapter, extending outward to the whole small-town community, that contribute to the maintenance of a local civic culture, rather paradoxically fortified by the still very "Soviet" character of small-town life.

Notes

1. This is not to deny that small towns may vary; for a portrait of an atomized small-town population in the mid-1990s, see Ashwin 1995.
2. Population figures are for January 2000.
3. For a description of the methodology, and the complete findings, see A.White 2004.

References

Aleksandrov, S. 1999. "Pod perebor gitarnykh strun." *Zubtsovskaia zhizn'*, February 4: 1.
Aleksandrova, N. 1999. "Zhenshchiny raiona, ob"ediniaites'!" *Nash put'*, September 17: 1.
Andreeva, L. 1999. "Sozdana Assotsiatsiia Zhenshchin achitskogo raiona." *Nash put'*, July 16: 1.
Ashwin, Sarah. 1995. " 'There's No Joy Anymore': The Experience of Reform in a Kuzbass Mining Settlement." *Europe–Asia Studies* 47, no. 8 (December): 1367–82.
Burdina, Ludmila. 1999a. "Sochetanie nravstvennosti, intellekta i talanta, ili neskol'ko slov ob odnom khudozhnike." *Zubtsovskaia zhizn'*, February 18: 4.
———. 1999b. "Tvorcheskie vstrechi s chitateliami." *Zubtsovskaia zhizn'*, February 20: 4.
Friedgut, Theodore. 1979. *Political Participation in the USSR.* Princeton, NJ: Princeton University Press.
Hann, Chris. 1996. "Introduction." In Hann and Dunn 1996, 1–26.
Hann, Chris, and Elizabeth Dunn, eds. 1996. *Civil Society: Challenging Western Models.* London: Routledge.
"Informatsiia: Rezul'taty oprosov." *Monitoring obshchestvennogo mneniia: ekonomicheskie i sotsial'nye peremeny.* 2003. March–April, 72–114.
Keane, John, ed. 1988. *Civil Society and the State.* London: Verso.
Kolesnikov, Andrei. 2003. "Sel'skii chas Vladimira Putina." *Kommersant,* July 18.
Kuteinikov, S. 1999. "Skhod reshil: tserkvi byt'!" *Zubtsovskaia zhizn'*, February 20: 1.
Ledeneva, Alena V. 1998. *Russia's Economy of Favours:* Blat, *Networking and Informal Exchange.* Cambridge: Cambridge University Press.
Mishler, William, and Richard Rose. 2003. *What Are the Political Consequences of Trust: A Russian Structural Equation Model.* Glasgow: University of Strathclyde (Studies in Public Policy, no. 374).
Nechaeva, L., M. Volkova, and I. Nozhkina. 2000. "Za muzhei spokoino." *Vestnik,* August 15: 2.
Nash put'. 1999. "Dushu 'lechat' pesni." March 5: 2.
———. 2000. "Imeet li pravo rabotat' s det'mi i v administratsii?" October 20: 1.
Pateman, Carole. 1988. "The Fraternal Social Contract." In Keane 1988, 101–28.
Petukhov, V. V. 2003. "Obshchestvennaia i politicheskaia aktivnost' rossiian: kharakter i osnovnye tendentsii." *Monitoring obshchestvennogo mneniia: ekonomicheskie i sotsial'nye peremeny,* September–December, 4–13.
Pickup, Francine. 2002. "Local Level Responses to New Market Forces in a City in the Russian Industrial Urals." Ph.D. dissertation, London School of Economics.
Pickup, Francine, and Anne White. 2003. "Postcommunist Livelihoods: Urban/Rural Comparisons." *Work, Employment and Society* 17, no. 3 (September): 419–34.
Putnam, Robert. 1995. "Tuning In, Tuning Out: The Strange Disappearance of Social Capital in America." *Political Science and Politics* 28, no. 4 (December): 664–83.
Rabo, Annika. 1996. "Gender, State and Civil Society in Jordan and Syria." In Hann and Dunn 1996, 155–77.

Rose, Richard. 1999. *Modern, Pre-Modern and Anti-Modern Social Capital in Russia.* Glasgow: University of Strathclyde (Studies in Public Policy, no. 324).

Rossiiskii statisticheskii ezhegodnik 2002. 2002. Moscow: Goskomstat.

Sabatini, Christopher A. 2002. "Whom Do International Donors Support in the Name of Civil Society?" *Development in Practice* 12, no. 1 (February): 7–19.

Salnikova, Alfiia. 1999. "Veteranov bespokoit sud'ba raiona." *Nash put'*, November 26: 12.

———. 2000. "Na raznykh poliusakh." *Nash put'*, March 17: 1.

Sampson, Steven. 1996. "The Social Life of Projects: Importing Civil Society to Albania." In Hann and Dunn 1996, 121–42.

Sedov, A. 2000. "Spasenie utopaiushchikh—delo ruk samikh utopaiushchikh." *Vestnik*, July 12: 3.

Seligman, Adam. 1992. *The Idea of Civil Society.* Princeton, NJ: Princeton University Press.

Sergeeva, N. 1999. "Materinskaia dver'." *Nash put*,' December 17: 10.

Shomina, Yelena, Vladimir Kolossov, and Viktoria Shukhat. 2002. "Local Activism and the Prospects for Civil Society in Moscow." *Eurasian Geography and Economics* 43, no. 6: 244–70.

Sverdlovskaia oblast' v 1995–1999 godakh. 2000. Ekaterinburg: Goskomstat.

Sztompka, Piotr. 1999. *Trust: A Sociological Theory.* Cambridge: Cambridge University Press.

Timkanova, T. 1999. "Otkrytie tsentra tatarskoi kul'tury." *Nash put'*, April 9: 2.

Trofimov, A. 2000. "Miloserdie zhivet." *Nash put'*, January 7: p. 2.

Uslaner, Eric M. 1999. "Democracy and Social Capital." In *Democracy and Trust*, ed. Mark E. Warren, 121–50. Cambridge: Cambridge University Press.

Vatolin, A. 1999. "A ty zapisalsia dobrovol'tsem v narodnuiu druzhinu?" *Nash put'*, February 25: 12.

Vestnik. 1999a. "Obrashchenie uchastnikov raionnoi konferentsii rabotnikov kul'tury zhiteliam Bednodem'ianovskogo raiona." February 5: 2.

———. 1999b. "Povernis' litsom k detiam." May 28: 1.

Vorob'eva, Galina. 1999. "Glavnoe—sokhranit' vse, chto znachimo, polezno dlia raiona." *Nash put'*, April 23: 1.

White, Anne. 1990. *De-Stalinization and the House of Culture. Declining State Control over Leisure in the USSR, Poland and Hungary, 1953–1987.* London: Routledge.

———. 1999. *Democratization in Russia: The Birth of a Voluntary Sector under Gorbachev, 1985–1991.* Basingstoke, UK: Macmillan.

———. 2003. "Mother Russia: Changing Attitudes to Ethnicity and National Identity in Russia's Regions." In *Gender and Ethnicity in Contemporary Europe*, ed. Jacqueline Andall, 179–98. Oxford: Berg.

———. 2004. *Small-Town Russia: Postcommunist Livelihoods and Identities. A Portrait of the Intelligentsia in Achit, Bednodemianovsk and Zubtsov, 1999–2000.* London: RoutledgeCurzon.

White, Jenny B. 1996. "Civic Culture and Islam in Urban Turkey." In Hann and Dunn 1996, 143–54.

Yamagishi, Toshio, and Midori Yamagishi. 1994. "Trust and Commitment in the United States and Japan." *Motivation and Emotion* 18, 129–66. Quoted in Uslaner 1999, 124.

Zhupikov, Anatolii. 1999. "Mir spaset krasota." *Vestnik*, June 3: 2.

Zubaida, S. 1992. "Islam, the State and Democracy." *Middle East Report* 17: 4–10. Quoted in Rabo 1996, page 158.

Zubtsovskaia zhizn'. 1999a. "Den' Pobedy v gorode i raione." May 14: 1.

Zubtsovskaia zhizn'. 1999b. "Nachalas' podpiska na gazetu *Zubtsovskaia zhizn'.*" March 26: 8.

Interviews

Ivanova, A. 1999. Zubtsov, April.
Kotkin, S. 1999. *Zubtsovskaia zhizn'*. Zubtsov, April.
Loginov, A. 2000. *Gorodok*. Achit, September.
Men'shikova, V. 2001. Russian Union of Soldiers' Mothers. Brussels. December.
Sokolova, N. 2000. *Vestnik*. Bednodemianovsk, July.
Surovatkina, V. 2000. Bednodemianovsk, July.
Vorob'eva, G. 2000. *Nash put'*. Achit, September.
Zhupikov, A. 2000. Bednodemianovsk, April.

Part IV

Concluding Thoughts

18

Russian Civil Society

Tensions and Trajectories

Lisa McIntosh Sundstrom and Laura A. Henry

Analyses of Russian civil society tend toward either extreme optimism or extreme pessimism based on the lens that the author uses to assess the scene. For example, aspects of the Soviet legacy such as continued low rates of participation in society and the weakness of society in relation to the state offer a bleak picture of social activism in Russia (Howard 2003). Yet the rapid increase in the number of nongovernmental organizations (NGOs) in Russia throughout the 1990s also marks an unprecedented effort to change the nature of state–society relations. More than a decade after the collapse of the Soviet system, the chapters of this volume, informed by recent research on the ground in Russia, provide us with a more complicated depiction of Russian civil society and contain analytical insights about how elements of change and continuity, tradition and innovation, coexist and interact in contemporary Russia.

A number of themes echo across the chapters to present a clear and convincing portrait of features common to Russian civil society regardless of issue area and geographic location. The authors have identified several key patterns in Russian civil society that continue from the Soviet and pre-Soviet periods and present obstacles to the development of a strong and democratic civil society. These widespread patterns include citizens' general reluctance to participate in civic associations, the weak institutionalization of Russian NGOs, the need for organized groups in society to communicate with the state via connections with key individuals, and the role of the state as the dominant actor in the political sphere. In addition to these patterns within civil society, other nonstate actors—namely, the mass media, organized crime, and the business sector—crucially shape the social context in which civil society operates. Identifying the ways in which these patterns occur and actors operate moves us closer to the goal, stated in the introduction, of not merely lamenting the undemocratic nature of civil society in Russia, as so many analyses have done, but revealing why it has the characteristics it does. These patterns and their context also are important because, although we insist that civil society cannot be considered democratic by definition, an interest in democratization remains one of the motivations for our study of Russian civil society development.

The contributions of Mary Schaeffer Conroy on the tsarist period and Alfred Evans on Soviet society present the historical and cultural context of civil society development in Russia. In so doing, they highlight the persistence of certain practices—such as the state's intolerance for autonomous social actors and dissent, the enduring importance of personal connections to government figures, and the difficulties of activism given the lack of informational and economic pluralism—in Russian political life under different regimes. Although some aspects of Soviet organized society were more active or beneficial than many previous studies have acknowledged, the contrast between Conroy's and Evans's chapters make it clear that the Soviet regime did manage to quash the limited amount of citizen activism that existed in the tsarist era, and such activism has not yet reemerged completely in the postcommunist period.

Yet a great deal has also changed in Russian civil society. This point is occasionally forgotten in the dominant academic discussion of civil society's weakness. The sheer number of organizations struggling to change state–society relations is the foremost difference. The role of foreign assistance in supporting many of these new nongovernmental organizations also presents an entirely new dilemma for Russian civic actors attempting to preserve their autonomy from the state while also building ties to local communities. Dialogue with the international community on issues such as feminism, domestic violence, disability, military service, and the environment has also profoundly altered the activities of some organizations working on these issues.

In the following sections, we elaborate on the enduring features and new challenges of Russian civil society development that are illuminated in the volume chapters, and we discuss some theoretical propositions that the chapters inspire. We end the chapter with speculation on the future fate of civil society in Russia and how Russian civil society can help us to reflect on the realities of civil society in Western countries.

Reluctance to Participate

Russian citizens' reluctance to become involved in political and social organizations has been well documented (Howard 2003; Mishler and Rose 1995, 6; Hemment 2004, 228). Howard (2003, 67) points out that postcommunist countries generally have much lower levels of membership in various organizations (with the exception of trade unions) than other postauthoritarian countries, with the average number of memberships for Russians standing at only 0.65 organizations per person.[1] Contributors to this volume—whether studying religion, women's rights, environmental organizations, or migrant groups—similarly have found a deep-seated disinclination to engage in "political" activities, especially in the form of protest. For example, Sperling states that "public forms of protest, such as demonstrations, which highlight both citizen activism and state accountability, are still quite rare in Russia's women's movement" (chap. 10). Reluctance to participate appears to be even greater in small towns and rural areas than in large cities. One pattern of participation that deserves note is that, as Johnson and others observe, Russian civil society has become disproportionately populated by women. This phenomenon arguably can be seen as reinforcing a gendered division of labor, in which civil society is a sphere of women's work, and thereby considered less important than the formal political sphere of men (chap. 16).

The factors behind this reluctance include citizens' experience with coerced mass mobilization in the Soviet era, their desire to retreat from politics after the pervasive ideology of the past, and, for many of those who were initially enthusiastic about the prospects for freedom in post-Soviet Russia, a disillusionment with the lack of political change that their activism brought about in the wake of the Soviet collapse. In addition, widespread distrust among Russians, not only of social organizations but of the public sphere in general, persists from the Soviet era (Rose 1996; Jowitt 1992). Evans notes that the difficulties of meeting even basic needs under the Soviet system led to "the perception of a wide gap between public norms and practical necessity, fostering an underground popular culture pervaded with cynicism concerning the validity of ethical guidelines for behavior outside the circles of intimacy and trust among family members and close friends" (chap. 3).

General depictions of Russian citizens as apathetic and apolitical, however, should not lead us to overlook the civic organizing that is occurring. As many of the volume's chapters have shown, the challenges of navigating life in postcommunist Russia have led a strong minority of citizens to band together to resolve their problems collectively. These small groups serve as "canaries in the coal mine," illuminating successful strategies of collective action while also pointing to features of the contemporary Russian political system that restrict civil society development.

Informal Networks

A number of the chapters have illustrated the influence of informal networks of citizens—that is, networks that have not institutionalized into formal organizations—on civil society development in Russia. For example, Stephen Wegren finds that residents of rural areas of Russia are much more likely to interact with family members than with friends and relatives and even less likely to interact with other village residents, evidence pointing to the persistence of kinship ties over impersonal varieties of public association. Several recent works have shown how such informal networks of friends or acquaintances are an enduring component of Russian society (Ledeneva 1998; Twigg and Schecter 2003). At least one author has posited that pacts between kin and fictive kin-based networks, otherwise known as clans, may contribute to the short-term stability of a political regime but do not promote democracy or long-term regime durability (Collins 2004, 244).

There is some disagreement, however, among the authors about whether informal social networks are a positive or negative attribute of civil society. That is, do informal networks contribute to the development of a public sphere of connectedness among citizens? Do they contribute, as Anne White states, to a "kind of civic culture, in the sense of social responsibility and a commitment to the well-being of the community" (chap. 17)? Or do informal networks, particularly clientelistic ties between citizens and government figures, in fact represent a corrosive, undemocratic bypassing of open political processes (chaps. 16, 6)? Does reliance on networks lead citizens to avoid dealing with important social issues by going "underground" to find informal means of accomplishing tasks? Can we equate informal networks with phenomena such as corruption and the weakness of the rule of law (Rose 1999a; O'Donnell 1996, 40–41)?

In fact, there may not be as much disagreement among contributors to this volume on the role of personal networks in civil society as it first seems. A closer look reveals that the authors who have examined informal networks are discussing very different kinds of relationships. The key feature in evaluating the role of these networks in encouraging broader-based social cooperation is whether or not they are based on exclusive ties. Anne White and Laura Henry, who both suggest positive effects of informal institutions on democracy and civic culture development, emphasize informal networks that are *not* based on kinship. White focuses on informal types of interaction among residents of small towns who are not related to one another, arguing that informal modes of interaction, such as conversations on the street or attendance at amateur concerts, lead to strong feelings of trust among small-town residents. White argues that Russians "clearly do mistrust institutions; however, it is not so clear that the resulting tendency to focus inward on informal networks of Soviet origin is an insuperable obstacle to the creation of civil society and the development of Russian democracy more generally." Henry points out that many grassroots environmental organizations are based on old Soviet-era informal survival networks, and argues that "if civic organizations are facilitated by social trust and norms of reciprocity, then Soviet-era networks, for example, may provide a basic building block for future civil society development" (chap. 13). Moreover, the dividing line between formal organization and informal network is often unclear. Henry finds, for example, that many of the most active grassroots environmental groups in Russia are created from informal groups of neighbors or friends (ibid.).

This question can also be asked of religious organizations. To what degree does the social trust generated within a congregation facilitate social cooperation that is not based on the exclusive ties of religious belief? Bacon argues that social capital developed in religious settings is valuable for civil society development, particularly in a country such as Russia where mistrust in other public institutions is high. This hypothesis is closely aligned to the "social capital" thesis of authors such as Robert Putnam and James Coleman, which emphasizes the importance of norms of trust that develop through regular social interaction in setting the foundation for political and economic institutions (Putnam 1993, 2000; Coleman 1988).

In addition, Moya Flynn, who directs attention to the positive aspects and considerable influence of informal migrant networks, including kinship networks, focuses on the impact of those networks on migrants' ability to survive in Russia and on the general governance of migrant issues—not on democracy per se. As Flynn points out, migrants' reliance on personal friends and family networks for support may be rooted in the well-documented mistrust of formal organizations that is part of Russian citizens'

Soviet legacy (chap. 15). It may be argued that mistrust of formal institutions, if it is sustained through the continuing reliance on informal networks, is in fact an inhibiting factor for democratic development. If citizens do not develop trust in their formal political institutions (see Rose 1999b, 20–21), they will continue to eschew engagement with the state.

Given these authors' findings, one reasonable hypothesis emerging from this volume is that informal kinship-based institutions may well contribute to citizen survival in situations of repression or scarcity, but they do not contribute to democratization of society or political institutions overall. A second hypothesis is that non-kinship-based informal networks in fact do contribute to a widening sense of community and social trust that encourages citizens to be involved in public life and therefore contributes to the democratization of society and politics. In any case, it appears that informal networks are in fact enduring behavioral and institutional phenomena in Russia. In many spheres and circumstances they define what citizens do and how they resolve collective problems. They therefore deserve study in their own right.

Louise Shelley, who studies a very specific kind of informal network—organized crime—and Janet Johnson, who mentions patronage networks of government officials and elite citizens, are referring to informal networks with entirely negative effects for democracy and civil society. These are corrupt patronage networks in which select groups of people, behind closed doors, are given special access to state resources. Such network interaction is obviously very different from gatherings of neighbors to clean the courtyard of their apartment or kinship and friendship networks that promote survival. These latter kinds of networks operate openly in society, within the law, and do not necessarily demand special favors from state officials. Networks of corruption, which are not publicly oriented and work against the rule of law, are clearly inimical to democracy.

Soviet Monopoly Organizations and Career Paths

Another enduring element of Russian civil society is that a number of prominent Soviet-era organizations constructed by the state to address social issues remain significant in people's lives today. Evans points out that many Soviet monopoly social organizations provided much-needed services to Soviet citizens facing issues of old age, disability, or the struggle of daily life. Of course, these organizations were not independent from the state and were seriously constrained by their attachment to it; yet many citizens did not think to question how compromised these organizations were. Organizations such as the *zhensovet* women's organizations and associations for the disabled or deaf conducted valuable work for the societal groups they were supposed to represent. They were imperfect but not worthless. These same organizations in many cases continue to offer crucial services to citizens suffering from the erosion of state welfare services, particularly in locations unlikely to host the NGOs that have arisen in the postcommunist era. Anne White notes that many of the strongest organizations in small Russian communities are former Soviet monopoly organizations, such as those for veterans, pensioners, and disabled people (chap. 17). She argues that the loss or weakening of these groups has had a negative impact on the civic life of many small towns (ibid.).

Evans points out that these organizations vary a great deal today in their level of activity, resource base, and degree of freedom to agitate on behalf of their constituents in opposition to the state (chap. 3). Some *zhensovety*, for example, are largely inactive, but many others provide services to disadvantaged groups of women by assisting them in finding employment, conducting charity work for poor families, or trying to assist victims of domestic violence. Soviet legacy organizations frequently maintain branches at the enterprise, raion, city, regional, and national level, constituting a network for potential mobilization. Their largely unchanged organizational structures are often a major advantage that these organizations possess over younger, independently formed groups. Several of the authors in this volume have argued that Westerners' (including foreign donors') frequent dismissal of these organizations as ineffective for civil society development is mistaken. Soviet-era organizations often worked and continue to work with the public directly a great deal more than many Western-style advocacy NGOs today or, as Evans states, the struggling pro-democracy dissidents of the late Soviet period (ibid.).

At the same time, however, state-organized "associations" from the Soviet period may crowd out other forms of civic organizations that could be more autonomous from the state and more responsive to memberships. Davis describes one major Soviet legacy organization—the Federation of Independent Trade Unions of Russia (FNPR)—as doing very little to help its constituents, but maintaining its status as the largest Russian trade union, possessing a strong organizational network, huge official membership, and favorable financial situation (chap. 12). Independent trade unions have struggled to compete with the advantages inherited by this Soviet behemoth. In spite of this, it is clear that a great many Soviet-era associations are recognized by significant numbers of Russians as useful service provision organizations. If they manage to attain some degree of autonomy, they may be an effective route for developing increased citizen interest in participating in public life.

In another illustration of the Soviet legacy, Laura Henry articulates a hypothesis about the correlation between a range of contemporary NGO activities and the professional backgrounds of the organizations' leaders. In her chapter on environmental NGOs, she posits that these professional backgrounds symbolize the leaders' orientations toward the Soviet past and their ability to gain access to key institutions, networks, and resources (chap. 13). According to Henry, grassroots organizations are most frequently led by educators who lament the breakdown of order in post-Soviet society and institutions but have great faith in the ability of the next generation to rebuild society if they have appropriate training and inspiration. Those who head "professionalized" environmental organizations tend to be scientific intellectuals who attempted to defend the environment during the Soviet era and are skeptical of state agencies' motives but somewhat detached from the general public. Leaders of government-affiliated NGOs have professional backgrounds in the Communist Party or bureaucracy and maintain the view that the state knows best and society should be loyal in fulfilling government directives. In this way, the habits of professional background—a connection from the Soviet past—contribute to shaping organizational leaders' views on how to develop civil society today.

Weak Institutionalization and Reliance on Personal Connections

Russia's new nongovernmental organizations generally possess insufficient material and human resources to allow them to become institutionalized—that is, to act as stable, recognized channels for societal constituencies to express their demands to the state and the wider public. Valerie Sperling identifies a common feature of most areas of civil society when she posits, in her chapter on Russian women's NGOs, that "perhaps civic activism in Russia is still closer to dissidence (individual forms of protest and action) than to the mass mobilization and institutionalization characteristic of civil society" (chap. 10). Peter Rutland concurs, arguing, "There is a contradiction . . . between the rapid appearance of civil society actors and their limited power in practice" (chap. 5). Stephen Wegren concludes that this problem is particularly pervasive in rural areas where the limited scale of NGOs given the size of the rural population and their chronic shortages of human and financial capital limits their overall level of institutionalization (chap. 8).

One aspect of weak institutionalization is the difficulty NGOs have in cultivating public awareness of and support for their activities. Compounding the problem of citizens' reluctance to enter the public sphere, Russian NGOs tend to have weak connections to public constituencies and typically lack serious outreach activities. For example, public demonstrations by NGOs or protest movements, which are aimed at the public as well as the state, are exceedingly rare (chap. 10; Henderson 2003, 114; Sundstrom 2001, 191). Consequently, public awareness of civil society is low. Henderson cites a 2001 survey that found 55 percent of respondents had never heard the term "civil society" and another in the mid-1990s in which 74 percent of respondents could not name a single charity (Henderson 2003, 55).[2]

Sperling, Henry, and others (Henderson 2003, 113) point out that part of weak civil society institutionalization is the lack of incentives for many Russian NGOs to build public constituencies. Mary Conroy's chapter describes the Soviet regime's early elimination of nascent nongovernmental charity associations, which often relied on funds from individual donors. In the contemporary period, financial hardship makes donations infeasible for most citizens and fundraising is further hampered by Russians' lack of familiarity with charitable giving, their uncertainty about the intentions of NGOs, and NGOs' inexperience with fundraising techniques. Civil society groups reliant on domestic resources tend to engage in more basic charity or "service provision" activity than foreign-funded NGOs (Henderson 2003, 111–13; Sundstrom 2001, 174–75; Hemment 2004, 234–35). However, Henderson points out that domestically funded organizations usually provide services to a "select number of acquaintances" rather than to an identified group in society as a whole (2003, 113).

Disincentives for public outreach are reinforced to a degree by the availability of foreign assistance for NGO activities, which we discuss below in more detail.

Reliance on personal connections as a means of access and influence is a constant theme in Soviet and Russian society, further impeding the development of stable, open channels of dialogue between organized civil society and the state. Evans notes that Soviet organizations' level of success in pressing for change in state policies seemed to depend on "ties with individuals in key posts of authority" (chap. 3). This continues to be the case in Russian civil society today. In order to influence government decision making, Russian civil society activists generally must identify individual allies within decision-making structures who can assist them. Sperling identifies this pattern in the cases of women's organizations (chap. 10), as does Sundstrom in a comparison of women's and soldiers' rights groups (Sundstrom 2005). One major consequence of this kind of political action based on personal connections (*sviazi*) is that activists find themselves immediately eliminated from policy influence when their particular contacts disappear from those structures. The importance of personal ties has also influenced relations between the state and businesses. Rutland points out that the reliance of elite businessmen, or oligarchs, on personal assurances from the Kremlin rather than on building organizations or championing the rule of law may undermine their positions of influence now that the Putin administration appears determined to rein in these actors.

Reliance on Foreign Funding

The lack of domestic nonstate resources for civil society development has led a significant proportion of nongovernmental organizations to seek foreign funding to support their activities (Henderson 2003; chaps. 10, 11, 13).[3] A recurring theme in many of the chapters of this volume is the impact that foreign (Western) assistance to Russian civil society is having upon its development. One phenomenon that several authors observe is that foreign assistance tends to shape NGOs' priorities and, since foreign grants are often the only readily available source of funding for NGOs, NGO leaders often become more responsive to the thematic emphases of Western donors than to the concerns of the domestic constituents on whose behalf they purportedly act. Sperling, Johnson (chap. 16), and other authors beyond this volume make this observation about women's NGOs (Richter 2002, 32, 36; Hemment 2004). Sperling notes that "there are clear incentives for women activists in Russia to address their English-speaking audiences abroad for support, rather than turning to their potential mass audience at home" (chap. 10). According to Johnson, "the reliance on foreign assistance also contributes to the biggest weakness of the Women's Alliance and other crisis centers, a problem typical of NGOs in post-Soviet society: the inadequate attention to recruiting constituents for their organizations" (chap. 16).

Although he is a consistent opponent of corporatist arrangements in which civil society would be heavily funded by the state, Larry Diamond points out that the major alternative means of financing for NGOs in postcommunist and developing countries today is through grants from foreign donor organizations, which also exert indirect pressure on NGOs to reshape their priorities (Diamond 1999, 252–54). As several authors of this volume testify, most NGOs seem to make the choice, when it is available, that foreign funding constitutes a less serious threat to their long-term autonomy than government financing does (chaps. 10, 16; see also Sperling 1999, Henderson 2003, and Henry 2004). Given the fact that being too reliant on the Russian state could potentially lead to complete co-option and disappearance of an NGO, while foreign assistance would not carry such a risk, this is an understandable choice.

One of the dangers of this phenomenon in Russian civil society is that it makes organizations and activists vulnerable to the criticism that they and their demands are creatures of foreign agitation and unsuited to Russian conditions (chaps. 9, 10). Some Russian environmental NGOs and researchers have even been accused of being spies for Western states (Henry 2004, 14–15). The cases of Grigorii Pas'ko and Aleksandr Nikitin, both of whom were reporting on radioactive contamination emanating from Russia's nuclear naval vessels, are the most serious and widely publicized examples of such harassment. Pas'ko was convicted of espionage in December 2001 and has now been released on parole but has been denied permission to obtain a foreign travel passport by two Russian courts in 2004 (RFE/RL 2004). Naval captain Aleksandr Nikitin was accused in 1996 of revealing state secrets to the Norwegian environmental organization Bellona but eventually was acquitted by the St. Petersburg Municipal Court in December 1999 (Yasmann 2004).

Although foreign funding has become the largest source of material support for civil society in Russia—in terms of overall amount supplied if not the number of organizations funded—various levels of government also continue to provide small amounts of funding and in-kind donations to Russian civil society groups. For some groups, the state's provision of small amounts of funds, office space, or conference facilities is crucial to their operation, especially in far-flung provinces of Russia, where foreign assistance is much less available than it is in Moscow. Yet as Sperling (chap. 10) and James Richter have pointed out, typically Russian state officials are much more willing to support basic charity services than more radical causes such as women's rights, which seek "to change the status quo" (Richter 2002, 40). In this preference for noncontroversial causes, state agencies typically support organizations such as those that distribute charity to veterans, disabled people, or orphaned children, although even these "privileged" groups struggle to locate resources. Groups that agitate for rights and freedoms are not favored recipients of state funding, especially in recent years under the Putin administration.

It is important here to mention the widely acknowledged scarcity of donations from individuals or private sector businesses to NGOs (chap. 10; Henderson 2003, 100–101). This has been blamed partly on the lack of an advantageous tax structure for Russian businesses donating to charities. It is also due to sociopolitical norms and the current politically repressive atmosphere in Russia that make agitation for even slightly controversial causes unpopular and now dangerous for business leaders (chap. 5). NGO leaders report that, like government officials, business leaders wish only to support popular, uncontroversial charity causes, in order to build positive public relations images (chaps. 5, 10).

Actors Shaping Civil Society: The Media, Organized Crime, and Business

Aside from the persistent patterns of behavior that characterize civil society in Russia, there are also a number of important nonstate actors that shape the environment in which civil society operates. Different authors include these actors in definitions of civil society to varying degrees; the media are generally conceived as wholly within the realm of civil society, while objections are made more frequently about criminal networks and business due to their pursuit of personal profit. These groups, however, are perhaps even more worthy of our attention due to their influence on the social conditions that affect the development of other types of cooperation in society. In other words, a free press, economic pluralism, and general adherence to the rule of law create a much more hospitable environment for the development of associations and networks than censorship, economic oligarchy, and pervasive corruption. To the degree that other actors in the public sphere affect governance and introduce corruption into social interactions, they shape the rest of civil society.

State and Citizen Attitudes toward the Media

Elements of the Soviet legacy extend not only to NGOs but also to practices in and attitudes about the mass media in Russia. Sarah Oates finds that one hindrance to the development of reasonably independent mass media outlets in Russia is that officials in government structures tend to view the media as a collection of "friends" and "enemies" rather than as a loyal opposition or Habermasian public sphere of debate. She compares this to the Soviet media environment, in which those media that were allowed to persist portrayed events through the official ideological lens of Marxism-Leninism (chap. 4). In addition, Oates's original survey data show that Russian post-Soviet citizens largely accept the media as a tool that power elites use to engage in state building. Most strikingly, her survey respondents prefer the "orderly" coverage provided by state-owned media outlets over the sometimes scandal-ridden news coverage of private outlets (ibid.).

By definition, state ownership of the media constrains the ability of the press to act as a watchdog of the state. Certainly, the more passive nature of news coverage of the conflict in Chechnya in the wake of state consolidation of the media speaks to the media's lack of independence (Lipman 2001). State influence on the development of the media in Russia is interesting not only in and of itself but also because of the media's expected role as a provider of independent sources of information to other civil society actors. Oates concludes that the Russian media in many ways lack "the power and ability to inform the public" and consequently the media's role as a facilitator of civil society is weak (chap. 4).

Criminal Network Ties to the State

Louise Shelley describes the organized criminal underworld in Russia, which emerged from the Soviet period, as an element of society that was not created by the state but has bypassed formal rules to form close ties to state officials that work to its advantage. As Shelley points out, one reason that civil society has a minimal impact on the state in present-day Russia is "not only because of the legacy of authoritarianism, but also because powerful local and national crime groups are closely tied to all levels of government" (chap. 6). While this volume does not consider criminal groups organized for their own profit as part of civil society itself, criminal group activities certainly impinge on civil society development in a number of ways. First, and most broadly, criminal groups intervene in governance at all levels of Russia, co-opting the role of civil society in swaying state policies for their own benefit, and at times openly threaten civic groups or journalists who stand in their way. Yet organized crime groups also substitute for state functions of providing security and funding to fulfill basic needs in society, changing the playing field for NGOs, making them irrelevant in some cases and acting as mercurial benefactors to civil society organizations in other cases. Finally, by exacerbating the level of corruption and violence present in state–society interactions, criminal groups lead citizens to be even more reluctant to address the state with their demands and concerns. As such, they are seriously impeding channels of healthy contact between civil society and the state.

Business and Civil Society

While profit-seeking corporations, small businesses, and other economic enterprises are generally excluded from definitions of civil society, business associations and networks of entrepreneurs often work together to influence state policy in a way that falls within our definition of civil society. In his chapter, Rutland takes the controversial stance that business can indeed be viewed as an element of civil society and even equates the fate of the oligarch Mikhail Khodorkovsky with the fate of civil society in Russia. While this volume's definition of civil society does not encompass individual actors in the economic sphere, Rutland's analysis offers a number of intriguing insights. First, the oligarchs' collective decision to forgo association building and networking in the postcommunist period and instead rely on personal connections with state actors in some ways set the stage for the fate of economic elites who dabbled in politics. Ultimately the state found it easy to accuse individual oligarchs, including Berezovsky, Gusinsky, and Khodorkovsky, of illegal behavior that had been tacitly accepted during the early 1990s. Second, the arbitrary treatment of these individuals, and the decision to use the state's taxation, security agencies, and the courts in politicized campaigns against them is indeed symbolic of the state's broader behavior toward autonomous political and social actors. This brings us to the final, crucial aspect characterizing civil society in Russia: its perilous and shifting relationship with the state.

Relations with the State

Undoubtedly the Russian state plays the dominant role in state–society interaction. The state's traditional monopoly on organizational resources has led to its continued control over many of the institutions and funds that are commonly associated with civil society development.

This collection of research has contributed new fuel to the ongoing debate over whether and how the state should be involved with civil society, and at what point civil society autonomy is compromised by too close a relationship between the two (Black 1988; Seligman 1992; Diamond 1999, 250–60; Hale 2002; McMann 2003, 242). A coherent system of governance can facilitate civil society development by promoting the enforcement of the rule of law and offering a framework for effective social activism. Jonah Levy's study of contemporary French politics, for example, concludes that "state intervention . . . can constitute an essential instrument of societal empowerment" (1999, 294). Examining the case of the United States, Theda Skocpol concludes, "The story of American voluntarism has been clearly one of symbiosis between state and society—not a story of society apart from, or instead of, the state" (1999, 70). Some scholars, such as Larry Diamond and M. Steven Fish, point out that government funding and a more corporatist rather than pluralist arrangement of relations between civil society and the state may be suitable for states in which liberal democracy has existed for a long time, such as in Western Europe, but that such close arrangements between state and society are dangerous for postcommunist states, in which there is a persistent history of an authoritarian state restricting independent society (Diamond 1999, 250–60; Fish 1996, 272–73).

Certainly the long-standing Russian tradition of statism, or *gosudarstvennost'*, which originated well before the Soviet period and is being revived under President Putin, does suggest that there is danger in NGOs becoming too closely intertwined with the state (chap. 16; Hale 2002, 310, 314–19; Squier 2002). Yet the actual relationship between state agencies and officials and social groups tends to be complex and ambivalent, with unpredictable consequences on social organizations. In his analysis of the Russian Orthodox Church, Bacon argues that while the church realizes the benefits of a close relationship with the state, it continues to guard its autonomy. Intriguingly, he also points out that the state's efforts to pass legislation favorable to the Russian Orthodox Church occasionally have unanticipated consequences, such as when new, rival religious groups are able to use the law to protect themselves from state harassment (chap. 7).

Some civil society organizations and networks are engaged in an effort to fill in for Russia's weakened social safety net and other eroding public services. Henry finds that some ecological organizations in Russia have discovered their niche in part through providing conservation services that the state fulfilled during the Soviet era but has failed to sustain during the post-Soviet period. From cleaning city parks to distributing public health information to patrolling against wildlife poachers, "instead of state–society engagement, environmental organizations are filling in for partially dismantled state bureaucracy and services" (chap. 13). Flynn argues that migrant groups have often stepped in to provide services that are not offered by the state such as information about housing and employment. Thomson, noting a similar pattern in disability organizations, refers to this behavior as "gap filling" on the part of nongovernmental organizations.

Several authors in this volume argue that organizations in Russian civil society are likely to make more progress in changing state policies and behavior in their issue areas by forming avenues of cooperation with state organizations than by opposing the state directly. This has been true particularly at regional and local government levels. Johnson describes a successful working group on domestic violence in the city of Barnaul, where NGOs have found that they have been able to change the local government's conduct on domestic violence by working in "constructive cooperation" with state representatives rather than through a purely adversarial approach (chap. 16). Sundstrom finds that soldiers' rights groups that locate allies within the state and participate in state bodies such as the Presidential Commission on Human Rights have historically achieved more success in their development as a movement, both in terms of policy change (however limited) and popular support, than those groups that see their role as one purely of protest (chap. 11). Thomson cites examples in which state officials have started family support groups on disability issues (chap. 14). Henry points out that while government-affiliated organizations appear to Westerners to be too close to their government sponsors, in terms of both a "revolving door" of members in administrative posts and their understanding of their primary role as one of helping the government, these government affiliates have the greatest influence on state policies as they are "well positioned to take on some of the functions of the former State Committee on Ecology" (chap. 13).

In the popular imagination and according to the language of East European dissidents in the late 1980s, civil society opposes the state and checks it (Geremek 1996, 241–43; Black 1988, 119; Ehrenberg 1999, 186–87). Yet there is ample evidence to suggest that we should be skeptical of Western theoretical and foreign assistance approaches to civil society that claim that Western nongovernmental organizations maintain a strict wall between themselves and the state in practice. NGOs and foundations in the West are often financed using large amounts of state funding, and there is indeed a great deal of exchange between the state and NGOs. Some of the most successful service provision NGOs in the West, such as domestic violence shelters and food banks, not to mention many public media outlets like Canada's CBC and the United Kingdom's BBC, are heavily funded by state agencies. This does not mean that they lack significant autonomy from the state. But promoters of democracy in Russia, both scholarly and practical, should admit honestly that Western civil society organizations also have difficulty achieving true engagement with the state without participating in partisan politics or sacrificing a certain amount of decision-making autonomy (chaps. 11, 13; see also Carothers 1999, 221). Certainly the state often maintains an ability and latent threat to withhold funding if these NGOs and media organizations adopt seriously antigovernment viewpoints. Yet in practice,

318 LISA McINTOSH SUNDSTROM AND LAURA A. HENRY

nongovernmental organizations face this kind of pressure from any large financial sponsor. We need only look at recent experiences in the Russian mass media to see that private-sector sponsors are also sometimes fickle in their patronage of civil society.

The difference between the situation in the West and the one in Russian civil society is one of legacy, and therein lies the danger for the basic autonomy of Russian civil society. In the past, especially during Soviet rule, citizens were trained to believe that the state was the primary source of legitimate authority. As a result, in the post-Soviet period many citizens continue to believe that the state's authority should be largely unquestioned, and that the state's imposition of order is more important than freedom or democracy. According to a Russian Center for Public Opinion Research (VTsIOM) study from 2000, 72 percent of respondents agreed that "order is more important even if one needs to limit democratic principles and individual rights" (Melville 2002).[4] In turn, occupants of bureaucratic and political positions also tend to believe in the state's extensive and unique role in governing all areas of society. These long-standing beliefs about democracy and freedom versus order have undoubtedly facilitated the recent moves by the Putin government to crack down on opposition movements and dissenting NGOs.

The volume's finding that cooperation with the state produces more results and is more feasible than unfettered independence or opposition suggests a gloomy future, at least in the near term, for Russian civil society. As Alfred Evans points out in his chapter on the Putin era, in recent years the Putin administration has shown an increasing tendency to work only with civic groups that are willing to be unswervingly loyal to the government's agenda, and to build institutions that are designed to control civil society rather than to engage with it (chap. 9). Indeed, Sundstrom points out in her chapter that although the soldiers' mothers' groups benefited from government and military contacts in the 1990s, they have since been shunned by government insiders and have adopted a much more adversarial stance against the government.

Johnson suggests that there may be a "third way" between state-organized corporatism and a strictly liberal model of civil society, in which the state and civil society collaborate on social issues by sharing responsibilities for providing services or solving problems, but the boundaries between state and society remain important and clear (chap. 16). She sees this arrangement as feasible and successful in her case study of domestic violence politics in Barnaul. Thomson's analysis implies that a model of state–society cooperation may also be possible in service provision sectors, such as those dealing with disability. It remains to be seen whether this modified civil society model can be replicated successfully in other areas, given the statist attitudes that tend to dominate in the Russian government and wider society and the trajectory of government policy on civil society at the national level. Whether or not these national trends will trickle down to local-level governments uniformly also remains unclear, but recent policies, mentioned in Evans' chapter on the Putin era (chap. 9), which have begun to centralize Russian government decision making, suggest that local governments' latitude for innovative alliances with civil society will be reduced.

Conclusion

In his chapter, Edwin Bacon asks whether civil society today is "settling into a more Russian form, where the role of the state removes a degree of independence, but nonetheless distinct groups and movements remain, with a voice, a legal identity, and—not universal, but nonetheless real in a number of cases—political influence?" The chapters in this volume have overwhelmingly answered "yes" to this question and provided fresh analysis of "really existing" Russian civil society by looking at diverse forms of social cooperation. The book thereby moves beyond paeans to the flowering of civil society in Russia and eulogies over its premature death. Instead, the authors have identified tensions and trajectories within civil society in order to understand why it is developing as it is and what the consequences of that development might be. Civil society in contemporary Russia is a unique amalgam of institutions, networks, and strategies that continue from the Soviet period and new social organizations, resources, and demands that have emerged in the postcommunist period. It is the adaptations and innovations that emerge out of actors' efforts to negotiate these tensions between the Soviet legacy and new challenges that create social and political change in contemporary Russia. As Alfred Evans discusses in his chapter on the Putin era, these tensions between old and new conceptions of civil society have become highly magnified in the current context of overt state threats to independently formulated civil society. It is unlikely that Russian civil society will revert to its entirely repressed Soviet form, with no independent civic activity permitted at all, given the tenacity of independent groups that have emerged over the past decade and international pressures upon the Russian state to uphold at least a semblance of democratic freedoms. Yet the past also strongly shapes Russian attitudes toward civil society and state control and suggests that there will be no major public protest against significant restrictions placed on groups that oppose government policies.

A careful examination of civil society development in contemporary Russia, in particular the perceived "weaknesses" of this process, also points to the need for a reexamination of certain fundamental beliefs about civil society in the West. Questions about the actual degree of autonomy that Western civil society actors have from the state, the role of personal networks as a basis for social cooperation, the importance of connections to key individuals for civil society groups' effectiveness, and the influence of external donors on the substance of groups' demands are insufficiently addressed in the current theoretical literature on civil society. While the constraints faced by civil society actors in the West are significantly less severe than those encountered by their non-Western counterparts, comparative research generates a fruitful debate about the essential and nonessential features of social cooperation and their impact on the political process. It is our hope that the chapters of this volume have provided important fuel for thought about these comparative questions.

Notes

The authors would like to thank Kelly McMann, Kathleen Collins, and Alfred Evans for their helpful comments and suggestions.

1. This figure places Russia somewhere in the middle of the postcommunist countries (ranging from Macedonia at 1.50 to Bulgaria at 0.35 memberships per person). These average membership numbers are much lower than those of postauthoritarian countries in other regions, which range roughly between 1 and 3 (Howard 2003, 82).

2. The first survey was conducted by the Charities Aid Foundation and the second by the Civic Initiatives Project Educational Development Center.

3. Existing scholarly studies differ in their findings on the extent of foreign funding among Russian NGOs. Some authors find that more than half of the NGOs they observe have received foreign funding (Sundstrom 2001; Henry 2004), while others find that half or fewer of the NGOs they observe have been funded by foreign donors (chap. 10; Henderson 2003, 100). It is clear that in most smaller cities and rural areas of Russia, only a minority of NGOs have received any resources from foreign donors, while in the larger cities—particularly Moscow and St. Petersburg—foreign funding is prevalent. Funding levels also vary drastically among types of NGOs, with "advocacy" groups such as women's, environmental, and human rights NGOs receiving much higher levels of foreign funding than basic charity or cultural organizations.

4. Hale (2002, 318), however, points to survey data such as that of Colton and McFaul (2001, 14–16), in which only 15 percent of Russians thought that the state should restore order "at all costs," while a majority believed that order should be restored "without violating rights."

References

Berman, Sheri. 1997. "Civil Society and the Collapse of the Weimar Republic." *World Politics* 49, no. 3 (April): 401–29.

Black, Antony. 1988. State, *Community and Human Desire: A Group-Centered Account of Political Values.* New York: Harvester Wheatsheaf.

Briggs, Xavier de Souza. 1998. "Doing Democracy Up Close: Culture, Power, and Communication in Community Building." *Journal of Planning Education and Research* 18: 1–13. Quoted in Putnam 2000, 23.

Carothers, Thomas. 1999. *Aiding Democracy Abroad: The Learning Curve.* Washington, DC: Carnegie Endowment for International Peace.

Chambers, Simone, and Jeffrey Kopstein. 2001. "Bad Civil Society." *Political Theory* 29, no. 6 (December): 837–65.

Cohen, Jean L., and Andrew Arato. 1992. *Civil Society and Political Theory.* Cambridge, MA: MIT Press.

Coleman, James S. 1988. "Social Capital in the Creation of Human Capital." *American Journal of Sociology* 94, Supplement S95–S120.

Collier, David, and James E. Mahon. 1993. "Conceptual 'Stretching' Revisited: Adapting Categories in Comparative Analysis." *American Political Science Review* 87, no. 4 (December): 845–55.

Collins, Kathleen. 2004. "The Logic of Clan Politics: Evidence from the Central Asian Trajectories," *World Politics* 56, no. 2 (January): 224–61.

Colton, Timothy, and Michael McFaul. 2001. "Are Russians Democratic?" Working Paper no. 20, Carnegie Endowment for International Peace (June).

Diamond, Larry. 1996. "Toward Democratic Consolidation." In Diamond and Plattner 1996, 227–40.

———. 1999. *Developing Democracy: Toward Consolidation.* Baltimore, MD: Johns Hopkins University Press.

Diamond, Larry, and Marc F. Plattner, eds. 1996. *The Global Resurgence of Democracy*. 2d ed. Baltimore, MD: Johns Hopkins University Press.

Ehrenberg, John. 1999. *Civil Society: The Critical History of an Idea*. New York: New York University Press.

Fish, M. Steven. 1996. "Russia's Fourth Transition." In Diamond and Plattner 1996, 264-75.

Geremek, Bronislaw. 1996. "Civil Society Then and Now." In Diamond and Plattner 1996, 241–50.

Gibson, James L. 2001. "Social Networks, Civil Society, and the Prospects for Consolidating Russia's Democratic Transition." *American Journal of Political Science* 45, no. 1: 51–68.

Gittell, Ross, and Avis Vidal. 1998. Community Organizing: Building Social Capital as a Development Strategy. Thousand Oaks, CA: Sage.

Hale, Henry. 2002. "Civil Society from Above? Statist and Liberal Models of State-Building in Russia." *Demokratizatsiya* 10, no. 3 (Summer): 306–21.

Hann, Christopher. 1996. "Introduction." In Hann and Dunn 1996, 1–26.

Hann, Christopher, and Elizabeth Dunn, eds. 1996. *Civil Society: Challenging Western Models*. New York: Routledge.

Hanson, Stephen E., and Jeffrey S. Kopstein. 1998. "The Weimar/Russia Comparison." *Post-Soviet Affairs* 13 (October–December): 252–83.

Hemment, Julie. 2004. "The Riddle of the Third Sector." *Anthropological Quarterly* 77, no. 2 (Spring): 215–42.

Henderson, Sarah L. 2003. *Building Democracy in Contemporary Russia: Western Support for Grassroots Organizations*. Ithaca, NY: Cornell University Press.

Henry, Laura A. 2004. "Changing Environments: Green Activism, Civil Society, and Political Transformation in Russia." Ph.D. dissertation, University of California, Berkeley.

Howard, Marc Morjé. 2003. *The Weakness of Civil Society in Post-Communist Europe*. New York: Cambridge University Press.

Jowitt, Ken. 1992. *New World Disorder: The Leninist Extinction*. Berkeley: University of California Press.

Ledeneva, Alena V. 1998. *Russia's Economy of Favours: Networking and Informal Exchange*. Cambridge: Cambridge University Press.

Levy, Jonah D. 1999. *Tocqueville's Revenge: State, Society, and Economy in Contemporary France*. Cambridge, MA: Harvard University Press.

Lewin, Moshe. 1991. *The Gorbachev Phenomenon: A Historical Interpretation*, exp. ed. Berkeley: University of California Press.

Lipman, Masha. 2001. "Russia's Free Press Withers Away." *New York Review of Books*, May 31.

McMann, Kelly. 2003. "The Civic Realm in Kyrgyzstan: Soviet Economic Legacies and Activists' Expectations." In *The Transformation of Central Asia: States and Societies from Soviet Rule to Independence*, ed. Pauline Jones Luong, 213–45. Ithaca, NY: Cornell University Press.

Melville, Andrei. 2002. "The Achievement of Domestic Consensus on Russian Foreign Policy?" Paper presented at the 43rd Annual Convention of the International Studies Association, New Orleans, Louisiana, March 24–27.

Mishler, William, and Richard Rose. 1995. *Trust, Distrust and Skepticism about Institutions of Civil Society*. Studies in Public Policy, no. 252. Glasgow: Centre for the Study of Public Policy, University of Strathclyde.

O'Donnell, Guillermo. 1996. "Illusions about Consolidation." *Journal of Democracy* 7, no. 2 (April): 34–51.

Putnam, Robert D. 1993. *Making Democracy Work*. Princeton, NJ: Princeton University Press.

———. 2000. *Bowling Alone: The Collapse and Revival of American Community*. New York: Simon and Schuster.

Richter, James. 2002. "Promoting Civil Society? Democracy Assistance and Russian Women's Organizations." *Problems of Post-Communism* 40, no. 1: 30–41.

RFE/RL. 2004. "Ecojournalist Loses Another Court Case." *RFE/RL Newsline*, August 13. www.rferl.org/newsline/2003/08/130803.asp. Accessed August 25, 2004.

Rose, Richard. 1996. "Postcommunism and the Problem of Trust." In Diamond and Plattner 1996, 251–63.

———. 1999a. *Modern, Pre-Modern and Anti-Modern Social Capital in Russia*. Studies in Public Policy, no. 324. Glasgow: Centre for the Study of Public Policy, University of Strathclyde.

———. 1999b. *New Russia Barometer: Trends since 1992*. Studies in Public Policy, no. 320. Glasgow: Centre for the Study of Public Policy, University of Strathclyde.

Sartori, Giovanni. 1970. "Concept Misformation in Comparative Politics." *American Political Science Review* 64, no. 4 (December): 1033–53.

Seligman, Adam B. 1992. *The Idea of Civil Society*. New York: Free Press.

Skocpol, Theda. 1999. "How Americans Became Civic." In *Civic Engagement in American Democracy*, ed. Theda Skocpol and Morris P. Fiorina, 27–71. Washington, DC: Brookings Institution Press.

Sperling, Valerie. 1999. *Organizing Women in Contemporary Russia: Engendering Transition*. Cambridge, UK: Cambridge University Press.

Squier, John. 2002. "Civil Society and the Challenge of Russian Gosudarstvennost'." *Demokratizatsiya* 10, no. 2 (Spring): 166–83.

Starr, S. Frederick. 1988. "Soviet Union: A Civil Society." *Foreign Policy*, no. 70 (Spring): 26–41.

Sundstrom, Lisa McIntosh. 2001. "Strength from Without? Transnational Influences on NGO Development in Russia." Ph.D. dissertation, Stanford University.

———. 2005. "Foreign Assistance, International Norms, and Civil Society Development: Lessons from the Russian Campaign." *International Organization* 59, no. 2 (Spring): 419–49.

Twigg, Judyth L., and Kate Schecter, eds. 2003. *Social Capital and Social Cohesion in Post-Soviet Russia*. Armonk, NY: M.E. Sharpe.

Yasmann, Victor. 2004. "'Spymania' Returns to Russia." RFE/RL Feature Article, April 13. www.rferl.org/features/features_Article.aspx?m=04&y=2004&id=4C58CAE8–20AF–4F94–8F83–96BB24DE8B6D. Accessed August 25, 2004.

Defining Civil Society

Laura A. Henry and Lisa McIntosh Sundstrom

Most scholars agree that civil society is an arena of activity that is distinguished from the private realm of the family, the self-interested behavior of the economic sphere, and the state. Yet they set different boundaries on the scope of citizen interaction that falls within that space. Larry Diamond argues that civil society is "the realm of organized social life that is voluntary, self-generating, at least partially self-supporting, autonomous from the state, and bound by legal order or set of shared rules," and it is distinct from society in general as it "involves citizens acting collectively in a public sphere" (1999, 221). Citizens' associations tend to be the most obvious element of "organized social life." Other analyses of civil society, such as that of Cohen and Arato (1992) explicitly include social movements as part of their definition although these movements are not an element of institutionalized political life. Others debate the question of whether social networks, organizations based on exclusive ties, or "uncivil" groups that pursue their aggrandizement through violent or illegal means should be included. We will briefly consider these debates.

The debate featured most prominently in this volume considers whether or not informal social networks should be included within the definition of civil society. Do informal social networks contribute to norms of trust, which many, particularly Robert Putnam, have connected to levels of citizen engagement and subsequently stable democracy and prosperous economies (Putnam 1993, 2000)? Looking specifically at postcommunist states, Marc Morjé Howard argues that reliance on personal networks leads to less involvement in voluntary organizations, and that this is deleterious for democratic development (Howard 2003, 107–8). He suggests that civil society and informal networks that build social capital are two distinct spheres, stating that although the two spheres are related and complementary, "civil society is generally viewed as a behavioral and institutional phenomenon, whereas social capital emphasizes the more amorphous 'norm' or 'value' of inter-personal trust" (ibid., 42).

Yet how do we know that formal organizations are inherently democracy-promoting, while interpersonal networks are not, unless we examine them? James Gibson combines the social capital and network approaches. Based on survey data from 1992–96, Gibson argues that the social ties and trust among those within personal networks are what allow for the development of civil society in Russia, commenting: "In general, social networks appear to be an important source of learning—from others and from experience—about the meaning of democratic institutions and processes. . . . Being embedded in social networks with high political capacity is perhaps a *necessary* but not *sufficient* condition for access to democratic ideas" (2001, 64). Gibson also suggests that these networks may evolve into broader and more impersonal formal organizations.

The question of social networks' contribution to civil society is often framed in terms of building social capital. In fact, there are social groups that may serve to build social capital without generating a platform for broader social cooperation and, therefore, without ultimately contributing to democracy. Exclusive ties based on ethnicity, religion, language, or kinship may serve to link small groups of people, while simultaneously limiting their interaction with the rest of society. This is the kind of social capital that some have called "bonding" (Putnam 2000, 22; Gittell and Vidal 1998, 8), and it has been described as being most helpful to people for "getting by" in situations of hardship rather than building democratic societies (Briggs 1998; Putnam 2000, 22–23). At the extreme, by positing a vision of state–society interaction based on ascriptive characteristics, the goals and behavior of these exclusive groups can undermine the very concept of civil society as the source of pluralism in the political system.

In the past decade, scholars have begun an energetic debate on whether or not to include "uncivil" elements in definitions of civil society (Berman 1997; Hanson and Kopstein 1998; Chambers and Kopstein 2001). For the most part, scholars have accepted that, while civil society as a whole often plays a democracy-supporting role, one cannot confine the definition of civil society to groups that are explicitly democratic without descending into teleological reasoning. In addition, such a view would gloss over many of the tensions within civil society that lead to social and political change. Revising his earlier theory of civic community that fused the concepts of social capital and "civicness," in a later work Putnam acknowledges that social capital can be "bridging" (inclusive) or "bonding" (exclusive) and can support both democratic and antidemocratic actions (2000, 22–23 and 355). Using similar logic, Larry Diamond urges a clear distinction between civil society and civic community, arguing that social organizations can act as advocates for the public interest in civil society and still may fail to generate social capital because they operate in undemocratic ways (1999, 226–27). Therefore, while the motivation for studying civil society often emerges from a concern for democratic politics, scholars should not assume that organizations, movements, and networks within civil society are inherently democratic. Certainly most groups are more likely to reinforce than to undermine transparent and accountable policy making, the free association of individuals, and the rule of law. Yet actors in civil society are not democratic by definition.

While we attempt to remain agnostic on the ultimate political impact of organizations operating within civil society, we do exclude those organizations, movements, and networks that employ violent means to achieve their goals. Organizations using violence operate outside the political process, reject the rule of law, and violate the basic norms of a civic sphere with the goal of physical destruction of other groups or individuals. This approach is destructive of civil society itself, in that it breeds fear among citizens and disrupts social ties. In order for civil society to grow and strengthen, there must be agreement in society that physical violence against other citizens is an unacceptable form of interaction. For this reason, revolutionary organizations using violence to bring about regime change are excluded from our concept of civil society.

One type of organization prone to using violence to achieve its goals in contemporary Russia is organized crime. We exclude these criminal groups not only because they employ violence, but also because they are profit-seeking organizations more similar to economic than civil society actors. We also exclude other business entities such as corporations and small businesses. Civil society does encompass, however, associations of business people, interest groups based on industries, and labor collectivities that emerge from the private sector to act within civil society by representing economic interests and influencing state policies.

An implication for comparative politics at stake in the debate over broader or narrower definitions of civil society is the applicability of the concept to non-Western societies such as Russia and other states of the former Soviet Union. The strongest argument against broadening the definition of civil society is that, if it were to include less formal varieties of social interaction, the concept could become meaningless and lose its explanatory power. In spite of the danger of "concept stretching" (Collier and Mahon 1993; Sartori 1970), however, there are sound arguments for eschewing narrow definitions of civil society—albeit in a careful way—if we want to understand civic life in other parts of the world. In particular, we wish to avoid the pervasive practice, especially among foreign donors in Russia, of identifying civil society as synonymous with nongovernmental organizations. In a volume devoted to examining what civil society means in non-Western settings, Chris Hann suggests, "the exploration of civil society requires that careful attention be paid to a range of informal interpersonal practices" (Hann 1996, 3). As a general rule, in applying a concept developed in the West in a non-Western context, we should be alert to practices and types of cooperation that are novel or endemic to that environment.

References

Berman, Sheri. 1997. "Civil Society and the Collapse of the Weimar Republic." *World Politics* 49, no. 3 (1997): 401–29.

Chambers, Simone, and Jeffrey Kopstein. 2001. "Bad Civil Society." *Political Theory* 29, no. 6 (December): 837–65.

Cohen, Jean L., and Andrew Arato. 1992. *Civil Society and Political Theory.* Cambridge, MA: MIT Press.

Collier, David, and James E. Mahon. 1993. "Conceptual 'Stretching' Revisited: Adapting Categories in Comparative Analysis." *American Political Science Review* 87, no. 4 (December): 845–55.

Diamond, Larry. 1999. *Developing Democracy: Toward Consolidation.* Baltimore, MD: Johns Hopkins University Press.

Gibson, James L. 2001. "Social Networks, Civil Society, and the Prospects for Consolidating Russia's Democratic Transition." *American Journal of Political Science* 45, no. 1: 51–68.

Gittell, Ross, and Avis Vidal. 1998. *Community Organizing: Building Social Capital as a Development Strategy*. Thousand Oaks, CA: Sage Publications.

Hann, Christopher. 1996. "Introduction." In Hann and Dunn 1996, 1–26.

Hann, Christopher, and Elizabeth Dunn, eds. 1996. *Civil Society: Challenging Western Models*. New York: Routledge.

Hanson, Stephen E., and Jeffrey S. Kopstein. 1998. "The Weimar/Russia Comparison." *Post-Soviet Affairs*, 13 (October–December): 252–83.

Howard, Marc Morjé. 2003. *The Weakness of Civil Society in Post-Communist Europe*. New York: Cambridge University Press.

Putnam, Robert D. 1993. *Making Democracy Work*. Princeton, NJ: Princeton University Press.

———. 2000. *Bowling Alone: The Collapse and Revival of American Community*. New York: Simon and Schuster.

Sartori, Giovanni. 1970. "Concept Misformation in Comparative Politics." *American Political Science Review* 64, no. 4 (December): 1033–53.

About the Editors and Contributors

Edwin Bacon is a Senior Lecturer in Russian Politics in the Centre for Russian and East European Studies, the University of Birmingham, England. He is the author of several books on Russian and Soviet affairs, including *Brezhnev Reconsidered* (2002), and has served as an expert adviser on Russia to the United Kingdom parliament.

Mary Schaeffer Conroy is a Professor in the Department of History, University of Colorado at Denver. Her books include: *Peter Arkad'evich Stolypin: Practical Politics in Late Tsarist Russia* (Westview Press, 1976); *In Health and In Sickness: Pharmacy, Pharmacists and the Pharmaceutical Industry in Late Imperial, Early Soviet Russia* (East European Monographs, 1994); and as editor and chapter contributor, *Emerging Democracy in Late Imperial Russia* (University Press of Colorado, 1998).

Sue Davis is an Assistant Professor of Political Science at Denison University. She is the author of *Trade Unions in Russia and Ukraine, 1985–1995* and *The Russian Far East: The Last Frontier.* She is currently working on a book manuscript about security issues in the Caucasus focusing on Georgia.

Alfred B. Evans, Jr. is a Professor in the Department of Political Science at California State University, Fresno. He has visited Russia frequently in the course of his research, twice with the support of grants from the International Research and Exchanges Board. He has published many journal articles and book chapters, and is the author of *Soviet Marxism-Leninism* and co-editor, with Vladimir Gel'man, of *Restructuring Soviet Ideology: Gorbachev's New Thinking* and *The Politics of Local Government in Russia*, His current research focuses on local government and civil society in contemporary Russia.

Moya Flynn is a Lecturer in the Department of Central and East European Studies, the University of Glasgow, Scotland, UK. Her main research interests concern the migration movements taking place in the Russian Federation and former Soviet Union and the situation of the Russian diaspora communities in Central Asia. She is author of *Migrant Resettlement in the Russian Federation: Reconstructing Homes and Homelands* (London: Anthem, 2004).

Laura A. Henry is an Assistant Professor in the Department of Government and Legal Studies at Bowdoin College. Her research interests include nongovernmental organizations, social movements, and political transformation in post-authoritarian states. She is currently working on a book based on her doctoral dissertation, entitled "Changing Environments: Green Activism, Civil Society, and Political Transformation in Russia."

Janet Elise Johnson is an Assistant Professor of Political Science at Brooklyn College. Her research has been published in the NWSA Journal, in an edited volume, *Post-Soviet Women Encountering Transition* (2004), and in her dissertation, "State Transformation and Violence Against Women in Postcommunist Russia." She is currently writing a book on the influence of global politics on the issues of domestic violence and trafficking in women in Russia.

Sarah Oates is a Lecturer in the Politics Department at the University of Glasgow, Scotland, United Kingdom. She has published widely on Russian elections and the mass media. Her current work focuses on the performance of the mass media in elections in several post-Soviet countries as well as the framing of terrorist threat in recent Russian and U.S. election campaigns.

Peter Rutland is a Professor in the Government Department at Wesleyan University. He is the author or editor of six books, most recently *Business and the State in Contemporary Russia* (Westview, 2001). He writes on Russia for the Jamestown Foundation's *Eurasia Daily Monitor.*

Louise Shelley is the founder and Director of the Transnational Crime and Corruption Center at American University and a Professor at the university's School of International Service. Professor Shelley has written widely on the problems of transnational crime, post-Soviet crime, and corruption.

Valerie Sperling is an Associate Professor of Government and International Relations at Clark University, in Worcester, Massachusetts. Her research interests include social movements, gender politics, and state-building in the post-communist region. Her book on the emergence and development of the Russian women's movement, *Organizing Women in Contemporary Russia: Engendering Transition*, was published by Cambridge University Press in 1999.

Lisa McIntosh Sundstrom is an Assistant Professor of Political Science at the University of British Columbia in Vancouver, Canada. Her areas of research include Russian women's and human rights organizations, democratization, and foreign democracy assistance. Recent publications include "Women's NGOs in Russia: Struggling from the Margins" (*Demokratizatsiya*, Spring 2002) and "Foreign Assistance, International Norms and NGO Development: Lessons from the Russian Campaign" (*International Organization* 59, no. 2 (Spring 2005). Her book on foreign assistance to Russian NGOs is forthcoming from Stanford University Press in 2006.

Kate Thomson, Ph.D., is a Lecturer in Sociology and Health Policy in the Faculty of Health and Community Care, University of Central England in Birmingham (UK). Her main research interests involve sociological and policy issues around disability, particularly learning disabilities, in a Russian, UK, and transnational perspective.

Stephen K. Wegren is an Associate Professor of Political Science at Southern Methodist University. He has published extensively on the political economy of Russia's transformation. His two most recent books are *Russia's Food Policies and Globalization* (2005) and *The Moral Economy Reconsidered: Russia's Search for Agrarian Capitalism* (2005).

Anne White is a Senior Lecturer in Russian and East European Studies at the University of Bath. She is the author of *De-Stalinization and the House of Culture* (Routledge, 1990); *Democratization in Russia under Gorbachev: the Birth of a Voluntary Sector* (Macmillan, 1999); and *Small-Town Russia: Postcommunist Livelihoods and Identities* (RoutledgeCurzon, 2004).

Index

Vremia, 59, 63, 64, 66
Vseobshchaia konfederatsiia profsoiuzov
 (VKP), 201
Vserossiiskii tsentry izucheniia
 obshchestvennogo mneniia (VTsIOM),
 162, 185, 318
Vsesoiuznyi tsentral'nyi sovet
 professional'nykh soiuzov (VTsSPS),
 199, 200, 201, 202, 203
Vucinich, Alexander, 41

W

wage arrears, 197, 201, 203, 204, 205
Walters, Philip, 37
Weiner, Douglas R., 47, 48
welfare, 3, 12, 40, 104, 144, 187, 198,
 204, 208, 229, 230, 231, 235, 236,
 237, 238, 242, 309
West, 7, 44, 48, 63, 73, 82, 111, 144,
 147, 165, 186, 198, 215, 224, 230,
 317, 319
Western donors, 132, 133, 134, 151, 161,
 163, 165, 166, 173, 184, 189–91, 235,
 266, 268, 272, 274, 276, 279, 286, 310,
 311, 312, 319, 325
 grants, 133, 151, 163, 166, 217, 221, 253,
 254, 273
White, Anne, 8, 45, 46
women in politics, 167–8
women, 7, 14, 19, 20, 22–3, 33, 40, 45, 100,
 139, 167, 168, 170, 186, 219, 270

women's groups, 7, 22, 23, 30, 40, 47, 95,
 106, 161–75, 184, 219, 254, 266–71,
 273–78, 311, 312
women's movement, 162–3, 165, 167, 169,
 172, 172, 175
World Bank, 75, 101
World War One, 23
World War Two, 38, 60, 293
World Values Survey, 112
writers, 20, 32, 35, 36, 42, 43, 229, 230, 294

Y

Yavlinsky, Grigory, 63
Yeltsin, 3, 61, 62, 64, 66, 73, 76–87, 102,
 113, 118, 129, 148, 153, 170, 203, 206,
 215
Yukos, 75, 81, 82, 86, 87, 89, 90, 91

Z

zemstvos, 14–15, 16, 17, 23
Zhenotdel, 33, 37
zhensovet, 40, 41, 309, 310
Zhirinovsky, Vladimir, 63
Ziegler, Charles E., 47
Zolotarev, Boris, 89
Zubtsov, 285, 288, 290, 292, 293, 294, 295,
 296, 297, 298
Zubtsovskaia Zhizn', 290, 291
Zudin, Aleksei, 84, 148
Zyuganov, Gennady, 64